Other Books by Dr. Gerald L. Kovacich and Dr. Andy Jones

Global Information Warfare: How Businesses, Governments, and Others Achieve Global Objectives and Attain Competitive Advantages by Dr. Andy Jones, Dr. Gerald L. Kovacich, and Perry Luzwick. Auerbach Publishers/CRC Press, 2002. ISBN 0-84931-114-4.

High-Technology-Crime Investigator's Handbook: Working in the Global Information Environment by Dr. Gerald L. Kovacich and William C. Boni. 1st ed. Butterworth-Heinemann, 1999. ISBN 0-7506-7086-X.

Information Assurance: Surviving in the Information Environment by Dr. Gerald L. Kovacich and Dr. Andrew J. C. Blyth. 1st ed. Springer-Verlag Ltd., 2001. ISBN 1-85233-326-X; 2nd ed. Springer-Verlag Ltd., 2006. ISBN 1-84628-266-7.

Information Systems Security Officer's Guide: Establishing and Managing an Information Protection Program by Dr. Gerald L. Kovacich. 1st ed. Butterworth-Heinemann, 1998. ISBN 0-7506-9896-9. 2nd ed. Butterworth-Heinemann, 2003. ISBN 0-7506-7656-6. Czech translation of first edition available.

I-Way Robbery: Crime on the Internet by Dr. Gerald L. Kovacich and William C. Boni. Butterworth-Heinemann, 1999. ISBN 0-7506-7029-0. Japanese translation available. T. Aoyagi Office Ltd., 2001. ISBN 4-89346-698-4.

The Manager's Handbook for Corporate Security: Establishing and Managing a Successful Assets Protection Program by Dr. Gerald L. Kovacich and Edward P. Halibozek. Butterworth-Heinemann, 2003. ISBN 0-7506-7487-3. The book's instructor's manual (ISBN 13: 978-0-750-67938-1; ISBN 10: 0-750-67938-7) is also available from Butterworth-Heinemann.

Mergers & Acquisitions Security: Corporate Restructuring and Security Management by Dr. Gerald L. Kovacich and Edward P. Halibozek. Butterworth-Heinemann, 2005. ISBN 0-7506-7805-4.

Netspionage: The Global Threat to Information by Dr. Gerald L. Kovacich and William C. Boni. Butterworth-Heinemann, 2000. ISBN 0-7506-7257-9.

Risk Management for Computer Security: Protecting Your Network and Information Assets by Dr. Andy Jones and Debi Ashenden. Butterworth-Heinemann, 2005. ISBN 0-7506-7795-3.

Security Metrics Management: How to Manage the Costs of an Assets Protection Program by Dr. Gerald L. Kovacich and Edward P. Halibozek. Butterworth-Heinemann, 2005. ISBN 0-7506-7899-2.

HIGH-TECHNOLOGY CRIME INVESTIGATOR'S HANDBOOK

Second Edition

HIGH-TECHNOLOGY CRIME INVESTIGATOR'S HANDBOOK

Establishing and Managing a High-Technology Crime Prevention Program

Second Edition

Dr. Gerald L. Kovacich

and

Dr. Andy Jones

ELSEVIER

AMSTERDAM • BOSTON • HEIDELBERG • LONDON
NEW YORK • OXFORD • PARIS • SAN DIEGO
SAN FRANCISCO • SINGAPORE • SYDNEY • TOKYO
Butterworth-Heinemann is an imprint of Elsevier

Senior Acquisitions Editor: Mark Listewnik
Acquisitions Editor: Jennifer Soucy
Acquisitions Editor: Pamela Chester
Editorial Assistant: Kelly Weaver
Senior Marketing Manager: Christian Nolan
Senior Project Manager: Paul Gottehrer
Cover Designer: Eric DeCicco

Butterworth–Heinemann is an imprint of Elsevier
30 Corporate Drive, Suite 400, Burlington, MA 01803, USA
Linacre House, Jordan Hill, Oxford OX2 8DP, UK

Library of Congress Cataloging-in-Publication Data
Application submitted

British Library Cataloguing-in-Publication Data
A catalogue record for this book is available from the British Library.

ISBN 13: 978-0-7506-7929-9

For information on all Butterworth–Heinemann publications
visit our Web site at www.books.elsevier.com

Transferred to Digital Priting 2009

Like the first edition, we dedicate this book to the security, law enforcement, and investigative professionals in every country who dedicate their lives to protecting their companies, their societies, their nations, and the world from the miscreants who use high technology to violate the laws, ethics, and morality of the human race.

Contents

Praise for the First Edition

High-tech crime remains a rapidly growing global menace. Read this book if you are interested in learning the basics of this type of crime and the professional tools and techniques used against it. Written by security professionals, federal/local government and corporate managers should read this book to understand strategies and methods needed to protect public and private resources from high-tech attacks. I especially would expect federal and local managers to be familiar with and follow the principles described in this book to protect taxpayer resources, and be aware of deficiencies and take corrective action. Other readers will gain better security awareness and the steps businesses are taking (or should be taking) to protect user/customer resources. After reading this book, I certainly have a better understanding of the difficulties my bank and credit union, for example, are facing to protect my money.

Reviewer Robert Setlow
Clinton, Washington, USA

Whether you're a law enforcement professional or corporate security professional, this book is one you should not just read, but thoroughly digest before stepping off the ledge into high-tech crime investigation. I've had both the satisfaction and frustration of managing investigations in both worlds during the past 16 years and have experienced firsthand the hazards and consequences that await the uninformed. If resources such as the *High-Technology Crime Investigator's Handbook* had been available when I first began working high-tech crimes in 1981, I would have gratefully traded the experience for the knowledge. The book is invaluable in educating law enforcement personnel in the interests and philosophy of private industry, as well as educating corporate security professionals in meeting the litmus tests for law enforcement involvement and successful prosecution. If you could choose to read only one book on high-tech crime investigations, this is it. Whether you are a private investigator, in law enforcement or corporate security, a criminal justice student, or just interested in the topic, this book is the book to read first—a must read.

Reviewer Jim Black
Colorado, USA

If you want to learn the principles of investigating computer crime, then this book is a must.

Reviewer Dr. Andrew Blyth
Cardiff, Wales, UK

For more reviews of the *High-Technology Crime Investigator's Handbook,* please visit www.amazon.com.

First Edition Foreword

It really came as a surprise to me.

I recently found myself with Jerry Kovacich drinking fine British beer in a fine London drinking establishment and he asked if I would pen an introduction to the new book he was writing with Bill Boni. I was certainly honored to be offered that task, but that wasn't the surprise. The surprise was the serendipitous timing of his request and the events that were surrounding me at the time. For, you see, a couple of my associates were themselves immersed in cyber-investigations.

Over the years I have had occasion to be on the trail of "bad guys," both within and outside of an organization, and I have found that, in most every case, the procedures followed on the part of the victim firm were ad hoc at best.

"What is your policy for dealing with serious external hacking?" I would ask.

"Uh, er...we don't have one," the senior security officer would say.

"Okay, how well tuned-in is your in-house counsel for these sorts of events?"

"He's a bean-counting lawyer.... He doesn't keep up on this sort of thing. What do you think we should do?" they would ask me.

So, it was odd indeed, that drinking fine beer with Jerry four thousand miles from home should coincide with two ongoing cases I was involved with.

In the first case, a large financial institution found itself under a fairly severe attack that had been going on for nearly two weeks. The security manager came from a legal/law enforcement background and had a healthy dose of street-fighting experience. He immediately commenced an internal investigation. Audit trails from all perimeter systems (firewalls, routers, etc.) and native host and applications were "turned up" to a greater degree of sensitivity, thus gathering greater amounts of raw audit data. Analysis was comprehensive in order to learn about the techniques of the intruder. They wanted, hopefully, to learn what his real goals were and what caliber of attacker they were dealing with.

Secondly, they quickly captured an IP address and began the laborious process of tracing and identifying the intruder who was making substantial progress through the company's very sensitive files. By using "street-smarts" pressure, he got the first ISP in the chain to carry on the trace to the next hop. He called the next hop during the night and was able to identify the real IP, real name, and real physical address of who had been breaking in. Throughout this process, police were neither notified nor invited to help.

Using additional investigative tools and by performing an extensive background check on their suspect, the company was confident to five-nines (99.999%) that they had the perpetrator. The security manager contacted some acquaintances and asked if they could make a house-call on the company's behalf. They did so, and in no uncertain terms, convinced the intruders it would be in their best interest to cease and desist their intrusions immediately. The not-so-subtle tactics worked.

Problem solved. Not one dime or ounce of time was spent with the police. Whether you approve of these actions or not is immaterial. The company was prepared to conduct an internal investigation without the participation of any outsiders, they implemented their plan, and within days it was over. Best of all, only a small number of top corporate officials ever knew there was a problem. No newspapers or Internet rumors. From the perspective of everyone throughout the company in 50 states and many foreign countries, it was business as usual.

The second case was handled a bit differently. Although a very large company with a large number of trade secrets, they had very little security process or technology in place. They became aware of their problem not because of electronic sensors picking up illicit and abnormal behavior as in the first case, but they had discovered that they had a malicious insider because of a disturbing e-mail that inquired why extensive hacking was coming from their IP address. After a scramble, they traced down some logs and manually found activities they couldn't explain; it did indeed seem that someone was hacking from inside their company.

Meetings were hastily called and the internal lawyer was endlessly stuck in a physical paradigm. He just didn't understand the power of their hacker and the technical limitations the company faced. Everyone did agree to no dealings with the police. They wanted to handle it themselves even though they had little clue as to what steps to take.

I helped them draw up a quick-and-dirty game plan, and we soon found that our likely disgruntled employee had one worked for the company that he was hacking into. Because of California law sensitivities, they did not take my advice: go lock up his machine, get a sector copy of the hard disk, and acquire some forensics tools to see what he's been hiding through erasure, deletion, or other disguise mechanisms. Human resources was appalled at our decision to fire the employee. They told us every reason in the book why we couldn't do what we knew we had to do to build a case against their hacker.

Intense frustration grew on all sides as it became quite clear that none of the senior management had ever considered or discussed the possibility they now faced. Time wore on, and it was at least three weeks before they all agreed on how to handle the case. It was quiet, politically correct, but more than 100 MB of information had been sent via ftp to the other company. They are still trying to figure out what happened.

Two different approaches, both in their own ways unsatisfactory: one in its outcome, the other perhaps in its method. And that is exactly why *High-Technology Crime Investigator's Handbook* is so valuable a contribution to field of information security and corporate asset protection management awareness. Very few companies have well thought-out plans on how to deal with contingencies such as I described above. While we have pretty well learned how to handle the Acts of God, such as hurricanes, floods, and fires, we are still in our infancy when it comes to coping with the Acts of Man.

What Jerry and Bill are providing you with is an excellent overview of the entire issue ranging from the new information age environment in which we all now live, who is doing what to whom, a basic outline on how to protect your information assets, and a look into the future.

Most companies I know are loath to enjoin law enforcement in an internal corporate investigation unless it becomes absolutely necessary. A majority of people I know say the police cannot be trusted to keep secrets. Public relations is a critical component of company image and spin control is hard enough without compromising leaks about embarrassing company events. Law enforcement is broadly viewed with technical disdain, often called clueless, mindless, or atavistic in their antedated approaches to cyber-investigations. In addition, you, as a private individual or company, often have a lot more leeway in the sorts of things you can do in an investigation. Due to legal procedural impediments faced by law enforcement, bringing in the police at too early a stage can doom a situation to failure.

Cyber-crimes involve technical staff, security management, senior executives, legal counsel, and often human resources. Because of the nature of the medium, the analyses and investigative processes are often nonlinear, and parallel tracks must be taken simultaneously. It is a complex process and must be planned for.

Whether you take every word of *High-Technology Crime Investigator's Handbook* and use it to gain a better understanding of this new information age environment and build it into your company's procedures or not is inconsequential. The point is that you build and install a process that is right for your company and your company's goals.

This book is also an "Internet crimes awareness handbook" for security professionals, law enforcement personnel, managers, and anyone else interested in this fascinating topic. You could not ask for two better guides than Jerry Kovacich and Bill Boni. I am proud to call them friends and colleagues who are making great contributions to the field.

Winn Schwartau

President, Infowar.Com, Inc., and author
His most recent book is *Time Based Security,* which
provides a quantifiable process and metric for
defining an organization's security level.

Second Edition Foreword

Today's cyber criminals, whether they are company employees, petty thieves, con artists, corporate executives, gang members, professional thugs, juvenile delinquents, government agents, international hackers, terrorists, or the like, are far better prepared to meet the challenges of their criminal "vocation" than those who investigate them. These criminals use all forms of modern high technology—computers, pagers, scanners, cellular phones, faxes, and color printers—to commit simple or complex crimes. Their use of modern processes, sophisticated devices, and high-technology equipment frequently gets in the way of, delays, or prevents detection.

It has been more than 5 years since the first edition of this book was published. Unfortunately, the world has changed little and the high-tech criminals of today are still usually better equipped than agencies responsible for enforcing the law and investigating criminal wrongdoings. Many federal, state, county, and local law enforcement agencies and civilian investigative organizations also continue to lag far behind in their procurement of and training in the use of high-tech equipment and methods for conducting high-tech-related investigations—at least compared with the global high-tech criminal. And yes, today these criminals all have a global reach.

During the last 5 or more years in the United States and other modern nation-states, the priorities of security and law enforcement professionals have drastically changed. This change was brought about by the events of 9/11. The already-limited resources of those who investigate high-tech crimes have been stretched further because of the global "War on Terrorism."

Many investigative units today have not had the resources to update procedures, processes, and tools to get the job done; however, there have been improvements, albeit slower than needed. Unfortunately, we continue to see prolonged investigations, delays in the preparation and delivery of investigative reports, challenges to collect and track data accurately, inadequate case management, poor development of statistical trends, and limits on comprehensive data analyses. Law enforcement officers excel at being investigators; however, intelligence collection and analysis are new skills that have to be learned, and they are needed these days to support high-tech crime investigators.

There are still managers and supervisors who oversee investigative units in law enforcement and other government and civilian business worlds who lack sufficient expertise or are hesitant to use many of the high-tech, automated tools and processes now available to the investigative and intelligence communities. In addition, there are still difficulties in presenting evidence in an understanding and convincing way to courts, juries, and so on; but again, we have seen improvements in this area. We will probably never encounter a situation that boasts the "ideal" investigative tools and environment, because budgetary considerations will always go to violent, physical crime investigations first. At least in those cases, high-tech support has been exploited, and it is making a great deal of difference in the investigation of violent crimes, primarily because of high-tech forensics.

Now that the War on Terrorism is upon us, the budgets for other-than-terrorist defenses and investigations, as well as the continued violent crimes, are receiving the most attention (as they should). Because of the limit on available resources, there will most likely be slow progress in the prevention and detection of other types of high-technology crimes and in conducting high-technology investigations, training, and providing support. Management is confronted with and under pressure from manpower reductions and frequent funding cuts and is constantly challenged to establish their priorities. Providing money for high-tech crime investigators' badly needed up-to-date resources, especially when the people and their elected leaders want to stop drugs, violent crime, terrorists, and gangs, remains a challenge. When these understandable pressures occur, it is difficult to make the case that these high-tech tools will help in the fight in these areas, especially because they relate to providing investigative services to corporations.

Quite often, updating statistical collection methods is nothing more than the development or implementation of a simple database or spreadsheet application. Most complex case management systems used by many agencies can be simplified and automated to provide a wealth of information with little or no effort. Most software applications produced today have excellent tutorials to help even the most high-tech illiterate high-tech crime investigator learn program basics and develop solutions to meet everyday business needs. These tools are being used more often these days and continue to provide good support for investigators. Such is the world in which those interested or charged with the responsibility of investigating high-technology crimes and criminals must work—the global information environment.

This book by Dr. Gerald L. Kovacich and Dr. Andy Jones, both experienced security professionals, accomplished authors, and lecturers on security-related topics, is unique. It not only provides a basic introduction to the world of high-tech crime, but more importantly, it is the only book I have found that has a primary purpose that is not about *investigating* high-tech crimes, but how to *establish and manage* a high-tech crime investigative unit. This is the main emphasis of this book and I highly recommend it for those who are responsible for establishing and managing such an organization, and for those who are interested in high-tech crime and the profession of the high-tech crime investigator.

Howard A. Schmidt
President & CEO R & H Security Consulting LLC
Former White House Cyber Security Advisor

Preface

This second edition of the *High-Technology Crime Investigators Handbook* has been completely updated; some chapters were eliminated, others were combined, and new chapters were added. The new chapters deal with the following:

- High-technology global threats
- Interviews and interrogations
- Computer forensics, including establishing and managing a computer forensics laboratory
- Pros and cons of outsourcing the high-technology investigative function
- Terrorism and its affect on the high-technology investigator
- Becoming a high-technology crime investigative consultant

As it was when this book was first published in the year 2000, high-technology crimes and other illegal activities in the global information environment continue to grow quickly. Because of the rapid integration and globally expanded use of high technology in our working and living environments, the targets of high-technology crime are becoming more plentiful and are susceptible to more sophisticated threats and attacks than ever before.

Colleges and universities are increasingly offering courses in nearly every aspect of high technology, and in recent years they have expanded their curricula on security, law enforcement, and investigations. Those courses related to high-technology crime investigations are not being expanded as rapidly as they should, but some progress is being made as some universities now even offer courses in computer forensics.

Although many of today's law enforcement and civilian training agencies provide basic and advanced instruction in modern methods and technologies, few offer in-depth, technical training in high-technology crime investigations, but that too has continued its slow improvement. For additional basic and more advanced instructions, one must look to the private sector and their sponsored security-related conferences held around the world.

Like the first edition of this book, the second edition has as its goals for readers to be able to:

- Gain an understanding of the global information environment and its threats
- Be more aware of high-technology incidents and their related investigations
- Be able to develop a basic plan to establish and manage a high-technology crime investigation unit
- Establish a high-technology crime prevention program
- Develop a high-technology crime investigation career plan
- Gain a basic understanding of the possible future world of high-technology crimes and their investigation

This book consists of four major sections incorporating 27 chapters. It is intended to provide a basic overview of the high-technology crime investigator's profession now and into the future. *This is not a "how to investigate high-technology crime" book, although an overview of that topic is presented.* This book is about working in the global information environment as a high-technology crime investigator and establishing and managing a high-technology crime investigation program.

For someone who wants to be a high-technology crime investigator, is new to this profession, or wants to know how to fight high-technology crime within a business or government agency environment, this book is for you. Also, it is hoped that this book offers tips and insights for the seasoned veteran, or at least provides some enjoyable reading.

Although there are only a small number of high-technology crime investigators who officially carry such a title (or a similar one), there is little doubt that there is a growing need for highly trained, technically competent high-technology crime investigators in the private and public sectors of every information-dependent, Information Age nation and corporation in the world.

We no doubt have a long way to go. This is obvious when some computer crime units are still using Microsoft's Windows ME and others are told to use confiscated software from the evidence locker to run their "new 500-MHz computers."

It is hoped that this book helps to focus attention and interest on the profession of the high-technology crime investigator. If we are to be successful in the 21st Century and rely on global information networks (the Internet; other international, national, and intranet networks; and global telecommunications systems), the professional high-technology crime investigator in concert with information systems security professionals must have the training, knowledge, and capabilities to protect this environment from the miscreants who now travel within the global information environment and attack their victims with impunity.

To those who will take up that gauntlet, we say again: Good luck and good hunting!

Dr. Gerald L. Kovacich   *Dr. Andy Jones*
Whidbey Island, Washington, USA   *Ipswich, England, UK*

P.S. For those of you who are curious regarding the change in co-authors, William C. Boni (co-author of first edition) has gotten extremely busy these past few years as Motorola Corporations' Chief Information Security Officer and Corporate Vice President. Dr. Jones, an old friend and prior coauthor, graciously accepted the challenge to coauthor this book and add his formidable expertise to this project.

Acknowledgments

This book was initially developed to fill a void in available books that provide an introduction to the "world of the high-technology crime investigator in the global information environment" and a basic approach to establishing and managing a high-technology crime investigative unit. Because of the popularity of the first edition and the support of our readers, we have written this "new and improved" second edition. To all those readers out there who made this book successful, we say a special thanks!

As for acknowledging the advice and support of others, we of course must always, in every book, thank our wives—Kath Jones and Hsiao-yun Kovacich—for their constant support, patience, and a nice cup of tea and a snack when it was sorely needed to keep us going. Without their wholehearted support, we probably would not have been able to complete this project and remain married!

We also send special thanks to:

- Motomu Akashi, security professional extraordinaire, mentor, great friend, and now retired (Thanks, Tom!)
- William C. Boni, Vice President and CISO, Motorola Corporation, one of the best and brightest in the profession today, and coauthor of the first edition
- Darrel Earnshaw, for his help and assistance
- Don Evans, who continues to be the InfoSec conferences' "workhorse" and a security professional even before computers used punch cards
- Edward P. Halibozek, Director of Security, Northrop Grumman Corporation, and a true security professional
- Andy Joyce and Mike Barbar, UK Avon and Sommerset police, for their input and for allowing us to include their material
- Breyan Littlefair, for his tolerance
- Steve Lutz, President, WaySecure, an international security consulting firm—the best in the business today!
- Don Rabon, Interim Director and Deputy Director for the Western Campus, North Carolina Justice Academy, for allowing us to quote

liberally from his excellent book *Interviewing and Interrogation* (Carolina Academic Press, 1992, ISBN 0-89089-488-4) and the author of *Investigative Discourse Analysis: Statements, Letters, and Transcripts* (Carolina Academic Press, 1994, ISBN 0-89089-569-4)

- Howard Schmidt, a true security professional, international security consultant, and good friend—even if we don't always agree!
- Jerry Swick, Senior Network Security Specialist/Investigator, Verizon
- Phil Swinburne, for his advice and support

As for our project team and publishing professionals at Butterworth-Heinemann—Mark Listewnik, Chris Nolin, Kelly Weaver, Paul Gottehrer, and Jennifer Soucy—we thank them for their continued support and professionalism shown in this and all our previous projects. You continue to excel!

This project also included many others at Butterworth-Heinemann who were on the project team for this book. We thank them for their professionalism and support on this project.

Lastly, we thank all of you who are reading this book. We hope that the information provided contributes to your professional success. Please send your comments to us through our publisher, Butterworth-Heinemann.

About the Authors

Dr. Andy Jones: During a full military career Andy Jones directed both intelligence and security operations, briefed the results at the highest level, and was awarded the MBE for his service in Northern Ireland. After 25 years service with the British Army's Intelligence Corps, he became a business manager and a researcher and analyst in the area of information warfare and computer crime at a defense research establishment. In September 2002, on completion of a paper on a method for the metrication of the threats to information systems, he left the defense environment to take up a post as a principal lecturer at the University of Glamorgan in the subjects of network security and computer crime and as a researcher on the threats to information systems and computer forensics. At the university he developed and managed a well-equipped computer forensics laboratory and took the lead on a large number of computer investigations and data recovery tasks. He holds a PhD in the area of threats to information systems. In January 2005, he joined the Security Research Centre at British Telecommunications to take up a post as a research group leader in the area of information security.

Dr. Gerald Kovacich: Over 40 years of counterintelligence/counterespionage, security, criminal and civil investigations, antifraud, information warfare, and information systems security experience in the US government as a special agent. He had also worked for numerous technology-based international corporations as an information systems security manager, information warfare technologist, investigations manager, and security audit manager, as well as an international lecturer, writer, and consultant on these topics in the United States, Europe, and Asia.

"Learning is not attained by chance. It must be sought for with ardor and attended to with diligence."

—*Abigail Adams*

"What is most obvious may be most worthy of analysis. Fertile vistas may open out when commonplace facts are examined from a fresh point of view."

—*L. L. Whyte*

"Knowing is not enough, we must apply. Willing is not enough, we must do."

—*Johann Wolfgang von Goethe*

PART I

Introduction to the High-Technology Crime Environment

This is the new high-technology crime investigators' crime scene.

The objective of this section is to provide professional high-technology crime investigators, managers, and supervisors, in either the business or government agency sectors, a basic understanding of the high-technology environment in which we live, work, and play. For high-technology crime investigators to establish and manage a high-technology investigative unit and to conduct high-technology crime investigations successfully, they must have a basic understanding of the topics discussed in Chapters 1 through 4.

In Chapter 1 we provide an overview of high-technology-related threats on a global scale. This is a new chapter, but it incorporates the discussion of basic computer systems (sometimes called *information systems*) from the first edition, which is an absolute necessity if the high-technology crime investigator is to be successful in establishing and managing a high-technology anticrime unit, to manage and supervise high-technology crime investigators, and to conduct high-technology crime investigations.

Chapter 2 was placed here based on feedback from some of our readers. In it we discuss what knowledge the investigator should have as a basic understanding of these miscreants, their motives, profiles, and philosophies. This chapter provides an overview of these individuals and groups.

Chapter 3 provides the high-technology crime investigator a non-technical overview of some of the basic methods high-technology miscreants use to conduct their criminal deeds.

Chapter 4 closes this section by providing an overview of the basic high-technology protection philosophies, methods, and processes that are used to protect the valuable assets of the global information environment's businesses and government agencies.

1

What Investigators Should Know About the High-Technology-Supported Global Environment and Its Threats

In this chapter we provide an overview of high-technology-related threats on a global scale. This is a new chapter, but it incorporates the first edition's discussion of basic computer systems, sometimes called *information systems,* which is an absolute necessity if the high-technology crime investigator is to be successful in establishing and managing a high-technology anticrime unit, to manage and supervise successfully high-technology crime investigators, as well as to conduct high-technology crime investigations. Although our discussion of high-technology crimes and establishing and managing a high-technology crime unit is focused primarily on the corporation, it is also generally applicable to government agencies, nonprofit businesses, and the like.

INTRODUCTION

The world continues to change and does so more rapidly than ever before. These rapid changes are driven by technology—high technology—based on the microprocessor, which is the engine for all high-technology devices. These devices are known as *computer systems, networked systems, information systems, knowledge-based systems,* and so forth.

For our purposes, let's just keep it simple and call computers, whether they be networked or standalone and regardless of their use or configuration (e.g., PDA, cell phone, notebook, networked or nonnetworked desktop), all *high technology.*

Although our discussion of high-technology crimes and establishing and managing a high-technology crime unit focuses primarily on corporations, the text of this book is generally applicable to goverment agencies, nonprofit businesses, and the like.

We will assume that the high-technology crime investigator has at least a basic understanding of computers and how they operate. This is necessary because the crime scenes encountered by the high-technology crime investigator will be high-technology based, as are the "victim's" high-technology devices. (If you need more information about how computers work, a basic "intro to computers" textbook will suffice; however the more one knows of high technology, the better. Much of this information was addressed in the first edition of this book and is not repeated here because we believe that, by now, you should be familiar with computers and their basic operation and know the difference between a bit, byte, RAM, ROM, TCP/IP, and so forth.)

THE GLOBALIZATION OF THE MARKETPLACE

Unless you have lived in isolation for the past several years, by now you have heard the term *globalization*. Some have grown to detest the use of the term as much as they have *paradigm shift*, which has also often been overused in the corporate world. However, the term *globalization* does convey a vision of an environment, one that most of us live in today. This single word helps us visualize what has gradually been taking place in the business world throughout the centuries and, more important, during the 5 years since we published the first edition to this book. By *globalization of the marketplace*, we mean that the world is now one big marketplace in which the businesses of the world buy, sell, and trade everything and anything.

> **Globalization:** the process by which social institutions become adopted on a global scale..., the process by which a business or company becomes international or starts operating at an international level.[1]

The *Global Competitiveness Report 2004–2005*[2] lists the top 15 most competitive nations:

1. United States
2. Finland
3. Germany
4. Sweden
5. Switzerland
6. United Kingdom
7. Denmark
8. Japan
9. Netherlands
10. Singapore

11. Hong Kong Special Administrative Region (SAR)
12. France
13. Australia
14. Belgium
15. Canada

These rankings are probably what you may have envisioned. (See the full report for more information and for the complete rankings of the nations.) The point of all this is that the world is rapidly changing, getting smaller and "connected" (Fig. 1-1). Furthermore, the more nations that become high-technology driven, the more the miscreants of the world will take advantage of this global environment to damage, steal, and destroy information and information systems of the globally dependent, high-technology-dependent corporations, small business, and the unsuspecting public.

So, because high technology provides the driver and support to global-ization—"the world talking to the world"—the world has "gone flat." In his book *The World Is Flat: A Brief History of the Twenty-First Century,* Thomas L. Friedman[3] provides a discussion of the ten "flatteners of the world":

1. When the walls (Berlin) came down and the windows (Microsoft) went up
2. When Netscape went public
3. Workflow software
4. Open sourcing: self-organizing collaborative communities
5. Outsourcing: Y2K
6. Offshoring: running with gazelles, eating with lions
7. Supply chaining: eating sushi in Arkansas
8. Insourcing: what the guys in funny brown shorts are really doing
9. In-forming: Google, Yahoo!, MSN Web Search
10. The steroids: digital, mobile, personal, and virtual

Figure 1-1 The world to talk to the world—from any place to anywhere.

By viewing this list, you can get some idea about how the flattening of the business world has taken place. The days of "stovepipes" (stand-alone entities within the corporation or within the global marketplace) in the business world are quickly ending. Businesses can no longer afford not to flatten their corporate structure and their part of the global environment if they are to compete successfully for their global market share.

> Your crime scene is no longer just a stand-alone, nonnetworked desktop computer system on some corporate desk in New York City. Now, that computer is networked to the other computers of the corporation's local area networks (LANs), wide area networks (WANs), the Internet, and from there to the world.

As a crime investigator, or even a high-technology crime investigator, you may be wondering what all this has to do with conducting investigations, even high-technology crime investigations. The answer is simple: The global business environment, with corporate computer tentacles attached to about everything and anything in the global marketplace, has become your crime scene; the *world* may now be your crime scene. A crime scene where, as a law enforcement officer, private investigator, or security investigator, you may lack not only jurisdiction but the global reach necessary to investigate a high-technology crime.

HIGH TECHNOLOGY IS RAPIDLY CHANGING THE WORLD

If you are involved in any activity in which high technology is used as a tool to help you accomplish your work, you will be aware of the tremendous and very rapid advances that are being made in this arena. It is something to behold.

If we look back at the 20th century, we see major high-technology inventions becoming commonplace (Fig. 1-2). Imagine what the 21st century will bring!

We are in the middle of the most rapid technological advances in human history, but this is just the beginning. We are not even close to reaching the potential that high technology has to offer, nor are we able to predict its affect on all of us—both good and bad.

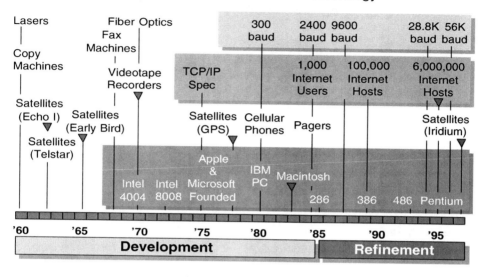

Figure 1-2 A brief history of 20th-century high technology.

"In 1994, people had to call the bank to check their balances. Or inquire in person, or wait for a paper statement to arrive in the mail. Baseball box scores were found in the newspaper. Weather forecasts came over the phone from the weather bureau, or on TV. Then along came the Internet and an experimental browser called Mosaic, followed by an improved browser from Netscape.

And if you had a computer, you discovered a new way to this cool, new thing called the *World Wide Web*. Mosaic and Netscape were the first popular connection to what came to be called the *information superhighway*. According to the Pew Internet & American Life Project, less than one in five Americans were online in 1995. Today, the majority of Americans are surfing the Web, exchanging e-mail, reading bank statements and ball scores, checking the weather. Today, Pew says, two out of every three Americans spend time online."[4]

It is said that there have been more discoveries in the last 50 years than in the entire history of mankind before that time. We just have to read the papers and the trade journals to look at every profession and see what high technology is bringing to our world. New discoveries are being made in medicine, and there are expanding online and worldwide information systems; we can now hold teleconferences across the country and around the globe. A short summary of the last few centuries of high-technology advances in calculators and computers have included the following[5]:

- John Napier shows how to multiply and divide using rods or bones.
- Blaise Pascal invents adding machine.
- G. W. von Leibniz invents the adding machine with geared wheels.
- Joseph Jacquard uses card-controlled looms to weave designs into cloth.
- Charles X. Thomas introduces the commercial calculating machine.
- Charles Babbage invents the "analytic engine," foreshadowing computers.
- George Boole publishes treatise on binary algebra.
- Charles Sanders Peirce applies Boolean logic to electric circuits.
- Lord Kelvin develops the analog computer to predict tides.
- Herman Hollerith conceives the idea of using punched cards for calculations.
- Hollerith's ideas are successfully applied to work of the US Census.
- Hollerith forms a company that later becomes IBM.
- George Stibitz creates the electrical circuit to apply Boolean algebra.
- IBM engineers and Howard Aiken of Harvard start on the Mark I computer.
- Alan Turing's "Colossus" computer breaks the German Enigma code.
- The Electronic Numerical Integrator and Calculator (or ENIAC) computer is built.
- Von Neumann, Goldstine, and Burks publish a paper on computer concepts.
- ILLIAC I is built at the University of Illinois using the Von Neumann design.
- The UNIVAC I machine is installed at the US Census Bureau.
- A computer beats a human player in a chess game.
- IBM unveils the FORTRAN programming language.
- Jack St. Clair Kilby of Texas Instruments invents integrated circuits.
- The Livermore Advanced Research Computer is built with transistors.
- The US Department of Defense creates the ARPANET computer network.
- Engineers at Intel invent the microprocessor.
- Nolan Bushnell introduces the "Pong" video game.
- Ray Tomlinson sends the first e-mail message using @ in the address.
- The first personal computers are introduced.
- The first time that a bar code is scanned in a supermarket.
- Cray Research sells the first supercomputer.
- A glove device to facilitate computer interaction is patented.
- George Lucas' computer effects in *Star Wars* revolutionize film making.
- The Pac-man video game is sold in Japan.

- Dan Bricklin and Dan Flystra write the software for the VisiCalc spreadsheet.
- IBM introduces the personal computer (PC), using the Microsoft operating system.
- The French postal and telegraph service hooks up the nation using the Minitel network.
- Internet emerges as the ARPANET splits civilian and military networks.
- Apple Computer introduces its Macintosh machine including a mouse.
- Microsoft introduces its first version of Windows.
- The World Wide Web begins.
- The Michelangelo computer virus is detected in United States.
- Broadband
- DSL
- Napster
- Computer glitch expected with new millennium
- WiFi
- New Centrino chip
- There are more than 353,284,187 Internet hosts
- Apple computers support Intel chips

Intel Keeps Moore's Law on Track

"Contradicting fears that the semiconductor industry's pace of development is slowing, Intel Corporation has announced it has achieved a milestone in shrinking the size of transistors that will power its next-generation chips.... It's created a fully functional 70-Mb memory chip with transistor switches measuring just 35 nm—about 30% smaller than those found on today's state-of-the-art chips. By shrinking the size of the transistors and other features etched into the silicon, more of the tiny devices can be squeezed onto a single chip. As a result, microprocessors become more powerful and memory chips can store more data without growing in size."[6]

Today's high-technology environment is based on the microprocessor—the "real" computer or, as some like to call it, the *computer engine*. Computers have been around for decades; however, they have become more powerful, cheaper, smaller, boast more features, are more connected nationally and internationally—and this trend is continuing. Computers have become an integral part, a necessity, in our society.

We have entered the Information Age and are moving into the Knowledge Age. In the United States and in other developed countries of the world, we have become information-dependent and high-technology-dependent societies. Today's cellular telephones are becoming complete information and communication devices that include the following wireless communications: voice mail, e-mail messaging, Internet access, video downloading, digital cameras, and digital music.

In the not-too-distant past, we moved on from feather pens and ink wells, to pencils and ballpoint pens, to typewriters, electric typewriters, correctible typewriters, and then the computer. During this high-technology evolution many new businesses were started based on the new high technology whereas others disappeared. For example, remember when people used carbon paper if they wanted extra copies? That industry pretty much disappeared with the advent of the copy machine. Today, these copy machines are more than just copying machines; they are part of networks, and some have been replaced by desktop computers.

Remember when computerized information stored on disk drives and tapes was supported by hard copies? This is no longer the case. Therefore, information is more at risk, miscreants can cause more damage and destruction, and the investigator lacks a paper audit trail on which to base investigative leads. Consequently, it is imperative, more than ever before, that the high-technology crime investigator have a basic understanding of computers, which are the basis of high technology. This knowledge should include the threats against computers, their vulnerabilities and risks, and what is being done to protect them and their information.

High technology is the mainstay of our businesses and government agencies. We can no longer function in business or government without them. Pagers, cellular phones, e-mail, credit cards, teleconferences, smart cards, notebook computers, networks, and private branch exchanges (PBX) are all computer based, and all are now common tools for individuals, businesses, public agencies, and government agencies. Criminals also are relying more and more on computers. As computers become more sophisticated, so do the criminals. As international networks increase, so do the number of international criminals and other assorted miscreants.

Finland to Adopt Mobile Broadband, Helsinki, Finland (Reuters)

"Finland will select a new wireless network technology from the United States next week in a move being watched by other European governments that are opening radio spectrum for mobile broadband Internet. Finland was the place where the European-invented Global System for Mobile Communications first went on the air in 1991, setting off a revolution in mobile communications. But this time around there is no European technology alternative."[7]

Because computers are becoming so powerful in terms of speed, storage capacity, memory, size, and their related software and networks, they have become more complex. No one can be a technical expert in all the various systems, software, and so forth; however, the high-technology crime investigator should maintain a current, basic understanding of today's high technology, how it functions, its vulnerabilities, and then rely on *trusted* and *experienced* specialists to assist in high-technology crime investigations.

PCs have changed our lives dramatically. The use of modems is now commonplace, and all newly purchased computers come with an internal modem preinstalled and ready for global access through the Internet or other networks. But wait! They are not the old 56K modems that run on the old telephone lines. They are now wireless modems that use broadband and DSL telecommunications links to the hooked-up world. Yet, "home computers" and long-distance telephone networks represent potentially the most serious and complex crime scenes of the Information Age, especially when coupled with wireless technology and high bit rates. Research shows that 8 to 16 megabits/second (Mbs) is possible, and this will surely increase as we make our way through the 21st century.

The Internet is the latest in a series of technological advances that is being used not only by honest people to further their communications, learning, and business transactions, but it is also being used with impunity by miscreants, juvenile delinquents, and others for illegal purposes. As with any technological invention, it can be used for good or illegal purposes. It all depends on the human being that is using the technology.

One should not be confused or clouded in one's investigative thinking by "high technology." The fact remains that high technology is just "tools of the trade" and will be used by honest people and criminals alike. The basic investigative questions of who, what, where, when, why, and how still apply. The basic investigative steps, seeking knowledge of the criminals' motives, still apply. The only real changes are the tools (computers, forensic software, and so on) and the new crime scene environment.

THE THREE BASIC STEPS OF COMPUTER OPERATIONS

The operation of the computer is based on three basic steps:

1. *Input*—Using some device such as a mouse, keyboard, or voice command, instructions are given to the computer through the application and operating system software.

2. *Process*—The information, or input, is processed according to the instructions entered and the applicable software used.
3. *Output*—Once processed, the information is output (e.g., to a disk, printer, the computer screen) based on the instructions that the computer was given.

So, from an investigative viewpoint, the very basic investigative steps can also be easily broken down into the same format. For example, the investigator would want to know what, who, when, why, where, how, and using which software information was inputted into the computer that instructed it to perform the way it did, and what was outputted to where.

"There's a new breed of crime fighter prowling cyber space: the hacker hunters. Spurred by big profits, professional cyber criminals have replaced amateur thrill-seeking hackers as the biggest threat on the Web. Software defenses are improving rapidly, but law enforcement and security companies understand they can no longer rely on technology alone to deal with the plague of virus attacks, computer break-ins, and online scams. Instead, they're marshaling their forces and using gumshoe tactics to fight back—infiltrating hacker groups, monitoring their chatter on underground networks, and when they can, busting the baddies before they do any more damage. 'The wave of the future is getting inside these groups, developing intelligence, and taking them down,' says Christopher M. E. Painter, deputy chief of the computer crime section of the Justice Department, who will help prosecute ShadowCrew members at a trial scheduled for October."[8]

The investigator must remember that the computer only does what its instructions tell it to do. In doing so, it can only take in so much input so fast, process only so much information, and output only so much information at some maximum speed. Such things as the computer's architecture, memory, storage, and program implementation determine what it can do and how fast it can do it. You may say, "Duh! No kidding!" Yes, this may seem obvious but, unfortunately, some miscreant (and not a security professional) first came up with the buffer overflow technique that made so many computers vulnerable to attack. Therefore, what happens when some high-technology parameter is exceeded may be the beginning of a modus operandi (MO) for committing a high-technology crime.

HIGH-TECHNOLOGY THREATS

To become familiar with this "new world, global threat environment," let's begin by looking at today's basic threats. Today's threats to high technology are often classified as natural (caused by nature) and man made.

Natural threats, such as hurricanes, earthquakes, tornadoes, and the like, are not discussed here. Our focus is on the man-made threats, those that are developed and used by today's collection of global miscreants (also called *malicious threat agents*). The miscreants' attacks are made easier by high technology vulnerabilities.

High-technology systems:

- Have inherent vulnerabilities (weaknesses) that are built into (generally by accident) the hardware and software
- Have vulnerabilities caused by human error in configuring the hardware or software
- Lack readily available security application software to protect them

Miscreants around the world know this, share information, and make it their goal to take advantage of these vulnerabilities to damage, destroy, or steal information. For a system to be secure, all weaknesses need to be protected and monitored at all times. Attackers can succeed if they find just one weakness in the security at the time that they make the attack.

However, you must keep an open mind when conducting your high-technology crime investigations. There may be times that what may look like a successful attack against a computer was in fact caused by human error.

Malicious threat agents (Fig. 1-3) are all driven by some form of catalyst, including events, high-technology changes, personal circumstances, and others. New techniques are constantly being developed by these global miscreants, and there is no end in sight. They are being fueled by hardware

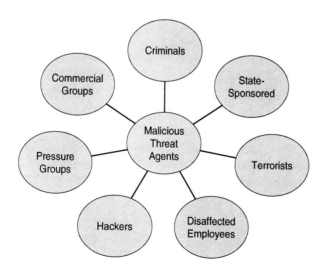

Figure 1-3   Primary types of malicious threat agents.

and software developers who pour out their products and seem to worry about security as an afterthought to be dealt with if a vulnerability is found in their product—to be fixed in the next version of their product. Even Bill Gates of Microsoft has said that security is important; however, Microsoft's products, which are global standards in many respects, continue to be found "buggy," and users are often required to download patches.

Most junk e-mail today emanates from Windows computers that "spammers" have hijacked and turned into spam "zombies" using security holes in Microsoft's operating system. What's more, Microsoft is blamed for wrecking efforts this past summer to create e-mail authentication standards. The company also stands accused of trying to neuter state antispam laws. And Microsoft has yet to win a lawsuit against a major spammer.[9]

As a high-technology crime investigator, you will be constantly faced with computer vulnerabilities and, worse than that, you will find that available security patches to known vulnerabilities are not always taken advantage of by the information technology (IT) staff of even major corporations. Yes, they are getting better at it, but they have a very long way to go as a group. Thus, fixes that are available are not implemented by the IT staff.

The former manager of computer security for Medica Health Plans said the company ignored repeated warnings that its information system was vulnerable to attack and abuse. The health plan's security engineer, until early 2004, said Medica didn't act on his recommendation to "lock down" the computer system and protect sensitive information, including personal information about Medica's 1.2 million members. That and other measures could have prevented two Medica computer administrators from allegedly sabotaging the company's computers and downloading data earlier this year.[10]

The lack of installing available security patches in a timely manner will add to your frustration as you investigate high-technology crimes. By the way, if you are lucky enough (sometimes luck plays a bigger role than good investigative technique) and identify the probable miscreant who is the reason for your investigation, you may find that the miscreant is in another country and extradition is not realistic or possible for one reason or another.

"Berlin, Germany (CNN)—A German court has convicted the teenager who created the Sasser worm that snarled tens of thousands of computers last year and sentenced him to 21 months' probation."[11]

Say you get really lucky and the miscreant is in your country. The district attorney may reject prosecution or the corporation may refuse to press charges because of the costs and associated bad publicity. Say the miscreant is prosecuted and found guilty. The "punishment" may be no more than a small fine or warning with probation to follow.

> "Leesburg, Virginia (AP)—A judge dismissed a felony spamming conviction that had been called one of the first of its kind, saying he found no 'rational basis' for the verdict and wondering if jurors were confused by technical evidence."[12]

A report by Symantec, as cited by SearchSecurity.com,[13] states the following:

- "Increase in malcode variants"
- "Increase in phishing threats"
- "Increase in vulnerability disclosure"

Other information provided in the report includes:

- "Microsoft's SQL server resolution service stack overflow attack was the most common for the period."
- "Denial-of-service attacks grew at an increase of 680% over previous reporting period."
- "Education was the most frequently targeted industry, followed by small business and financial services."

A paper entitled *Computer Attack Trends Challenge the Internet Security*[14] states the following:

- "Antiforensics are being used to mask attacks."
- "Automated attack tools can vary their behavior."
- "Modularity of attack tools make it easier to upgrade them."

The article, although written several years ago, is still valid today. It further states, "The level of automation in attack tools continues to increase. Automated attacks commonly involve four phases, each of which is changing. These phases include scanning for potential victims, compromising vulnerable systems, propagating the attack, and coordinated management of attack tools."[14]

We can provide more examples, but you get the idea. The bottom line is that there appears to be no end to high-technology crime in sight, and the need for those in the high-technology crime investigative profession will continue to grow.

CASE EXAMPLE: DON'T RUSH TO JUDGE

When you are concerned with what appears to be attempted or actual unauthorized access, how do you know it is some form of malicious attack that adversely affects information protection? You must consider the affect that human error and computer misconfiguration may have on the issue. So although the intrusion detection software may detect what appears to be an intrusion, you need to determine whether it really was an actual penetration or a denial-of-service attempt. To illustrate this point, we present the following real-life example.

A large international corporation called in an information systems security consultant and explained they were under attack by their competitor, who was headquartered in another country. They were ready to file a lawsuit against them because they appeared to be accessing their systems without authorization and perhaps performing a denial-of-service attack as well. Furthermore, the attack appeared to be coming through a third party in a third country in an apparent attempt to hide the origin of the attacks. This situation is not unusual and was considered a further indication of the covert attacks by their competitor.

The consultant traveled to the country of the competitor and that of the third party, and talked to law enforcement authorities on the best course of action. The consultant also discussed the matter with the apparently unwitting third party whose systems were being used as the conduit for the attacks. While collecting audit trail evidence and conducting detailed analysis of the third party's system configuration, it was determined that the third party had business relationships and was networked with both parties. It was further determined that the systems were misconfigured in such a manner that they caused the problems being experienced. Thus, there was no attack! Can you imagine the consequences of a lawsuit if the "victim" corporation had hastily filed the lawsuit and the subsequent cause of the attacks were determined? Because the unwitting third party did not request any assistance from the security consultant, the matter was dropped.

Can you think of any events that would make this a more complex and perhaps an international criminal matter? What if the competitor had bribed the third party's system programmer or others to misconfigure the system so, if caught, it would look like human error? As with any investigative matter, proving intent is a key issue.

OTHER AREAS OF INTEREST

The following are examples of related matters that may help you understand today's high-technology environment:

- "Digital Evidence: Today's Fingerprints: Electronic World Increasingly Being Used to Solve Crimes—Police and prosecutors are fashioning a new weapon in their arsenal against criminals: digital evidence. The sight of hard drives, Internet files, and e-mails as courtroom evidence is increasingly common."[15]
- "FBI Shuts Down Public E-mail System; Washington (AP)—The FBI said Friday it has shut down an e-mail system that it uses to communicate with the public because of a possible security breach. The bureau is investigating whether someone hacked into the www.fbi.gov e-mail system, which is run by a private company."[16]
- "Feds Launch Internet Crime Crackdown; Washington (CNN)—Federal agents armed with search warrants conducted raids in three states Wednesday as part of a nationwide crackdown on the theft of copyrighted materials through the Internet, the Justice Department announced. Individuals were being questioned after six searches by investigators in Texas, New York, and Wisconsin, authorities said. No immediate arrests were expected, but charges stemming from the investigation were likely to be filed later, they said. In a separate federal operation aimed at combating Internet fraud and curbing junk e-mails or spam, agents were concluding 'Operation Slam Spam,' which officials could announce as early as Thursday."[17]
- "Germany Proposes Hefty Fines for Spammers; Berlin, Germany (Reuters)—People sending junk e-mail, or spam, in Germany will face fines of as much as 50,000 euros ($65,190) according to a draft law agreed to by Germany's ruling coalition of Social Democrats and Greens. 'Spam e-mail is a big problem. It causes economic problems and costs people a lot of time,' Daniel Holstein, a research associate for the Greens, the junior partner in the government, said on Friday."[18]
- "FBI Cuts Carnivore Internet Probe: Commercial Software Now Used for Investigations; Washington (AP)—The FBI has effectively abandoned its custom-built Internet surveillance technology, once known as Carnivore, designed to read e-mails and other online communications among suspected criminals, terrorists, and spies, according to bureau oversight reports submitted to Congress. Instead, the FBI said it has switched to unspecified commercial software to eavesdrop on computer traffic during such investigations and has increasingly asked Internet providers to conduct wiretaps on targeted customers on the government's behalf, reimbursing companies for their costs."[19]
- "Federal Bounty May Nab E-mail Spammers; Washington (AP)—What would it take to get someone to turn in one of those spammers who send millions of unwanted e-mails? At least $100,000, the Federal Trade Commission figures. Six-figure incentives are the only way to persuade people to disclose the identity of coworkers, friends, and others they know are responsible for flooding online mailboxes with

unsolicited pitches for prescription drugs, weight loss plans, and other products, according to an agency report Thursday. The commission said a government-funded reward system could work if the payoff was between $100,000 and $250,000—higher than rewards in most high-profile criminal and terrorism cases."[20]

- "New Bill Targets Some Peeping Toms: Hidden Cameras Found on Warships; Washington (AP)—Camera phones may make great Christmas gifts, but people better not use them for peeping-Tom photos on federal property."[21]

- "State Spam Law Ruled Unconstitutional; Rockville, Maryland (AP)—A judge has ruled that the antispam law in Maryland—the first state law to penalize senders of junk e-mail—is unconstitutional because it seeks to regulate commerce outside the state's borders. Last week's ruling, which threw out a lawsuit against a New York e-mail marketer, effectively overturns Maryland's 2002 Commercial Electronic Mail Act.... Congress and more than three dozen state legislatures have passed laws to corral spam, the popular term for junk e-mail advertising. Appeals courts have upheld laws in California and Washington that were declared unconstitutional by lower courts on grounds similar to the December 9 ruling in Maryland."[22]

- "Bush Pressed for More Net Security; Washington (Reuters)—Computer security experts, including former government officials, urged the Bush administration on Tuesday to devote more effort to strengthening defenses against viruses, hackers, and other online threats."[23]

- "Experts: Cyber-Crime Bigger Threat than Cyber-Terror—As David Perry left a cyber-security conference in Luxembourg in 2004, an airport terminal handling international flights was in chaos. A network worm known as Sasser was scorching the world's computer systems and had knocked out the airport's reservation desk, stranding delegates in the terminal."[24]

- "Geolocation Tech Slices, Dices Web; New York (AP)—Type 'dentist' into Google from New York and you'll get ads for dentists in the city. Try watching a Cubs baseball game from a computer in Chicago and you'll be stymied. Preexisting local TV rights block the Webcast. The same technology is also being used by a British casino to keep out the Dutch, and by online movie distributors to limit viewing to where it's permitted by license, namely the United States."[25]

- "Study: Spam Costing Companies $22 Billion a Year; New York (AP)—Time wasted deleting junk e-mail costs American businesses nearly $22 billion a year, according to a new study from the University of Maryland."[26]

- "Survey: Thousands Leave Laptops, Mobiles in Cabs; Amsterdam, Netherlands (Reuters)—An estimated 11,300 laptop computers, 31,400 handheld computers, and 200,000 mobile telephones were left in taxis around the world during the last 6 months, a survey found on Monday."[27]

- "Information and Identify Theft Legislation Impairs Industry's Ability to Support Judicial and Legal System—Four leading security associations announced the formation of a new coalition to advocate a Six Point Identity Protection Program to help prevent identify theft without hampering the ability of private investigators to support the judicial system, legal community, law enforcement, corporate security, and private citizens, including assisting victims of identity theft. The founding members of the new coalition are the National Council of Investigation and Security Services (NCISS), ASIS International, Security Companies Organized for Legislative Action (SCOLA), and the International Association of Security and Investigation Regulators (IASIR)....The Six Point Identity Protection Program includes
  - Conducting thorough credentialing of new accounts and those where a review indicates a new check is in order
  - Denying Internet sales of personal identification information to the general public
  - Increasing penalties, such as fines and jail sentences, for the misuse of personal information
  - Enacting legislation requiring data providers to notify customers of breaches
  - Prohibiting use of social security numbers on identification documents such as health care insurance cards, drivers' licenses, and state permits
  - Allowing access to personal data for licensed individuals who can demonstrate a need and have submitted to a background investigation."[28]
- "Geeks Gather at 'What the Hack': Computer Security Conference Aims to Erase Stereotypes; Liempde, Netherlands (AP)—There are hundreds of tents on the hot and soggy campground, but this isn't your ordinary summertime outing, considering that it includes workshops with such titles as 'Politics of Psychedelic Research' or 'Fun and Mayhem with RFID.' This is the 3-day 'What the Hack' convention, a self-styled computer security conference dealing with such issues as digital passports, biometrics and cryptography."[29]
- "UK Military: iPod Is Security Risk; London, England (Reuters)— Music fans, beware: Britain's Ministry of Defense has become the latest organization to add the iPod to its list of high-tech security risks. The pocket-size digital music player, which can store thousands of songs, is one of a series of banned gadgets that the military will no longer allow into most sections of its headquarters in the UK and abroad. Devices with large storage capabilities—most notably those with a universal serial bus (or USB) plug used to connect to a

computer—have been treated with greater suspicion of late by government agencies and corporations alike. The fear is that the gadgets can be used to siphon information from a computer, turning a seemingly innocuous device into a handy tool for data thieves."[30]

- "Survey: Hackers Target Flawed Backup Software; Washington (Reuters)—Flawed backup software has emerged as the latest target for hackers looking for corporate secrets, according to a survey released on Monday. The survey by the nonprofit SANS Institute found new holes in widely used software products, even as computer users are getting better at patching some favorite hacker targets. Attackers are now focusing on desktop software, like Web browsers and media players, that might not get fixed as frequently as Microsoft Corp.'s Windows operating system and other software widely used by business, the cyber security research organization found. More than 422 significant new Internet security vulnerabilities emerged in the second quarter of 2005, the cyber security research organization found, an increase of 11% from the first 3 months of the year."[31]

These snapshots of the global working environment provide you with some understanding of the high technology, miscreants, and issues facing today's high-technology crime investigator. Based on the past and the trends of today, the challenges facing the high-technology crime investigator will continue to grow. So far, the high-technology crime investigators are outgunned and outclassed!

SUMMARY

Computers are electrical devices that, when broken down into basic components, are fairly easy to understand. Computers and the microprocessor (the heart of the computer system) drive much of today's processes. These systems are growing in power, connectivity, and speed, while their prices are declining. This means that it will be an increasingly more difficult job for the high-technology crime investigator to conduct high-technology crime investigations. Therefore, the high-technology crime investigator must work harder and smarter.

The globalization environment, coupled with increased dependency on high technology with inherent vulnerabilities, offers many challenges to the high-technology crime investigator. Our dependency on high technology continues to grow to such an extent that any failure of the hardware and/or software has major personal, business, national, and international repercussions. The challenge to high-technology crime investigators is to maintain a working knowledge of high-technology tools and their changes so they can successfully conduct high-technology crime investigations.

REFERENCES

1. Microsoft Corporation. (1999). *Encarta World English Dictionary* (p. 759). New York: St. Martin's Press.
2. *Global Competitiveness Report 2004–2005.* www.weforum.org/site/home public.nsf/Content/Global+Competitiveness+Programme%5CGlobal+Compe titiveness+Report
3. Friedman, T. L. (2005). *The World is Flat: A Brief History of the Twenty-First Century.* New York: Farrar, Straus, and Giroux.
4. Almasy, S. *The Internet Transforms Modern Life.* www.cnn.com/2005/TECH/internet/06/23/evolution.main/index.html
5. www.worldhistorysite.com/gateway.html
6. *Intel Keeps Moore's Law on Track.* www.cnn.com/2004/BUSINESS/08/29/intel.chips.ap/index.html
7. *Finland to Adopt Mobile Broadband.* www.cnn.com/2005/TECH/06/15/finland.mobile.reut/index.html
8. www.businessweek.com/magazine/content/05_22/b393 5001_mz001.htm?chan=tc
9. www.salon.com/tech/feature/2005/01/19/microsoft_spam/ print.html
10. Medica Ignored Warnings, Says Ex-Employee. Glenn Howratt, Star Tribune.
11. www.cnn.com/2005/LAW/07/08/sasser.suspended/index. html
12. www.cnn.com/2005/LAW/03/02/spam.trial.ap/index.html
13. Symantec. www.searchsecurity.techtarget.com/originalContent/0,289142,sid14_gci1125934,00.html?track=NL-105&ad=529860
14. Housebolder, Houle, & Diugherty. (2002). *Computer Attack Trends Challenge the Internet Security.*
15. Coren, M. (2005). *Digital Evidence: Today's Fingerprints: Electronic World Increasingly Being Used to Solve Crimes.* www.cnn.com/2005/LAW/01/28/digital.evidence/index.html
16. *FBI Shuts Down Public E-Mail System.* www.cnn.com/2005/TECH/02/04/fbi.email.ap/index.html
17. Frieden, T. *Feds Launch Internet Crime Crackdown.* www.cnn.com/2004/TECH/08/26/cybercrime.probe/index.html
18. *Germany Proposes Hefty Fines for Spammers.* www.cnn.com/2005/TECH/internet/01/28/germany.spam.reut/index.html
19. *FBI Cuts Carnivore Internet Probe: Commercial Software Now Used for Investigations.* www.cnn.com/2005/TECH/internet/01/18/fbi.carnivore.ap/index.html
20. *Federal Bounty May Nab E-Mail Spammers.* www.cnn.com/2004/TECH/internet/09/17/ftc.spambounty.ap/index.html
21. *New Bill Targets Some Peeping Toms: Hidden Cameras Found on Warships.* www.cnn.com/2004/LAW/12/09/video.voyeurs.ap/index.html
22. *State Spam Law Ruled Unconstitutional.* www.cnn.com/2004/LAW/12/14/spam.lawsuit.ap/index.html
23. *Bush Pressed for More Net Security.* www.cnn.com/2004/TECH/internet/12/07/tech.security.reut/index.html
24. Coren, M. *Experts: Cyber-Crime Bigger Threat than Cyber-Terror.* www.cnn.com/2005/TECH/internet/01/18/cyber.security/index.html
25. *Geolocation Tech Slices, Dices Web.*

26. *Study: Spam Costing Companies $22 Billion a Year.* www.cnn.com/2005/ TECH/02/03/junk.email.ap/index.html
27. *Survey: Thousands Leave Laptops, Mobiles in Cabs.* www.cnn.com/2005/ TECH/ptech/01/24/taxis.lost.reut/index.html
28. *Information and Identify Theft Legislation Impairs Industry's Ability to Support Judicial and Legal System.*
29. *Geeks Gather at "What the Hack": Computer Security Conference Aims to Erase Stereotypes.*
30. *UK Military: iPod is Security Risk.*
31. *Survey: Hackers Target Flawed Backup Software.* www.cnn.com/2005/TECH/ internet/07/25/hackers.backup.software.reut/index.htm

2

High-Technology Crime Miscreants: Profiles, Motives, and Philosophies

This chapter discusses miscreants and their motives, profiles, and philosophies. It provides an overview of these individuals and groups so that the investigator will have a basic understanding of them as they conduct their high-technology crime investigations.

INTRODUCTION

As a high-technology crime investigator, it is imperative that you know your adversaries—what makes them "tick," so to speak. By understanding their motivations and philosophies, and being able to categorize them, you can more easily identify them and determine why they committed the crime (e.g., violation of regulations or violation of corporate policies). It should also help determine their basic MO.

It is also important for the high-technology crime investigator to understand the history of such high-technology crimes and to look at the development of crime trends to assist you better in predicting the challenges of the future, which will be discussed in some detail in Part IV of this book. After gaining an understanding of the history of high-technology crimes, driven of course by advances in computers, and using the threat agent identification noted in Chapter 1 (see Fig. 1-3), we will discuss the miscreants' profiles, motives, and philosophies in more detail.

"**Miscreant:** somebody who does wrong, a villain, wrongdoer, or generally malicious and contemptible person"[1]

A BRIEF HISTORY OF HIGH-TECHNOLOGY CRIME AND ITS ASSOCIATED MISCREANTS

As stated earlier, the environment is really the only major difference between high-technology criminals and other miscreants found in every society today. The change in environment does not change the type of people or their motives. They are still the same scoundrels who want something someone else owns; or, out of jealousy or just plain meanness, they want to deprive the owner of that thing of value. Some miscreants may even want, and will try, to kill someone through telemedicine by changing test results (e.g., changing a positive test for cancer to negative or changing the drugs that are to be prescribed to a patient). So soon we can probably add murderers to our list of criminals traveling the Internet, along with spies, terrorists, pornographers, environmental extremists, and their ilk.

The juvenile delinquents, economic and espionage spies, hackers, PBX and cellular phone fraudsters, sexual deviants, and other miscreants that commit high-technology crimes generally represent a cross section of those that have been around for probably as long as humans have been around. As soon as one human had something considered of value, some other human would try to find a way to get it or destroy it. It seems to be part of the "evolution" of human beings, for the problem is not confined to the high-technology environment, nor is it confined to any one nation-state. It is a global problem.

> Crime has never been the sole possession of any one race, religion, society, community, or nation, and a pervert has always been a pervert, seeking sexual gratification by illegal means and in illegal ways.

Known generally as *malicious threat agents* (see Fig. 1-3 in Chapter 1), all these miscreants pose threats to the businesses, government agencies, and honest citizens in today's high-technology environment. Let's take a brief look at the history of high-technology crime to assist in understanding these "high-technology criminals."

In the 1970s, high-technology crimes such as computer frauds were rare, and those that did occur were rarely reported, because companies and government agencies did not want the public to lose confidence in them and in their newly installed computers. After all, they were touting the dawn of the computer age, at a cost of millions of dollars.

Perpetrators generally were computer specialists: programmers, computer operators, data entry personnel, systems analysts, and computer managers—insiders. After all, they were the only ones who knew how to operate and use the technology and the only ones who were able to gain physical access to it. Thus the threats were internal, because there were very few dedicated physical connections of these systems to the outside world. In addition, these early computer systems cost millions of dollars, were extremely heavy, and thus were difficult to move. So, even their physical theft was generally not an issue. As technology and the systems evolved, limited networking took place, but most connections occurred via ARPANET (the "father" of the Internet). Therefore, the vast majority of threats were from insiders.

The only real threat to these systems were the spies from the old Cold War period who stole, misappropriated, or illegally diverted shipments of computer schematics and computer systems. They then reverse engineered them to make, for example, copies of IBM mainframes. This type of malicious threat agent (state-sponsored spies and thieves) lasted throughout the Cold War period. Today, this is less of a state-sponsored issue because computers are more readily available to everyone.

In the 1980s, the type and frequency of high-technology crimes changed as a result of the advent of the PC, telecommunications advancements, and networking. Types of internal perpetrators were expanded to include other employees who had access to computer terminals (generally dumb terminals connected to mainframe computers): workers who were motivated to commit policy violations or violate laws, workers who were suffering from financial or personal problems, or workers who were disgruntled, bored, tempted by curiosity, or challenged. The '80s were also the time of the external hackers and their "powerful" 300-baud external modems.

With the advancement of the Internet, telecommunications systems, cheaper and more powerful computers, more powerful modems, dial-up systems, and computer bulletin boards, high-technology criminals had more opportunities to commit their crimes; both the availability of the tools and access to the systems increased. During this period, external threats began to grow. Most information systems security (InfoSec) professionals during the 1980s and early 1990s placed the threats at approximately 80% internal and 20% external.

In the 1990s and into the 21st century, international high-technology crime and frauds developed and will continue to develop, as a result of increased international networking—the global information infrastructure (GII), which is based on the Internet. Also, the "new" technologies of the 20th century's PBX and cellular phones, personal digital assistants (PDAs), and such, all of which are computer based, brought with them the telecommunications criminals, which have increased in number as the technology became cheaper, more powerful, and more widely used.

These "new" perpetrators generally were the same as those of the past, but they now included more international criminals, hackers, and phreakers, because of the ease of international access.

With the integration of telecommunications and computers, along with the integration of government agencies and businesses into the Internet, threats now represent at least an equal split between internal and external threat agents—50% internal and 50% external. There may even be a slight edge toward external threat agents because of today's reliance on the Internet and other corporate and externally connected networks.

The high-technology, microprocessor-based trends of the 20th century continue unabated into the 21st century. We've seen more and more powerful, smaller and smaller, more and more integrated devices. Cellular phones are now also cameras, "notebook computers," and Internet devices with the same capabilities (e.g., Internet and browser capabilities, search engines, e-mail) as the larger notebooks, desktops, and the old legacy systems of 20 years ago.

REQUIREMENTS TO COMMIT A HIGH-TECHNOLOGY CRIME

To commit a high-technology crime and/or violation of regulations or corporate policies, three requirements must be met. According to the Association of Certified Fraud Examiners and members of the criminology profession, these three requirements are the same regardless of the crime to be perpetrated.

1. *Motive*—If one is not motivated to commit a crime, that person would not commit a crime.
2. *Rationalization*—One must be able to rationalize the crime to be committed. For example, many "devoutly" religious people (e.g., terrorists, although their application of religious tenets may be questionable) have committed crimes. One has to wonder that, if they were so religious, how could they commit such a crime when they also believe they go to hell and suffer eternal damnation for such crimes? They rationalize that what they do is not in violation of God's law (or God will forgive them). If they cannot rationalize or justify the act, they will not commit the crime. The rationalization need not be logical or make any sense to anyone else, but the miscreant must believe it.
3. *Opportunity*—The last part of this triad is *opportunity*. If one is motivated and can rationalize a high-technology crime, but knows that there is no opportunity to commit that crime (or no opportunity to commit that crime without getting caught), the perpetrator won't commit the crime, unless he wants to go to prison.

Motive + Opportunity + Rationalization = High-Technology Crime

When discussing this "triad," it is important to remember that as human beings we all would probably commit a crime under the "right" circumstances.

AN EXAMPLE OF A CORPORATE EMPLOYEE AND THE "CRIME TRIAD"

Let's say you have a family with kids who are growing up and getting ready for college. You have a mortgage, car payments, and all the other bills associated with caring for and raising a family. You've worked for a company for about 25 years and you are 54 years old. Now let's say that your boss calls you into his/her office one Friday; he/she tells you that the company is downsizing, and they are terminating your employment. You are told the company is terminating more than 500 people and, according to federal law, your boss is giving you your 60-day notice. You know you are going to have difficulty finding another job, especially at your age, and your skills are somewhat outdated—not in great demand. You don't know how you're going to make it. You know it's a good possibility that, to survive, you are going to have to dip into the kids' college funds. You also realize that you'll have to sell one car because you can't afford two—never mind other financial concerns. In other words, in about 60 days, your entire world will be turned upside down. Is this picture gloomy enough for you? It happens every day. It may even have happened to you at least once.

For most people, this scenario is enough to start them thinking somewhat negatively about where they work and the people they work with. However, just to push you over the edge, let's say that Monday morning, on your way out the door to go to work, you glance at the business section of the newspaper and discover that the company you work for has just posted record-breaking earnings. You read on and learn that the company president is getting a $2.5 million bonus and all executive managers are getting $1 million each for saving the company so much money over the years and for increasing sales and profits.

You now decide to get what you can from that company during the next 60 days. You deserve it. You gave them your blood, sweat, and tears for 25 years, and they are where they are today partly because of you. And what did they give you? The boot! So now, you have *motive* and *rationalization*. When it comes to opportunity, some people use violence (e.g., a postal worker kills the manager who yelled at him), and others use fraud, theft, or whatever opportunity is presented.

In today's world of information and information systems, some ways of getting back at the company include using its computers to misappropriate items for resale; damaging, destroying, or modifying information; or stealing information, hardware, or software to sell (e.g., trade secrets, employees' private information to some "spam" company, mailing lists, customer's lists).

We know how vulnerable computers are and how easy it is for an authorized company system user to have access to sensitive information online. After all, he or she is an "insider" and is "trusted." So, stealing vital information for resale may not be too difficult. In other words, the *opportunity* is there.

The triad "bar" for some is higher than for others. In our case example, the situation is now a matter of survival—a basic and extremely strong human trait. Yes, we all have our limits. As a high-technology crime investigator, keep the triad in mind as you investigate a high-technology crime and try to identify the traid as you search for your suspect.

INSIDER THREATS

Insider threats are still the most serious. The highest risks are from the employees, the individuals who have authorized access to the physical and intellectual property of their employer. Furthermore, they are *trusted*.

Who Is an Insider?

An insider is an employee or a contracted employee who works for a company or government agency. To make a clearer distinction, an insider is defined, at least for our purposes, as someone who receives payment directly from the business or government agency that employs him.

Position of the Insiders

The insider who threatens the company is basically anyone who has access to the high technology, intellectual property, and other sensitive information stored in high-technology equipment (e.g., such as information system networks) as well as input documents or output documents. As a high-technology crime investigator, one basic investigative rule is to find the person who has access.

Remember that those we tend to trust the most are still human beings with the same needs and frailties as others. They are not immune to temptations and should never be discounted as potential suspects in a high-technology crime. Some examples of those who have possibly more access than others and thus may be considered a greater threat include, but are not limited to, the following:

- *Auditors*—Auditors have the authority to gain access to many sensitive areas and a great deal of sensitive information. Furthermore, they conduct audits of computers, PBX systems, and other high-technology processes (depending on the business) that identify areas that lack adequate controls. They are some of the most trusted employees within a business.
- *Security personnel*—Security personnel are the people on the defensive frontlines protecting corporate assets against high-technology crime.

They, like the auditors, know what areas are vulnerable, where security may be weak, and what security controls are in place in all areas of the business. They, like the auditors, are the most trusted personnel within a business. (But, who watches the watchers? Nobody!)

- *Marketing personnel*—The marketeers have access to computer systems, dial-out access to the PBX, cellular phones, pagers, and so on, both in the office and when they travel on company business. They have access to customers' listings, long-range plans, and marketing concepts now and into the future (which is valuable information that can be sold to unethical competitors, especially to those overseas who are immune to the laws of the nation-state where the victim corporation is located). Remember that "globalization" has increased the potential customers of competitors' information and can be easily sent via e-mail attachments from anywhere *to* anywhere in the world.

- *Accountants/financial personnel*—Accountants and financial specialists have access to automated financial accounts, check-writing capabilities, financial analyses of the business, accounts payable, accounts receivable, and other financial information. In many companies, these personnel are also responsible for distributing and controlling company credit cards.

- *Management*—Managers have access to sensitive information and finances (via their budgets), and they generally have more access authority with regard to information systems. Also, they have the authority, or at least the power, depending on the management level, to waive controls—physical, administrative, and logical.

- *Inventory/warehouse personnel*—These individuals have access to physical property and inventory records maintained on the business' computer network. High-technology devices are always a tempting item for misappropriation or theft.

- *Human resource staff*—These people have access to much of the company's information. At a minimum they have information concerning salaries, home addresses, social security numbers, and other information of a private nature that is worth money to businesses building marketing databases of potential customers. In companies going through downsizing, human resource personnel have been known to sell computerized listings of these individuals for various purposes (e.g., spamming, identity theft, and the like).

Insider Motivations, Rationalizations, and Opportunities

Some possible motives of insiders include financial gain, revenge, challenge, curiosity, losing one's job, and so on. Some of the possible rationalizations could be the following: they are underpaid, they didn't get their deserved or expected promotion, their work goes unrecognized, they need money to support their family, they feel they should "get their share," and so forth. Opportunities include lack of audit trails, no access controls to systems or files, lack of separation of duties, lack of monitoring, no method of accountability, lax assets protection controls, and so on.

Insider Threat Recognition

There are various threat indicators that could indicate whether an employee has perpetrated or intends to perpetrate a high-technology crime. Some characteristics or profiles of an insider threat include:

- Bankruptcy
- Pending divorce
- Unexplained wealth
- "Big" spending
- Constant complaining
- Hostility
- Emotional instability
- Signs of extreme stress
- Profound personality changes
- Expressed feelings of being victimized by peers, employers, or an organization
- Always at work, never takes a day off

Insider threats, in addition to disaffected employees, may also include all the groups identified in Chapter 1:

- Criminals
- Terrorists
- State-sponsored agents
- Hackers
- Pressure groups
- Commercial groups

OUTSIDER THREATS

Who Is the Outsider?

As mentioned earlier, outsiders have always been a threat, especially now that corporations rely increasingly on the Internet, global networks, cellular phones, PBX systems, and so forth. In the past, there have been far more documented high-technology crimes perpetrated by insiders than outsiders. However, there is growing evidence that outsider threats may have increased to equal or surpass insider threats, as more and more computers are networked both nationally and internationally, cellular phones are used outside protected areas, and other devices allow for direct inward system access. A further defined list of potential outsider miscreants includes the following:

- Hackers
- Phreakers
- Vendors
- Ex-employees
- Employees of associated businesses
- State sponsored (e.g., foreign government agents)
- Customers
- Subcontractors
- Terrorists
- Contractors (e.g., maintenance personnel)
- External auditors
- Consultants
- Political activists
- Criminals in general
- Pressure groups (e.g., environmentalists)
- Commercial groups (e.g., financial, aerospace, competitors)

There are a number of business and technological developments that have increased the outsider threats:

- The growth of the number of computers internationally continues to increase unabated.
- Computer literacy worldwide continues to increase, thus there are more potential miscreants.
- Telecommunications and networked computers continue to increase worldwide.
- More and more people are telecommuting.
- Increased outsourcing is occurring.
- The use of technologies such as electronic data interchange (EDI), electronic funds transfer (EFT), and point of sale (POS) systems is increasing.
- Strategic, advanced systems are becoming increasingly the target of others as economic competition grows (e.g., Netspionage).
- Terrorism is growing, and it is only a matter of time before terrorists begin targeting computers as targets of opportunity.
- Some agents of nation-states are selling their computer expertise to the highest bidders for illegal system penetrations.
- High-technology devices are being integrated into one device, thus expanding the vulnerabilities of all individual devices into one. For example, a cell phone with a camera allows the photographing of sensitive information in the corporation and then sending it through

the cellular telephone to unauthorized personnel—all without any controls to prohibit such methods.

- Malicious software has become increasingly more sophisticated, allowing for more powerful attacks against assets protection systems (e.g., firewall penetration software).

Outsider Motivations

Many outsiders share the same motivations as insiders. In addition, other motivations of outsiders include the following:

- Revenge of a former employee
- Competitors wanting inside information
- New employees who provide information relative to their previous employer
- Former employee curiosity about their previous access ID and password still being valid
- Political agenda
- Environmental activists attacking corporations who they believe are harming the environment
- Nationalistic economic pressures
- Espionage
- Information warfare

WHO ARE THE HIGH-TECHNOLOGY MISCREANTS AND OTHERS ON THE INTERNET?

High-technology criminals are the miscreants who use computers and telecommunications systems as their tool and as the target for unlawful, immoral, and/or unethical purposes. They can be anyone—the "normal" employee, organized crime members, white-collar workers, drug dealers, people in debt, people wanting to show how smart they are and how dumb you are, people wanting revenge, greedy people, anyone, under the right circumstances. They can be anyone who has the *motive, opportunity,* and *rationalization* for perpetrating their criminal act.

HACKERS, CRACKERS, AND PHREAKERS, OH MY!

The Hackers

One of the biggest challenges facing security, high-technology crime, and law enforcement professionals today is the hacker. This is not only because of some of their increasingly sophisticated methods, but also because of their sheer numbers.

Initially, hackers were just considered intelligent kids who experimented with computers.[2] News reporters played up their stories, and the term *hacker* began to be used as a label, not for the computer enthusiasts who loved learning new things and programming computers, but for those who illegally accessed computers for their personal pleasure, for vandalism, and, later, for criminal purposes.

This general term for those who break into computer systems (gain unauthorized access), now predominantly via the Internet, may be incorrect, but it has stuck and is now part of the Internet culture. Some have tried, unsuccessfully to differentiate between hackers and the miscreants on the Internet, but to no avail.

Hacker Profile

It is generally agreed among those dealing with hackers that the average United States hacker profile in the 20th century was a white male, young (14 years–mid 20s), intelligent, an avid computer enthusiast, introverted, insecure, and from a middle- to upper-middle-income family (as profiled by Kovacich and others in the early 1980s).

This was logical when one thinks that, at the time, because the majority of US citizens were white, only families with sufficient income could afford computers, and these were primarily two-income families with both parents working. So, to help "junior" to prepare for college and the future, computers were bought. Some parents probably believed that it was a good way for junior to stay out of trouble, and it was the modern equivalent to the babysitter. Furthermore, those who were more extroverted generally had friends, more activities, and social events to concern themselves with. Thus the insecure, introverted boy took refuge with his computer—his friend.

> The hacker profile has changed as networks went global, with hackers being primarily white being the biggest change. Now, hackers are from almost every modern or even "semimodern" nation-state of the world. However, hacking still remains a primarily "male-dominated sport."

It is beyond the scope of this book to try to explain why it is that hackers are predominantly male. It may stem from the fact that the computer field seems to be of interest more to males than to females. It may be that males prefer violence, possibly stemming from the "caveman" days of hunting, protecting their turf, and so on. Many a hacker began with computer games, and computer games have grown graphically more violent throughout the years. Suffice it to say that today's hackers are using more sophisticated attacks. They are intelligent but not necessarily overly so, because today's hacking tools require little expertise when compared with the 20th-century attack software. Since going more global as a result of the Internet, there are many more hackers who are older, who may work as threat agents for competitors, and who may be state sponsored in global information warfare.

Motivations of the Hacker

In the opinion of security professionals and the hackers themselves, the 20th century hackers tended to agree that computer hackers are mostly motivated by their desire to:

- Learn about computers as a hobby
- Defy authority
- Respond to a challenge
- Try to "beat the system"
- Cause disruption
- Show contempt for others
- Show how smart they are

However, during the late 20th and into the 21st century, hackers have gradually become more malicious and tend to want to cause more destruction of information and systems, taking advantage of a system's known vulnerabilities to cause wanton destruction and chaos for no logical reason. These low-life, no-life miscreants are basically divided into two categories: (1) juvenile delinquents who would be spray-painting walls with graffiti and breaking windows for "fun" if it were not for the Internet and other networks, and (2) the more dangerous individuals who have a cause or are a type of mercenary being paid by a nation-state or competitor.

United States Department of Justice Hacker Profile

Several years ago, the US Department of Justice (http://ed.harrison.net) described the hackers as the following:

- Between 15 and 45 years old
- Predominantly male, with the number of females increasing
- Having no prior criminal record
- Someone who targets business and government agency systems
- Bright, motivated, and willing to accept challenges
- Fearful of ridicule, exposure, and loss of status
- Someone who usually works alone, but is socially "normal"
- Someone who holds a position of trust, is usually the first to arrive at work, and is the last to leave
- Someone who views criminal acts as a game

It does not appear that much has changed during the last 15 to 20 years.

Psychological Perspectives of the Hacker

During the late 20th century, Dr. Jerrold M. Post, Director of Political Psychology Programs at George Washington University, described hackers as follows:

- They are creative, individualistic problem solvers, but from a psychological perspective they are arrogant, loners, and from a broken or troubled home.
- They seem to suffer from lower self-esteem, have a need to draw attention to themselves, and they seek the recognition of their peers.
- Hackers perceive themselves to be intelligent but poor achievers in school—often perceived as misfits, nerds, weirdos. They are misunderstood, looking for challenges, usually between 12 and 28 years old, from dysfunctional families, and are inept from a social perspective.
- They are motivated by challenges, excitement, and want to learn for intellectual satisfaction.
- They do not consider themselves thieves, but "borrowers." They may be addicted or obsessed by computers.
- They consider themselves civil libertarians, Robin Hoods, and electronic freedom fighters—and maybe sometimes they are.

Do you believe that this description is still valid today? We believe it is, but it no longer describes the vast majority of hackers, as was the case in the 20th century. Hacking has gone global as systems have gone global. Furthermore, the attacks appear more vicious, paralleling some societies that also appear to be becoming more vicious, self-serving, and of the "What's in it for me?" generation.

A Brief History of the Types of Hackers

It is important for a high-technology crime investigator to understand the history of high-technology crimes. Therefore, the following is offered to provide one view of that history and some perspective regarding the changes that have taken place throughout the years. Hackers have been categorized into three basic types[2,3]:

1. *The Curious*—those who break into computers to learn more about them
2. *The Meddlers*—those who break into computers because they are interested in the challenge of breaking in and looking for weaknesses in the system
3. *The Criminals*—those who break into computers to commit a crime, to act for personal gain

The Curious Hacker   It is generally agreed that the first true hackers came from the Massachusetts Institute of Technology (MIT) in the 1950s and

'60s. Many of that initial group belonged to MIT's Technical Model Railroad Club (TMRC). These hackers had an insatiable curiosity—the kind that caused them to wonder what made things work and how to make them operate better. So they took things apart to see how they worked and then found ways to make them work better. They naturally gravitated to the computer. These early hackers were ones who enjoyed learning about computers and how to expand the computer's capabilities, as opposed to those who wanted to learn just enough to get by for their classes. They began to develop their own terminology. For example, they called a piece of equipment that didn't work *losing*. A ruined piece of equipment was called *munged* (aka mash until no good). Someone who insisted on studying for their course was called a *tool*. Garbage was *cruft*.[2]

The term *hack* had previously been used to describe MIT college pranks. However, members of the TMRC used it in a more serious vein as it related to their computer and computer programming exploits, which were clever, innovative, had style, and so forth. The "hacker ethic" was defined as follows: "Access to computers—and anything which might teach you something about the way the world works—should be unlimited and total. Always yield to the Hand-On-Imperative!"[4]

Their philosophy was one of sharing, openness, decentralization, and getting their hands on machines at any cost to improve themselves and to improve the world. They believed that computers could do much to improve the world. Rules that prevented them from taking matters into their own hands were not worth discussing, not to mention abiding by them. They believed that information should be free; they mistrusted authority. They believed they should be judged on their skills and not by their degrees, age, race, or position. They believed that art and beauty can be created on a computer and that computers could change lives for the better. They were young, intelligent free spirits who lived for the computers they learned from and modified, and for the software that they wrote and made more and more efficient.[2]

> As computers improved, proliferated, and became less of a novelty, the types of hackers also began to change. With the new, modern computers of the 1970s came passwords, software licenses, copyright notices, protected programs, and other controls that were totally contrary to the hackers of old.

As computers began playing a more and more important role in our daily lives, our dependency on them continued to increase. We could not take chances that unauthorized users would gain access to them. To safeguard these computers and their information, additional security controls were put in place. Thus began the adversarial relationship between hackers and the people responsible for safeguarding the computers and the information stored, transmitted, and processed therein. Although this relationship started during earlier years, a line was now drawn in the sand. This didn't deter the hackers. In fact, it probably increased their eagerness to break into the computers. This was an increased challenge to their egos and their talents—like a bullfighter waving a red cape in front of the bull. How could these young bulls resist?

The Meddler—The Juvenile Delinquent The next generation of hackers had the spirit of the older hacker generation, but was more active in computer penetrations. Some called this type of hacker the *meddler*.[4] The meddler is a hacker who is inquisitive and an irritant to the staff of the computer system he attempts to penetrate. This person normally tries to uncover information about a system, such as the type of system, the passwords for it, how it works, what type of software it uses, the telephone number to dial in to it, and so forth. After discovering the information, the hacker will then try accessing the system without authority. This inquisitive person in the days of "dial-ups," and before the Internet expanded into what it is today, would often use a "hacking software" product that was known as a *war dialer* that continuously dialed telephone numbers, looking for the computer modem tone. Then the hacker used various types of software (or just guessed) to identify a user's identification and passwords to gain access.

Today, these miscreants, using search tools such as Yahoo, Lycos, and Excite; search the Internet for hacking tools; download hacker software programs (or security programs that have been turned into hacking tools); identify a target; and then just execute the programs. Although this is a very simple process, it continues to work.

The meddler is interested in the challenge of trying to break into the systems and, once in, to discover its uses, how it operates, and generally to learn as much as possible about it. This type of hacker has even been known, on occasion, to identify vulnerabilities, correct them, or recommend corrections to the computer operations staff—not so much out of kindness, but out of ego by "kicking sand in their faces." Many of these hackers, like those before them, are the type to take apart a clock, radio, or other piece of electronic equipment just to see how it operates. They, too, are not only curious, but usually have no intention of destroying the system's software, files, or information stored on the computer. The primary difference between these hackers and earlier hackers was that they accessed computers without any approval or authority. If they were challenged, they became the juvenile delinquents of the Internet.

The True Criminal Element This generation of hackers began to gain unauthorized access to computer systems in violation of the computer crime laws that were rapidly being ratified by many modern nation-states in the 20th century. Some of these threat agents began to destroy information, steal information, and damage system files. Additionally, their use of the systems cost the owners money. Initially, and to some extent today, computer costs were generally charged back to customers directly or indirectly through budget allocations. Previously it was based on time on the systems. The use of the computer literally meant that time was money! However, with the expansion of more powerful, cheaper, and more sophisticated systems, charging for system time is basically a thing of the past. Therefore, hackers who are being tried in court these days are more apt not to be charged with using computer time, but for damages caused (e.g., denial-of-service attacks, such as when a corporation's customers or employees could not access the system and thus the corporation lost money because their customers couldn't purchase items online, employees could not work, and thus productivity was lost).

In the past, as these criminals began to penetrate computers, they bragged about their exploits to fellow hackers via hacker bulletin boards. These hacker computers linked through telephone lines enabled them to "talk" to one another. It is interesting to note that many of the hacker bulletin boards had better security than the billion-dollar corporation systems they had penetrated! Now these hackers, along with the true hackers and meddlers, often operate their own Web sites on the Internet.

These penetrations and subsequent unauthorized entry and manipulation of computer files, such as those of TRW credit records, caused more harm and increased publicity. Because of public outrage and legislation, hackers began to face confiscation of their equipment by federal and local law enforcement officials, many times to the surprise of the parents who saw their son's or the family's computer being carted away as evidence.

Although there are still those computer and telephone hackers who fit the profile of the hackers of the '50s, '60s, and '70s, the late 1980s saw two new types of hackers. The first type includes the international hackers, who began penetrating computers in the United States from as far away as Europe. The case that gained the most publicity was one in which a hacker was traced from Lawrence Berkeley Lab to Hannover, Germany.[5] It was subsequently determined that this hacker was being paid by the KGB to break into US computers. Hacking had become an international "profession!" The other type of hacker is the one who began penetrating the telephone switching systems for the sole purpose of initially using and subsequently selling toll-free international telephone calls to anyone with $15 or $20. They became known as the "phreakers."

The new challenge is to inhibit these hackers and phreakers who are causing annual losses in the billions of dollars. Jerry Swick, former senior investigator at MCI, said:

> According to law enforcement and private sector experts, business losses from telecommunications fraud are estimated at more than $4 billion per year. The average loss per incident to users exceeds $50,000. Telecrooks, hackers, and "phone phreaks" are invading corporate telephone and voice messaging systems at an unprecedented rate. This type of activity disrupts an organization's valuable communications network and causes losses of

revenue. Telecommunications fraud creates an expensive problem that affects consumers, and your businesses. As the telephone becomes more integrated into the Internet, this will open up an entirely new source of threats, vulnerabilities, and risks.

International Hacker Criminals Both home-grown and international hackers have increased in number as access to the Internet exploded around the world. Some have targeted systems in the United States, especially those of the Department of Defense. These juvenile delinquents and foreign government information warriors have become more sophisticated, better equipped, and more vicious than their predecessors. It was rumored that a group of Dutch hackers had offered their support to Iraq during the first Persian Gulf War. They have denied making any such offer. The financial systems of the United States have come under increased attacks, and some of the most serious are from Russia's criminal elements.

Adding to the global aspects of today's hacker criminals is their use by competitors to steal company-sensitive information from their competitors, generally with immunity as they sit in other nation-states. As the global marketplace becomes broader and more competitive, we expect to see a steady increase in the amount of high-tech crimes being conducted around the world. In addition, the Internet and other global networks are being used by one nation-state to attack the networks of other nation-states. Taiwan and China are a good example of such attacks.

The Phreakers

Although the term *phreakers* has generally faded from our vocabulary (as has the term *crackers,* which is synonymous with hackers), particularly as a result of the change from analog to digital communications technologies, they are still out there, even though much more emphasis is being placed on Internet miscreants than phreakers. While the hackers were busy breaking into computer systems, the phreaker was busy breaking into telephone switching systems and making telephone calls around the world without paying for them. One of the first to gain notoriety was called "Captain Crunch." He allegedly found that a free whistle enclosed in each box of cereal, when held to the telephone handset, made the same sound as the telephone switching equipment. It provided him the ability to make free long-distance telephone calls. Another was known as "The Cracker." This person, at the age of 14, began to explore telephone switching systems.[6]

The phreaker is a hacker who specializes in telecommunications hacking. They prefer PBXs and telephone switches. When writing to one another and others, they exchange the letter "f" with "ph," which is why they are known as phreakers (similar to those who are "phishing" and not "fishing" for information). Today, these juvenile delinquents and criminals pose some of the most serious challenges to security and law enforcement professionals. Some of them have skills that rival those of the engineers working for telecommunications corporations.

These hackers and phreakers formed "hacker gangs" and often were at war with each other. Some shared information and others were rivals. The rival gangs often attacked each other as the street gangs of today. Gangs such as Masters of Deception, Legion of Doom, and numerous others were loosely formed groups of young hackers who enjoyed the camaraderie of sharing information and attacking systems together.

With the merging of computers and telecommunications devices, the term *phreaker* may no longer be relevant. We prefer to call them *miscreants* and group them with the hackers.

PROFILE OF THE HIGH-TECHNOLOGY AND INTERNET FRAUDSTERS

Technology fraudsters, like other technocriminals previously discussed, can be anyone—organized crime members, white-collar workers, drug dealers, people in debt, people wanting revenge, greedy people—anyone, under the right circumstances.

Don't forget that high-technology fraud offenders differ little from the "average" person. According to some studies,[7] most offenders commit fraud for the same reasons most criminals commit crimes, as we previously discussed: motive, opportunity, and rationalization. Studies also indicate that most computer crimes have been committed for personal financial gain, followed by being intellectually challenged, to help the organization, and as a result of peer pressure or to gain peer recognition.

HIGH-TECHNOLOGY TERRORISTS

For technology-driven terrorists, the Internet may soon become the vehicle of choice, as car bombs are today. Terrorism is basically the use of violent and terrifying actions for political purposes, as by a government, to intimidate the population, or by an insurgent group to oppose the government in power.

Terrorists are defined based on your point of view and interests. For example: The Federal Bureau of Investigation (FBI) defines terrorism as "...the unlawful use of force or violence against persons or property to intimidate or coerce a government, the civilian population, or any segment thereof, in furtherance of political or social objectives."

- The Central Intelligence Agency defines international terrorism as "...terrorism conducted with the support of foreign governments or organizations and/or directed against foreign nations, institutions, or governments."

- The US State Department and Department of Defense define terrorism as "…premeditated, politically motivated violence perpetrated against a noncombatant target by subnational groups or clandestine state agents, usually intended to influence an audience. International terrorism is terrorism involving the citizens or territory of more than one country."

A terrorist, then, is one who causes intense fear—one who controls, dominates, or coerces through the use of terror. With more and more businesses, government agencies, and users becoming more and more dependent on the Internet, it is just a matter of time before Internet terrorism becomes viable and terrorists begin committing their acts. However, instead of car bombs, they will be using logic bombs and viruses.

WHY USE TERRORIST METHODS?

Terrorists, of the type that we understood prior to 9/11, generally use terrorism when those in power do not listen, there is no redress of grievances, and/or when individuals or groups oppose current policy. They find that there is usually no other recourse available. A government may want to use terrorism to expand its territory or influence another country's government. The advent of the fundamentalist terrorists who have dominated the current environment has different objectives and works on significantly different values to those we have had to deal with in the past. It is likely that, in the future, as we get to understand their high-technology capabilities better, we will have to reconsider what the threats actually are from this now dominant group.

WHAT IS A TERRORIST ACT?

What is a terrorist act? Generally speaking, it is what the government in power says it is. Some of the questions that come up when discussing terrorism are:

- What is the difference between a terrorist and a freedom fighter?
- Does "moral rightness" excuse violent acts?
- Does the cause justify the means?

RESULTS OF TERRORIST ACTIONS

Terrorist acts cause an increase in security. They may cause the government to decrease freedoms of its citizens to protect them. This, in turn, may cause more citizens to turn against the government, thus supporting the terrorists! It also causes citizens to become aware of the terrorists and their demands.

We can see the beginning of this trend in the United States and in Europe. We are willing to give up some of our freedom and privacy to have more security and personal protection, such as increased airport security searches and questioning of passengers.

Terrorists cause death, damage, and destruction as a means to an end. Sometimes, these acts may cause a government to listen, and they may also cause social and political changes. Current terrorist targets have included transportation systems, citizens, buildings, government officials, military barracks, and embassies.

TERRORIST TECHNOLOGY THREAT ENVIRONMENT

Today's terrorists are not only using technology to communicate (e.g., e-mail), and high-technology crimes to fund their activities (e.g., credit card fraud, illegal bank money transfers), they are beginning to look at the potential for using technology in the form of information warfare against their enemies. It is estimated that this will increase in the future.

Because today's technology-oriented countries rely on vulnerable computers and telecommunications systems to support their commercial and government operations, this is becoming a concern to businesses and government agencies throughout the world. The advantage to the terrorist of attacking these systems is that Internet terrorists acts can be carried out with little expense by very few people and can cause a great deal of damage to the economy of a country.

They can conduct these activities with little risk to themselves, because these systems can be attacked and "destroyed" from the base of a country friendly to them. In addition, they can do so with no directly attributable loss of life, thus escaping the extreme backlash against them if they had destroyed buildings with much direct loss of life. However, at this time, they want more carnage, more people in fear, and more blood on the television news. Therefore, their attacks will probably continue primarily to be those of car bombs and suicide bombers. However, when they find a way to penetrate networks to modify controls over nuclear reactors, power grids, water control, air traffic control, and so forth, to cause massive human carnage and economic destruction within a nation-state, it is probably only a matter of time before they use it. The key now is for them to use whatever means they have to cause carnage and chaos. Thus far, blowing themselves up with others seems to be their preferred method of destruction.

HIGH-TECHNOLOGY ECONOMIC AND INDUSTRIAL ESPIONAGE ON THE INTERNET—NETSPIONAGE

When we look at rapid, technology-oriented growth, we continue to find nation-states of "haves" and "have-nots." We also see corporations that conduct business internationally and those that want to do so. International economic competition and "trade wars" are increasing. Corporations are finding increased competition as a result of globalization and are looking for that competitive edge, that competitive advantage.

One way to gain the advantage, that edge, is through industrial and economic espionage. It is true that both forms of espionage have been around since there has been competition. However, in this Information Age, competitiveness is more time dependent, more crucial to success, and has increased dramatically, largely because of high technology—the technology based on the microprocessor. Thus, we see the increased use of high technology to steal that competitive advantage and, ironically, these same technology tools are also what is being stolen! In addition, we now have more sensitive information consolidated in large databases on Internet networked systems with security that is often questionable.

INDUSTRIAL AND ECONOMIC ESPIONAGE DEFINED

To clarify what we are talking about here, definitions of industrial espionage and economic espionage are in order. Industrial espionage is defined as an individual or private business entity sponsorship or coordination of intelligence activity conducted for the purpose of enhancing a competitor's advantage in the marketplace.

According to the FBI, economic espionage is defined as "government-directed, sponsored, or coordinated intelligence activity, which may or may not constitute violations of law, conducted for the purpose of enhancing that country's or another country's economic competitiveness."

TRY CATCHING THESE MISCREANTS!

During the days of the Cold War, ex-KGB, ex-CSR, and ex-GRU (as well as active) agents were professionals, but the most dangerous were the computer scientists with doctoral degrees who were trained by the KGB, GRU, and others. They have many decades of experience, and they reverse engineered IBM mainframes in the "good ol' days"; these were the individuals who InfoSec professionals feared most. These are the ones who, without sheer luck and/or a lot of money spent on security, were not caught.

If they were caught, it was almost impossible to investigate the crime and build a case that would stand up in court. In addition, lack of jurisdiction was always a barrier that could never be penetrated. For example, try having a KGB-employed Russian computer scientist operating in Moscow arrested. This was impossible! Times have changed from those Cold War days, only in that the number of these highly trained hacker criminals has expanded to include other nation-states as they expanded their high-technology base.

PROPRIETARY ECONOMIC INFORMATION

This new world environment makes a corporation's proprietary information more valuable than ever. When we talk about proprietary economic information, we are talking about, according to the FBI, "...all forms and types of financial, scientific, technical, economic, or engineering information including but not limited to data, plans, tools, mechanisms, compounds, formulas, designs, prototypes, processes, procedures, programs, codes, or commercial strategies, whether tangible, or intangible...and whether stored, compiled, or memorialized physically, electronically, graphically, photographically, or in writing." This assumes that the owner takes reasonable measures to protect his information and that it is not available to the general public. These types of information are key targets for industrial and economic espionage agents, and much of this information is now available via the Internet.

ECONOMIC ESPIONAGE VULNERABILITIES

The increase in economic espionage is also largely the result of corporate vulnerabilities to such threats. Corporations do not adequately identify and protect their information, nor do they adequately protect their computer and telecommunications systems.

Even today, corporations often do not have adequate security policies and procedures, and employees are not aware of their responsibilities to protect their corporation's proprietary information. Many employees do not believe they have any information worth stealing or believe, "It can't happen here."

Therefore, the combination of the following all add up to some very dangerous times for those with information worth protecting and major challenges to the security, high-technology crime investigator, and law enforcement professionals with the responsibility for that protection and investigating incidents:

- A nation's or corporation's information that is valuable to other nations and businesses
- The amount of money that some are willing to pay for that information
- The increase in miscreants willing to try to steal that information
- The increase in Internet ports to businesses and government agencies
- The vulnerabilities of systems on the Internet
- The lack of security as a high priority for businesses and government agencies
- The ability to steal that information on a global scale

When corporations fail to protect their information adequately, they are taking risks that will, in all probability, cause them to lose market share, profits, and business, and help weaken the economic power of their country.

INFORMATION WARRIORS AND CYBER WARRIORS

Information warfare (also referred to as *information operations*) is the term used to define the concepts of 21st-century warfare, which will be electronic and information systems driven. Because it is still evolving, the definitions and budgets are "muddy" and dynamic.

In the United States and other modern nation-states, government agencies and even departments within the Department of Defense (US Air Force, US Navy, Office of the Secretary of Defense, National Security Agency, US Army, and so on) all seem to have somewhat different definitions of information warfare and information operations. As you would expect, these agencies now define information warfare in terms of strictly military actions as information operations; however, this does not mean that the targets are strictly military targets.

> Information warfare, as defined by the US Defense Information Systems Agency (DISA), is "actions taken to achieve information superiority in support of national military strategy by affecting adversary information and information systems while leveraging and protecting our information and information systems."*

The federal government's definition of information warfare can be divided into three general categories: offensive, defensive, and exploitative.

1. *Offensive*—Deny, corrupt, destroy, or exploit an adversary's information, or influence the adversary's perception.
2. Defensive—Safeguard ourselves and allies from similar actions (also known as *information warfare hardening*).
3. *Exploitative*—Exploit available information in a timely fashion to enhance our decision/action cycle and disrupt the adversary's cycle.

In addition, the military views information warfare to include electronic warfare (e.g., jamming communications links), surveillance systems, precision strike (e.g., if you bomb a telecommunications switching systems, it is considered information warfare), and advanced battlefield management (e.g., using information and information systems to provide information on which to base military decisions when prosecuting a war).

---

*This definition seems to be a good "summary" definition of all the federal government agencies' definitions noted earlier.

Some may wonder how they can be involved in a country's information warfare activities. After all, isn't that between governments and their military forces? Nothing can be further from the truth. During World War II, the Allies bombed cities and private factories of the Axis forces. Today's and tomorrow's cities and private factories are on the Internet—a nation's information infrastructure—and its Web sites. The Chinese of the People's Republic of China have the view, as do most other countries, that information warfare will include the civilian community:

> The rapid development of networks has turned each automated system into a potential target of invasion. The fact that information technology is increasingly relevant to people's lives determines that those who take part in information war are not all soldiers and that anybody who understands computers may become a "fighter" on the network. Think tanks composed of nongovernmental experts may take part in decision making; rapid mobilization will not just be directed to young people; information-related industries and domains will be the first to be mobilized and enter the war.[8]

Based on a combination of the definitions noted earlier, one can look at information warfare as being a factor in information, systems, and telecommunications protection. The information warriors, cyber warriors, techno-spies, Internet terrorists, or whatever one wants to call them, present additional increased challenges to all those on, attached to, or concerned with making the Internet a safe place to travel, visit, and maintain as a free space for sharing information and learning.

Remember that these armies of information warriors are looking at the targets presented along the Internet, and the first of these are commercial, or nonmilitary. The weapons that they will use can be categorized as attack, protect, exploit, and support weapons systems. They have the funding and identification of targets, and they are developing plans and sophisticated application programs to attack a nation's information infrastructure, which includes those on the Internet.

SOPHISTICATED DRUG DEALER USE OF HIGH TECHNOLOGY

The following quote is provided to give the high-technology crime investigator some perspective regarding the use of high technology to commit a crime:

"'Drug traffickers no longer use telephones or radios. They have become sophisticated using equipment that codifies their messages,' Also Demoz, head of the Latin American and Caribbean division of the United Nations Drug Control Program (UNDCP), told Reuters. Julio Cesar Araoz, head of Argentina's drug enforcement agency, said, 'Drug-trafficking organizations have globalized their task and use high technology,' and said similar tactics should be used by governments to fight the drug war. 'Latin America and the Caribbean should likewise have a globalized reaction based on international cooperation. And we have to use the same technology as the traffickers, because otherwise it looks like a lost battle,' he said."[9]

SUMMARY

One should not be surprised to see that those who are interested in adult or child pornography, racism, bigotry, perpetrating frauds and scams, and others whose behavior has been termed unacceptable by most societies, are involved in high-technology crimes. They are also the ones out there "surfing" the GII, Internet, National Information Infrastructure (NII), and companies' high-technology systems.

They are not unique. High-technology crime investigators have come across these types of people prior to the construction of any high-technology networks, devices, and equipment. The high-technology crime investigator will find these same types of people on the GII and Internet, and using other high-technology equipment for the very same reasons that they used other techniques and methods in the past. They are the same people, thus not unique to the high-technology environment.

The high-technology investigator should know that there are those employees and outsiders who, for reasons including sexual gratification, "buying" that get-rich scheme, and out of curiosity, are willing to open business or government agency doors leading to a perceived wealth or justifications for their actions. For those who don't open the door, there are those who use tactics, tools, and techniques to break down the door.

The high-technology investigator, to be successful, must know "what makes people tick." Again, people are people; only high technology and its environment has changed. In addition, the high-technology crime investigator should have a basic understanding of the techniques used by these miscreants.

REFERENCES

1. *Microsoft Encarta World English Dictionary*, 1993–2003. New York: St. Martin's Press.
2. Levy, S. (2001). *Hackers: Heroes of the Computer Revolution, update edition.* New York: Penguin Books.
3. Kovacich, G. L. (1993). *Hackers: From Curiosity to Crime.* In The White Paper. Association of Certified Fraud Examiners.
4. Steele. (1983).
5. Stoll, C. (1989). *The Cuckoo's Egg.* New York: Doubleday.

6. Landreth, B. (1985). *Out of the Inner Circle: A Hacker's Guide to Computer Security.* Microsoft Press.
7. Association of Certified Fraud Examination. (1995). Fraud Course.
8. The British Broadcasting Corporation summary of world broadcasts. Translated from the *Jiefangjun Bao* (newspaper). Beijing, China, June 25, 1996, p. 6.
9. www.infowar.com

3

The Basic Techniques Used by High-Technology Crime Miscreants

This chapter provides the high-technology crime investigator with a non-technical overview of some of the basic methods high-technology criminals use to conduct their criminal deeds.

INTRODUCTION

There is no doubt that high-technology crimes are increasing, especially in the more high-technology-dependent corporations, government agencies, and societies, which are more vulnerable to threat agents. Before discussing the ways that high-technology miscreants attack high-technology systems, a summary of the reasons why these attacks are gaining in number and are successful is presented to provide additional background information prior to beginning to explain the methods that are being used and why they are being used. These reasons were valid more than 5 years ago and are still valid today.

High-technology security problems have increased and high-technology criminals are successful for several reasons, including the following:

- A more distributed computing network environment no longer controlled in one room with dumb terminals in office areas
- More networking both nationally and internationally
- Blurring of computers and telecommunications systems (e.g., a PBX is a computer, a cell phone is an Internet device and a camera)
- The capability for more remote systems maintenance (If access codes are known, anyone who knows them could take over the system.)
- Cheaper hardware, software, and communications; thus, more available to more people

- Poor high-technology security because it is still not redesigned from the initial stages and is a rather low priority (but it is moving up the priority chain)
- More individuals growing up with high technology have turned into high-technology criminals and vandals (Why break a business' store windows and spray paint walls when they can break Microsoft Windows and "spray paint" Web sites?)
- Less morality and social pressure to conform to societies' standards
- Opportunity for global criminal gains with little international recourse by law enforcement agencies
- General standardization on specific hardware and software (e.g., TCP/IP, UNIX, browsers, and Windows XP environments that have known vulnerabilities that are found and exploited before vendor patches are developed and implemented)
- Systems are generally easier to use
- More hackers, although most are much less technically competent than in the past
- Few, but smart, very sophisticated miscreants with a great deal of technical competency
- More integration of the high-technology devices (e.g., PBX, computer, cell phones, digital cameras, Internet devices, pagers)
- Law enforcement and high-technology crime investigators lack the training, knowledge, budget, and other resources to deal adequately with high-technology crimes

INTERNAL AND EXTERNAL ATTACKS

In the previous chapter we discussed the various types of miscreants who are committing high-technology crimes. Again, it is important to stress these are the same people and type of miscreants who, in most cases, would have conducted these criminal acts regardless of a high-technology environment. They would have found some way to perpetrate their deeds. We're talking about the criminal element and not the usual juvenile or young adult hacker who does it as a "hobby."

The high-technology environment has provided these miscreants, in many cases, a new and better opportunity to commit their crimes. This is the result of a different, more complex, and difficult type of required security environment. It is no longer just a physical environment. It is a "cyber space" environment—more complicated, relatively newer, and one in which there are concerns about security but not a great deal of good high-technology security in most businesses and government agencies.

Since the US government passed the Computer Security Act of 1987 with the goal of protecting the sensitive information processed, stored, and transmitted by government systems, we still find the majority of these systems have not met the spirit and intent of this law. However, there have been some improvements.

The high-technology crime investigator must continue to stick to the investigative basics when investigating such crimes because the miscreants will continue, for the most part, to stick to their previous objectives of fraud, theft, and destruction, but in the high-technology environment.

"Under Siege in Dulles By New-Generation Hackers—The hackers used to be the little guys, scampering around unleashing viruses and furtive attacks against Web sites. It was a nuisance, but big government and commercial sites generally could chase them away."

"International Business Machines Corp. released a report saying 'criminal-driven security attacks' jumped 50% in the first half of this year compared with last year. IBM's global security intelligence team detected more than 237 million security attacks worldwide in the first 6 months, including 54 million against governments, 36 million against manufacturers, and 34 million against financial services"[1]

HIGH-TECHNOLOGY MISCREANTS' BASIC APPROACH TO ATTACKING NETWORKS*

High-technology criminals who attack through high-technology systems, especially those that are networked, for example, to the GII, Internet, and other systems, generally use a common attack philosophy and methodology. Their sequence of attacks usually follows the scenario depicted in Figure 3-1.

- Identify the target (this could also be a file, company, government agency, network) then research it. If it is connected to the Internet, research it as much as possible by doing a search using one or more of the search engines that can be found on the Internet, collect information, and gather documentation and system identification.
- For various computer hardware and software, excellent sources of information are the computer emergency response teams (CERTs) announcements notifying all those on their Internet subscribers' list as to new-found system vulnerabilities and how to eliminate or at least mitigate the new-found vulnerabilities. Normally, attackers keep up with these vulnerabilities from the CERTs and use them to attack systems faster than the Internet-targeted businesses or government agencies can patch the systems against the vulnerabilities!
- Use basic hacker software tools and techniques and begin the attack. Once inside, the attackers steal, modify, or destroy information, or make use of the facilities (e.g., processor power or storage).
- Depending on his objectives, the attacker may:

---

*Emphasis is placed on those related to the internet because, for high-technology crime investigators and others, the Internet is the "hot" high-technology crime environment, as well as where law enforcement at all levels of government are concentrating much of their efforts (e.g., on child pornography and hackers).

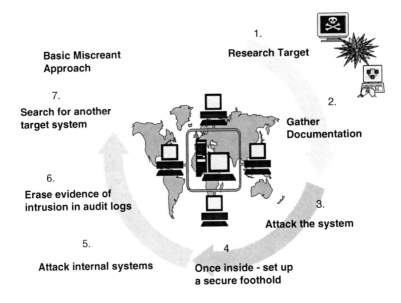

Figure 3-1   General attack methodology by a miscreant.

○ Install a covert backdoor that circumvents protection systems to reenter the system later.
○ Search for other systems that are networked to the system just penetrated and attack them in a similar manner.
○ Log off the system. (The attacker may or may not erase the audit trail records identifying what he did.)

BASIC USE OF PHYSICAL AND HUMAN INTELLIGENCE COLLECTION METHODS: THEFT AND SOCIAL ENGINEERING

Based on the general systematic approach just presented, the attacker must gather information about the target from some source or sources. Let us use the example of a high-technology criminal whose goal is to obtain information about a company. Again, we go back to the GII, NII, and Internet, because these massive networks are excellent examples of the high-technology environment in which miscreants will ply their trade now and into the future. It is where high-technology crime investigators are expected to spend a great deal of their investigative time.

The Internet itself provides an excellent vehicle for the attackers to share and collect information on a global scale. They can use the Internet to search out their targets and to share information about that target and attack techniques with other miscreants around the world.

The information miscreants share may not be about Internet-connected networks or breaking into computer systems. The information they share may be about how to make fraudulent long-distance calls; provide PBX voice mail box access codes; and how to clone cellular phones, listings of credit card numbers, details of their owners, and even where to buy and sell specific types of drugs. Remember that these massive networks are global *communications* systems. Thus, the high-technology criminal uses them as they would a telephone, telegraph, or letter a few years back.

You may recall watching a typical television drama in which the police, trying to catch a criminal involved in fraud, drug dealing, and so forth, covertly take the person's garbage and sift through it for information that can be used to help their investigation. High-technology criminals often use the same technique. They frequently rummage through the trash bins of their target, looking for clues to assist them in successfully attacking that target. This has been called *dumpster diving* and is one reason why some corporations actually secure their garbage!

So, what are these "dumpster divers" looking for? They are seeking information that will tell them more details about individuals, the organization, and the computing environment of the target. For example, there may be boxes in the trash that had been used to transport new computer hardware and software. One of the boxes may have been used to ship the target's new Internet firewall product, its new network server, routers, and switches, as well as the new version of their operating system.

> Sometimes it may be necessary to gather information directly from the target, whether it is a business or government agency. The basic methods for doing so are by personally collecting the information on the target's site, through theft, social engineering, or a combination of both.

In addition, they will look for memos, telephone books, anything with names, job titles, and telephone numbers that may give a hint regarding the user IDs and passwords people may be using, and possibly passwords themselves. This information can also be used for social engineering.

Even expired passwords provide good information because they may indicate a pattern that would allow easy guessing of the new password. For example, if I am required to change my password every month, I may choose a word with a sequential set of numbers. So when I have to change my password I use "password2" in February. Then in March, when I am again required to change my password, I use "password3." This meets the security requirements to change passwords on a monthly basis as well as the security requirement to use alphanumeric characters for my passwords, but it also means anyone who finds my old password could easily predict my current and future password.

The information also may be gathered by posing as an employee, a prospective employee, vendor, or even as a janitor on a night shift (when there are probably fewer people around). All it takes to obtain almost unrestricted access to a target site is getting hired by the janitorial service or finding out what work clothes the janitors use and stealing a set or buying a similar set. Photo ID badges used by the organization pose little deterrent to a determined Internet criminal. With just a little bluffing (using social engineering techniques), he may tell the security guard that he is a new employee, and he has an appointment to get an ID badge in the morning. In the interim, the janitorial company has told him to sign in as a visitor. More likely than not, the guard will allow access for the single evening, which may be all that is required.

This is only one way of "social engineering" your way into the targeted facility. The objective is to convince someone to allow you access to the target facility. Once inside, you have many hours to find information that will assist you in breaking in the company computer network, system, and the like. If you are lucky, maybe someone even left their computer operating and connected to the organization network at the end of the workday. Such a lucky break will allow the fortunate intruder to act as an "authorized" user with access to the system.

> "Researchers from a little-known security software company named Sunbelt Software have seemingly uncovered a criminal identity theft ring of massive proportions. During the course of one of their recent investigations into a particular Spyware application (rumored to be called CoolWebSearch), they've discovered that the personal information of those 'infected' was being captured and uploaded to a server." (Massive spyware-based identity theft ring uncovered arstechnica.com, Clint Ecker).

Social engineering is used quite often for gathering information necessary to attack a system successfully on the Internet. Social engineering is nothing more that the ability to "con" information out of someone and/or make them do what you want them to do. For example, taking an organization's phone book out of a dumpster may give the Internet robber the names of people who may have the information required to break into a major network or application containing the most critical information of the organization.

Another approach that has been used is to call during nonbusiness hours, the later at night the better, because all the higher-level managers, if not all managers, will most likely have gone home. The miscreant calls the systems operations group, which typically works 24-hours-a-day, and tells them he needs access to their maintenance port to do some online maintenance. The miscreant then gives them as the name of "his" company, their primary computer vendor (e.g., Sun, IBM—whatever works)!

You know what systems they have from documentation you obtained in your previous searches or by calling up someone in the target corporation and asking her what computers the company is using. Again, social engineering techniques apply. You can say you are a high school student looking for a company for your high school science class to tour that has a certain type of computer. Normally, you will be referred to the public relations or marketing people. In either case, these individuals have been known to give out a great deal of information.

You can also pose as a computer salesman, or anyone else who can get information because of who they claim to be. The most essential skill for social engineering is the ability to make other people believe what that person is telling them.

If the operations person is hesitant in providing that information, some nice talking may work: "Look, I understand your concern and I appreciate your position, but we both have our jobs to do. Mine is to do some system maintenance for you. Your company called in the first place, so it's not like I want to be here this late at night either. Look, is Bob Johnson there? (You found Bob Johnson's name in some target documentation and discovered that he was director of operations.) His name is listed on the work order with telephone number 234–2345."

Normally, it's the specific and detailed nature of the information provided to the contact that causes them to believe the request is legitimate. After all, how could anyone know that much information unless they were legitimate? Remember that the purpose of reception staff and help desks is to help, so it is natural that they will do their best to assist anyone making an inquiry!

If this approach does not work, then some intimidation may work: "Look. If you don't give me the information I need to perform the maintenance, I really don't care. I can go home early, no problemo! Let me have your name and position please so that when my boss or this Johnson guy asks why the work wasn't done, I can tell them to talk to you. I don't care!" This technique works quite often, and once you are in, you are in! If none of these techniques work, maybe it is time to try an easier target.

Unless the high-technology criminal has specifically targeted a business or government agency, the Internet robber will generally move on to an easier target. After all, he wants to spend time online "playing" with systems and cruising the Internet for other systems to attack. Most high-technology criminals don't want to be delayed by spending their time talking to people and researching ways to get the information they need to mount a successful attack.

Social engineering works because people basically think other people are honest and, unless they had a guidance and awareness briefing on what to say and *what not to say*, they are normally very helpful and provide the requested information.

OTHER COMPUTER-RELATED TECHNIQUES USED BY BOTH INSIDERS AND OUTSIDERS

The description in the previous section of techniques centers around a social engineering attack approach. However, in today's globally connected information environment, it appears to be more common to use readily available hacker tools that have been downloaded from some Internet Web sites that are "hacker based."

In the good ol' days of hacking systems, the techniques listed here were some of the most common methods used by threat agents. Many are still valid today and are presented for that reason.

- *Data diddling*—Changing data before or during entry into the computer system (e.g., forging or counterfeiting documents used for data entry, exchanging valid disks and tapes with modified replacements)
- *Scavenging*—Obtaining information left around a computer system, in the computer room trash cans, and so forth
- *Computer manipulation/data leakage*—Removing information by smuggling it out as part of a printed document, encoding the information to look like something different and removing it from the facility (With current technologies such as universal serial bus (USB) memory devices and storage devices such as the iPod, the untraceable removal of information, in large quantities, has never been simpler.)
- *Computer manipulation/piggybacking and impersonation*—Physical access (e.g., following someone in through a door with a badge reader), electronically using an employees' user ID and password to gain computer access, tapping into the terminal link of a user to cause the computer to believe that both terminals are the same person
- *Computer manipulation/simulation and modeling*—Using the computer as a tool or instrument to plan or control a criminal act
- *Wire tapping*—Tapping into a computer's communications link to read the information being transmitted between systems and networks

These definitions are the generally accepted definitions used by the FBI and others. The FBI provided these definitions in 1979. Obviously, not much has changed over the years!

SYSTEM MANIPULATION

Many software applications have been written and techniques used by the high-technology criminal. The terms for these types of application programs have become standardized throughout the years. Most high-technology criminals use a variation of hacker tools, but they generally can be classified as follows:

- *Trojan horse*—This is the covert placement of instructions in a program that causes the computer to perform unauthorized functions but usually still allows the program to perform its intended purpose.

This is the most common method used in computer-based frauds and sabotage.

- *Trap doors*—When developing large programs, programmers tend to insert debugging aids that provide breaks in the instructions for insertion of additional code and intermediate output capabilities. The design of computer operating systems attempts to prevent this from happening. Therefore, programmers insert instructions that allow them to circumvent these controls. High-technology criminals take advantage of these trap doors or create their own.
- *Logic bombs*—This is a computer program executed at a specific time period or when a specific event occurs. For example, a programmer would write a program to instruct the computer to delete all personnel and payroll files if her name were ever removed from the file.
- *Computer virus*—This is malicious code that causes damage to system information or denies access to the information through self-replication.
- *Computer worms*—Worms are pieces of self replicating code.

USING THE GII, INTERNET, AND NII TO SEARCH FOR TOOLS

When high-technology criminals need tools to attack their targets, especially those on massive, global networks, they usually come from three sources:

1. Friends
2. Themselves
3. The Internet

The first two sources speak for themselves, so only the Internet is addressed here. Very little equipment or skills are needed these days to attack systems on the Internet. The high-technology crime investigator must remember that these are just some examples and are far from all inconclusive. Some "network patches" have been developed by manufacturers and others that defend against such attacks. Furthermore, new vulnerabilities, patches, and attacks seem to be identified on what seems to be a daily basis. To obtain hacking tools from the Internet, the criminal must have access to the Internet, which is usually through some Internet service provider (ISP), and for our purposes that is assumed. Once on the Internet, the attacker points the mouse to the search icon and then types in "hacker," "hacker software," "Warez," or specific tools that the Internet threat agent heard about. Then, the Internet threat agent must be able to download the tool. This is also generally an easy task, because often the attacker only has to click on

the download icon. The Internet threat agent then identifies the target
or randomly attacks various targets by executing the attack tools programs. On the plus side, not all hackers are nice to each other, and it is
not unheard of for a hacker tool that has been downloaded to a system
to do more than it was intended to.

ATTACK TOOLS FOUND ON THE INTERNET AND USED PRIMARILY TO ATTACK INTERNET-CONNECTED TARGETS

Most high-technology criminals use common and readily available programs found on the Internet. Many of these programs were created with
the intention that they would be used by systems administrators to assist
them in identifying the vulnerabilities of their systems so they could subsequently "patch the holes." Let's look back at some of the common tools
used only about 5 to 10 years ago.

- *SATAN, or Security Administrator Tool for Analyzing Networks*—
  This is a testing and reporting tool that collects a variety of information about networked hosts. SATAN was developed for security
  administrators to assist them in identifying vulnerabilities in their
  systems that would require patching. This tool is also commonly
  used by hackers to identify and then attack the vulnerabilities of networked systems. This public domain tool can be found and downloaded from numerous sites on the Internet.
- *COPS, or Computer Oracle and Password System*—COPS is a publicly available collection of programs that attempts to identify
  security problems in a UNIX system. COPS does not attempt to
  correct any discrepancies found; it simply produces a report of its
  findings.
- *ISS, or Internet Security Scanner*—This software program checks
  from the beginning to the end of a set of Internet Protocol (IP) logical
  addresses on a network to determine which systems, by address, are
  on the network.
- *CRACK*—Crack is a software program that attempts to guess passwords based on dictionary entries, user ID, and user name, and
  requires a password file (/etc/passwd). The new version can be used
  across an entire network.
- *FBRUTE*—This software program can decrypt encrypted password
  software. It uses a dictionary and is similar to CRACK.
- *RootKit*—According to BellCore, this tool was first noticed about
  1993. It targeted specific systems (originally, SunOS 4.1.X); the new
  version targets Linux. It is used as a "patched" login that allows any
  ID to access the systems through a backdoor password. It is a combination of attack programs.

- *Tripwire*—This software program checks files and directory integrity. It is a utility that compares a designated set of files and directories with information stored in a previously generated database. Any differences are flagged and logged, including added or deleted entries. When run against files on a regular basis, Tripwire enables you to spot changes in critical system files and to take immediate and appropriate damage control measures. Tripwire is also available on the Internet.
- *Finger*—This is a UNIX protocol that can be used to obtain information about users logged on to a system. It provides information that can be used by attackers, such as when the account was last used and from what location the user last connected.

Some techniques used by these programs and tools have been taken to a more sophisticated level and have become more advanced and automated. Some of these include the following:

- *Keystroke sounds*—Attackers armed with electronic equipment that costs less than $10 can sniff out what's typed on keyboards simply by recording keystroke sounds using software and off-the-shelf tools to record keystroke sounds. They then turn them into a transcript that's accurate 96% of the time.[2]
- *Foistware* —This is software that adds hidden components to your system on the sly. *Spyware* is the most common form of foistware. Foistware is quasilegal software bundled with some attractive software or other bait. The stealth process is installed without your knowledge. Sneak software often hijacks your browser and diverts you to some "revenue opportunity" that the "foister" has going.[2]
- *Instant messaging, internet relay chat (IRC), and point-to-point (P2P) file-sharing networks*—These three Internet services rely on cozy connections between your computer and other computers on the Internet. If you use them, the special peer-to-peer software that you install makes your machine more vulnerable to hostile exploits. Just as with e-mail, the most important thing to be wary of is attachments and Web site links.[2]
- *E-mail*—E-mail messages themselves are now used as attack vectors, even though its more common to use attachments. The hostile content can be embedded in the message. Another trick is to combine the two vectors, so that if the message doesn't get you, the attachment will.[2]

Then, of course, there are the phishing and pharming aspects of it all. Phishing attacks use both social engineering and technical subterfuge to steal consumers' personal identity data and financial account credentials. Social engineering schemes use "spoofed" e-mail messages to lead consumers to counterfeit Web sites designed to trick recipients into divulging financial data such as credit card numbers, account user names, passwords, and social security numbers. Hijacking brand names of banks, e-retailers, and credit card companies, phishers often convince recipients to respond. Technical subterfuge schemes plant crimeware onto personal computers to steal credentials directly, often using Trojan key logger spyware. Pharming crimeware misdirects users to fraudulent sites or proxy servers, typically through domain name server (DNS) hijacking or poisoning.[3]

As if that is not enough, there are legal issues and controversies behind peer-to-peer networking: ...files shared on peer-to-peer networks are copies of copyrighted popular music and movies in a wide variety of formats (MP3, MPEG, real media [RM], and so on). Sharing of these copies is illegal in most jurisdictions. This has led many observers, including most media companies and some peer-to-peer advocates, to conclude that the networks themselves pose grave threats to the established distribution model.[4]

There are numerous methods used today to attack individual systems, ranging from home systems to massive corporate and government networks. You can learn more about these latest techniques and stay current in them to help you with looking for the MO when conducting a high-technology crime investigation by doing an online search using such terms as *malicious codes, hacker tools,* and similar phrases.

> "New Internet Worm Targeting Windows; Seattle, Washington (Reuters)—A new Internet virus targeting recently uncovered flaws in Microsoft Corp.'s Windows operating system is circulating on the Internet, an antivirus computer software maker said on Monday."[5]

SOME ADDITIONAL COMMON METHODS OF INTERNET ATTACK

Some of the more common Internet attack methods can cause millions of dollars in lost revenue resulting from denying use of Web sites and high costs for recovery and repair, and modifications of Web sites can also cause embarrassment to their owners. Distributed denial-of-service attacks, phishing, pharming, spoofing, session stealing, and other attack methods have been plaguing the Internet. There are patches and remedies to avoid being the victim of most of these common attacks; however, history has repeatedly shown that many businesses and government agencies have not installed the fixes (or not installed them quickly enough), including many US Department of Defense systems. There is no excuse for such lack of security. Ironically, the US Department of Defense is supposed to defend this nation but can't seem to defend their own systems!

Denial of Service

Denial of service means to block use of the Internet or related system. There are various methods to deny service or access to a system on the Internet. One example is to send a big ping packet. The attacker sends a packet (ICMP echo request), for example, bigger than 65,507 bytes (ping −1 65510 target system). The reassembled fragments overflow the TCP/IP stack. This attack works on various hardware; however, vendors and others have been developing patches to prevent such a denial of service.

Web Server Modifications

Attacking Web servers has been a fad among many of the miscreants on the Internet, generally the juvenile delinquents. It's equivalent to juvenile delinquents spray painting a wall, building, or sign with graffiti. However, in the hands of someone more devious, it can be used for making political statements, to divert others through links to a competitor's site, and many other devious schemes that are only limited by the high-technology criminal's imagination.

The problem is that common gateway interface (CGI) scripts allow for the creation of Web pages, but these CGI scripts are vulnerable (phf, AnyForm, FormMail, convert.bas, .bat files, custom scripts, and so on).

> "Suspected Hacker Taps into Military Records; San Antonio, Texas (AP)—A suspected hacker tapped into a military database containing social security numbers and other personal information for 33,000 Air Force officers and some enlisted personnel, an Air Force spokesman said Tuesday."[6]

IP Fragmentation

This attack method is accomplished by making a fragment so the TCP header is split between two fragments—fragment 1, part of the TCP header; fragment 2, the rest of the TCP header with the port number. For example, in fragment 1, put in a "phony" port (e.g., port 80). In fragment 2, use the TCP header with port 23. When the fragments reconnect, the port number is overwritten.

Password Sniffing

One technique to attack a system successfully on a busy subnet is to change the system configuration to make it a network sniffer. Thus, the attacker can collect user IDs and passwords flowing through the network (Fig. 3-2).

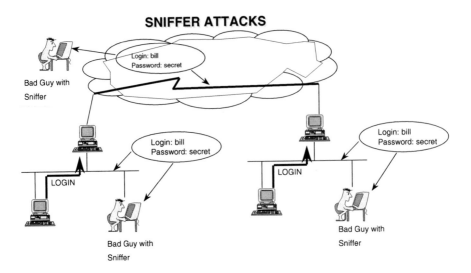

Figure 3-2 A simplified example of "sniffing."

ISP Attack

With this type of attack, the attacker sends a false message, usually to numerous servers that support newsgroups and "convinces" them to send back information (e.g., server passwords).

Spoofing

This method of attack requires the prediction of future sequencing numbers. The attacker spoofs the trusted system into believing that the attacker's system is another authorized trusted system, while simultaneously blocking that other trusted system (Fig. 3-3).

War Dialers

Prior to the widespread adoption of the Internet, dial-up systems were the predominant method for high-technology criminals and authorized users to gain remote access to a business or government agency computer system. Today, this is still possible; however, it is not as prevalent now that the ubiquitous Internet exists. In the old days, hackers wrote programs in languages such as BASIC to find the modems those computers use to communicate and record their telephone numbers for later attack. This method was made famous by the movie *War Games*. These days, the programs are more commonly written in Java or C.

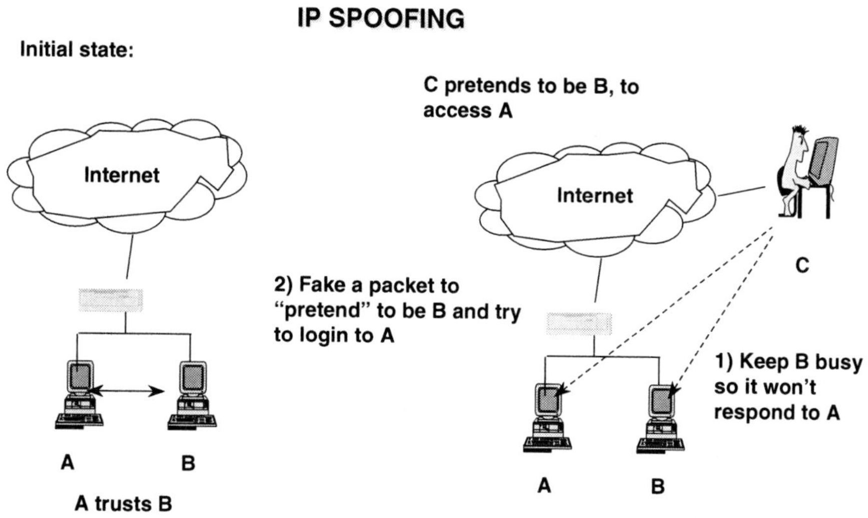

IP SPOOFING

Initial state:

C pretends to be B, to
access A

Internet

Internet

C

2) Fake a packet to
"pretend" to be B and try
to login to A

1) Keep B busy
so it won't
respond to A

A   B

A trusts B

A   B

Figure 3-3   A simplified example of "spoofing."

After identifying a modem for a computer system through its dial tone, the hacker then used various other programs or manual guessing to identify a user ID and password that would allow system access. Some systems can still lead the hacker to an Internet ramp.

OTHER METHODS, TOOLS, AND TECHNIQUES

As you should know by now, there are numerous techniques, methods, tactics, and tools available to anyone on the Internet, as well as other sources, such as hacker magazines and computer magazines, that discuss Internet hardware and software vulnerabilities. We again emphasize that the high-technology crime investigator should become familiar with the basic information provided on various hacker sites. The methods are constantly changing and improving as Internet security improves. Attacks by malicious agents continue to be an ongoing challenge for everyone on the Internet.

"Car Computer Systems at Risk to Viruses; Helsinki, Finland (Reuters)—Here's a new excuse for not getting to work on time on a Monday morning: My car caught a virus. Car industry officials and analysts say hackers' growing interest in writing viruses for wireless devices puts auto computer systems at risk of infection. As carmakers adjust onboard computers to allow consumers to transfer information with MP3 players and mobile phones, they also make their vehicles vulnerable to mobile viruses that jump between devices via the Bluetooth technology that connects them."[7]

EXAMPLE OF HACKER NAIVETÉ

One hacker advised others via e-mail to rent a cheap room at a hotel—"rundown motels that you take hookers to." He also stated that the motel owners probably wouldn't remember you, they hardly ask for identification, don't take credit cards, and want cash payment. Then go to the room and dial in to an ISP using a hacked trial (e.g., free use of ISP access to the Internet for a specific period of time by using the ISP's CD that normally is given away through the mail) account, but never your own. If traced back, they investigators would "hit a dead end." This miscreant also recommended that one should use different hotels and different accounts. Furthermore, one shouldn't brag. This individual also recommended using a laptop and not using a motel, but using universities and libraries that have phone jacks. "Bring a bunch of textbooks and you'll fit in with everyone else with a laptop there."

If you are investigating a hacker and traced the hack to a motel, library, or a public room of a university, think of the steps that you would take to investigate such a case. Is this miscreant correct in his thinking or has he watched too many movies that included a "short-time" motel with a sleazy desk clerk, partially unshaven, smoking a beat-up cigar, sweating, and wearing a sleeveless T-shirt. The clerk takes the money and throws the guy a key. In this type of motel, favored by prostitutes, drug addicts, winos, and the like, would this miscreant, probably a young white male with a computer under his arm, blend in? (You might ask yourself how good an idea it is to walk into a hotel like this with a nice shiny laptop.) Such indications are useful to a high-technology crime investigator in that they indicate the level of expertise one is dealing with—in this case, probably a juvenile miscreant.

ELECTRONIC MAIL

E-mail is used to send and store written communications through computer networks. Aside from the normal fraudulent uses of e-mail, it can also be used to transmit and distribute a virus. However, in the past, the virus has been a program that the receiver overtly implemented by accessing mail (e.g., the mail attachments).

There are some indications that it is possible to send covert instructions and viruses through the "cookies" that are constantly being requested of users by various Web site vendors, news agencies, marketing companies, and so forth. Using e-mail through such systems as the Internet does provide a vulnerability in that the true sender of the message can be disguised, spoofed, or anonymous. This method could work well to assist in economic sabotage of a business. In addition, because a sender's identity can be disguised, he can safely forward sensitive business information to an unauthorized address. Again, old theft and fraud schemes in new ways.

CELLULAR TELEPHONES: CLONING AND OTHER FRAUDS

Cellular telephones, like any high technology, are both a target and the tool of the high-technology miscreant. In the past, it was big business to clone phones and, even today, stolen phones are excellent communication devices used by criminals not only for making illegal, long-distance telephone calls, but also to communicate such things as drug deals and other criminal activities with impunity.

> "New Virus Found in Phone Messaging: 'Commwarrior.A' Is a Virus Designed to Spread Through Multimedia Messages and Drain Phone Batteries; Helsinki, Finland (Reuters)—A new mobile phone software virus started spreading this week via messages containing photos and sounds, the first of its kind and a threat to cell phones globally, data security firms said on Tuesday. The Commwarrior.A virus tries to replicate itself by sending multimedia messages to people on the phone's contact list, and tries to do the same via Bluetooth wireless connections with other devices, eventually draining the battery."[8]

When we think of cellular phones, we usually don't think of computers and information protection in the "systems" sense. However, as the divisions of hardware begin to blur, as they are integrated into communications networks, we must begin focusing on all aspects of information storing, processing, and transmitting. To do otherwise would be a disservice to our companies and our profession. After all, cell phones are information systems too. All one has to do is look at the increase in the number of wireless communications (e.g., cellular phones replacing cameras, e-mail devices, Internet search engine tool), all of which provide great challenges to the high-technology crime investigator.

THREATS, VULNERABILITIES, AND RISKS

What are the threats to this new communications tool? Why and how are they vulnerable to criminals? How much of a risk is a business taking by using these devices? The following may help answer some of these questions.

"Wireless Web Puts Personal Data at Risk; Atlanta, Georgia (CNN)—What comes to mind when you think of wireless Web surfing? It may not be security, or lack of it. There are nearly 30,000 public wireless "hot spots" in the United States at places such as parks and cafes, but there's more to consider than just where to log on. The convenience comes with a caveat. 'Understand that the information you're sending is very similar to standing up here in the park and shouting out all the information. Would I normally do that?' said Richard Rushing, a wireless expert with security firm Air Defense who visited an Atlanta park to show security vulnerabilities."[9]

The Federal Communications Commission (FCC) rulings on listening in on the airwaves state that you can listen, but you can't use the information received for personal, professional, or monetary gain. How hard is it to scan the cellular airwaves and listen to the conversations? According to John Beecher (personal communication), a Los Angeles-based telecommunications expert, you can easily purchase the necessary equipment for about $200 at your local electronics store (Fig. 3-4). In addition, your cellular phone can be easily modified to pick up cellular phone conversations. If you know how to reconfigure your telephone in maintenance mode, you

Figure 3-4 Photo of a scanner that can pick up cellular phone information.

can reconfigure it to act as a listening device on cellular phone frequencies. The maintenance mode passwords are readily available in published documents relating to cellular phones. However, this approach is more difficult than using scanners to pick up cellular phone conversations.

According to Beecher, the new cellular phones make it more difficult to listen in on conversations. However, the new phones are not a quantum leap in protection, but do provide better security. (We are generally talking about analog cellular phones, and we are now very much into the digital era. The whole situation has changed and the intercept of calls and details have changed. However, it is presented here to help you understand the history of this problem.)

Cellular phone carriers have established monitoring processes that look for individual cellular phone usage patterns. When a phone exceeds the normal pattern (e.g., many calls in one day to overseas numbers when you never called overseas before), the carriers will normally suspend that phone service and notify the customer. This abnormal increase in phone usage is known as *spiking*. The criminals who clone these phones are aware of the monitoring process. They may just take their chances and use the phone as long as they can, or they may keep the number of calls low so as not to attract attention. Because of the difficulty in identifying these criminals, most of them appear to continue to use the phones as long as they can. Some criminals clone the phones and sell them to others such as drug dealers, operators of prostitution rings, gambling rings, and so on. These people then use the phones, which are difficult to trace, to transact their illegal business.

Tech helps protesters get creative, changing how protests are organized: Technology has changed how protests are organized. Activists are using the Internet to arrange housing for out-of-towners, organize a mass-flash of underwear emblazoned with anti-Bush messages and tell protesters what to say if they're arrested. ("I am going to remain silent. I would like to speak with a lawyer.") There are at least two Web guides for protesters packed with calendars of events and dining guides, including dumpster-diving tips for those on a tight budget.

In one instance, a company purchased several new cellular phones that were held in reserve for issue later. While the phones were still in their original boxes and never assigned, the company received a bill from their carrier that included more than $6000 in charges to the phones still in their boxes! The carrier was informed and the company was not charged for the calls, many of which were to overseas locations. The carrier absorbed the costs as a "normal" part of doing business. However, those charges are eventually passed on to all the customers through rate increases.

A cellular phone can "leak" information without the knowledge of the sender or receiver. For example, several years ago at a security conference in San Francisco, one of the authors and a friend were in the hallway outside a conference room. The friend turned on his phone and, as he was about to dial a number, he heard a conversation between a US military captain and a US military general in Washington discussing sensitive contract information and contract bids of potential contractors. This happened purely by accident, but it proves one very important point: high technology can be vulnerable in ways that we may least expect.

Another major threat to cellular phones is theft. Cellular phones are stolen and used by the thief until the user and/or the carrier terminate the phones. A criminal may sell time on the phone so people can call nationally or internationally. This type of operations is known as a *call–sell operation*. The cellular phone owner picks up the costs or the carrier may pick up the costs. These costs can amount to thousands of dollars in a matter of 1 or 2 days. The phones can still be sold and used again after they have been cloned, as described previously.

> "FCC Goes After Cell Phone Spammers; Washington (AP)—The Federal Communications Commission on Monday published a list of domain names to which telemarketers may not send e-mail without permission from cell phone subscribers."[10]

With basic scanning equipment, an outsider can "listen in" on cellular phone calls and obtain sensitive company information. Remember, as business competition increases, especially in this slow economy, the incentive to learn more about what the competition is doing is increasing. This threat may be one of industrial espionage (one company seeking information from another company) or economic espionage (a foreign government seeking information from a company).

Cellular phone calls that are personal and not related to company business can be made by authorized employees. The employee may even let friends and family members make calls on the phone. Employees who are issued a cellular phone can sell it to criminals and subsequently report it stolen.

According to the US Defense Security Service Report on "Cellular Phone Vulnerability," the cellular phone has three major vulnerabilities:

1. Ability to monitor your conversations while using the phone
2. Ability to turn the phone into a microphone to monitor conversations in the vicinity of your phone while the phone is inactive
3. Ability to clone the phone number so that others can make calls and charge them to your account

"High-Tech Phones Bring Virus Potential; Stockholm, Sweden (AP)— Malicious programs that can delete address books. Junk messages that flood a cell phone's inbox. Stealthy code that uses Bluetooth wireless technology to sneak onto handsets."[11]

CLIP-ON FRAUD

Telecrooks are always looking for innovative ways to steal telephone service. They are driven by the free services and the profit to be derived from the illegal activity. A vast majority of telabuse is committed through customer premise equipment. Hackers will continue to take advantage of the vulnerabilities of unsecured PBXs and communications networks.

Although it's essential that network risk management strategies continually be considered, let's not forget some of the old fraud methods. Clip-on fraud, which was prominent in the '70s and ebbed in the '80s, has made a comeback big time. It is unknown exactly how much clip-on fraud has cost our industry, but hundreds of thousands of dollars in illegal calls are currently being rung up.

Typically, the way clip-on fraud works is a telecrook will attach a butt phone to the copper connectors in a b-box, which is generally located on a sidewalk. The b-box serves as a junction for the phone lines to hundreds of homes and businesses in a particular area. Once inside the b-box, the telecrook clips on to the phone lines and finds a dial tone. A newer variation of clip-on fraud involves the use of a cordless telephone and a portable battery. After the base station is connected to the terminals in the b-box, the phone moves with the telecrook, allowing him to operate in a secure location 200 to 300 feet from the terminal, reducing the possibility of detection. In more sophisticated cases, the phone line's dial tone is forwarded to a nearby pay phone. In either scenario, after having established a base of operation, the call–sell operation begins when people line up to pay for calls. The vast majority of clip-on fraud cases have occurred in southern California, with its vast immigrant population. Telecrooks have a ready market of people wanting to make inexpensive international calls to their friends and families. This fraud primarily occurs on the weekends in light industrial or commercial areas.

Clip-on fraud activity shows up as direct-dial calls on the customers' bills. When customers receive their bill they are confused and do not realize they have been victimized. A company in Los Angeles racked up more than $30,000 in fraudulent long-distance calls, not realizing that telecrooks clipped on to their phone lines from a b-box located blocks from their location. Moreover, to make matters worse, the company's ability to conduct business was affected because their lines were tied up. It is important to note that, the FCC has ruled clip-on fraud that can be proved to be on the local exchange carrier's (LEC's) end of the demarcation line is the responsibility of the LEC. This ruling establishes an important precedent when trying to resolve billing issues.

> Clip-on fraud is a complicated problem and is not easily detected. The users and carriers are at risk and should consider some basic security measures.

LECs are upgrading security at the b-boxes in the affected areas. Monitoring for suspicious activity on the network and international call blocking are among the practical ways in attempting to get a handle on the problem. Most important, users should check monthly bills for any unauthorized calls. It is clear that no one solution will prevent clip-on fraud from occurring. A company should tailor security measures to the way they conduct business, because what works for one may not work for all. A collaborative effort on the part of both local and long-distance carriers as well as the customer is very important. (This information was provided by Jerry Swick, a professional high-technology crime investigator.)

INFORMATION OF INVESTIGATIVE INTERESTS

There is test equipment that is used to poll cellular phone cells. If you identify such equipment in the hands of someone who is not employed by the carrier, or some related, legitimate cellular phone business, you can assume the equipment is stolen and is being used for illegal purposes.

If you seize a phone and it is necessary to determine its original destination, the manufacturer should be able to tell you the identity of the phone and its destination. For example, Motorola maintains centralized records in Arlington Heights, Illinois.

> "Internet Infection Holds Files 'Hostage'—Computer users already anxious about viruses and identity theft have new reason to worry: Hackers have found a way to lock up the electronic documents on your computer and then demand $200 over the Internet to get them back."[12]

Check also for the serial numbers on the phone. Obviously, if they are not there or are written over or scratched out, the phone was probably stolen. In addition, an FCC sticker is required. In one case, the lack of the FCC sticker enabled investigators to obtain a felony conviction in Illinois.

If the phone has a locked code or codes, the manufacturer may be able to unlock it. In addition, and under certain circumstances, they may even be able to determine the last number called. As a minimum, don't do anything to the phone because this may erase the number. Contact the manufacturer or your carrier to determine whether either one of them can help you.

If it is important to identify and trace phone numbers called by the cellular phone you have seized, remember that the phone stores telephone numbers to make calling more convenient for their owners. Contact the manufacturer for assistance if you don't know how to recover those numbers from the phone without destroying relevant evidence.

COLORED BOXES AND TELECOMMUNICATIONS FRAUD

Over the years, phreakers and others have devised various electronic boxes that emulate various sounds used by the telecommunications networks. These "colored boxes" allow the user to circumvent the normal controls and billing for such things as long-distance calls. The following nontechnical descriptions are provided:

- *Blue box*—This box allows the user to make long-distance toll calls for free (Fig. 3-5).
- *Red box*—This box simulates the signals made by coins in a pay phone.
- *Black box*—This box simulates the toll call being terminated. Thus, a toll was no longer being recorded; however, the parties could continue talking (Fig. 3-6).
- *Yellow box*—This box indicated "supervision status" to the telephone system.

Other colored boxes have been identified throughout the years and the boxes sometimes were called different colors by different phreakers. For example, some call the silver box the predecessor to the blue box; however, some call the silver box the box that can change specific traffic-signaling devices. Others colored boxes are white, beige, green, and a rainbow of colors, according to at least one individual. For additional information on these devices, use your search engine and search the Internet and hacker/phreaker sites.

PBX ATTACKS

The PBX can be attacked like any other computer and for various reasons, such as to gain outside calling access to make toll-free calls, take over

Figure 3-5   A blue box.

Figure 3-6   A black box.

a PBX, read other people's voice mail, and so forth. Figures 3-7, 3-8, and 3-9 depict the three basic methods and reasons a PBX is attacked.

CASE EXAMPLE: AN ONLINE COMPUTER IS ALWAYS UNDER ATTACK

If you are investigating any type of high-technology crime in which the crime scene is a corporate computer linked to the "outside world" (e.g., the Internet), then you should assume that the computer is going to be under attack and may be constantly under attack. For example, using a common firewall product, we turned on a computer for approximately 3 hours a day. During one day, the firewall log showed 20 potential attacks, most of which were probes against the computer caught by the firewall and hopefully rejected. The attacks were traced to Beijing, Shanghai, New York City, Philadelphia, and Warsaw. They were multiple attacks, and some tried hiding by going through San Jose, California, through Chicago, Illinois, back to San Jose and up through Seattle, Washington. In one week, this one computer had 225 potential attacks, and 1354 for the month.

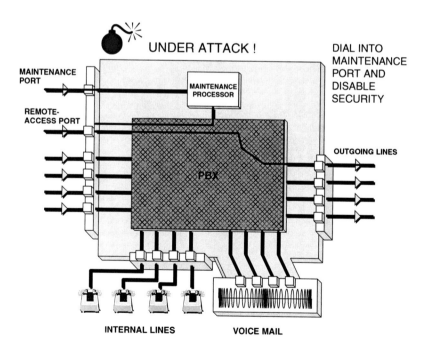

Figure 3-7 Dial in to the maintenance port and disable security.

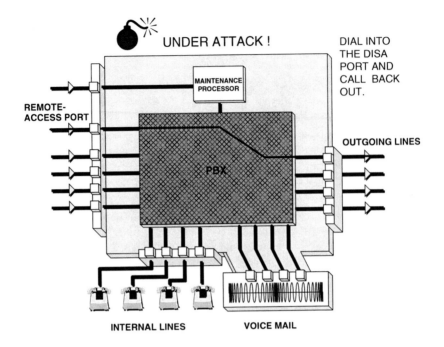

Figure 3-8   Dial in to the DISA port and call back out.

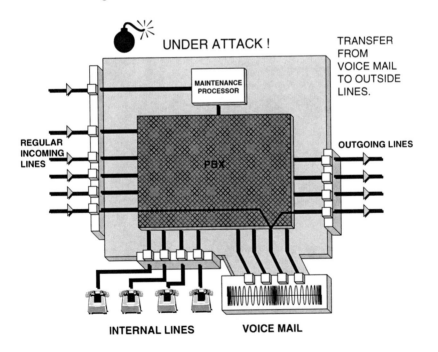

Figure 3-9   Transfer from voice mail to outside lines.

This is not unusual, because these probes are generally nothing more than downloaded hacker software sent over the Internet to probe online computers. That is just the first step. Once the initial probe is successful, and depending on the miscreant's objective, a successful probe may lead to compromising a computer and using it as a gateway to attack other computers, probe networks, destroy information, steal information, and the like. These probes are also a good way to collect data to be used for one of today's biggest crimes—identity theft.

SUMMARY

High-technology devices have become both essential and convenient business communications tools not only for legal businesses, but also as tools involved in illegal activities. The basic techniques and methods are well known. Whether a miscreant is attacking a PBX, Internet site, cellular telephone, or computer, the high-technology crime investigator must learn their attack techniques and work with the individuals responsible for the protection of these valuable business and government agency assets. In addition, the high-technology crime investigator must understand these techniques to conduct successful high-technology crime investigation.

Overview of Attack Trends by the CERT Coordination Center[13] (see www.CERT.org for more information on this and other related topics) stated that they saw the following trends related to threat agents:

- Automation, speed of attacks
- Increased sophistication of attack tools
- Faster discovery of vulnerabilities
- Increasing permeability of firewalls
- Increasingly asymmetric threat
- Increasing threat from infrastructure attacks

REFERENCES

1. www.washingtonpost.com/wp-dyn/content/article/2005/08/04/AR200508 0400429.html
2. www.personaltechpipeline.com/170704253?cid=RSSfeed
3. www.antiphishing.org
4. http://en.wikipedia.org/wiki/Peer-to-peer
5. *New Internet Worm Targeting Windows.* www.cnn.com/2005/TECH/internet/ 08/16/microsoft.worm.reut/index.html
6. *Suspected Hacker Taps Into Military Records.* www.cnn.com/2005/TECH/ ptech/08/23/hacker.military.records.ap/index.html

7. *Car Computer Systems at Risk to Viruses.* www.cnn.com/2005/TECH/08/01/viruses.cars.reut/index.html

8. *New Virus Found in Phone Messaging: "Commwarrior.A" Is a Virus Designed to Spread Through Multimedia Messages and Drain Phone Batteries.* http://money.cnn.com/2005/03/08/technology/personaltech/mobile_virus.reut/index.htm?cnn=yes

9. *Wireless Web Puts Personal Data at Risk.* www.cnn.com/2005/TECH/internet/06/21/hotspot.hacking/index.html

10. *FCC Goes After Cell Phone Spammers.* www.cnn.com/2005/TECH/ptech/02/08/cellphones.spam.ap/index.html

11. *High-Tech Phones Bring Virus Potential.* www.cnn.com/2004/TECH/ptech/12/27/cell.phone.viruses.ap/index.html

12. *Internet Infection Holds Files "Hostage."* www.cnn.com/2005/TECH/internet/05/24/internet.ransom.ap/index.html

13. CERT Coordination Center. *Overview of Attack Trends.*

14. (May, 1993). *Orange County Register Newspaper.*

4

The Basic Information Systems Security Techniques Used to Defend Against High-Technology Crime Miscreants

Part I culminates in a chapter that provides the high-technology crime investigator with an overview of the basic high-technology protection philosophies, methods, and processes that are used to protect the valuable assets of business and government agency global information environments.

INTRODUCTION

The high-technology crime investigator must understand the InfoSec policies, procedures, processes, and plans in place that relate to the high-technology crime and the high-technology crime scene, as well as any other applicable assets, protection policies, procedures, and so forth. Just as any investigation has to do with elements of proof based on the violation of laws, a high-technology crime investigator is also required to be familiar with corporate policies and procedures, as well as whatever government laws have been violated. This is one of the first steps, because if no corporate "rules" or government laws have been violated, why are you, the high-technology crime investigator, conducting an investigation? Also, in understanding the basic concepts of information and information systems protection, the high-technology crime investigator who is undertaking a high-tech crime investigation should identify the vulnerabilities of InfoSec that allowed attempts to gain unauthorized access to valuable assets (or successful infiltration).

BASIC INFOSEC CONCEPTS

Several terms are used interchangeably to describe the protection of information systems and the information they store, process, and transmit.

Among the more common are computer security, information systems security (or InfoSec), information systems protection, assets protection as they relate to high technology, network security, Internet security, and systems security. It is important for high-technology crime investigators to understand the high-technology protection concepts used today if they are to assist successfully in protecting the high-technology (corporate or government assets) and related systems used to process, store, display, and transmit information. In these types of cases, high-technology or IT specialists along with InfoSec specialists must be used. Their assistance in identifying protection mechanisms, vulnerabilities that allowed the crime to take place, and the like, will be useful in conducting a successful high-technology crime investigation.

"Feds Recruiting Hackers at Defcon; Las Vegas, Nevada (Reuters)—Attention hackers: Uncle Sam wants you. As scam artists, organized crime rings, and other miscreants find a home on the Internet, top federal officials are trolling hacker conferences to scout talent and talk up the glories of a career on the front lines of the information wars. 'If you want to work on cutting-edge problems, if you want to be part of the truly great issues of our time... we invite you to work with us,' Assistant Secretary of Defense Linton Wells told hackers at a recent conference in Las Vegas."[1]

The basic InfoSec philosophy and its concepts require that there be a balance between ease of use, costs, capability, flexibility, and performance and protection requirements. So, as a high-technology crime investigator, don't expect a foolproof high-technology system to be in place.

There are three basic InfoSec principles that form the foundation of an InfoSec program. The first is *access control*. Access control is the first line of defense of high technology, for without access controls, either physical, logical, or a combination thereof, the opportunities to conduct high-technology crimes are drastically reduced—not eliminated, but reduced.

Access controls include physical access through gates, guards, badge readers, smart cards, biometric devices, and the like. When physical access has been overcome, the individual then has access to the high technology (e.g., telephone, cellular phone, computer workstation, or other high-technology devices). The next hurdle for the miscreant to overcome is obtaining the personal identification number (PIN), user ID, password, or whatever the InfoSec hardware and/or software require to gain access to the high-technology asset (e.g., hardware, software, or computerized information). So, from a high-technology crime investigator's viewpoint, one of the first questions that should be asked when conducting a high-technology crime investigation is: Who had access that could have been used to perpetrate the crime being investigated?

The second InfoSec principle is *individual accountability*—a major pillar of an InfoSec program. Individual accountability means that all actions related to the high-technology device, system, or whatever, can be traced back to a specific individual. However, individual accountability requires such policies, procedures, and processes as separation of functions, unique user ID and password for each individual, unique biometric scans for each individual, unique PINs, unique badges and card readers for each individual, and so forth.

As businesses and government agencies downsize and look for more and more ways to gain efficiencies in their processes, it is not uncommon for employees' responsibilities to cloud or even eliminate the separation of function concept. That is why such things as passwords, smart cards, and PINs are, by policy, never to be used by anyone other than the person to whom it was assigned. If individual accountability is nonexistent or questionable, the possibility of successfully identifying the high-technology criminal and having sufficient evidence for disciplinary action and/or prosecution is drastically reduced.

When conducting a high-technology crime investigation, the investigator should be sure to ask a series of questions related to separation of functions; sharing of passwords, PINs, and so on; and policy and procedures. If the administrative security documentation (policies, procedures, employee acknowledgment statements) related to the investigation are old, inadequate, or nonexistent, the opportunities for taking disciplinary action or prosecuting an employee are, generally, drastically reduced, if not eliminated all together. Therefore, as you conduct the investigation, continue to coordinate with applicable corporate staff members (e.g., legal staff) to determine whether the investigation should continue as you begin to find that some "elements of proof" or support to elements of proof are not in place. Thus, the individual or individuals may not be identified and, if identified, the elements of proof may not be provable.

If passwords were shared by two or three employees and there was corroborating evidence, there may still be some hope that the miscreant can be identified. However, this is very unlikely because company lawyers and prosecutors often shy away from high-technology cases in the first place. When you add the other complications, they may not want to support disciplinary action or prosecution.

The third principle is *audit trails*. When we speak of audit trails, we are talking about historical records in any form. These include, for example, closed-circuit television videotapes, hard-copy sign-in records, computer historical records of which user ID accessed which files or networks or of who made what telephone calls through the PBX or cellular phone, and any other records that can help identify the miscreants and prove or disprove allegations against individuals.

When it comes to computerized records, generally they fall short of meeting the needs of a high-technology crime investigation. They may show the user ID that accessed the system, systems, network, or database as well as what time of day or night. However, they usually do not provide the detail that shows exactly what specific information in a database was accessed, modified, deleted, or manipulated.

Most of today's modern InfoSec systems have the *capability* to provide a great deal of detail; however, most of the IT people who operate, maintain, and otherwise support the business or government agency will only "turn on" the minimum audit trail features they can get away with. They will continually argue that detailed monitoring adversely affects the performance of the systems and that the record keeping takes up too much storage space. They are correct to a point, and generally management will side with them and take the risk that detailed audit trail records will not be needed.

For a high-technology crime investigator, audit trail records are like fingerprints and footprints at the crime scene. If properly noted in sufficient level of detail, they can often be the piece of evidence that leads to suspects. So, when conducting a high-technology crime investigation, you should ask a series of questions related to audit trail records. All applicable audit trail records should be considered and protected as evidence.

INFOSEC PROCESSES OR FUNCTIONS

The InfoSec program is separated into several basic functions (see Figs. 4-1 and 4-2):

- *Physical security*—Physical security refers to those barriers and devices that help protect assets. They include such things as guards, fences, alarms, closed-circuit television cameras, and sensors. In most companies, physical security is the responsibility of the corporate security department and the chief security officer (CSO).
- *Personnel security*—This may include background investigations on potential employees and other screening processes. Also, this is generally the responsibility of the CSO.
- *Administrative security*—As its name implies, administrative security consists of the administrative processes, policies, and procedures related to InfoSec. The department responsible for InfoSec generally establishes these policies and procedures. They, depending on the business culture, corporate structure, agreements, and company policies, may or may not coordinate them with the CSO.
- *Communications security*—This generally refers to the encryption of the information transmitted via telecommunications links and can be the responsibility of the InfoSec organization or business security management.

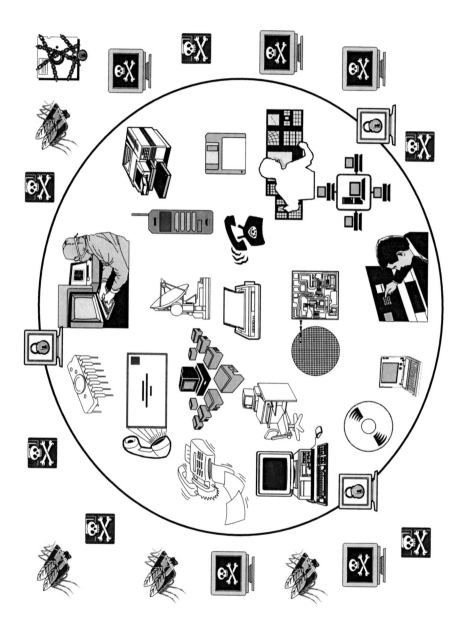

Figure 4-1   The InfoSec environment of today.

Improve Survivability By Extending Focus

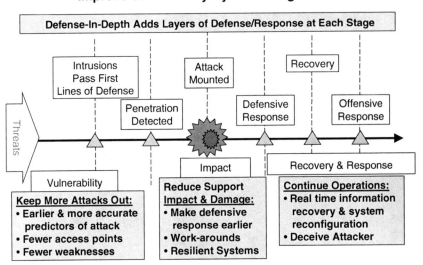

Figure 4-2   A defense process to protect valuable assets.

- *Risk management*—The management of risks associated with high technology is generally everyone's responsibility when using or making decisions relative to any high technology. Formal risk assessments and analyses vis-à-vis high-technology protection generally falls within the purview of the InfoSec organization.
- *Disaster recovery/contingency planning/emergency planning*—Planning and preparing for actions to take in the event emergencies or disasters strike (e.g., hurricanes, earthquakes, hacker destruction of the business' database) and how to recover from such disasters generally falls within the InfoSec organization's purview for high-technology devices and computerized information. All other such planning is usually the responsibility of the CSO. Often the high-technology portion is integrated into the overall related plans of the CSO.

"Microsoft Unveils PC Security Service: Software Maker's Subscription Plan Includes Anti-virus Updates; Rollout Seen by Year-end; Seattle (Reuters)—Microsoft Corp., the world's largest software maker, unveiled Thursday plans to launch a computer subscription service that would include anti-virus and security updates for personal computers."[2]

THE INFORMATION SYSTEMS SECURITY OFFICER (ISSO)

The ISSO leads the InfoSec effort for a business or government agency. Today, some of these positions are identified as chief information security officer (CISO) or other similar name. The ISSO position can be summarized as follows: To direct, supervise, manage, and administer an InfoSec program that minimizes threats, vulnerabilities, and risks to the company's sensitive information and high-technology assets.

INFOSEC AND ISSO GOALS AND OBJECTIVES

The ISSO, through the InfoSec program, generally has some stated goals and objectives. The following are examples of some goals and objectives that may be used by an ISSO:

- To administer an innovative InfoSec program that minimizes risks at least impact to costs and schedules, while meeting all requirements
- To enhance the quality, efficiency, and effectiveness of the organization
- To identify potential problem areas and mitigate them before customers identify them
- To enhance the company's ability to attract customers because of the ability to protect their information efficiently and effectively
- To establish the organization as the InfoSec leader in the industry

RISK MANAGEMENT

The risk management process is crucial to an InfoSec program to establish and maintain an InfoSec program at least cost while protecting the high technology. Risk decisions are based on

- *Threats*—Man-made or natural occurrences that can cause adverse affects to systems and information when combined with specific vulnerabilities
- *Vulnerabilities*—Weaknesses that allow specific threats to cause adverse affects to systems and information
- *Impacts*—The effect that a threat exploiting a vulnerability would have
- *Risks*—The chances that a specific threat can take advantage of a specific vulnerability to cause adverse affects to systems and information

The assessments can be qualitative, quantitative, or a combination of both. They often result in a formal report and include identifying costs and benefits.

> "Passport ID Chips May Not Be Secure; Washington (AP)—The Bush administration opposed security measures for new microchip-equipped passports that privacy advocates contended were needed to prevent identity theft, government snooping, or a terror attack, according to State Department documents released Friday. The passports, scheduled to be issued by the end of 2005, could be read electronically from as far away as 30 feet, according to the American Civil Liberties Union, which obtained the documents under a Freedom of Information Act request. Though the passports wouldn't include transmitters of their own, they would have antennas to allow a reader to capture the data. The ability to read remotely, or "skim," personal data raises the possibility that passport holders would be vulnerable to identity theft, the ACLU said. It also would allow government agents to find out covertly who was attending a political meeting or make it easier for terrorists to target Americans traveling abroad, the ACLU said."[3]

OTHER ASPECTS OF AN INFOSEC PROGRAM

There are many aspects of InfoSec, depending on the business, sophistication of the InfoSec program, and, more important, how management perceives its importance and allocates resources for it.

Security verifications and validations must be part of a good InfoSec program and include ensuring:

- InfoSec is in place where needed.
- InfoSec systems are active (configured and operating per security parameters).
- InfoSec is cost-effective.
- New technology products are evaluated for risks and cost-effectiveness.

INFOSEC ORGANIZATION

There is a continuous debate regarding where the InfoSec responsibility/ organization should be located. Regardless of its reporting structure, it should include developing, implementing, maintaining, and administering a companywide InfoSec program that includes all plans, policies, procedures, assessments, and authorization necessary to ensure the protection of customers' and the company's systems and information.

Its operations should include the following:

- All functions and work that are routinely accomplished during the course of conducting the organization's security business
- System access administration and controls to include the direct use and control of systems' access software, monitoring their use, and identifying access violations
- Access violation analyses to identify patterns and trends that may indicate an increased risk to systems and/or information
- Coordinating of computer crime and abuse inquiries with the high-technology crime investigator when indications of intent to damage, destroy, modify, or release to unauthorized people information of value are noted
- Disaster recovery/contingency planning to include directing the development and coordination of a companywide program to miti-gate the possibility of loss of systems and information, and ensure their rapid recovery in the event of an emergency or disaster
- An awareness program established and administered to all system users to make them aware of InfoSec policies and procedures that must be followed to protect systems and information
- An evaluation of all systems' hardware, firmware, and software for impact on security systems and information; where applicable, risks assessed and results reported to management for risk decisions
- Systems' compliance inspections, tests, and evaluations conducted to ensure that all users and systems are in compliance with security policies and procedures
- Projects initiated for the purpose of continuous improvement

---

"Thwarting I.D. Theft, Part I—An in-depth survey conducted on behalf of the Federal Trade Commission found that nearly 10 million Americans were victimized by ID theft in 2003—almost five% of the population. ID theft tops the list of frauds reported to the FTC last year, with complaints up 15%. This could mean the crime itself is becoming more common or that people are get-ting more diligent about reporting it—or both. Identity fraud costs consumers roughly $5 billion dollars each year. Businesses eat another $48 billion."[4]

PREVENTIVE CELLULAR PHONE FRAUD MEASURES

With the advent of cellular telephones and the integration of other func-tions into what has become a multifunctional device, this device offers many opportunities to support the commission of a high-technology crime as the target or "victim," and is a tool to be used by miscreants to commit high-technology crimes.

Cellular phone-related crimes cannot be eliminated, but they can be reduced if some simple steps are taken.

- Ensure cellular phones are adequately justified.
- Establish and enforce good security policies and procedures.
- Brief phone users on security requirements.
- Approve phone numbers to be called in advance.
- Limit call areas only to those required for business.
- Coordinate with cellular phone provider to establish billing thresholds.
- Secure the phone out of sight when not in use.
- Don't make a call if suspicious people are near you.
- Use encryption when possible to protect sensitive information.
- Actively monitor the billings and verify the legitimacy of the calls.

"Introducing the New McAfee Wireless Home Network Security—Now you can keep your wireless home network and data safe, complementing your antivirus and firewall protection. Wi-Fi networks are a huge convenience, but they can also be open targets for the new wave of "wireless" hackers. Your new PC may be loaded to the hilt with security software, but if your wireless network is not protected, you could still be vulnerable. Protect your Wi-Fi from hackers who can hijack your connection to use your bandwidth, steal your data as it travels over the airwaves, insert viruses and other malware into your network, or even launch widespread Internet attacks from your service. Lock down your wireless now with the proven security of McAfee" (e-mail communication received from McAfee, September 2005).

SECURITY REQUIREMENTS FOR VOICE MESSAGING OPERATIONS

The uses of telecommunications systems continue to grow rapidly. One aspect is the company-owned telecommunications switch. These PBXs play an important role. They give the companies control over their voice and data communications networks that were not possible just a few years ago. These modern telephone switches are nothing more than "just another computer." However, as with any computer, they come with the potential for exploitation by hackers or, in this case, phreakers.

Although most companies are beginning to secure their computer networks that are "attached" to the outside world, many of them have failed to realize that the PBX is also a computer that must be secured. In many companies, the organizations responsible for "normal" computer systems are not the same as those responsible for the PBX. This has historically been the case because computer systems were maintained and operated by data center people whereas telephone systems were maintained and supported by the telecommunications people.

Although in the past, communication between the two groups was not that necessary for both groups to get their respective jobs done, this is no longer the case. Companies have been slow to recognize the need to integrate these two segregated groups into one. The lines between telephone switches and other types of computers are rapidly blurring.

Although telecommunications people didn't concern themselves that much with any types of threats (other than such things as fire, flood, and so forth), the computer technicians have for some time been concerned with both the internal and external threats to their systems. Telephone technicians, until the advent of the computer-based PBX, were primarily concerned with ensuring the phone systems were operational. When a company purchased their PBX, little attention was paid to securing the system from phreakers. In fact, even the PBX suppliers paid little attention to the threats to the systems. They did not provide any type of training or awareness briefings to their customers related to the features of the PBX that are vulnerable to exploitation by phreakers, primarily because many of them were not aware of the threats themselves!

It's amazing that companies had to learn the hard way all over again. They did not seem to, and some still do not, take the hard-learned lessons of securing their computers and use those techniques to secure their PBX.

The penetration of a PBX still appears to be primarily for using its DISA feature to dial through the switch to a long-distance number, with the charges being picked up by the owner of the PBX. The penetration of the PBX to use and store messages in vacant voice mailboxes, and listening to and destroying messages of a voice mailbox that has been penetrated, is becoming an ever-increasing threat.

The following security requirements are provided to assist the high-technology crime investigator in understanding the protection that should be in place, thus helping to minimize the opportunity for miscreants to take advantage of the system. This in turn will lead to less high-technology crime investigations.

Telephone Voice Messaging Operation

While conducting a PBX or other type of high-technology communications-related crime investigation, one should look at the security or protection policies that govern how such high technology is to be controlled. The following is an example of one such policy.

APPENDIX 4-1

1.0 Policy

This document outlines the minimum-security requirements for telephone voice messaging (TVM) systems that support the services of voice mail, call answering, mailboxes, and call processing.

The security controls for TVM must, with reasonable dependability, prevent (1) unauthorized access to company information during or resulting from the processing of such information and (2) unauthorized manipulation of the system that could result in the compromise of company information.

The company's PBX security controls and operating procedures must be documented in writing and approved by security personnel. The purpose of the documentation is to ensure that all security aspects of the systems are addressed, to serve as a baseline for investigation in the event of a penetration or attempted penetration, to assist in conducting a risk analysis, and to assist in conducting damage assessments in the event information or equipment is stolen or damaged.

2.0 Requirements

Requirements are provided using the following 13 sections as the baseline for a procedures document:

2.1 Identification

This section provides basic TVM system, user, and management identification.
  2.1.1 Provide a unique name for the system.
  2.1.2 Identify personnel responsible for maintaining controls and safeguards.
    • System security manager
    • Security custodian and alternates
    • Owners of hardware and software resources
  2.1.3 Specify physical locations of resources.
  2.1.4 Specify the location of all users.

2.2 System Usage

This section describes TVM system purpose, sensitivity levels of the information processed, type and usage of electronic media, and the specific mode of operation.
  2.2.1 Describe the specific services of voice mail, call answering, mailboxes, call processing, and so forth, provided to each users (or group of users).
  2.2.2 Indicate the days and hours of operation.
  2.2.3 List the highest sensitivity level of company information transmitted/stored in mailboxes.

2.3 Hardware

This section identifies TVM system equipment, hardware layouts, configurations, and disconnect methods.
  2.3.1 Provide a current list of equipment that includes manufacturer model and serial number (and, optionally, any company property tag numbers).

2.3.2 Describe company and noncompany premises where all hardware components for the system reside.

2.3.3 Provide an inventory of the type and size of internal memory.

2.3.4 Provide an inventory of the type and usage of storage media.

2.3.5 Describe all removable/nonremovable media used.

2.3.6 Describe configuration management techniques in place to
ensure that all hardware components function in a cohesive,
identifiable, predictable, and reliable manner.

2.4 Software

This section describes TVM operating system and application software.

2.4.1 List all installed software, including vendor and release numbers.

2.4.2 Describe operating system security/protective features.

2.4.3 Describe messaging software security/protective features.

2.4.4 Specify the telephone time-out interval and method of warning established for interactive voice messaging.

2.5 Teleprocessing

This section describes TVM communication capabilities and circuits.

2.5.1 Provide current network diagrams, schematics, and floor
plans of the systems and telephones, as well as capabilities
and restrictions on the use of cellular phones, company-
owned pagers, and so forth, as applicable.

2.5.2 Describe the methods of restricting voice messaging to company use only.

2.5.3 Describe techniques for the safe storage of all incoming/outgo-
ing message traffic against power or equipment failure, power
surges, or power spikes.

2.5.4 Describe configuration management techniques in place to
ensure that all elements and components function in a cohesive, identifiable, predictable, and reliable manner.

2.6 Personnel

This section describes the TVM system personnel access controls.

2.6.1 Describe the security responsibilities of the following personnel:
- System security manager
- Security custodian and alternates
- Owners of hardware and software resources
- Users of mailbox information

2.6.2 Describe supplemental custodian and user security awareness and training.

2.7   Physical

This section describes the physical security measures to protect the TVM system.

    2.7.1   Describe the system hardware and media access controls in place during working and nonworking hours.

    2.7.2   Describe how all teleprocessing circuits are physically secured against tampering.

    2.7.3   Provide evidence that information carrying sensitive information is not connected to systems that are not approved to transmit sensitive company information.

    2.7.4   Provide evidence that connectivity to nonsensitive systems/telephone equipment outside of approved company areas is accomplished with controls in place that would preclude the intentional and/or accidental introduction of sensitive company information.

2.8   General Access Controls

This section describes TVM controls that restrict access to the system, such as passwords, detection of unauthorized use, and sign-on/sign-off procedures.

    2.8.1   Describe the method for user identification and authentication of employees using the system from outside company facilities.

    2.8.2   Describe the method for user identification and authentication of employees from within company facilities, including the following:

- Authorized user identification
- Restrictions on use of guest mailboxes
- Automatic password/PIN expiration interval
- Password/PIN minimum length
- Password/PIN change interval
- Nonworking hours for restricted mailbox access
- User failed logon suspense criteria

    2.8.3   Describe procedures for periodic review of user mailbox access and call processing authorization.

    2.8.4   Describe mailbox group list update procedure upon notification of an employee organization reassignment.

    2.8.5   Describe mailbox access list update procedures upon notification to or by an employee of intent to terminate employment.

    2.8.6   Describe method to prevent audible disclosure of passwords/PIN codes (e.g., conference speaker phones).

2.9   Operating Procedures

This section describes TVM system startup, in-process, and shutdown procedures used for sensitive processing.

2.9.1   Discuss how security-approved procedures will be used to enforce continuity, accuracy, and protection of mailbox information.

2.10   General Storage, Protection, and Control

This section describes TVM methods of marking, handling, storing, and controlling system media and information.

2.10.1   Describe provisions during call answering and call processing for system identification as a company "business-use-only" system.

2.10.2   Describe companywide method to enforce labeling of voice mail as company sensitive.

2.10.3   Describe how the owner of each message contained in a mailbox is identified.

2.10.4   Describe method for safeguarding operation system software, messaging software message distribution lists, and mailbox contents.

2.11   Audit Trails

This section lists, describes, and provides exhibits of all automated and manual audit trail records to provide a documented history of TVM system use, violations, and maintenance.

2.11.1   Describe audit trail reports/logs used to capture accesses to the system, attempts to break in, attempts to bypass established system parameters, accesses to another user's mailbox without proper authorization, and so on.

2.11.2   Describe the review process for reports/logs. Show how all anomalies or violations of security policies and procedures are evaluated, how the reason for them is determined, and what corrective action will be determined and taken.

2.11.3   Provide examples of the following minimum set of audit trail logs and reports:
- Custodian acknowledgment statement
- User acknowledgment statement
- System access list
- Mailbox group list request
- Mailbox access change request
- Vital software index

2.12   Subcontracting

This section describes TVM arrangements for subcontracting time and/or services as applicable.

2.12.1   Identify all authorized subcontractors, vendors, or other noncompany personnel who interface with this TVM.

2.12.2 Describe the voice messaging services and features authorized for subcontractors, vendors, or other noncompany personnel.

2.12.3 Describe security restrictions unique to noncompany personnel, how they are enforced, and so forth.

2.13   Emergency Plans

This section describes TVM procedures to identify, recover, and protect information during system crashes, security violations, or other emergencies; and the backup recovery process for information processed on the system.

2.13.1 Specify and prioritize vital system software, messaging software distribution lists, and mailbox information.

2.13.2 Provide a list of personnel to notify in case of emergency; include telephone numbers, fax numbers, home addresses, and so forth.

2.13.3 Specify emergency procedures for protection of hardware, system software, messaging software, distribution lists, mailbox information, and audit trials.

2.13.4 Provide evidence of periodic testing of backup procedures.

2.13.5 Provide procedures for rapid resumption of vital voice messaging functions.

2.13.6 Document procedures for long-term restoration of normal messaging service levels.

Voice Mail Summary

The establishment of a security policy and procedures documentation for each PBX will help mitigate but not prevent attacks by external and internal threat agents. However, by establishing such policies and documentation, the major security threats, vulnerabilities, and risks, and applicable countermeasures must be addressed by the PBX staff. This can then form the baseline on which to develop a more secure system.

Voice Mail Protection

As with cellular phones, protection methods can be used to minimize losses and damage to voice mail systems. They are the following:

- Use long and complex passwords.
- Lock out all unused mailboxes.
- Search unused boxes for messages.
- Eliminate their use by ex-employees.

- Don't store personal information.
- Don't store sensitive information.
- Ensure audit trails are in place and active.
- Review audit trails often.

PBX PROTECTION

To assist in protecting the business PBX, the following four measures should, at a minimum be in place:

1. Adopt a corporate remote access policy.
2. Audit existing system software for configuration and compliance with InfoSec policy.
3. Establish and maintain a process to maintain a secure PBX.
4. Implement remote maintenance port protection, install call accounting software, and continuously monitor the PBX's parameters.

E-MAIL PROTECTION

To minimize electronic mail problems, don't execute programs received in the mail, verify the sender's identity, and establish and maintain current security policies and a user awareness program.

> "Insecure high-tech devices such as USB flash drives and media players are being used in 84% of companies, but little is being done to address the information security risks that they present, according to a survey by mobile security firm Pointsec. The use of USB-connected devices such as memory keys and flash drives is rising in the workplace, and companies need to be aware of how easy it is for staff to use them, lose them, or take competitive information away on them, says Pointsec."[5]

NEW MISCREANT TECHNIQUES BRINGS NEW DEFENSIVE METHODS

One of the changes brought about by more and more sophisticated threat agent techniques is that as more security is installed to protect systems and their information, the more miscreants find ways around or through these defensive walls. Then the defenders find stronger defensive mechanisms. This has started an entire new business of corporations developing and selling high-technology defensive products. Now, even home computers, notebooks, and soon cell phones will require defensive software. These products, which are pretty much a necessity for even home computers, include

- Personal firewalls
- Antispam software
- Antivirus and antiworm software
- Antispyware

> W32/IRCbot.worm! is a medium-risk worm for home users. You can be infected simple by going on line. Once infected, your computer may start continuously (e-mail communication received from McAfee, October 7, 2005.)

> "Microsoft: MSN site hacked in South Korea; WASHINGTON (AP)—Microsoft acknowledges that hackers booby-trapped its MSN Web site in South Korea to steal passwords from visitors. The company says it was unclear how many Internet users might have been victimized."[6]

PROTECTING SEMICONDUCTORS—MICROCARVING

In the past, the theft of microprocessors was rampant. However, most of this is now history because massive numbers of microprocessors are available and their prices have been drastically reduced during the last few decades. However, for those high-technology crime investigators who may still become involved in the investigations of the thefts of semiconductors, the following information was gleaned from the Internet (source unknown) and may be of use to you:

> Selling stolen semiconductors is about to get a lot harder. An electronic industries association has adopted a new technology called *Data Matrix* that engraves an indelible microscopic code on the outside of chips. It works like a tiny barcode but contains 100 times as much information. That lets manufacturers mark each chip with individual serial numbers. Thieves can't remove the code without ripping off the chips' casings, which in most cases would destroy the devices. (Source unknown)

SUMMARY

The high-technology crime investigator should have a basic understanding of the functions of the business or government agency InfoSec program. The investigator will need to develop a relationship with and work closely with the members of the InfoSec organization. The key InfoSec principles are access control, individual accountability, and audit trails. This applies to all high-technology equipment, including computer networks, PBXs, cellular telephones, PDAs, Blackberrys, and other devices. InfoSec functions, duties, and responsibilities will vary depending on the culture and management support given to it.

REFERENCES

1. *Feds Recruiting Hackers at Defcon.* www.cnn.com/2005/TECH/internet/08/11/fed.scout.hackers.reut/index.html
2. *Microsoft Unveils PC Security Service: Software Maker's Subscription Plan Includes Anti-Virus Updates; Rollout Seen by Year-End.* http://money.cnn.com/2005/05/13/technology/microsoft_antivirus.reut/index.htm?cnn=yes
3. *Passport ID Chips May Not Be Secure.* www.cnn.com/2004/TECH/ptech/11/29/electronicpassports.ap/index.html
4. *Thwarting I.D. Theft, Part I.* www.foxnews.com/printer_friendly_story/0,3566,149468,00.html
5. www.out-law.com/php/page.php?page_id=securityrisksofus1118667763&area=news
6. *Microsoft: MSN Site Hacked in South Korea.* www.cnn.com/2005/TECH/06/02/ms.hack.ap/index.html

PART II
High-Technology Crime Incidents and Crime Investigations

High-technology crime is often about following the money trail.

The objective of this section is to provide an overview of high-technology crime investigations and evidence collection methods. It includes a sampling of actual high-technology crimes.

Although the primary purpose of the book is to provide a basic framework for establishing and managing a high-technology crime investigative program for a corporation, with some insight into the profession of the high-technology crime investigator, as well as an overview of the global information environment where the investigator will work, it would not be complete without at least an overview of actual cases of high-technology crimes.

Chapter 5 provides an overview of the important concepts associated with "computer forensics." It describes the potential sources of evidence available in the typical microcomputer, how to conduct a search for evidence, and a method of conducting a search in a systematic and effective manner.

Chapter 6 presents what to do and, just as important, what *not* to do when responding to high-technology crime scenes.

Chapter 7 includes a discussion about collecting high-technology crime scene evidence, a crucial part of any high-technology investigation.

After the investigator responds to the high-technology crime scene, there are witnesses and victims to talk to and, subsequently and hopefully, the miscreant will be interrogated. Chapter 8 provides a basic discussion of interviews and interrogations that can be used by high-technology crime investigators.

No book on high-technology crime is complete without addressing the computer forensics aspects of high-technology crime investigations—the topic of Chapter 9.

Chapter 10 provides a basic discussion of how to establish and manage a computer forensics laboratory based on real-world experience; it is not a theoretical discussion.

Chapter 11 presents a range of cases that illustrate the types of incidents that may be encountered under the general grouping of high-technology crimes. Although not exhaustive, they do provide a sense of the many challenges that face high-technology crime investigators in both the public and private sectors.

5

Investigating High-Technology Crimes

This chapter provides an overview of the important concepts associated with computer forensics. It describes the potential sources of evidence available in the typical computer, whether it is a desktop, a laptop, a handheld device, or a hybrid; how to conduct a search for evidence; and a method of conducting a search in a systematic and effective manner.

INTRODUCTION

Before we begin, we must note that the information provided is not all inclusive, because operating systems, applications, and hardware are constantly changing. Therefore, the information presented should be used as a guide. Specific systems require specific forensic procedures.

Government and public agencies, businesses, and individuals increasingly rely on a wide range of computers, often linked together with networks, to accomplish their missions. Because computers are now ubiquitous, they are often a highly productive source of evidence and intelligence that can be obtained by a properly trained and equipped investigator. Creating and equipping a high-tech investigative unit to be capable of competently searching the most commonly used types of computer is essential.

In many cases these days, a suspect will have used a computer to plan the crime, to keep records of acts in furtherance of a crime or conspiracy, or to communicate with confederates about details via e-mail, a message board, or (increasingly these days) voiceover IP with tools such as Skype.* In other crimes, the computer will play a more central role, perhaps serving as the vehicle for an unauthorized intrusion into a larger system from which valuable files or other information is downloaded or tampered with.

---

*Our identification of specfic hardware or software by no means should imply any recommendation for or against it, but merely identify it as an example.

Surprisingly, even many sophisticated criminals who are highly computer literate remain unaware of the amount of information that is stored on the computer (including their own computer), and the many software tools and utilities available that allow evidence to be recovered from various types of storage media, including hard drives and random access memory. Therefore, every investigation of a crime or of unauthorized activity should now be based on the assumption that some effort will be invested in examining computers and computer records to locate relevant evidence that will prove or disprove allegations or suspicions of wrongdoing.

SIGNIFICANCE OF COMPUTERS IN CRIME AND INVESTIGATIONS

Whether computers are themselves used as the tool to commit a crime or merely contain documents, files, or messages discussing the plans, computers can provide a wealth of useful information if they are properly exploited. A major barrier to obtaining and preserving this potentially valuable evidence is the relative lack of knowledge and skill of many corporate and law enforcement investigators concerning high technology—computer technology. This lack of familiarity and experience hampers the investigator's ability to conduct effective searches or even to consider that the computer may be a source of evidence. When the crime scene itself is a computer or when the evidence related to the illegal or unauthorized activity is stored on a computer, there is no substitute for the use of "computer forensics" to gather relevant evidence.

> *Webster's New Collegiate Dictionary* defines forensics as "belonging to, used in, or suitable to courts of judicature or to public discussion and debate."[1] Thus, *computer forensics* is a term that we define as describing the application of legally sufficient methods and protocols and techniques to gather, analyze, and preserve computer information relevant to a matter under investigation.

Operationally, computer forensics encompasses using appropriate software tools and protocols to recover, search the contents of magnetic and other storage media, and identify relevant evidence in files, fragments of files, and deleted files, as well as any information that may be found in slack space, swap files, temporary files, deleted files, and free or unallocated space. Each of these areas merits some discussion.

Slack Space

Most computer operating systems divide up the available storage media into manageable "chunks," which are called *clusters*. For most computers, clusters come in various sizes, ranging from 12k to 16k to 32k. When an application creates a new file, the minimum number of clusters that are necessary is assigned to the new file. However, if the file doesn't completely fill a cluster with data, there will be an area *between* the last byte of file data (the end-of-file marker) and the "physical" end of the assigned cluster size, which is known as the *slack space*. In some computers, as much as 20% to 30% of the total space allocated to files may actually be unused—slack space. As files are written to and deleted from the clusters, there will be times when the length of the file that replaces a previous deleted file will be shorter; data elements from the old, deleted file will remain and can be recovered. By the way, if you didn't know it, deleting a file does not actually delete it; it only changes the first character of the filename and flags that the space it used to occupy is now available for use again. Searching this much space can be very tedious effort, but with the proper software utilities it can sometimes be a very productive source of information.

Swap Files

To operate more efficiently, many operating systems create a data cache or buffer in RAM to speed up processing. In doing this, the computer does not need to access the hard drive to read data; it merely restores it from the RAM cache. This cache (or buffer area) is called the *swap file* in Windows (from the concept that the file is "swapped" in or out of RAM as needed). When Windows is open, the dynamic swap file is changing constantly as new files are opened and closed. When Windows closes normally, these files are written out to the hard drive and are stored in a swap file. In most desktop computers, the swap files may be as large as 600 to 700 MB, which means that a great deal of information may be stored in the swap file. If Windows has been shut down improperly (e.g., loss of power), then the entire swap file may be recoverable from the hard disk drive of the microcomputer in file "386.swp."

Temporary Files

Many applications create temporary "working" copies of the files that are created or used by the user. These files are typically "deleted" by the operating system when the user closes the application or exits the program. Many common tasks also create temporary files. For example, when a document or file is printed, the operating system typically creates a print spool file that is also deleted when the print operation is completed. These temporary files are created using "free" or "unallocated" space on the attached storage media, and are then "deleted" when no longer needed. There is a very good chance that evidence may be recovered from these areas through a careful search with disk-editing software or by using customized forensic search utilities.

Deleted Files

Many investigators and sophisticated computer users understand that files are not physically removed from storage media when they are "deleted." Rather, what happens is that the operating system flags the files (and thus the associated storage space allocated to that file by the file allocation table) as "open" or "available for use." This means that when the system needs to store a new file, this space may or may not be used, depending on a number of variables. If the file has been very recently "deleted," it may well be fully recoverable through the use of file recovery utilities. Older Microsoft Windows operating systems were notorious for the way in which they allocated storage space, which resulted in a rich source of potential evidence for the investigator. The more recent versions are considerably more efficient in the way they deal with storage space, and as a result are much more likely to overwrite any previously used space before they look to other areas of storage. The result of this is that there is now a far greater likelihood that potential evidence from deleted files may be overwritten and lost.

Remember, though, that, particularly when a file consists of multiple clusters (e.g., a big file), it is still possible that significant "chunks" of relevant evidence/data may still be discoverable through the use of disk-editing tools or specialized computer forensic software. It's also important to consider that the huge number of temporary files generated by Windows and its applications may be fully or partially recoverable and thus could provide important evidence if properly searched.

Free or Unallocated Space

As noted earlier, the portion of the storage media (e.g., the hard disk, floppy disk, or other drive) that has not been assigned or allocated to existing files and documents is called *unallocated* or *free space*. Even though it appears empty to the casual user, it may contain a wealth of material that could be relevant to an investigation. Although it is possible to search the unallocated space using a disk editor, given the rapidly increasing size of hard drives (often more than 300 GB), the task can be compared with draining a swimming pool using a bucket; it can be done, but it takes a very, very long time. As a practical matter it has become important to use specialized search utilities to filter these vast holdings and to find the character strings that indicate useful evidence.

Now that we have a baseline operational definition of computer forensics, it may be more apparent why a working knowledge of the concepts and applications of the technology and practices are vital to the success of high-technology investigation units. The balance of this chapter provides an overview of the recommended roles, responsibilities, and capabilities of computer crime investigative resources in a high-technology investigations unit.

We will also look at basic concepts that provide a foundation for understanding the process and the technologies involved in preparing and searching computer media for electronic evidence. Given that there are a large number of competitive forensic software products, we describe the generic processes that are pertinent to all, rather than focus on any one specific tool.

ONE APPROACH TO RETRIEVING AND PRESERVING ELECTRONIC EVIDENCE

This section includes a systematic approach to retrieving and preserving electronic evidence—how to recover deleted information, identify and recover hidden password data, and avoid inadvertent destruction or contamination of evidence.

Computers in Crime

There is sometimes a tendency to consider a crime a "computer crime" or high-technology crime because a computer was used in the commission of the crime or was a target of the crime. Although this is true, it is only part of the story. As computers and technology are increasingly integrated into our everyday lives, it is increasingly true that computers, PDAs, mobile phones, iPods, and the paraphernalia of everyday modern life must be considered during the investigation of any type of crime.

In addition to this, the definition of computer crime contained in the applicable statutes varies widely from state to state and country to country. In some states and countries, using a computer to defraud or commit other crimes may make it a special type of violation. There are also computer crimes that are specified by federal legislation, such as attacks upon or misuse of federal government-owned systems. *Computer crime* is defined as "any illegal act for which knowledge of computer technology is used to commit the offense."[2]

As previously stated, there are many and varied statutes. In Europe, despite attempts to harmonize computer crime law, most countries still have different interpretations. Each of these statutes and national laws has different elements of proof. It is vital that the investigator be familiar with the language and elements of relevant statutes that would likely include federal and national laws, as well as state laws in which the organization has offices and conducts operations.

Computer fraud is defined as the use of a computer with the intent to commit a fraudulent act: "Any defalcation or embezzlement accomplished by tampering with computer programs, data files, operations, equipment, or media, and resulting in losses sustained by the organization whose computer system was manipulated."[3]

Elements of proof include knowingly having accessed or otherwise used a computer, without authorization or having exceeded authorization, with intent to commit a fraudulent act.

VIOLATIONS OF ORGANIZATION POLICIES

In contemporary organizations, whether government, nonprofit or business, it is likely that computers are widely used and critical to daily operations. In most North American organizations, every staff member has one or more individually assigned computers, perhaps including a designated laptop for travel, desktop workstation for in-office work, and a palmtop/PDA. In addition to these systems potentially being used to commit crimes, they may also be used to commit acts that are not crimes, but are in violation of the organization's policy or procedures. For example, most organizations have explicit policies that prohibit downloading or viewing of pornography onto the organization's computers.

Other organizational policies may include instructions that direct employees not to send threatening, harassing, or sexually explicit e-mail messages to coworkers. When an employee is known or suspected to have engaged in such a prohibited activity, the evidence to prove this or other serious policy violation may exist on the hard disk drive or other media. This evidence, which may be discovered through a skillful examination of these media, can be used to significant effect during interrogations.

Although policy violations are normally less serious than crimes, organizations are now often held to a very high standard of proof in situations when an employee is terminated for violating a policy. Given the increased volume of wrongful termination lawsuits, evidence recovered from computers may be essential both to prove the violation as well as shield the organization against trivial wrongful termination suits.

SEARCHING A COMPUTER: WARRANTS AND POLICY ISSUES

Law enforcement investigators will most likely need a search warrant to obtain evidence from a personally owned computer unless it has been seized at a crime scene under pertinent authority. In exceptional circumstances, it is possible that the system owner may indulge a request for a consent to search, but it's not very likely that any criminal or anyone involved with any serious offense will be so cooperative.

In the private sector, obtaining *physical* access to a target computer may be simple. However, the investigative unit manager must ensure that the company policy framework supports a legal search so that any evidence that is discovered can be used. Typically, employee handbooks and other policy pronouncements should contain language that explicitly states that the company owns the computers used by the staff and the data they contain.

Any management communication should be phrased in terms that make it clear that the organization reserves the right to inspect the computer at any time for any legitimate business purpose, including investigating known or suspected violations of company policies or relevant laws. The language should also advise employees that they have no reasonable expectation of privacy in using the machine and that if they choose to use the computer for personal communications or other purposes, they do so at their own risk.

If the company does not have such a policy and procedure, it is possible that an employee might be able to sue the organization for violation of privacy, especially in states like California, where there is an explicit state constitutional right to privacy. In any event, consulting with corporate counsel or other company attorney prior to initiating a search is an important element of every investigation.

Some of the issues to consider in planning a computer search are as follows:

- Why is the system being searched?
- What evidence is expected to be recovered?
- Is there a specific time period in which a search is most likely to be productive?
- How long should the investigators wait before informing the suspect?

OPERATIONS PLAN

As with any serious effort, remember the six Ps: Prior preparation and planning prevents poor performance. As with any other search, a computer search requires careful planning. The bigger the systems, the more important it is to plan.

The following sections should be considered for inclusion in a written computer search/investigative plan:

- Objective (relevant to private sector/corporate organizations)
- Jurisdiction
- Call signs
- Frequencies
- Investigative agencies
- Command post

- Communications (relevant to private sector/corporate organizations.
- Logistics
- Assignments
- Hospitals
- Locations (relevant to private sector/corporate organizations)
- Floor plans (relevant to private sector/corporate organizations)
- Maps
- Assembly area
- Teams
- Resources, such as manpower, budget, equipment, and so on (relevant to private sector/corporate organizations)
- Surveillance options, such as type of business, public access, hours of operation, number of employees, and so on

Planning for the search should include specific information to cover most search aspects and contingencies, including:

- Who will bring the warrant?
- Who will bring the tool kit?
- Who will make out the evidence tags?
- Who will search the systems?

Are you considering printing out a hard copy of the contents of the hard drive? It is not something that you would normally consider these days. A 4-GB drive could hold approximately 1,000,000 printed pages, or enough hard-copy pages to fill more than 400 drawers of filing cabinet space! However, there are times when you may need to consider doing this or doing at least a partial print.

THE SEARCH PROCEDURES

Prior to searching a computer for evidence, it is important to know the violation of law or company policy on which you are going to base your search, the warrant (if necessary), and associated effort. After this is established, the plan is developed, and the team is briefed, you are prepared to conduct the search. Never forget that once you start the search and seizure, you need to be prepared to throw the plan out the window and adapt to changing situations. The reality of the situation may be different from what you expect.

Each search must be addressed individually. Even after conducting hundreds of searches, never be complacent; never take anything for granted. Criminal users of computers are becoming more sophisticated, and their application of security features is constantly improving.

As an example of how sophisticated operators may prepare, consider this posting extracted and paraphrased from an actual posting to an Internet-distributed "spy" list. Although the "advice" was posted a considerable time ago and its reference was last, it is still just as valid today and the investigator should bear it in mind:

"Destroying Information on a Storage Media—Use an AC current bulk VCR tape eraser from Radio Shack. Just lay the unit on the hard drive and it'll clean the hard drive with magnetic pulses. Make sure to leave it on for at least 10 minutes. This procedure will leave no traces. Use it as an emergency disk crasher in the event you need to make an immediate and permanent erasure of sensitive data. Keep the unit on standby next to the computer. If it is ever needed, turn it on and place it on top of your computer case, and within seconds the hard drives will be corrupted beyond repair. If the computer is later seized for inspection or as evidence, the hard drives will be unusable and corrupted.

Antiseizure Device—As an additional safeguard, you can install a booby trap switch that turns the system on if the computer case is removed or tampered without the "proper" opening method. This requires a small 12-volt dry-cell battery (w/small-drain 12-volt charger tapped into the unit's power source) connected to a $39 inverter (installed inside the tower computer case). Use a switch located on the computer cover that will trip if the "proper" deactivation procedures are not followed. Use a regular on/off switch inside one of the unused floppy plates that can be accessed to turn on the deactivator (on/off switch) prior to opening. If this isn't done (and only the owner would know to do this), when the cover is removed, the unit activates (switch is closed to inverter and it operates as a self-contained power source), and 15 seconds later, the hard drives are trashed. Tape the AC erasure unit to the underside of the hard drives using duct tape or use nylon tie straps."

Comments: Avoiding this trap is difficult for the computer investigator. Unless forewarned by informants or the suspect, the technician is likely first to learn of this system when the case is removed. Quick removal of the extraneous equipment may not be possible before significant corruption has already occurred.

In an article published in *Wired Magazine,*[4] the following advice was given with regard to pagers: "Be sure to yank the batteries if you're about to be nabbed. During an arrest, cops can scroll through the information on your pager without a warrant. As for PDAs, Just say no; do not give permission for a search.... Speaking of portable electronics, here's some free advice: Don't let 'em search your car. Once you do, the cops will legally have permission to search the memory or storage of whatever electronics you've got stashed away."

With regard to "no-knock" searches, the article comments: "Conservative activists may hate this, but 'no-knock' searches, where Kevlar-clad goons toting M-16s break through your front door without warning, aren't going away. If anything, the Justice Department seems to think they're even more necessary when dealing with computer crimes. ...Technically adept computer hackers have been known to use 'hot keys'—computer programs that destroy evidence when a special button is pressed. If agents knock at the door to announce their search, the suspect can simply press the button and activate the program to destroy the evidence," the manual (2001 update of the US Department of Justice guidelines for police and prosecutors in cases involving computer crimes) says:

In an online discussion about the destruction of data, the following comments were made:

Commentator 1: "Defense has a policy of destroying any hard drive with sensitive data if it is to be removed from its secure area. I've put sledge hammers through many a hard drive in my time...its a big company...they can afford it!"

Commentator 2: "How would a small stick of C4 placed on the [hard drive] do? Would the resulting explosion guarantee destruction of the data? I saw this thing on A&E about the FBI HQ [headquarters] and how they have this huge forge at the basement that they use to destroy all the files and documents that get put in the trash. Would a [hard drive] getting incinerated at high heat work? Interesting stuff this data forensics is...."

Commentator 3: "I have a solution to the destroying of [hard disk drives]— easy as 1, 2, 3: (1) Obtain large acid-resistant bucket, (2) place large quantity of sulfuric acid in the bucket, and (3) place [the hard disk drives] in the bucket, add acid and [hard disk drives] to taste. Let simmer/boil/crackle until happy."

There is plenty of information and advice out there regarding ways to prevent an investigator from getting access to data. The investigator should bear in mind that the measures you may encounter from desperate individuals are as wide as their imagination.

A HIGH-TECHNOLOGY CRIME SCENE

Figures 5-1 through 5-5 depict a general crime scene that you, the high-technology investigator, may observe during an investigation. Assuming the systems were running at the time of the search, would you know what to do and in what order?

Figure 5-1 shows what could be three standalone microcomputers. However, two of them are actually part of a LAN that includes several other systems in a different room. They are running Microsoft Windows

Figure 5-1   An example of a high-technology-related crime scene.

98 and Windows 2000, each system has a separate output to a telephone line, and one is also used as the interface to the Internet.

Figure 5-2 provides a different angle of some of the hardware. At first glance the desktop contains an inkjet printer and scanner. On the work area are monitors, mouse interfaces, and keyboards. Under the work area are the three CPUs, a hub, an "A/B" switch, a box for CDs, and a toolbox. The bookshelf contains a large selection of computer-related books. The cupboards above the work area contain spare hard disks, system boards, CDs, floppy disks, cables, and a range of related paraphernalia. The filing cabinets contain a mixture of personal documents, and computer and systems-related documents. The books and documents may provide an indication of some of the applications on the network.

The systems look alike; however, the one on the left is a standalone system that is connected via a separate phone line to the Internet, the system on the right is the server, and the one in the middle is a workstation. What, at first glance, may be a normal setup may not be. The CD box or anyone of the devices may actually be an explosive device that could possibly even be triggered remotely. as the high-technology crime investigator, you must be cautious when you approach a high-technology

Figure 5-2   A different angle of the hardware.

crime scene just as you would when you conduct drug searches of a "meth" lab.

Figure 5-3 provides a closer look at the power and data cables. When you try to understand which system is connected to what, or when you want to disconnect the cables prior to transporting the system, it is important to photograph the cables in situ and to label them so that you can reconnect them correctly later.

What should be of interest to the high-technology investigator, besides the desktop system and LAN hardware is that the notebook obviously indicates mobility, which means that it is reasonable to consider that it may be used at other locations. So much for stating the obvious. However, one must understand the reason for this mobility on the part of the high-technology criminal. Is it for the convenience of working at home, at another location, on the road? Probably. And this means there may be more evidence in the car, in the home, in other offices, or in other locations to which the suspect may have access. Having good sources and detailed information from those sources before conducting the search would obviously greatly enhance the ability of the investigator to collect all relevant evidence during the search.

If a source is being used to gather information, be sure to spend time with the source, show the source pictures of hardware, and try to determine what is at the crime scene. If a notebook computer is there, can

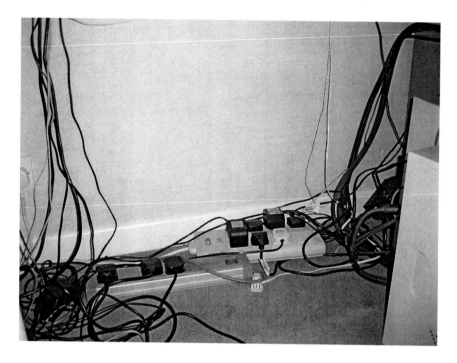

Figure 5-3   A closer look at the power and data cables.

Figure 5-4   A closer look at the crime scene.

Figure 5-5   A notebook system that includes an external hard disk caddy, diskettes, CD case containing applications on CDs, a wireless telephone, and an indication of an internal modem attached to the telephone.

the source determine why a notebook computer is being used? Where it is being used? Are there any other possible details about the systems (e.g., applications, versions, brand names, models, and so on)? The notebook pictured in this series of figures has USB ports, which means that it may have a range of associated devices, such as a cellular phone or Blackberry.

SUMMARY

High-technology crime investigations are still based on the basic investigative techniques that have been developed over time for all types of crimes—answering the questions of who, where, when, why, what, and how.

High-technology criminals are increasingly installing more sophisticated security systems, including strong encryption systems. Such devices will require expertise, and perhaps some lateral thinking, to access them. Some miscreants have focused on methods of destroying evidence if law enforcement or investigators attempt to investigate the system.

The challenges to high-technology crime investigators are many and increasing quickly. Only through constant training will investigators have any hope at all of keeping up with these changes, including searching media for evidence. The key to successful searches is to know the technology, have a plan, use common sense, and use a specialist who is an expert in the technology and accompanying software to be searched.

REFERENCES

1. *Webster's New Collegiate Dictionary.* www.m-w.com
2. McEwen, J. T. (1989). National Institute of Justice/Issues and Practices, Dedicated Computer Crime Units. Washington, DC: The National Institute of Justice.
3. Association of Certified Fraud Examiners. *Computer Fraud* [teaching course].
4. www.wired.com/news/politics/0,1283,41133,00.html

6

Responding to High-Technology Incidents and Crimes

This chapter looks at the considerations that a corporation and the high-technology crime investigator must address prior to an incident if they are to be successful in responding to high-technology crimes. It also looks at the actions that need to be taken immediately after an incident is detected.

INTRODUCTION

The ability to respond to high-technology incidents and crimes in an effective and efficient manner requires preparation. The preparations and related activities for investigating high-technology crimes fall into three areas:

1. Actions that are taken before the incident
2. Investigation activities
3. Postincident activities

The information that is given here is, by the very nature of the problem, generic. The range of incident types and the different levels of severity of an incident will mean that each case has to be addressed individually, but they all have a number of features in common. These phases are addressed below as we break down the whole investigative process into the main components.

PREINCIDENT PREPARATIONS

There are steps that can be taken prior to an incident occurring. The rationale for this is that the way in which a corporation or the high-technology crime investigator responds to an incident depends, in part, on the forethought that has gone into the configuration of the system that may be a miscreant's target, in addition to the plans and procedures that have been put in place before the incident occurs.

In the worst-case scenario, imagine the problems that an investigator might have if no audit information were being collected and stored or if users were allowed to share login IDs. Prior preparation and planning can vastly improve the likelihood of a successful investigation and can shorten the time that it takes to respond effectively to an incident.

> In order for there to be any realistic chance of a successful investigation into a high-technology crime, it is essential that the corporation has taken steps to ensure that, in the event of an incident, it will be able to contain the situation and preserve the necessary information (potential evidence) in a form that will not only allow the investigator enough information to be effective, but also to have it in a form that is evidentially sound and can be used, if necessary, in any subsequent prosecution.

To investigate high-technology crimes successfully, the IT staff and security staff (e.g., high-technology crime investigator) of the corporation need to be aware of the legal requirements for the capture and preservation of the evidence. They also need to be aware of the legal issues that will affect the actions that they take during the immediate aftermath of the discovery of a high-technology crime. Often, it is no use collecting the evidence in an evidentially sound manner if it has been contaminated by the staff or other individuals before the proper investigation starts.

At all times during the process, there are decisions to be made. The first of these will probably be to decide what is more important—the continuity of the operation or the capture and preservation of the evidence—but this is dealt with on a case-by-case basis. If the system is critical to the corporation (perhaps a military command and control system or an air traffic control system), it may be imperative to continue to operate and accept that evidence may be lost or destroyed.

Another decision that may have legal implications is that of whether to shut down the system and capture what evidence is already there or allow the system to continue to operate and attempt to gain more evidence with regard to the activities of the attacker. One of the legal implications here is that if the system is allowed to continue to operate and the miscreant uses it as a conduit to attack another system, the corporation may be liable for the damage that is caused to the second system (owned by another), because the organization was aware of the illicit activity and could have prevented it from occurring by preventing access to the system or shutting down the system. After the appropriate decisions have been made, the next phase to be undertaken is the investigation, and this may well take place at the same time as the restoration phase (i.e., bringing the systems back to their preattack configuration—perhaps with better security software installed).

According to Rowlinson,[1] there is a 10-step process that can be used by a corporation to make sure that it has taken a range of measures that, in the event of an incident, makes them capable and prepared for the collecting and storing of the information that will be required for a successful investigation. The steps that he defines are as follows:

1. *Defining the business scenarios that require digital evidence*—You will never be able to identify or capture all the scenarios that may occur, but you should be able to select and address those that are considered to be the most likely or those that cause the corporation the most concern. The scenarios that will be most significant to the corporation will depend on the type of corporation, the type of systems that are used, and the way in which they are used. The benefits of defining these scenarios will include
   - *A reduction in the impact of computer-related crimes*—If you have thought about the factors that will affect the likelihood of an incident and the impact of such an incident on the business, you will have enhanced the awareness of the corporation to its vulnerable points and the steps that can be taken to minimize the likelihood and level of impact of an incident.
   - *Legal requirements*—By understanding the legal requirements for the storage, handling, and disclosure of information, it will be possible to organize the storage to retain the information that is likely to be required and weed out information that is not required or should not be held, and to store it in such a way that any legal requirements can be met without undue disruption to the business.
   - *Production of evidence*—It may be necessary to be able to demonstrate compliance with a range of regulatory or legal requirements or to produce evidence for use in internal disciplinary or external criminal or civil cases. Each of these cases may require different types of information to be stored. If a range of scenarios have been considered, the correct data can be identified and stored appropriately to meet these potential requirements.
2. *Identifying available sources and different types of potential evidence*—Undertaking this process will, in itself, aid a subsequent investigation because the potential sources of information will have already been identified. The very act of identifying the information sources may help to highlight gaps in the information that is currently being collected and allow for changes in the type of information collected, the positioning of sensors, and the procedures that are created to ensure that the level and type of information that will, potentially, be required for any investigation is available.
   Issues that need to be considered include the format of the data, the length of time that it is stored, the locations where it is

stored, the way in which it is controlled and who has access to it, other sources of information required, how it should be made available for an investigation, in what form, and whether there are any legal or regulatory constraints on its release (Data Protection Act, Basel II Accord, Sarbanes Oxley, human rights legislation).

3. *Determining the evidence collection requirement*—By considering the issue in advance with the investigators, the system administrators and the legal team, there is the opportunity to determine the type and range of information that could and should be collected. When the likely scenarios have been identified and the potential sources of information have been isolated, it will be possible to determine the evidence collection requirements.

    Issues that need to be addressed when determining the requirements for evidence collection include how the evidence can be collected without undue interference with the business process, managing the cost of the collection and storage of information for any potential investigation in proportion to an incident, the legality of collecting the information required for a successful investigation, and whether there will be sufficient information available to allow for a successful investigation.

    After these factors have been considered, it will be possible for the corporation to understand the economics of the data storage and evidence collection requirements and to determine whether they already can collect or can arrange to collect all the information required. If they do not collect all the information that is likely to be necessary, then a business decision needs to be made on the economics of collecting and storing any additional information.

4. *Establishing a capability for securely gathering legally admissible evidence to meet the requirement*—This includes the planning to ensure that the tools and facilities are in place to make sure the information is collected in an appropriate manner and the members of the staff are suitably trained, aware, and practiced in the requirements so that any evidence collected and stored is done so in a manner that will make it admissible in any legal or internal disciplinary proceedings.

    The issues that need to be considered here are whether the information has been collected in a manner that is legal and whether it has been stored in such a manner that it will be admissible in court. Consideration will have to be given to the way in which the data are collected. For instance, does the corporation have the right to monitor and collect e-mail? Have the corporation's Internet and e-mail usage policies been written in such a way that the e-mail belongs to the corporation and not the individual? Consideration will also have to be given to storage methods and practices, and to which members of staff who will have access to the stored records.

5. *Establishing a policy for the secure storage and handling of potential evidence and ensuring that it is properly and regularly tested*—It is only by planning the correct storage and handling of the information in advance that its usability as evidence can be assured. One must ensure that audit and other logs, as well as any other relevant information, are stored in such a manner that they cannot be tampered with or modified, and that they are stored in a physically secure and safe manner.

6. *Ensuring that the monitoring of systems and networks is targeted both to detect and to deter major incidents*—This step should be part of the normal security procedures implemented to protect the systems, but input from an investigator may provide a different viewpoint and improve the defenses and the monitoring systems that are put in place.

   Activity monitoring will be guided by a range of factors that are indicative of different types of activity. For example, fraud activity may be indicated patterns or variations in patterns in financial data, whereas the leakage of IPR from a corporation may be revealed by checking information contained in e-mail messages and attachments, copying files to removable media, or printing documents. The abuse of privileges on a system may be indicated by changes in individuals' authorities and access rights or their access of files and areas of the system they do not normally need to access. It is only by understanding what the investigator will need to look for that the appropriate monitoring can be instigated. Remember that the monitoring and analysis of systems and the storage requirements that result have a cost. Also remember that trying to monitor *everything* is pointless because the recovery of any significant information from huge volumes of stored data will be difficult and expensive.

7. *Specifying the circumstances in which an incident should be escalated to a full, formal investigation*—By considering this in advance, it is possible to think about the subject rationally and to get the necessary input from all parties that will be affected or involved. This is a much better time to consider the issues, rather than having to make on-the-spot decisions when the pressure is on during an incident.

   Ensure that the policies for incident management contain the relevant detail for the conditions when incidents will be escalated, and note the individuals who should be informed/involved in the identified scenarios.

8. *Train all relevant staff in incident awareness*—By undertaking this activity, all those members of the staff who are likely to be involved will understand their role in the digital evidence process and the legal requirements for the collection and storage of evidence. This

is an obvious preparatory step. It is not possible to train staff and ensure they have an awareness of the role they will play in the process after it has started. By then, it is too late.

9. *Documenting an evidence-based case, and describing an incident and the impact*—By documenting a case, you will be providing a template for the processing and reporting of a real incident, and you will provide the staff with a memory aid for any investigation. It will also provide management with an opportunity to consider the range of impacts that may affect them and allow them to think about the decisions and the actions they will need to take to address the variety of scenarios.

10. *Ensuring there is a legal review of the procedures that are developed*—This will facilitate any action that is taken in response to an incident. By getting a legal review of the policies and procedures that have been put in place to make sure they are legally sound and address all the issues, the corporation can have confidence that the steps that have been implemented are effective and correct. Legal advice that might be sought includes potential liability that may result from an incident, legal or regulatory constraints that must be taken into account, methods for dealing with members of staff, and any other areas that should be considered that have not been identified until the legal review.

RESPONSIBILITIES AND DUTIES

Another area that must be addressed in advance is the allocation of duties of the people who may have responsibilities during an incident and the documenting of these duties. For example, as the manager or team leader, you should consider defining the roles of the following groups: users, system administrators, security staff/other high-technology crime investigators, incident team, public relations (PR) staff, and management.

The Users

The users will need to be trained and educated so that they know when and how to identify and report security problems and incidents. It is only if the users (your most numerous and, usually, the best sensors on the system) are conscious of the indicators of any potential incident that they will be able to adopt the appropriate procedures and report unusual activity. If a user spots unusual activity and knows the procedures that should be followed and who to report the activity to, then many incidents can be stopped before they become serious. In the event of an incident, the users need to know who to report it to, what they should report, when they should report it, and what immediate actions they should (or should not) take.

System Administrators

System administrators will need to understand audit and other system logs, reports of incidents that are made to them, as well as evidence preservation. With this understanding, they will be able to decide whether the action required is within their purview or whether it is necessary to initiate incident procedures. Although the system administrator is "king" of the system, he or she cannot be everywhere at all times. System administrators will be most effective if they can understand what the users (or others) are reporting to them. System administrators need to know

- Who might report to them
- What immediate actions they should take
- Who they, in turn, need to report it to
- What they should report and when

Security Staff/High-Technology Crime Investigators

These individuals will need to understand the meaning of reports that they receive, and they will need to make decisions regarding whether an incident has taken place. They need to be able to identify the type of incident that has occurred. They will have to decide whether the incident lies within their area of responsibility, expertise, and jurisdiction; whether they need to inform external agencies; or whether they need to activate a security incident team. They then have to know how to escalate the activities that are taking place and set in motion the action that is required.

Incident Team

The incident team, which will be led by the high-technology crime investigator, will consist of applicable members from management, the legal staff, human resources staff, PR staff, the security staff, the system administrators, and the users. These team members will have to be able to undertake the management of an incident and must have the experience of having worked together. This experience can only be gained by having practiced and exercised together through a range of scenarios.

The PR Staff

The PR staff will have to be capable of dealing with the management and release of information relating to the incident. It is essential that, in the event of a significant incident, they act as the single conduit for the release of information about the incident to the public. Their role should not be to minimize the incident (doing this has a nasty habit of backfiring when the full scope eventually comes out). If they are to carry out their task effectively, they will have to be able to interact with the incident team and have some understanding of the meaning of the information they are given and its significance. Two of their tasks are (1) to take some pressure off the investigators and (2) to control the release of information to protect the image (and, if appropriate, the share value) of the corporation.

Management

The management team will have to be able to understand the information that is being reported to them and make effective and appropriate decisions regarding the approach to the incident, the scope of the investigation, and the probable business implications. They may need to authorize the actions of the relevant groups involved and interact with external agencies and corporations.

It is only with exercise, education, and training that the relevant members of staff will be capable and confident of carrying out their duties during an incident and be able to work together effectively as a team. This can only be achieved over a period of time and must be undertaken as a part of overall system and security management and incident preparation.

TRAINING

In the preceding paragraphs there have been numerous references to training and staff awareness. This is not something that can be addressed in a single session; it is achieved and maintained through an ongoing program of targeted training and awareness sessions. If staff members are fully trained and aware, they will be better prepared to identify that an incident is occurring and to handle an incident when it occurs. At the Global Enterprise Corporation (GEC; a fictitious corporation used to facilitate discussion of the investigation and high-technology crimes and described in Chapter 12), this is an integral part of the corporate disaster, recovery, and emergency planning program and plans and is the responsibility of GEC's CSO.

THE INCIDENT HANDLING PLAN

When you have developed and documented your plans for information collection and handling, storage, staff training, and incident escalation, you will need to put together a plan for the actual handling of an incident. The resources that will be available to manage an incident will need to be clearly defined in terms of the staff and equipment, together with details of when and how to contact the relevant members of the staff. The incident handling plan should also detail the different roles and responsibilities of those involved. Given the range of possible scenarios, this can never be precise, but it will prevent gaps from occurring in the actions that are taken. It will also prevent an individual or group from "hijacking" the handling of an incident, which may happen when you get strong characters involved who either have their own agenda or think that they "know it all."

Only when you have taken these or similar preparatory steps suitable for your corporation will you be able to have any confidence that it is prepared for an incident. Do not be under any illusions as to whether there will be an incident. There will. It is just a matter of time before it happens.

When an incident does occur, the preparatory steps that you have put in place will mean that you have a much greater chance of managing it successfully and concluding a successful investigation. You should be able to determine what happened, when it happened, what damage took place, what you need to do to restore the system, and (if you are lucky) who did it. Although it may be tempting to dive straight into the investigation, there are a number of things that you need to do before you start.

IDENTIFICATION OF AN ATTACK

Although the preparation that has been undertaken is vital in minimizing the effects of an attack and allowing for a return to normal operations as rapidly as possible, after the incident has occurred, the first thing that has to be done is to determine whether it was an accident or an attack. If an attack has taken place, then the type of attack should be identified before steps can be initiated to contain it. A number of the most commonly seen types of attack are detailed in the following paragraphs.

Malicious Software Attack

Probably the most common and best known type of attack is a malicious software attack. In the past we would probably have referred to this as a *virus attack,* but in reality, in recent years, the distinction between viruses,

Trojan horses, and worms has become blurred. There are a huge number of different types of malicious software, and attacks by many of them are characterized by the speed with which they can spread between systems. Among the normal system security measures, those responsible for day-to-day protection of these valuable assets will have taken antivirus measures (hopefully). In the event of failure of the assets protection measures, an early identification of this type of attack is essential to prevent the spread to other systems and to minimize its impact. The early identification of this type of attack will most likely occur if system users are trained and aware of the characteristics of such an attack. A large number of potential attacks can and will be prevented if users are trained in "digital hygiene" and are, for example, aware that they should not open unsolicited e-mail.

Good examples of the types of malicious software that exploit e-mail as a vehicle to attack systems are the "Anna Kournikova e-mail worm," which was written using a Visual Basic worm generator and was released on to the Internet in February 2001.[2] This virus spread rapidly, prompting a large number of firms to shut down their e-mail servers as a precaution. Also, one report estimated that the "I LOVE YOU" virus will cause economic damage of up to least $10 billion before the virus and its variants are eradicated.[3] According to *Computer Economics*,[4] the "I LOVE YOU" virus, which was spread by e-mail, affected 78 million people globally.

The questions that might be generated by this type of incident include the following:

- How many systems have been affected?
- What is the likely damage as a result of the incident?
- Have any data on the system been destroyed or compromised?
- What steps need to be taken to restore the system?
- How long has the malicious software been present on the affected systems and has it affected the backups?

System Intrusions

System intrusions are most often characterized as the "hacking attack" on a system. In reality this might be true, but you should bear in mind that it is also just as likely that the "intrusion" will have been initiated by an insider abusing the privileges he or she has on the system. The characteristics most often seen for this type of attack are deleted, unexplained, additional, or modified files; additional accounts on the system; and unaccounted disk or memory usage.

The questions that might be generated by this type of incident include:

- What security measures are likely to have been breached?
- How did it occur?

- What is the likely damage as a result of the incident?
- Have any data on the system been compromised, stolen, or tampered with?
- What steps need to be taken to restore the system?

Denial of Service

The name pretty much defines this type of attack. The most obvious characteristic of a denial-of-service attack is that systems and services that would normally be expected to be available will not be or will have a reduced availability, and systems may crash. This type of attack is often mounted against corporations by individuals and groups that have a disagreement with the corporation or a grudge against them. In the past, a denial-of-service attack would have been mounted from a single source, but more recently, distributed denial-of-service attacks have been launched from a large number of systems against single targets. A distributed denial-of-service attack attempts to bring down a site by overloading servers with requests for information.

Examples of this type of attack can be seen in the case of the Arab satellite television network Al-Jazeera,[5] which sustained more than 2 days of continuous distributed denial-of-service attacks against its English and Arabic language Web sites in March 2003. The powerful and coordinated attack on Al-Jazeera's Web sites started on March 25, shortly after the network had published photographs of US soldiers taken prisoner by Iraqi forces. (More information of this type of attack and related information warfare concerning terrorism can be found in our book *Global Information Warfare.*[6])

Many of the more recent denial-of-service attacks have been initiated by organized crime to blackmail corporations for the equivalent of "protection money." The case reported by the *E-Commerce Times*[7] involving the credit card processor Authorize.net, one of the backbones of the Internet, gave details of the launch of a denial-of-service attack against the credit card processor that took place over a period of several days and was accompanied by an attempt to extort money to halt the attack. Another report published in *IT Week* in March 2005[8] indicated that companies were being advised to ensure that their systems were protected against denial-of-service attacks because of the growing problem of online blackmail. A spokesman for the UK-based research corporation, QinetiQ, was quoted as having stated, "When blackmail is linked to a denial-of-service attack, you know that [the criminals] will have a real source of professional expertise behind them." The spokesman went on to state that the year before (2004), many online bookmakers had been targeted by blackmailers who had threatened to disrupt their Web sites by launching denial-of-service attacks.

The questions that might be generated by this type of incident include the following:

- What proportion of the bandwidth is being compromised?
- Is the attack being launched from a single source or multiple sources?
- Can the sources of the attack be determined?
- Is the corporation the specific target of the attack or one of a number of targets?
- What steps need to be taken to restore the system?

System Abuse

The type of activity that may constitute e-mail abuse includes using the corporation's resources to carry out a personal business, sending and receiving pornographic images or text, harassment, stalking, or a number of other activities, depending on the acceptable usage policy that is defined by the corporation. This type of attack is normally mounted by individuals who are acting on their own. An example of this type of attack can be seen in the case of an Australian man who was jailed for 3 months for sending offensive e-mail, and making abusive and threatening phone calls.[9] He pled guilty to stalking and using the public network to carry out the offense. After being jilted by his girlfriend, he retaliated by making abusive phone calls—sometimes as many as 40 in a day. In addition, he also started to send threatening e-mail containing explicit photos of him and his ex-girlfriend. In a period of 1 month, he sent approximately 60 explicit photos to people associated with his ex-girlfriend.

The questions that might be generated by this type of incident include the following:

- Are copies of the offending e-mail or other material available on either the server or the client?
- What material has been sent or received?
- Is the suspected individual the sole user of the computer and could anyone else have had access to the computer?
- Is there any history of this type of activity by the individual or within the corporation?
- Is there an identifiable victim?

Intellectual Property Theft

The type of activity that may constitute intellectual property theft includes the copying, printing, or e-mailing of information that is of value to the corporation. This type of attack is normally mounted by individuals who are acting on their own and is most often seen when an individual is about to leave the corporation to join a competitor or set up their own company. The type of information that might be stolen includes customer lists, research, development data, and business plans (e.g., marketing, strategic, tactical, and annual plans of a proprietary nature).

CONTAINMENT

After an attack has been identified, steps can be initiated to start to contain it and to minimize the effects. The containment process allows the corporation to take measures to protect other systems that may be at risk from the attacker and to limit the damage that is caused. Remember that the decisions made in order for the containment to be carried out may affect the subsequent collection or validity of evidence for any subsequent investigation, prosecution (if the miscreant is an insider or outsider), or other disciplinary action (if the miscreant is an insider).

The steps that need to be taken to contain an incident will vary depending on:

- The type of attack taking place
- The type of high-technology crime committed
- The type of high-technology equipment or devices
- The configuration of the systems

The actions that you need to take for a virus attack will be different from those taken for an intrusion into your systems or a denial-of-service attack.

Malicious Software Attack

The containment action for an attack by malicious software is to isolate the affected systems. After the systems are isolated and further spread of the malicious software is prevented, then the collection of information and/or cleaning of the systems can be carried out. After this has been accomplished, it will be possible to restore the systems. However, if cleaning the systems is not complete, reinfection will almost certainly occur.

System Intrusions

The containment of a system intrusion depends on the decision of the high-technology crime investigator, with input from the incident management team, because there are two possible courses of action. The first, and most often adopted approach, is to isolate the affected system, both logically and physically as soon as an incident is suspected. This should preserve any evidence of an attack that exists on the system and, by preventing any access to the system, should prevent anyone from removing or modifying it. The second option, which has its own risks, is to allow the system to continue to operate without interference but to monitor all activity, including incoming and outgoing traffic. This allows the high-technology crime investigator (supported by the incident team) to monitor what the attacker is doing and to work out what their methods and intentions are.

Denial of Service

There is no real containment action that can be taken against a denial-of-service attack, because the attack will most likely be external to the system. The denial-of-service attack normally consumes the communications bandwidth between systems. The action required here is for the service provider to try and identify the source of the attack and get it blocked. However, with the modern version of this type of attack—distributed denial of service—the attack is mounted from a large number of separate systems, making it difficult to block. With this type of attack, it may be necessary to take more drastic action, such as changing the ISP that is used, until effective action can be taken.

ESCALATION

It may seem strange to discuss the escalation of an incident before an investigation has started, but it is useful to have considered what types of incidents will require escalation before you have to deal with one. After all, you do not want to set in place major incident procedures for the misuse of a standalone PC, which can probably be dealt with by the security officer and the system administrator. Or, consider the scenario of calling the chief information officer (CIO) of a multinational corporation during the weekend to tell him that you need his authority to deal with the disciplining of a staff member who has unauthorized software on their PC. You will soon be looking for another job.

The planning that goes into the subject of escalation should address:

- The types of incidents that will require escalation action
- The procedure for escalating an incident
- When the escalation procedures should be initiated
- Who can initiate an escalation

- Who is to be involved and how they can be contacted
- The method that will be used to contact them (phone, pager, e-mail)

BRIEFINGS BEFORE THE INVESTIGATION STARTS

After an incident has been discovered, but before any full investigation gets underway, there will potentially be a series of briefings that needs to take place. In some cases these will be perfunctory and a number of groups may have to be briefed together. After all, time will normally be of the essence. So who needs to be briefed? There may well have been some sort of briefing from the users to the system administrators, depending on who noticed the incident. After the alarm has been raised, the procedures that have been developed should be implemented and followed. This should provide you, the high-technology crime investigator, with a consistency of approach and allow people to get on with their tasks, rather than second guessing what needs to be done.

Management will need to be briefed on what has happened to get an idea of the likely impact of the incident and to decide on what action to take, remembering that in some incidents there is no option but to ensure that law enforcement is involved.

The following groups all require briefing, at the appropriate time, before they take up their roles in response to an incident.

- *The incident team*—If activated, as soon as it is formed and ready to take over the management of the incident, the incident team will have to be briefed on what is known or suspected to have happened and what is required of them. Individuals may have already been briefed in their other roles but must be briefed in the new role.
- *The PR team*—If it is likely to be a major incident or one that will be of interest to the media, the PR team will need to be briefed at an early point so they can start to prepare news releases and act as an informed interface with interested parties. This will take the pressure off the investigative team and allow team members to concentrate on their own tasks.
- *The high-technology crime investigator*—What does the high-technology crime investigator need to know? In reality, anything that is relevant to the investigation. He will certainly need to know
  - What is thought to have happened
  - Whether anyone is suspected of involvement in the incident
  - Which sites or systems have been affected

  The high-technology crime investigator will need a clear briefing on the scope of the task that is to be to undertaken, decide who will be taking part in the investigation, have as much information available on the systems that are known to have been affected, and the authority to conduct the investigation.

A description of the incident will assist investigators in deciding the line of inquiry they will follow and the type of information that they are going to have to look for. The types of crimes that may be encountered will range from:

- Hacking
- Denial of service
- Improper use of the facilities
- Fraud
- Blackmail
- Theft
- Pedophilia
- Smuggling
- Drug crimes
- Many others

You will need to consider the implications of each type of incident or crime and the basic approach to the investigation. It is also vitally important that the information provided be separated into facts, speculation, and theories. Often, what was thought to be factual in the "heat of the moment" turns out to be conjecture, causing problems for the team.

EQUIPMENT AND TOOLS

When the high-technology crime investigator knows the background of the incident/crime and the type of systems that are involved, he or she should be able to determine the equipment and tools needed. The type of "kit" needed should include, at a minimum, items such as:

- Evidence bags and labels (How embarrassing is it to have to send out for items like these?)
- Adequate communications equipment
- Camera to record the crime scene
- Flashlight
- Incident logs to record actions and decisions
- Adequate transport if equipment is likely to be seized and removed from the scene
- Packing material for seized equipment
- Search warrants (if required) or letters of authorization (the last thing you need is someone obstructing the investigation because they do not recognize the authority that you are operating under)
- Antistatic wrist band
- Gloves
- Indelible pens

- Notepads
- Screwdrivers (cross-head and straight)
- Pliers
- Seals
- Tape
- Imaging equipment

When investigating any high-technology incident or crime, having the correct tools at hand is important. If the investigation is on your own premises, this should not be a problem, because you are operating within your own infrastructure, you most likely know the people involved, and you already have the appropriate tools on-site. If, however, the investigation is taking place at another location, it is essential that the high-technology crime investigator be properly briefed and prepared with the appropriate authority, knowledge, and tools to achieve a successful conclusion.

DEFINE AND DOCUMENT THE CASE

It is important that every case is documented from the very beginning. This aids the investigator in the event that the case needs to be peer reviewed to ensure that no aspect of the investigation is overlooked. It is sensible to document all cases to the same standards. Although this may seem to be "over the top" for what appears to be an internal discipline case of someone abusing their privileges, you will look very silly when it turns out to be a major fraud case if you have failed to handle evidence or document your actions properly. Also, by documenting the process from the very beginning, it sets the process for the entire investigation. Good, comprehensive, and accurate documentation will also provide evidence for aspects such as supporting the chain of custody of the evidence.

During an investigation, evidence may pass through the hands of several people. Unless the evidence is correctly documented at all stages, it will be impossible to track its location and to prove that it has been properly stored and handled at all stages, that it has not been contaminated, and that the chain of custody has been maintained at all times. The level of information recorded should include details of when, where, and by whom the evidence was seized. Remember that taking photos, videos, or making sketches of the scene can be invaluable in reconstructing the scene or in highlighting details that were missed when the equipment was seized.

A record should be maintained of where the material is stored and any "hand-overs" to other individuals or agencies. If material is handed over from an individual or agency to another, signatures should be obtained. The items that have been handed over, the location, date, and time of the hand-over should be recorded. If copies of material are made, the copies should be labeled with an identifier, the name of the individual who made the copy, and the time and date the copy was made. The case documentation should have an entry made to record the fact that a copy was made, including the date, time, and name of the person making the copy. An MD5 hash of both the original and the copy should be made and recorded. They should be compared to verify that the copy is an exact replica of the original.

Remember also that besides the chain of custody to show who had the evidence at what time, date, and so on, the evidence must always be kept secure so that no one can later legitimately claim that the evidence may have been tampered with.

Throughout all stages of the investigation, it is essential that detailed notes are maintained of who is carrying out the work, what information is found, any conclusions that are made, and the supporting evidence for those conclusions.

All this documentation will be of use to the investigating officer when the time comes to present any evidence, which may be several days, weeks, or months after the investigation took place. If the documentation is not comprehensive and complete, being able to present clear and supportable evidence will be extremely difficult.

SECURING THE SCENE OF THE INCIDENT

Before the investigation can get underway, the scene of the incident must be secured to ensure that no contamination takes place during the time between the detection of the incident and the start of the investigation. Depending on the scenario, either within the corporation or outside its jurisdiction, securing of the crime scene will require differing considerations—if you control the environment and control access to the area, or if the scene is outside the corporation. In the latter case you may have to rely on others, and it may not be possible to obtain jurisdiction. Remember at all times to keep management informed, but also note that the legal requirements may override the needs of management in serious crimes. It may be illegal to take action that may impede, stop, or fail to report an investigation. The most often encountered scenario that this applies to is cases in which child pornography images are discovered.

THE FIRST RESPONDER

Much as the name suggests, the first responder is the person with some knowledge and authority who is the first to arrive at the scene of an incident. An individual who is properly trained will be able to take the appropriate measures to ensure that the scene remains sterile and is not subsequently contaminated. It cannot be stated strongly enough that the first responder has a huge responsibility to ensure that the scene of the crime is not contaminated and that as much evidence as possible is preserved for any future investigation.

So what steps should the first responder take? There are a set of internationally accepted principles that must be adhered to whenever possible:

- When dealing with digital evidence, all general forensic and procedural principles must be applied.
- Actions taken to secure and collect electronic evidence should not change that evidence.
- When it is necessary for a person to access original digital evidence, that person should be trained and experienced for the purpose.
- All activity relating to the seizure, access, storage, or transfer of digital evidence must be fully documented, preserved, and available for review.
- An individual is responsible for all actions taken with respect to digital evidence while the digital evidence is in their possession.
- Any agency that is responsible for seizing, accessing, storing, or transferring digital evidence is responsible for compliance with these principles.

These are clear, commonsense principles that have been developed and agreed upon by professional investigators and legal professionals to ensure that evidence is collected and preserved in such a manner as to prevent its contamination.

THE INVESTIGATIVE PROCESS

The investigative process is made up of a number of phases, each of which need to be planned and prepared for. Although each of the phases are linked, they can, in a number of ways, also be planned for and considered separately. Each of these phases needs to be planned and the relevant preparations, such as policy preparation, training and skill practice, and tool acquisition, need to have been made. For the purposes of completeness and because planning is required for each of them, all the phases are mentioned here, although they will be dealt with in detail in later chapters.

Information Collection

The collection of information is the foundation of everything that may happen during the investigation of an incident. If the collection of information that may be used as evidence is not properly planned and thought out, any subsequent investigation will be made more difficult and less likely to be successful. The planning and preparation for this phase should include:

- Ensuring that the InfoSec and audit policies within a corporation encompass the collection and storage of data that may be required for investigations
- Ensuring that appropriate and adequate sensors and data collection tools are in place or available
- Ensuring that sensors are located at suitable points on the networks
- Ensuring that tools are available to view and interpret the information collected by the sensors
- Ensuring that staff have received adequate training and have had the opportunity to gain necessary experience

Information Preservation and Recovery

After an incident has occurred, the first phase that must be addressed is the preservation and recovery of the evidence. If the recovery is not carried out using the right staff with the right tools and observing the correct procedures, it may be a waste of time. The aftermath of an incident is not the right time to start to consider the issue. The planning for this phase should include:

- The training of staff
- Policies for the safe and effective recovery of data
- Appropriate and adequate data recovery tools

Examination

After the available information has been collected and recovered correctly, it needs to be examined and the relevant elements of information identified and isolated. It is only with training and experience that the person carrying out the examination will be able to determine the elements of the collected data that are likely to provide the information required for the specific investigation. The planning for this phase should include staff training and practice of examining systems to gain experience and appropriate tools to carry out the examination of the available data.

Analysis

The analysis phase is when the information that has been collected, recovered, and examined is analyzed. This evidence may be in the form

> *Computer forensic analysis* is the term used to describe the thorough and painstaking examination of digital evidence in all formats for all applicable devices.

of digitally stored documents, photographs, sounds, videos, spreadsheets, databases, Internet history files, or any other recording in digital form. It also includes the retrieval of these documents or recordings after they have been deleted, fragmented, or encrypted. The analysis stage is when all the knowledge and experience of the investigative team and available experts are applied to the information. This stage includes an evaluation of what has occurred and what action needs to be taken next, both for the pursuit of the perpetrator and the repair and restoration of the system, equipment, or device. The planning for this phase should include staff training and practice to gain experience and to ensure that the appropriate tools are procured to carry out the analysis of the available data

Reporting

It may seem strange to "plan" the reporting of an incident that has not yet happened, but thought applied to it in advance will make the whole process much easier. The preparations for reporting include consideration of who the report will be produced for, the types of information that should be included, and the aspects of the incident that should be addressed. In preparing for this and in producing reports on the material that is examined during practice sessions undertaken to gain experience, the investigators will produce reports that can be examined and discussed by all interested parties. These reports will be examined to ensure that they contain the relevant levels of information and that they are in a suitable format and language. The reports that have been developed during this period can then be used as the template for the actual investigation.

SUMMARY

This chapter has looked at a range of steps that can be taken to reduce the likelihood of an incident occurring. If an incident does occur, this chapter has examined how to make available the information that is likely to be required during any subsequent investigation. It has also addressed how to minimize the impact of an attack. We addressed the policy, procedural, and training issues that must be tackled if a corporation is to be able to identify an incident when it does occur (and, once again, it is worth stating that incidents will happen; it is only a matter of time until they do), to be able to capture and store, in a forensically sound manner, any information that may be of use in an investigation.

REFERENCES

1. Rowlinson. (2004). A Ten-Step Process for Forensic Readiness. *International Journal of Digital Evidence, 2*(3).
2. Leyden, J. (September 14, 2001). Anna Kournikova Virus Author Stands Trial. *The Register.*
3. Weil, N. (May 8, 2000). "Love Bug" Virus Costs Expected to Reach $10 Billion. *INFOWORLD.*
4. *Computer Economics.*
5. Roberts, P. F. (March 26, 2003). Al-Jazeera Hobbled by DDOS Attack. INFO-WORLD.
6. *Global Information Warfare.* Auerbach/CRC Press.
7. Regan, K. (September 23, 2004). DDoS Attack Stalls Web Credit Card Transactions. *E-Commerce Times.*
8. Neal, D. (March 8, 2005). Online Blackmail Grows: Extortion Threat is Growing Menace. *IT Week.*
9. Oates, J. (May 14, 2004). Jilted Lover Jailed for Email Stalking. *The Register.*

7

The Collection of Evidence

This chapter looks at the issues that need to be addressed in the collection of digital evidence relating to an incident. We look primarily at the seizing of evidence from a PC that relates to a suspect, because this is one of the more probable scenarios in a high-technology crime investigation, regardless of whether the PC is a personal home computer, a laptop, or one used by an employee within the organization. Later in the chapter we address the issue of recovering evidence stored on networks.

INTRODUCTION

To say that the process of legally seizing evidence is crucial to any high-technology crime investigation is like saying that the Pope must be Catholic. For without evidence, even with an identified suspect, and often with the suspect's confession, the case may never proceed past the investigative state because corroborating evidence is required by the legal system in many countries.

The process used to collect evidence legally varies from country to country; however, assuming that the country has a rather mature legal process that protects the rights of its citizens, then the high-technology crime investigator must follow certain investigative steps. These steps may include such things as determining the probable cause for a search, obtaining a search warrant, and the like.

HOW DO YOU GO ABOUT SEIZING THE EVIDENCE?

It is fine to go in and seize any or all the computers in the vicinity of the crime, but unless you follow a set of defined procedures, this may be a waste of effort. If the equipment and information are not handled properly, then any evidence that is derived may not be admissible as evidence in legal procedures. In the following paragraphs we look at the procedures and good practice that should be adopted to ensure the collection of evidence is effective and has the maximum benefit.

The seizure procedures start from when the crime scene is controlled—in other words, the point in time when you have removed or excluded any individual from access to the crime scene and have pre-served the scene so that any information found is not contaminated. Efforts must be made to ensure that any actions that the investigative team takes do not subsequently contaminate the evidence. The steps that need to be taken will always vary, depending on what is found at the scene.

THE LAW

You should always remember that if the equipment and information are not seized in accordance with relevant laws, company policy, or both, any evidence acquired may be inadmissible in court or other proceeding. In the United States, the two most obvious laws that need to be taken into account are the Fourth Amendment and the Electronic Communications Privacy Act. In the United Kingdom, the main ele-ments of law that are relevant are the Data Protection Act, the Criminal Procedures and Investigation Act of 1966, the Protection of Children Act, and the Criminal Evidence and Procedure Act.

THE FIRST RESPONDER

As mentioned in Chapter 6, the first responder is the individual (or group of individuals) who is the first to arrive on the scene of the crime and who has some authority to start to deal with the incident. The first responder may not be a member of the investigative team. He or she must have the author-ity to take control of the scene and must have sufficient knowledge of the legal and company policy requirements to take the correct initial steps.

> The primary duty of a first responder is to secure the scene of the incident and ensure that no unauthorized personnel tamper with or contaminate any potential evidence.

It is essential that, in addition to the suspect and other people encountered at the scene, the first responder ensures that other individu-als involved in the investigation are controlled and do not take any actions that will compromise the evidence. We have all encountered the computer literate but not forensically aware law enforcement or security officer who turns the system on to "have a quick look to see if I can find any evidence" and subsequently contaminates or destroys potential evidence.

The first responder can, if he or she has the appropriate knowledge, also perform a useful role in acting as the on-site representative for the investigation. Remember, this person may not be part of the normal inves-tigative team. If the responder has suitable training and knowledge, the responder will also be able to carry out an initial reconnaissance and advise the incident response team regarding the conditions at the site. The first responder must also be able to provide the team with details of the type of equipment and the quantity of storage media visible on-site.

The first responder must be able to recognize that relevant evidence can be found on a wide range of devices, including magnetic, optical, and solid-state media, and hard copy. The responder must also understand that potential evidence may be volatile and, if not handled or protected appropriately, it may be lost.

All efforts must be made to ensure that contamination does not occur during the collection of the evidence. If the personnel at the scene are correctly trained and follow the procedures, then the likelihood of any possible contamination will be reduced. Again, as previously mentioned, if the collection of evidence is comprehensively documented, it will aid the investigators in proving they did follow the appropriate procedures. It will also help to prove that any evidence subsequently used is not contaminated.

Remember that it is the integrity not only of the digital evidence that has to be protected, but also that of any physical evidence such as DNA, fingerprints, or even blood. With this in mind, any equipment that is used to handle or store the seized equipment should be, if possible, disposed of or cleaned thoroughly prior to its reuse. It is risky to clean items after use and then put them in storage, because contamination may occur during such storage. Any magnetic media used to create copies should be wiped and checked prior to use.

HEALTH AND SAFETY

At the scene of the incident, investigators should take care that they do not endanger either themselves or others on the scene, and they should be aware that the items they are seizing may be hazardous, as they may be biologically or chemically hazardous. It is also not unknown for a computer to be booby-trapped to destroy potential evidence or the computer itself. If there is any suspicion that the system has been booby-trapped, then appropriate action should be taken and the scene cleared until the computer is made safe.

A GUIDE TO SEIZING EVIDENCE

If the investigation of the incident has identified a suspect and requires the seizure of potential evidence from a computer or computers, then consideration should be give to what items are relevant and should be seized. The items listed here are intended as a guide. When you arrive at the site to be searched, you may find other items of relevance and interest. A thorough search of the entire area should be carried out to ensure that any relevant items are not missed. Items that should be seized, if you are dealing with a PC or a small LAN include:

- Main unit—the part that most people would call the computer. This is the box that normally contains the CPU, the motherboard, the hard disk, floppy disk, and the CD/DVD drive.
- Monitor, keyboard, and mouse
- The leads that connect the individual elements together
- Any external power supply unit or uninterrupted power supply unit
- Any external hard disks. External hard disks may appear in many shapes and forms, and a variety of sizes.
- Floppy disks
- LS 120 disks
- Dongles (memory sticks). The storage capacity of memory sticks is currently 512 MB, and they have been incorporated into a number of everyday objects, such as wrist watches and ladies earrings.
- Modems
- Digital cameras
- Memory SIMMs (single in-line memory modules). Some digital devices have removable memory storage SIMMs. SIMMs can be fitted into cameras, PDAs, and mobile phones. SIMMs that are currently available can store as much as 1 GB of data.
- Backup tapes
- Jazz/zip drives
- PCMCIA devices. PCMCIA devices have been developed for a wide range of applications, including network connection, modems, "click disks," Bluetooth, and wireless devices.
- Any hard-copy printouts, documents, diaries, books, or notes that are relevant

PROCEDURES FOR SEIZING A STANDALONE COMPUTER

The steps detailed here are intended to provide guidance on the issues that need to be considered during the collection of evidence. Again, from the very start, ensure that you document the scene. Photograph, videotape, or draw a diagram of the scene. Make notes of any actions that you take and any changes that these actions cause to the system. For example, if an indicator light goes off when you disconnect a cable, you should make a record of this.

Try to determine the mode that the computer is in. Is the computer switched off, switched on, or in "sleep mode?" The actions that you take at this point will differ depending on what state the computer is in. If the monitor is switched on and the screen is blank, then the computer is either switched off or in sleep mode. Check the system box for indicator lights. If they are on then, the system is probably on; if there are no indicator lights, do not presume that the computer is switched off. Move the mouse slightly without pressing any of the buttons. If the screen does not change, then

- Document the state of the system. If possible, this should include photographing or drawing diagrams of all connections to the computer.
- Remove the power source from the computer. Conventional wisdom is that you remove it from the back of the PC, not the wall socket. If the system is a laptop, remove the battery (or batteries) from the laptop as well.
- Remove any floppy disks that are present in the drives, and bag and tag them separately.
- Remove any dongles, and bag and tag them separately.
- If external storage devices are connected (DVD/CDs, tape drives, external hard disks), remove their power source, disconnect them, and bag and tag them separately. *Do not attempt to remove any media that they may contain.*
- If the system has an internal DVD/CD, do not attempt to remove it.
- Check for modem or network connections. If any are found (and there is a strong probability that there will be some form of connectivity), try to identify either the telephone number or the IP address.
- Disconnect the external connections.
- Label each cable as it is removed from the system with details of the device that it connected to the computer and which end connects to the device.
- Record any details of make, model, or serial number that are visible.
- Document any damage that is apparent.
- Bag and tag all items (Remember to tag the bag, not the item.)

If the screen changes and displays either running processes, data, or a logon prompt, look at the information available on the screen. If there appears to be a process or processes running that may indicate the destruction of evidence is occurring, do the following:

- Immediately disconnect the power supply.
- Take a photograph or document any information that is on the screen.
- Document the state of the system. If possible this should include photographing, videotaping, or drawing diagrams of all connections to the computer.
- Remove the power source from the computer. Conventional wisdom is that you remove it from the back of the PC, not the wall socket. If the system is a laptop, remove the battery (or batteries) from the laptop as well.

- Remove any floppy disks that are present in the drives, and bag and tag them separately.
- Remove any dongles, and bag and tag them separately.
- If external storage devices are connected (DVD/CDs, tape drives, external hard disks), remove their power source, disconnect them, and bag and tag them separately. *Do not attempt to remove any media that they may contain.*
- If the system has an internal DVD/CD, do not attempt to remove it.
- Check for modem or network connections. If any are found (and there is a strong probability that there will be some form of connectivity), try to identify either the telephone number or the IP address.
- Disconnect the external connections.
- Label each cable as it is removed from the system, with details of the device it connected to the computer and which end connects to the device.
- Record any details of make, model, or serial number visible.
- Document any damage.
- Bag and tag all items. (Tag the bag not the item.)

If the monitor is switched off, do the following:

- Record the fact that the monitor is switched off.
- Switch the monitor on.
- Record the fact that you have done this.
- When the screen has warmed up, if there are data or a login screen visible, carry out the steps described earlier for monitor on, information present.
- If no data or login screen are visible, follow the steps described earlier for monitor on, but no data or logon screen visible.

PROCEDURES FOR COLLECTING EVIDENCE FROM A NETWORK

In most cases it is neither practical nor sensible to attempt to seize an entire network to collect and preserve evidence, unless it is the organization that is suspected of carrying out the crime. Even then, careful thought should be given before such a radical step is taken. In the early days of computer crime investigations (1990), at least one company was severely affected by the seizure of their computers.[1] This case occurred in Austin, Texas, where the US Secret Service raided a company called Steve Jackson Games. At the time, the firm was preparing to market a new Dungeons and Dragons-type game called GURPS Cyberpunk.

When federal agents raided the company's headquarters, they seized the computers the company was using to create the game and to maintain a bulletin board system for communications with its customers. During the raid, the Secret Service agents also confiscated company records and software. No one was ever charged with any offense relating to the computers that had been seized. Thus, the company suffered damages by not being able to adequately operate without their seized property.

When dealing with systems that are part of a LAN or WAN, a range of additional skills will be required by the investigator at the scene. There may be management decisions that need to be made because the actions that need to be taken for the preservation and collection of evidence may have a significant business impact. In most cases it will be specific information required by the investigator to assist in the investigation. This may include configuration information, access logs, audit logs, account details, intrusion detection system (IDS) logs, files stored on the system, and a host of other possible information.

Always bear in mind that the volume of information available from a network may be huge and could create problems with both the capture and storage of the information. Do you have the capacity to store and analyze terabytes of information? Also, the information may be transient. Some information is only stored for a limited period of time before it is overwritten. Once again, in these cases, comprehensive and accurate documentation of the steps taken to collect the evidence may be essential.

In most cases, the shutting down of systems and the seizing of hardware and software will also be based on a business decision. It is usually better if the system can be left running until any relevant information can be collected. This will go against the normal instincts of the system administrator, who will, in all probability, want to turn off the system, reload from a clean backup, and restore the system. If possible and practical, before the system is shut down, a bitmap image of the storage media should be made to capture any deleted files and to preserve the time stamps on files that have been made by the system. A record should also be made of the system clock time, and any discrepancy between this and a known and trusted time source should also be noted.

It is particularly important to remember that, particularly on a large network, the information required for the incident investigation may be transitory and may not achieve the requirements for legal admissibility. Always bear in mind that:

- Evidence from the network can be easily altered or deleted, and such modifications and deletions may be undetectable.
- Because a running network will be altering files in the course of its normal operation, files that are copied during the process of capturing evidence may not be accurately copied or copied at all if an update of the file is taking place when it is being copied.
- The format in which potential evidence is stored may be different than the format in which it is displayed.
- The use of system backups should be considered, even if they have not been made and stored in a forensically sound manner. They may

provide corroboration of the evidence taken during the investigation and may provide intelligence for the investigation.

If it is not possible to create a bitmap image and the live system has to be worked on to gain information, then a record should be created of all actions that are taken on the live system. One tool that can achieve this is the UNIX script command, which will create a permanent record of the actions taken. Many investigators now also take the precaution of videotaping their activities and the screens during the investigation to allow them to demonstrate to a court what actions they took and what effects those actions had.

If, during the examination of a live system, any unknown processes are found running on the system, they should be dumped to disk using a suitable tool. Forensically sound images should be made of activity logs and any files that appear to be suspicious or have been tampered with. An MD5* or similar hash should be made of both the original file and the copy, and both hash values should be recorded.

As mentioned earlier, the decision to keep the system running after an incident will normally be a business decision (unless keeping it running is at the request of the investigative team or law enforcement). The potential ongoing damage to the system and an evaluation of the cost benefit of capturing the attacker versus the cost of the damage that is being caused must be considered. Also consider potential liability from third parties affected as a result of actions taken by the attacker that could have been prevented if the system had been isolated or switched off.

If the system is kept live to gather intelligence on the attacker, then all logs that are made relating to that activity should either be stored in an encrypted form on the system or stored on media that cannot be detected or modified, to prevent the attacker from altering or destroying the logs to cover their tracks.

OTHER ELECTRONIC DEVICES THAT MAY CONTAIN RELEVANT INFORMATION

Before dealing with individual devices, it is worth remembering that they may, potentially, have wireless links to another computer or device in the area (Bluetooth, wireless, or infrared).

Mobile Phones

Mobile phones contain records of calls that have been made, received, and missed. They may also contain other information such as address books, diaries, and text messages, and they may have the potential to store data in a manner similar to a computer. In fact, many of them can be connected to computers to "share" files, so the phone may, in fact, contain any of the

---

*See http://www.webopedia.com/TERM/m/md5.html for further explanation.

types of information that you might find on a computer. A number of the phones are fully Internet capable and can be used for browsing, sending e-mail, and downloading.

The first responder should not try to access the mobile phone. If the suspect is present at the scene, he should be asked for any security code or PIN, but under no circumstances should you allow him to have access to the phone. If possible, attempt to identify the make and model of the phone. The area should also be checked for anything that may contain a security code for the phone (the handbook, diary, filofax, notebook). If there is any information on the screen, this should be recorded, either by making a note of the information or, if possible, by taking a photograph of the screen (take care to ensure that data are readable). Collect any peripheral devices, manuals, and software that may relate to the phone. Bag and tag the phone, remembering that there may be a requirement to obtain physical evidence from the phone or peripherals (fingerprints or DNA). Finally, document any actions that have been taken.

The type of evidence that may be found on a mobile phone includes:

- Numbers that have been called, received, or missed
- Contact details, including names and addresses as well as phone numbers
- PIN numbers or passwords for other devices and accounts
- E-mail and internet browsing history
- Short message service (SMS) messages sent and received
- Documents, applications, and images

Pagers

Pagers are small, portable devices used to receive numeric, alphanumeric, and/or voice messages, and they may contain messages that are of interest. The first responder should not try to access the device, but should identify the make and model. Again, record any information visible on the screen either by photographing it or making a note of it. If the suspect is present, do not allow him to handle the pager. Collect any peripheral devices, manuals, and software that may relate to the pager. Bag and tag the pager, remembering that there may be a requirement to obtain physical evidence from the phone or peripherals (fingerprints or DNA). Finally, document any actions that have been taken.

Blackberry Devices

Treat a Blackberry device (e-mail devices and related services) in the same way that you would a pager.

PDAs

PDAs, in many respects, are like a small handheld computer, but the procedures for handling them should be similar to those for mobile phones, pagers, and Blackberry devices. The first responder should not try to access the PDA. If the suspect is present at the scene, he should be asked for any passwords or security codes (PINs), but under no circumstances should you allow him to have access to the PDA. If possible, attempt to identify the make and model of the PDA. The scene should also be checked for anything that may contain a password or security code for the PDA (handbooks, diaries, filofax, notebooks). If there is any information on the screen, this should be recorded, either by making a note of the information or, if possible, by taking a photograph of the screen (again, take care to ensure that data are readable). Collect any peripheral devices, manuals, and software that may relate to the PDA. Bag and tag the PDA, remembering that there may be a requirement to obtain physical evidence from the PDA or peripherals (fingerprints or DNA). Finally, document any actions that have been taken.

The type of information that may be found on a PDA includes:

- Documents, applications, and images
- Voice or text messages
- E-mail and Internet browsing history
- Contact details, including names, addresses, and phone numbers
- Passwords
- PINs for other devices and accounts

Land-Line Telephones

Land-line telephones may have memories that contain lists of favorite numbers; calls made, received, and missed; and messages. Such devices should be handled basically as you would other communication devices (e.g., cellular phones).

Answering Machines

Answering machines are the land-line telephone equivalent of the mobile phone voice mail capability. The answering machine may be an integral part of the telephone or a separate device. It may contain messages (current or deleted) that have been left for the suspect and caller ID information as well. Again, as evidence, handle as you would other communication devices (e.g., fingerprints, DNA).

Fax Machines

Fax machines may contain messages that have been sent or received by the suspect, stored messages, transmission logs, speed dial lists for numbers that the user of the fax calls regularly, and details of the numbers that have been called. The type of information that may be found on a fax machine includes:

- Copies of faxes that have been sent or received
- Transmission logs
- Clock setting
- The fax header line

Photocopiers

Modern photocopiers may have access control systems and may contain their own internal hard disk, which could contain an image of any material that has been copied.

> Many modern printers incorporate a scanner/copier and a fax function in the one device.

Dictaphones

Dictaphones record voice messages on either a cassette tape or (more commonly these days) on digital media. They may contain any messages that the suspect has recorded or, if digitally based, any other type of data that can be stored on a computer.

Digital Cameras

Digital cameras store photographs in a digital medium, rather than on the now-old-fashioned light-sensitive film. Digital cameras contain memory modules that may not only contain images, both static and video, but sound bits and any other type of file that could be stored on a computer as well.

Internet-Capable Digital TVs

Internet-capable digital TVs may contain information such as e-mail, browsing history, and preferences (e.g., "favorites" or some configuration information such as default Web pages). Hence, you may have some indication of the user's habits.

Batteries and Mobile Devices

Please note that when bagging and tagging any mobile device, the investigator must remember that most of them have batteries with a limited life and, in most cases, when the battery goes, some or all the information stored in the device could be lost. Care should be taken with the handling of these devices to ensure that the batteries are kept charged until data recovery can be undertaken. Don't just bag and tag the device with all the other items and hand them over to the laboratory for processing at some time in the future. Make sure that whoever receives them understands their "life expectancy" and the requirement to maintain the charge on the batteries.

SUMMARY

This chapter provided sound guidance for collecting evidence from a range of devices. We provided a framework from which an investigator can work and raised a number of issues that must be considered if evidence is to be captured in a form that is forensically sound and useful in identifying what has happened and who has carried out the actions that resulted in the incident. Remember, each incident should be considered unique, and your procedures must change based on the changes in laws, company policy, and of course, the changes in high-technology devices.

REFERENCE

1. Leccese, M. (1990). Hackers Under Attack. *Boston Phoenix.*

8

Interviews and Interrogations

This chapter discusses techniques and issues that should be considered to gain the maximum benefit from the interviews and interrogations of high-technology crime witnesses, victims, and suspects who would obviously have information that could assist the investigation.

INTRODUCTION

As a high-technology crime investigator, you should also have the basic experience and knowledge of any investigator as they relate to interviews and interrogations. Although this may be a high-technology crime investigation, the majority of basic investigative techniques still apply, including how to obtain information from people.

Always remember that in any investigation, the initial contact with a witness, victim, or suspect, if correctly exploited, can be of huge value. With luck, you will have the element of surprise on your side and may obtain information that would not be so easily obtained at another time. However, there is a danger here: If the suspect can show he was in a shocked and disoriented state or his legal or human rights have been contravened, then any evidence gathered may be inadmissible. (In the United Kingdom, Section 78 of the Police and Criminal Evidence [PACE] Act may be invoked and the evidence struck out under the fairness rule, especially if cautions were not given at the correct times or if the suspect turns out to be a juvenile.)

In terms of catching the criminal off guard, remember that most perpetrators do no expect to get caught. Although you should never rely on this, it is possible during the initial contact that you will be able to obtain information from a suspect he or she would not be prepared to give up if he or she had time to consider his situation and the benefit of legal representation. (A lawyer will normally advise that a suspect should not incriminate himself.) This is no way intended to suggest that a suspect should be denied his legal and human rights; it is just the reality of the situation. Remember that if the information is not obtained in an appropriate manner and is later needed in a tribunal or criminal case or often even a company disciplinary hearing, it will be tainted and of little use to you, as would any information that you obtained as a result of that information.

When you bear in mind that Internet-related evidence is potentially highly volatile and may be lost if prompt action is not taken to preserve it, then any delay in capturing it may result in the loss or corruption or contamination of potential evidence. As early as possible in the investigation, you need to establish whether potential evidence is stored on systems other than the one you are investigating (perhaps at the ISP or at a site that has been used to store data). It is always worth trying to determine who the suspect uses as an ISP and to ask for any passwords. You cannot rely on obtaining this information, or of it being correct if it is given, but it is worth a try.

If you have the jurisdiction to do so, ensure that you remove the suspect from the computer or any other electronic media or evidence source he or she may be able to influence, and do not forget to carry out a search of the suspect. There may be information that can be recovered during a search of the environment that the suspect may attempt to dispose of if he were given the time and opportunity.

Try the sticky fingers test and run your finger around the edge of the monitor to see if any Post-It notes that were attached have been recently removed.

In the UK and many other jurisdictions, it is not only essential, but also good practice that all activities at the search scene are recorded, including any questions, answers, and cautions against self-incrimination.

Also, do not forget that it may be possible and sensible to question other people who are at the scene who may have had access to the system, who may have observed the suspect while he was conducting the crime, or who may have other information to offer. They may be able to provide information about facets of the system that the investigator would otherwise be unaware of, or they may be able to give details of the activity the suspect undertook prior to the arrival of the first responder. It may be that the other people at the scene can provide considerable detail relating to both the actions of the suspect and other activity that took place on the system or at the scene. It may also be necessary to obtain traditional forensic samples from them such as fingerprints and DNA to exclude them from any evidence gathered.

With good questioning, it may be possible during the initial contact with the suspect to gain some impression of the level of skill he or she possesses, whether he or she appears to be working on his or her own, his or her state of mind, or some indication of his motivation. It may also be possible to gain some insight into the intention of the suspect; however, do not forget the previously mentioned caveats regarding cautioning suspects and their rights.

WHO, HOW, WHERE, WHEN, WHY, WHAT

There is a difference, in fact several, between conducting an interview and conducting an interrogation.[1] It depends primarily on the willingness of the individual to whom you are talking.

- Interview
  - Involves a witness
  - Involves a victim
  - No Miranda warning (in the United States)
  - General information
  - Less demanding
  - Casual
  - Interview in the field
  - Information not known
- Interrogate
  - Involves a suspect
  - Involves custody
  - Requires Miranda rights
  - Specific facts
  - More demanding
  - Highly structured
  - Interrogate at the office
  - Confirm known information
  - Pin-down approach

Remember that the techniques used will depend on the individuals being interviewed and how willing they are to cooperate with you in your high-technology crime investigation. Generally, witnesses and victims tend to cooperate whereas suspects do not.

During your interviews and interrogations, try to obtain answers to your basic questions. For example,

- Who?
  - Who witnessed the crime being committed?
  - Who was the victim of the crime?
  - Who committed the crime?
- How?
  - How was the crime committed?
- Where?
  - Where was the crime committed?
  - Where was the victim?
  - Where were the witnesses?
  - Where was the suspect?
- When?
  - When was the crime committed?

- Why?
  - Why was the crime committed? Revenge? Greed?
- What?
  - What crime was committed?
  - What corporate policy, government regulation, or law was violated?
  - What are the elements of proof that must be considered?

DEALING WITH VICTIMS

If you have identified victims, it is also worth questioning them at the earliest opportunity to gain any information they may have. The questions for the victim will, in most cases, be very similar to those you would ask of the suspect. If you know where the attack was launched from and what the target is, you will have narrowed down the volume of information you have to process to gain the evidence you require. Keep notes of any conversations and remember that you may be required to disclose them, by law, in many jurisdictions. You will ask different questions, depending on the type of crime. For e-mail crimes you might ask:

- What is the name of your ISP?
- What is your e-mail address?
- Is your e-mail account software or Web based?
- Do you have the e-mail address of the person who sent you the e-mail?
- Are the offending messages saved on your computer?
- When and how did you notice the offending e-mail?

For IRC crimes you might ask:

- Who is your ISP?
- What is the name of the chat room?
- Do you know the name of the server?
- Who operates or moderates the chat room?
- What is your nickname?
- Do you know the nickname of the person who has committed the crime?
- Do you keep a log of your chats?
- What has happened?

For newsgroup-related crimes you might ask:

- Who is your ISP?
- What is the name of the newsgroup?
- Is your newsgroup's access software Web based?
- Which newsgroup service do you use and is it based at your ISP?
- What is the name of the posting?
- When did you notice the event?

For Web-related crimes you might ask:

- Who is your ISP?
- What happened?
- What is the address of the Web site?
- When did you visit the Web site?
- What happened?

DEALING WITH WITNESSES

Witnesses are important to solving your high-technology crime investigation successfully. They provide information that may lead to suspects and solving the crime, and they may corroborate information previously obtained about the crime.

Witnesses basically fall into two categories: willing and unwilling.

A willing witness is the most useful; however, one must also question whether the witness' cooperation is done for some ulterior reason, such as identifying a potential suspect to "get even" as a result of some conflict between the witness-identified suspect and the cooperative witness (i.e., "frame the suspect").

An unwilling witness is one who may not want to get involved, may be a friend or relative of the suspect, may fear retribution, or some other unknown reason. In such cases, you should determine the reason for their lack of cooperation. In addition, you may have to resort to using interrogation techniques (the kind you would use on an uncooperative, aka lying, suspect) instead of interview techniques. The questions you ask depend on the matter being investigated, but essentially you want information from the witness that will answer who, how, where, when, why, and what questions.

PERSONAL DESCRIPTIONS

Whether you are talking to a victim or witness about a suspect, personal descriptions of the suspect are important. Unfortunately, many witnesses or victims often see the same event in different ways, and thus there may be some conflict in their various observations. Because of the usually anonymous nature of a high-technology crime, the suspect's personal description may be impossible to state until that person is actually identified. When a personal description can be obtained from a victim and/or witness, lead the victim or witness through some basic descriptions that will help describe the suspect (see Appendix 8-1).

DEALING WITH SUSPECTS

When dealing with a suspect, always remember that if there is any indication from the suspect that he or she was not working alone, it may be necessary to take immediate action to broaden the scope of the investigation. You may want to try and gain an impression of whether your suspect is the main instigator or whether one of the others involved was the driving force.

If the suspect is providing information, it may be opportune to gain any information that you can about what the target was, what the intended attack route was, and the methods that were to be used. However, caution should be exercised, because this level of questioning should normally be saved for a formal interview and should, unless you can justify it, be the subject of a formal (in the United Kingdom) taped interview. If you do too much at the scene then, for example, in the United Kingdom, Section 78 of the PACE Act comes into play (Why were the suspects not afforded the chance to have legal advice?) and may make any information gained inadmissible. Similarly, in the US, the US Constitution and Bill of Rights apply.

The range of questions you might want to ask the suspect will depend on the type of crime suspected. There are some questions that you will want to try and get answered no matter what the manner of the crime, and then there are other questions specific to the type of crime. The questions listed here are based on the *UK Avon & Somerset Police Force Interview Guide*[2] compiled by the Force's high-technology unit. (We appreciate their help and assistance and their permission to incorporate portions of the guide in this chapter.)

- Basic questions
  - What type of computer is it?
  - What is the make?
  - What model is it?
  - What is the processor type?
  - What is the size of the memory?
  - How many hard disks are there and what is their size?
  - Did you buy it new?
  - How old is it?
  - What is the operating system?
  - What types of software are on the system and who installed it?
  - Where did you get it?
  - Who has access to the computer and how often?
  - How do they access it (accounts/passwords)?
  - What equipment is connected to the computer?
  - Are there any other computers connected to the suspected system?
  - Who set up the peripherals and any network connections?
- Data storage
  - Where do you store information on your computer?
  - Do you have any external storage such as zip drives, jazz drives, external hard disk, floppy disks, CDs, USB drives, or storage with the ISP?

- Do you use any specific software to copy files to these external storage drives?
- Who set up these storage devices?
- What do you store on them and how often do you use them?

- Encryption
  - Do you use any form of encryption?
  - If yes, what type of encryption do you use?
  - Why do you use it?
  - What is the password or pass phrase for it?
  - Where are the passwords and pass phrases stored?

- Evidence elimination software
  - Do you use any software to clear traces of your activity from the system?
  - What type of software do you use?
  - How do you use it?
  - How often do you use it?
  - Why do you use it?

- Internet use
  - Which service provider do you use for access to the Internet?
  - What do you use the Internet for?
  - How often do you use it?
  - How do you connect to the Internet (modem, broadband, TV access, satellite, mobile)?
  - Do you have access at work/home (depending on the location of the suspect system)?
  - Do you have free access or do you pay for it?
  - What user names and passwords do you use to connect to the Internet?
  - Do you use any antivirus software?
  - How often do you update it?
  - Is it always active?
  - Have you ever had a virus on the system?
  - Do you use any firewall software?
  - Is it always active?
  - Do you defragment your hard disks?

- Web browsing
  - What software do you use to browse the Internet?
  - Which sites do you regularly visit?
  - How did you get to know about the sites that you regularly use?
  - What search engines do you use?
  - What links have you saved in your "favorites" location?
  - How are they organized?
  - Have you created any Web pages?
  - Where are they hosted?
  - What are their URLs?
  - Are they paid or free?

- o What is the content of the Web page?
- o How long has it been running?
- o What software did you use to create it?
- o What are the user names and passwords?
- File sharing
  - o What software do you use for file sharing?
  - o What are the user names and passwords?
  - o How often do you download files?
  - o What types of files do you download?
  - o How often do you upload files?
  - o What types of files do you upload?
  - o Where do you get them?
- E-Mail crimes
  - ° What is the name of your Internet Service Provider (ISP)?
  - ° What is your e-mail address?
  - ° What is the password for your account?
  - ° Is your e-mail account software Web based?
- IRC crimes
  - ° What software do you use?
  - ° Who is your service provider?
  - ° What is the name of the chat room?
  - ° Do you know the name of the server?
  - ° Who operates or moderates the chat room?
  - ° What is your nick name and password?
  - ° Do you get involved in private chats?
  - ° How do you arrange them?
- Newsgroup-related crimes
  - ° What software do you use?
  - ° Who is your service provider?
  - ° What are the names of the newsgroups that you access?
  - ° Is your newsgroup access software or Web based?
  - ° What do you use the newsgroups for?
  - ° What user names and passwords do you use?
- Web-related crimes
  - ° Who is your ISP?
  - ° Which Web sites have you attacked? (It is often the case that the focus of the investigation to be on the current attack, but it may be very interesting and helpful to discover if this was a specifically targeted attack or part of a wider campaign.)

CASE STUDY: COMPELLING SUSPECTS TO PROVIDE ACCESS INFORMATION

The following information (from Don Ingraham, Assistant District Attorney, Alameda County, California, USA, now retired) provided the authors supporting information that can be used to obtain a court order to compel a suspect to provide system access information.[*]

Problem: May a suspect, whose computer is in the possession of law enforcement to be searched, be lawfully ordered to divulge the password?

Caveat: This opinion does not address the risk that a suspect might use the opportunity to command destruction of the potential evidence, which actually occurred in a case entitled the Equity Funding Case.

Conclusion: Yes, if the fact of his divulgence is immunized and not used as evidence of his authority and control of the computer. A password authorizes the computer to access and recover the specified files. It does not create the data; it simply permits access to data already in existence. Such data were not created under compulsion, but speak for themselves, just like writing exemplars, blood samples, or fingerprints.

Analysis: There are at least three decisions of the United States Supreme Court and a recent decision of an appellate division in California that suggest such an order can be made and enforced through a court's contempt authority:

In *Fisher v US (1976), 425 US 391, 48 LED2 39,* the suspect gave his attorney invoices and an IRS summons for his records, and the attorney entrusted them to the accountant on whom the summons was served. Such disclosure does not involve Fifth Amendment self-incrimination, because "…a party is privileged from producing evidence but not from its production." There is no violation of the attorney–client privilege, because these records could have been seized from the suspect if he still had them; there is no violation of the fourth amendment if the summons is so narrowly drawn as to be limited to materials of significant relevance to the investigation.

US v Doe (1983), 465 US 605, 79 LED2d 552, reversed a lower court's suppression of the business records of the suspect in a government contracting fraud investigation, including the records of his bank accounts in the Grand Caymans. The records sought were created voluntarily. The US Supreme Court affirmed the lower court's conclusion that the act of enabling their production would permit the inference that the suspect could be identified with them, and therefore the suspect would be entitled to immunity regarding their acquisition. In other words, we could not use his compliance with the order as proof of complicity in the crime the records will be used to prove.

Footnote 13 to this opinion (*79 LED2d 561*) clarifies this restriction: "by producing the documents, respondent would relieve the Government of the need for authentication…[which would] establish a valid claim of the privilege against self-incrimination. This is not to say that the government was foreclosed from rebutting the respondent's claim by producing evidence that possession, existence, and authentication were a "foregone conclusion." Clearly, independent proof on those critical points would have to be established by other evidence.

Doe v US (1988), 487 US 201, 101 LED2d 184 takes it a bit further. Doe appeared before a federal grand jury looking into oil cargo manipula-

---

[*]This unique approach may or may not be upheld in court, depending of course on the court, judge, precedence, etc.

tion and other offenses. He produced his records of some accounts in the Caymans and swore he had no others but refused to sign an authorization for those banks to reveal any other accounts he had on the basis of the Fifth Amendment. He was properly ordered to do so, again with the restriction that the fact of his compelled act could not be used to establish the accuracy of those records or as an admission of his authority over those accounts.

The California case (Los Angeles), *People v Sanchez (1994), 24 CA4 1012,* which relied on the US Supreme Court decisions, was a murder case. Sanchez killed his fiancee. His written plans for her murder were found in his room by his sisters after his arrest. They placed them in an envelope and turned them over to the trial court. The judge properly turned the plans over to the prosecution because they were voluntarily written and their disclosure involved no action by the defendant.

Under the reasoning of those decisions, the analogous, compelled divulgence of a computer password simply accomplishes the recovery of preexisting information, and therefore does not compel self-incrimination. However, the fact that the suspect provided the government access cannot be used as proof of his control or of its authenticity.

SUMMARY

This chapter included pointers regarding the type of information that could potentially be gained from the appropriate questioning of a suspect at the earliest opportunity. The rights of the suspect must be acknowledged and respected at all times, or the information that you gain and any subsequent discovery may not be admissible. The potential gains can be significant. Do not put too much reliance on the information that is obtained from the suspect because, if he or she is astute, he or she may take the opportunity to misdirect and obstruct the investigation, providing the investigator with misleading information.

The chapter has also looked at the early questioning of the victim and others who were present at the scene to gain information that may aid the conduct of the subsequent investigation. The information acquired may provide valuable leads. If questioning is left to a later date, the information may have been forgotten.

APPENDIX 8-1

INVESTIGATIVE DESCRIPTIVE AID TO ASSIST IN PERSONAL DESCRIPTIONS

Some basic traits that a high-technology crime investigator can use to assist witnesses and victims describe a suspect are as follows[3]:

Forehead

- Slope
  - Receding
  - Medium
  - Vertical
  - Prominent
  - Bulging
- Height
- Width
- Peculiarities

Nose

- Root
  - Flat
  - Small
  - Medium
  - Large
- Line
  - Concave
  - Straight
  - Convex or hooked
  - Roman
  - Aquiline
- Base
  - Turned up
  - Horizontal
  - Downward
- Length (in proportion to entire face)
  - Forehead
  - Nose
  - Mouth and chin
- Projection
  - Long
  - Medium
  - Short
- Width of head
  - Narrow
  - Medium
  - Wide
- Peculiarities

Ears

- Lobe

- o Descending
- o Square
- o Medium
- o Gulfed
- Antitragus
  - o Horizontal
  - o Oblique
  - o Size
  - o Nil
  - o Small
  - o Large
- Shape
  - o Round
  - o Triangular
  - o Rectangular
  - o Low set
  - o Normal
  - o Close to head
  - o Protruding from head

Lips

- Length
  - o Long
  - o Medium
  - o Short
- Thickness
  - o Thin
  - o Medium
  - o Thick
- Position
  - o Normal
  - o Protruding lower
  - o Protruding upper

Mouth

- Size
  - o Small
  - o Medium
  - o Large

Chin

- Slope

      ° Receding
      ○ Normal
      ○ Jutting or protruding
- Size
  - Small or pointed
  - Large or square
- Length
  - Small, short
  - Long, pointed
- Peculiarities
  - Dimpled or cleft chin
  - Double chin

Face and Head

- Shape of face
  - Round
  - Square
  - Oval
  - Broad
  - Long
- Shape of head
  - Round
  - Egg shaped
  - Flat in back
  - Flat on top
  - High on crown
  - Bulging in back

Other physical features

- Weight
- Color eyes
- Color hair
- Type of hair
- Peculiarities

REFERENCES

1. Rabon, D. (1992). *Interviewing and Interrogation*. Durham, NC: Carolina Academic Press.
2. UK Avon & Somerset Police Force High-Technology Unit. *UK Avon & Somerset Police Force Interview Guide.*
3. Federal Bureau of Investigation. *Personal Descriptions, Portrait Parle or Speaking Likeness: FBI Visual Instruction.*

9

An Introduction to Computer Forensics

This chapter provides a discussion of computer forensics, defines and discusses what is meant by the term *computer forensics,* and describes its role in high-technology crime investigations.*

INTRODUCTION

As with most things in computer science, there are a range of views and interpretations of words and terms, and so it is with the term *computer forensics.* What is meant by that term may depend on who you are talking to. The following explanation is one of the more comprehensive that exists. The definition incorporates all aspects of the investigation and includes the collection of evidence, its preservation, examination, analysis, and presentation, and is derived from the Information Security and Forensics Society (ISFS).[1]

> Computer forensics is the science of obtaining, preserving, and documenting evidence from digital electronic storage devices, such as computers, PDAs, digital cameras, cell phones, and various memory storage devices. All must be done in a manner designed to preserve the probative value of the evidence and to ensure its admissibility in legal proceedings.

THE STAGES THAT MAKE UP THE FORENSIC PROCESS

As indicated in the previous definition, the computer forensic process can be broken down into a number of distinct stages. These are described in more detail here:

- *Evidence collection*—The collection of any digital information that may be used as evidence must be carried out by trained staff and must follow

---

*Due to the importance of computer forensics in high-technology crime investigations, it is handled here to support and compliment other related chapters in this book. Any redundance will hopefully help strengthen your knowledge of this important topic.

recognized and accepted procedures so that its value as evidence is preserved for use in any legal or disciplinary proceedings. (Refer to Chapter 7 for a discussion of equipment and data that may be relevant.)

- *Preservation of evidence*—This factor is fundamental in all computer forensics activities. If potential evidence is not preserved in a forensically sound manner, then it may have little or no value in any criminal or civil proceedings, although it may still be used as intelligence to inform the investigation. The preservation of evidence must be conducted by staff members who are trained and skilled in the required techniques and use of the appropriate tools to preserve the evidence in an unaltered condition. Procedures that have been developed and tested and are known to be accepted by the courts should be followed whenever possible. The preservation of evidence must be considered at all stages of the investigation.

- *Examination of evidence*—The examination of evidence must be conducted by staff members who are trained and experienced, and who use tools that have been tested or accepted by the courts as providing information in a true form. Any data produced for use as evidence must be capable of being reproduced by another investigator. The examination of the devices for evidence must be conducted in an in-depth and comprehensive manner. The examination of the evidence should, whenever possible, be carried out on an image of the original material rather than the original material itself, although it is accepted that, in exceptional circumstances, this may not be possible.

- *Analysis of evidence*—The analysis of evidence is the forensic phase during which the information that has been preserved and examined is interpreted to draw conclusions and to determine the truth of what has occurred in the period leading up to and during an incident. This will normally take place in the computer forensic laboratory and consideration should be given to ensuring that any results are documented and can be recreated by another investigator.

- *Presentation of findings*—The presentation of the findings of the analyzed data is as important as any other phase of the forensic process. If the findings are not presented in a coherent, comprehensive, and believable form, then the effort that has been taken during the preceding phases will have been wasted.

Evidence collection → Preservation of evidence → Examination of evidence → Analysis of evidence → Presentation of findings

---

Always remember that evidence that is being presented must be:

- *Admissible*—It must conform to the relevant legal rules within the jurisdiction.

- *Authentic*—The evidence that is presented must be traceable back to the incident.
- *Complete*—The evidence must cover all aspects of the incident, not just those that address one perspective.
- *Reliable*—It must be provable that all aspects relating to the evidence have followed appropriate and relevant guidelines and procedures, and that the evidence being presented is authentic.
- *Believable*—The people to whom the evidence is being presented must find the evidence both understandable and believable.

If the evidence does not have all of these characteristics, it will fail to achieve its purpose.

WHO WILL DIRECT THE COMPUTER FORENSICS EFFORTS?

At the very earliest point possible, the high-technology crime investigative manager or investigator must decide who will be responsible for directing and conducting the high-technology crime computer forensics effort. This will depend on what is known at the time and, in part, what resources are available. Obviously, if a high-technology crime investigator is not on staff, one may have to rely on the corporation's investigator supported by applicable members of the IT staff.

High-technology crime investigations and computer forensics should not be conducted by noninvestigative professionals. If specialists are required, they should be under the direct supervision of the high-technology crime investigator. Neither IT nor audit personnel have sufficient expertise in interview and interrogation techniques, evidence collection and preservation, and the like, to perform the investigation correctly or, acting alone, conduct computer forensics.

Always remember that when an incident is detected, you, as the high-technology crime investigator, will be in a reactive mode.

When an incident occurs, you will be under pressure to do something (anything) and "solve" the problem (or make it go away). You will probably not have all the facts and will probably have little idea of the scope of the problem. The decisions that you and executive management make at this point are critical. The indications may be that you are dealing with a simple case of an insider who has been abusing his or her privileges and has been accessing material he or she should not have (snooping).

A decision to allow the technical staff to have a "quick look" and carry out an initial inquiry may result in potential evidence being contaminated before a real investigation can get started. Even if it is eventually determined that the incident was an internal user abusing user privileges, there may issues that place prosecution or other disciplinary action at risk. Also, what if this was only the tip of the iceberg, and the incident was actually far more serious? What if the situation was serious enough to end up in an industrial tribunal or in a criminal court? A mistake in the way that the investigation is run and the information is dealt with at this point will probably result in any evidence being inadmissible.

> If your preparation and planning have been done properly, you will have procedures in place and your investigative staff will know what they have to do. They will also have been trained to be able to carry out the initial investigation, with the preservation of evidence in mind, and will have the tools to carry it out.

At some point in an investigation, you may have to make a decision on whether you should be using internal resources or whether you need to involve external resources (experts in specific areas) or law enforcement resources for your computer forensics. This will not normally be an easy decision, because the perception is that once you have involved law enforcement, you have lost control of the situation. Organizations normally want to keep their problems "in house" and deal with them without publicity or outside organizations being involved. After all, the news that a company has been "hacked" or that there has been an insider perpetrating a fraud is not likely do anything to enhance its image or the confidence of the shareholders or customers. A good example of this is the case in which CITIBANK was hacked by the Russian hacker, Vladimir Levin.[2,3] In this case, when the information about the hack became public, the share price was, certainly in the short term, severely affected.

Unfortunately, it may not be possible or sensible to take the option of keeping the matter "in house." What if the attack on your organization were only a small part of a much wider attack on the infrastructure, and each individual element of that infrastructure were keeping the information to himself? What if your staff members do not have the skills or the authority to carry out an effective computer forensics effort? As the corporate high-technology crime investigator, you will be responsible for making a recommendation to executive management regarding whether to call in local law enforcement for computer forensics and help with your investigation. You may also hire an outsource investigative firm with experience in conducting computer forensics and high-technology crime investigations.

GUIDELINES

There are a number of sets of guidelines that are very well thought out that detail the way in which a computer forensic investigation should be conducted and that provide advice on things to be considered when carrying out an investigation. These guidelines are freely available, but perhaps not well-known, because, unless you know a little about computer forensics and high-tech crime, you are unlikely to be aware of them or know the organizations that produce them. Excellent examples can be found on the Web site of the UK National High-Technology Crime Unit (NHTCU; www.nhtcu.org), which is the Association of Chief Police Officers (ACPO) good practice guide for computer-based electronic evidence, and on the US Department of Justice, Computer Crime and Intellectual Property Section Web site (www.cybercrime.gov/s&smanual2002. htm). The first is a document that has been produced for use by UK law enforcement officers, has been well thought out, and is widely accepted. The second is for use by US law enforcement officers. Another comprehensive set of guidelines for investigations is the Hong Kong *Information Security and Forensic Society (ISFS) Computer Forensics, Part 2: Best Practice* document.[4] Although these documents have been produced, certainly in the first case, for use by law enforcement officers, they are available to all investigators and provide the best baseline from which internal procedures can be developed for all investigations.

As an example, the ACPO good practice guide outlines the following guidance for personnel attending the high-technology crime scene or making initial contact with the victim. This is a good baseline for commercial and other types of investigation.[*]

- *The principles of computer-based evidence*—The principles of computer-based electronic evidence that must be borne in mind.
- *An overview of computer-based electronic investigations*—The different roles that a computer may play in a crime, in its commission, as a repository for evidence, or as a target
- *Attending crime scenes*—Guidance on the measures that need to be taken to deal with a wide range of different types of equipment.
- *Investigating personnel*—Guidance on the preparation and planning that must take place prior to and during an investigation, and advice on the thought that should be given to the types of equipment that should be taken along to the scene of the crime, which personnel should be selected to carry out the investigation, what records to keep, and considerations for interviewing suspects as well as the subsequent storage of material
- *Evidence recovery*—Guidance for the staff who are involved in the recovery of computer-based evidence
- *Welfare and health and safety considerations*—The issues that should be taken into consideration for the welfare of staff members who are involved in the investigation of electronic evidence
- *Control of child pornographic images*—Comprehensive guidance on the special steps that must be taken throughout an investigation that involves images of child pornography

---

[*]Summarized from www.acpo.police.uk/asp/policies/data/gpg_computer_based_evidence_v3.pdf

- *External consulting witnesses*—Guidance for the selection and use of people who possess specific skills that cannot be found within the organization
- *Disclosure*—Guidance on the appropriate measures for the disclosure of computer-based evidence and those that take into account the issue of the volume of evidence that may be involved
- *Handling instructions, mobile phones*—Guidance on the specific measures that should be taken when mobile phones are being handled
- *Initial contact with the suspect, suggested questions*—Guidance on the type of question that can be asked of a suspect during the initial contact.

Although the guidance provided in these documents is not necessarily provided in great detail, it does give the high-technology crime investigator a framework that covers all the essential aspects of a high-tech crime scene, including computer forensics. The book is not intended to be a comprehensive instruction book that covers all aspects of high-tech crime, but is more of an *aide memoire* to prompt the reader to consider all the issues that are covered. This is a very sensible approach given the rapid changes in technology that occur.

> It is easy, when thinking of computer forensics, to fall into the trap of thinking in terms of the seizure and analysis of a single computer and, as a result of this, not to consider the whole picture and develop a strategy for an investigation.

It is increasingly common these days to have considerably more complex scenarios to deal with that involve large networks and a number of miscreants who have been working together in the commission of the crime.

STRATEGY FOR AN INVESTIGATION

As you will have gathered from the previous examples, it is important to develop a strategy for every investigation that will allow it, if necessary, to be escalated and to bring in external experts or other agencies. The strategy does not need to be detailed, but should at least consider the options and ensure that, if needed, the points of contact and contact details for other agencies have been identified. Do not forget that for the investigation to be successful, it may involve additional resources other than those from your own organization. After an investigation is underway is not the best time to discover that you do not know who the law enforcement points of contact are. It is far better to have developed a relationship with them and for them to have some knowledge of your organization prior to being called in.

PROCEDURE FOR A FORENSIC INVESTIGATION

The procedures that are defined and followed for the forensic investigation of a high-technology crime will ensure that the investigators operate in a professional, competent, and coherent manner. They process information in a manner that has been tested and accepted in the courts. The aspects that are detailed here describe the issues for which procedures should be developed:

- *Physical examination of the scene*—The physical examination of the scene of the incident, including not only the equipment that is potentially involved in the incident, but also the environment
- *Collection of relevant items*—To provide a framework to ensure that all relevant items are taken into consideration and that nothing is overlooked; to provide the investigator with a logical set of guidelines for dealing with incidents, no matter what the scale
- *Photographs*—To provide guidance on the photographs that are required, to ensure that a consistent approach is taken to all investigations
- *Disassembly*—To ensure that the disassembly of equipment is undertaken in a safe and consistent manner and that it meets any regulatory requirements for the preservation of the evidence and continuity of evidence
- *Secure storage*—To provide the guidelines to ensure that any equipment is stored in an appropriate manner to ensure that it is both safe and complies with the appropriate regulations
- *Tools for the job*—To ensure that any tools that are used are both appropriately licensed and are suitable for the purpose in that they have been tested or accepted in the courts
- *Virus checks*—To ensure that appropriate antivirus measures are in place and followed to ensure that the evidence does not become contaminated and that the actions taken by the investigators are not affected by a virus
- *Imaging*—To ensure that the copy of the system that is made is conducted using predetermined procedures and tools and is done to a standard that is acceptable to the courts
- *Search and recovery of evidence*—To ensure that guidelines are in place for the search for and recovery of evidence and to outline for investigators what actions they can take and when and under

what circumstances they can be taken; to provide a crib sheet for the investigator to ensure that all potential evidence is considered and that any relevant material is recovered

- *Analysis of evidence*—To ensure the analysis of the evidence is conducted using the correct practices and that any evidence discovered will be correctly documented so that any other person who examines the evidence will be able to recreate the findings
- *Safe storage*—The safe and secure storage of equipment and data in the care of the investigation team to ensure that any material handled by the investigation team will have the chain of evidence preserved and will not become contaminated. (It is only when an organization has procedures that it can follow and that can be demonstrated that the investigator can be confident that the process is suitable and adequate.)
- *Presentation of evidence*—A vehicle for the capture of experience that has been gained by current staff and others who have input to the production of the company and investigative policy. The policy will include guidance and templates for the production of reports and for the preparation of material for presentation at a tribunal or in the courtroom. It would be a massive waste of effort to carry out an exhaustive investigation but fail to present the findings of the investigation in a form that is acceptable and understandable.
- *Peer review*—To define under what circumstances a peer review should take place and who should carry out the review

Other issues that you will need to keep in mind include:

- *Verification, or check, check, and check again*—At each stage in the process, you will need to verify that the actions that have been taken are appropriate and that the correct level of detail has been recorded.
- *Evidence handling*—After the evidence has been collected, you need to ensure that it is handled appropriately at all times. This may seem obvious, but when you are working in a busy laboratory, with several cases potentially being processed at the same time, care will have to be taken to ensure that they are kept separate and that the continuity of handling is maintained.
- *Know your limits*—There is always a temptation to carry on with an investigation and to try to achieve what is required. Given the requirement to carry out a thorough investigation and the desire to do your best, there will always be the temptation to go the extra step and try to do something that you do not have the skill or experience to do to the proper level of scientific integrity. Always remember that whatever you do, you may have to stand up in a court of law and justify what you have done, and if you do not have the skill

and experience to back up the actions that you have taken, you may devalue any evidence that you have gained by your actions. In its simplest form we are back to the equivalent of the untrained investigator turning on the computer to "see if there is anything on it." The level may be very different, but the outcome could be the same.

- *Sources of advice*—Always keep up to date with sources of advice that are available to you so that, when you need assistance and expert guidance, you will have the contacts available and the relationships established. The very act of keeping up to date with sources of advice will mean that the staff are keeping up to date with significant developments.

- *Note taking and recording*—You can never take too many notes. There may be significant delays between the investigation of an incident and its coming to court or a tribunal. If you have made full notes of every step of the process, it will remove any need to rely on memory and will improve the credibility of the evidence if you can demonstrate the care and completeness of the processes that have been applied to all aspects of the collection, handling, and analysis of the evidence.

- *Case law*—Make sure that your staff keep up to date with relevant case law. It is pointless to go through the whole evidence collection and analysis process to discover, when it has been completed, that it does not meet the current requirements that have come about as the result of recent case law and will not stand up in court. Also remember that technologies and forensic tools are continuing to develop and that case law can also work to your advantage as more cases are tried and issues that affect you are tested in the courts. Always coordinate with your company's legal staff!

- *Communication*—You will need to keep on top of the communication issues throughout the whole of the investigation. You will need to make sure that you have provided adequate communications to ensure that all phases and aspects—from the initial reporting of the incident, through the briefing of the investigation team, team communications while they are deployed to collect the evidence, the recovery of any material, its handoff to the laboratory, to the contact with the legal team and the PR team—are addressed.

PURPOSE OF THE INVESTIGATION

When the incident has been detected and the decision is taken to start an investigation, the purpose that the investigation will serve must also be considered. It may well be that as the investigation progresses and more facts are known, the purpose will change, but the person or team that is tasked to carry out the investigation must have clear direction. Are they investigating an incident to find out what has happened, are they looking for what has gone wrong, or are they trying to identify the culprit? After all, if you do not have a clear idea of what you are trying to achieve, how will you know when you have got there?

> As the investigation progresses, the purpose may change as the investigation develops. It may be that when you have found out what has happened, you have enough information to try to identify who the culprit is, or when you have found out what happened, you turn the investigation to find out why the incident occurred.

Always try to keep an open mind as you investigate, because an investigator who is trying to prove what he thinks has happened will potentially make mistakes and ignore facts that do not support theories. This is not to say that you should not use your experience and knowledge to help you in your investigation.

BUSINESS DECISIONS

There are a range of factors that will influence the type and extent of an investigation. They vary from the purpose and importance of the high-technology system that is under attack, to the type of attack and external environmental factors, such as attacks on other systems that have taken place in the past or are currently taking place. As a result there may be a number of pressures that will be applied to direct the investigation. An example of this might be that the system under attack is critical to the well-being of the organization, but it is only the latest in a series of attacks in the same business sector.

From a company point of view, the restoration of service is the main driver, because downtime normally means lost income. However, a law enforcement point of view might be that a more thorough investigation and capture and preservation of evidence will help to detect the perpetrator and prevent future crimes. Both are valid ambitions, but which is correct? The answer is that they are both correct and that the solution (in most countries) may well be a compromise.

At the end of the day it is not normally in the interests of the law enforcement community to make a company bankrupt. This would tend to return us to the time 10 years ago when people would not discuss potential high-technology crimes with law enforcement. One interesting development has taken place in the UK, where the NHTCU has developed and implemented a "confidentiality charter" (www.nhtcu.org/nqcontent. cfm?a_id=12445&tt=nhtcu) that can be used in a relationship with the commercial sector. This allows a company to engage in a dialogue with the NHTCU, to inform them when attacks have happened, and even to solicit their support in an investigation, but it does not commit the organization to the case being taken to court if the organization does not agree to do so. By introducing the charter, the business sector has gained far more confidence that that they will not lose control of an investigation.

The security staff will want to get to the bottom of the problem and may be reluctant to turn the systems off in the first place, because this can alert an attacker to the fact that he has been detected and can make it more difficult to observe the miscreant's actions or trace him or her. After the system has been turned off, the security staff will want to keep it switched off for as long as it takes to preserve the evidence, determine what has happened and how it happened, and then make sure that it cannot happen again. It is unlikely that business managers, the board, or shareholders will agree with this approach, because the company is losing business all the time the system is switched off. But who makes the decision when to turn it back on?

Who takes the risk that the culprit may not be caught and, as a result, is free to come back and cause the same problem again? The answer, as stated elsewhere, is that it will be a business decision, and it should be made by the managers of the organization. When all is said and done, and no matter how frustrating it may be to the security staff or the investigators, everything they do is to support and maintain the organization's ability to carry out its business. If the business decision is to take a course of action that is less than ideal for the investigation, then the investigators will have to learn to live with it.

THE FULL INVESTIGATION

Who Will Carry Out the Full Investigation?

Your policies should outline who should be called to investigate a range of the types of incidents that have been anticipated; however, each case will have to be judged on the information that is available at the time and the members of staff who are available at the time. The procedures that determine who will make the decision to investigate are detailed elsewhere in this book, but after the decision has been made, everyone must respond to support the person or group that has been selected to carry out the investigation.

What Resources Will Be Available?

This will depend on the severity of the incident and a range of other circumstances, as well as the priority that has been allocated to the case. The level of resources that will be required should have been identified during the initial phase of the investigation.

When the full investigation starts, it may end up that it will follow one of several routes. It may turn out to be a security investigation into a breach of the organization's security. This type of outcome will normally occur when a virus infects the system, a Web site is defaced, an unexplained system failure occurs, a loss or compromise of information is detected, or when, at the time of the investigation, there is no obvious culprit, either internal or external. The conventional security investigation will try to determine the cause of the breach in security, to find out what has happened, how it happened, whether there is anyone responsible, and what the impact has been.

An investigation that results in an industrial tribunal will take place when there has been some type of employee malfeasance that does not constitute a criminal offense or that the company chooses to deal with internally rather than through the criminal justice system. This may seem an odd statement, but if the company is the victim of the activities of an employee, it may choose not to press criminal charges against the member of the staff and deal with it internally, rather than risk any potential bad publicity that may result from a court case. In some cases, such as pedophile investigations, the company will have no choice but to involve law enforcement, because a failure to report the crime makes the people who have been involved in the investigation guilty of criminal offenses.

An investigation that results in a criminal prosecution normally occurs when the attack is perpetrated by someone outside the organization or when the attack is so serious that the organization passes the investigation over to law enforcement.

For Whom Is the Investigation Being Conducted?

One of the factors that must be considered is whether there is a time limit for the investigation. Any investigator who has carried out an investigation into a high-tech crime will be happy to tell you that time is one of the major enemies. At what point do you stop? A law enforcement-led investigation will have a clear view of the level of effort that is required. They will investigate an incident until they have sufficient evidence to obtain a conviction against the perpetrator.

This is a realistic and pragmatic approach, but it does not deal with any possible intelligence that may be on the disk that was not a part of the evidence that is being used for the prosecution. Given the limit to the resources that will be available, all organizations will have to make similar decisions with regard to any investigation. On the plus side, should the investigator ever have any slack time, the evidence can be revisited to gain more intelligence. Having carried out the investigation and determined what has happened and identified the likely miscreants, the next phase of activity is the chase.

THE CHASE

For the investigator, this is normally the most exciting part of the investigation. After the actions that occurred have been analyzed and a suspect has been identified, the chase begins. Whether the suspect who has been identified is internal to the organization or external, the next phase of the investigation can begin. What must be taken into consideration is, what is your remit for conducting the chase? Will the chase only involve investigations in one country or are there other jurisdictions that must be considered? Is there a requirement for additional assistance and where can this be obtained? Is this case likely to be significant enough to gain access to these (scarce) resources?

The questions that must be asked are how much of your available resources are you going to expend on the chase and what is the benefit? These may seem trite questions, but you need to bear them in mind. It is very easy to get tunnel vision when the chase starts, and to carry on regardless, even when the investment in effort can never be balanced against any possible outcome. This may sound like a very commercial consideration, but it equally applies to law enforcement and, to a lesser degree, to other government agencies. Finite resources must be used to the best effect and this may involve making decisions on the cases that can be won or are important enough to pursue no matter what.

RESTORATION

Within an organization, the restoration of the system will almost certainly commence as soon as the evidence has been preserved. After the decision has been made that it should be brought back into service (remember that this will normally be a business decision, rather than an investigative one), the system should be returned to an operational state. There will always be a risk in doing this, because it will normally be brought back into service before the evidence that has been collected has been analyzed and the full facts of the incident are known. This means that the system may be brought back into service with the vulnerabilities or procedural shortcomings that allowed the incident to occur in the first place.

When the incident has been dealt with and the investigation is in hand, then the final action that needs to be taken is the "lessons learned" process. At the end of the day, something that should not have occurred took place, and there should be a review of the events that took place and where the systems that were in place failed or were inadequate to deal with the situation. It may be that the processes that are in place need to be changed or that new procedures or safeguards need to be put into place to ensure that a similar event does not occur in the future.

> If the security system has failed, then it may be necessary to carry out a full review of the polices and procedures that are in place.

THE ANALYSIS

Each of the types of incidents described here will have a set of characteristics that may have left traces of evidence, and although some of the evidence may be common to many or all of the types of incident, some will be specific to just a few or only to one type. This chapter does not deal with all types of crime, but those detailed in the following list are provided to give the investigator an indication of the types of files that may be relevant to different crimes.

Hacking

- Swap file
- Scripts
- Executable programs and source code
- Internet activity logs
- Config files
- IP addresses, logon IDs and passwords
- Manuals and technical documents
- Chat logs, instant messages, e-mail

Denial of Service

- Swap file
- Internet activity logs
- Executables or source code
- IP addresses, logon IDs, passwords

Improper Use of Facilities

- Swap file
- Internet activity logs

- Audit logs
- Configuration files
- User account files
- Executables or source code

Identity Theft

- Swap files
- Internet activity logs
- Images of documents, identity documents, and signatures
- Executables for credit card number generation
- Documents related to multiple identities

Blackmail and Extortion

- Swap files
- User account details
- Internet activity logs
- Text files and letters
- Images
- Chat logs, instant messages, e-mail

Murder and Violent Crimes

- Swap files
- Internet activity logs
- Address books
- Diaries
- E-mail
- Letters
- Memos
- Financial records
- Legal documents
- Medical records
- Telephone records

Smuggling

- Swap files
- Internet activity logs
- Contact details

- Accounts
- Spreadsheets
- Route plans

Child Abuse

- Swap files
- Internet activity logs
- Address books
- Diaries
- Image files (both still and movie)
- Chat logs, instant messages, e-mail
- Text and word files
- Digital camera software
- Games

Theft

- Swap files
- Text and word files
- Images
- Diagrams
- Spreadsheets
- Databases
- E-mail

Drug Crime

- Swap files
- Internet activity logs
- Address books
- Contact details
- Chat logs, instant messages, e-mail
- Accounts
- Images of prescription forms
- Chemical formulas
- Drug-related "cookbooks"

Fraud

- Swap files
- Internet activity logs

- Address books
- Diary, calendar
- Chat logs, instant messages, e-mail
- Audit logs
- Accounts
- Text files
- Letters and templates
- Other people's credit card information/accounts
- Accounting software and accounts on financial systems
- Images of documents, identity documents, signatures
- Currency
- Checks
- Money orders

Online Auction Fraud

- Online auction account data
- Diary, calendar
- Address book
- Other people's credit card information/accounts
- Paypal or similar account details
- Multiple identity information
- Digital camera, images
- Internet activity log
- Telephone records
- E-mail
- Letters and templates
- Testimonials or ratings
- Chat logs

Although this is not a definitive list, it should act as an *aide memoire* and a basis for lists of your own.

EXAMINATION OF PDAS

PDAs require special procedures and care to ensure that any evidence or intelligence is not lost or compromised. Almost all the current PDAs have an encryption system available to the user.

Different procedures need to be followed depending on whether the PDA is switched off or on when it is found. If the PDA is switched off, then the current recommended procedure is that it should *not* be switched on, because the very act of turning the power on will change one or more files on the device and result in the potential evidence being changed. If the PDA receives power via replaceable batteries, those in the PDA should be replaced with a fresh set. Any leads and the cradle should be seized, and the PDA should be installed in the cradle until it can be investigated.

If the PDA is switched on, then the current recommended procedure is that it should not be switched off, but the screen should be photographed to capture any information that is visible. The cradle and any related leads should be seized, and the PDA fitted into the cradle until it can be examined. To prevent the PDA from going into sleep mode or activating the screen saver, the screen should be tapped at regular intervals. If the skills required to examine the device properly are not available within the investigation team, a suitable expert should be brought in to carry out the examination.

EXAMINATION OF MOBILE PHONES

Although PDAs and mobile phones may appear different, they are now, in many cases, totally identical in their capabilities, functionality, and the problems that affect them. The examination of mobile phones should consider that any interaction with the handset may result in contamination of potential evidence. As with PDAs, the mobile phone will probably hold a SIMM. Consideration should be given by the investigator regarding whether the phone should be turned off when it is seized, to prevent changes to the information available being made by incoming voice, SMS, or e-mail messages. If the decision is made to keep the phone turned on, the investigator should ensure that the power supply is available to maintain the unit in a charged state.

EXAMINATION OF FLASH MEMORY MEDIA

Increasingly these days, there is an ever-expanding range of what are commonly referred to as *flash media* memory devices that will be encountered in an investigation. These devices are the memory modules commonly found in digital cameras, mobile phones, and PDAs, and items such as iPods and MPEG players. The devices are normally accessed by either connecting directly to the computer through a USB or firewire connection, or by placing them in a reader device. There are at least seven major different types of memory media currently available, some of which have write-protect tabs and some of which do not. If there is a write-protect tab available, you should take the same precautions that you would with any other removable media and ensure that the reading device cannot write to this type of media when the tab is in the protected position before connecting the actual device that contains the evidence. If there is no write-protect tab on the memory device, then use an operating system that does not require a disk write to function or that has a recognized "write blocker" in place to prevent writing to the media.

CASE STUDY 1

One example of the complexity that an investigation can encounter is the "Drink or Die" case.[5,6] This case was about the activities of a large group of mostly computer literate individuals, many of whom had privileged access to systems as system administrators, who created a massive software piracy ring. The investigation into this group was started in the year 2000 by the US Customs Service, as part of Operation Buccaneer, and resulted in the arrest of more than 60 people in the United States, Britain, Norway, Sweden, Finland, and Australia.

The scale of the losses to the computer industry as a result of this group's software-cracking activity was massive. In March 2005, two of the individuals involved in the UK were finally convicted at the Old Bailey in London. The number of systems that were involved and the volumes of information that had to be examined to gather the evidence was vast. One early report in January 2002 stated that after the arrest of 30 of the people involved in the case in the United States, more than 200 computer hard drives had been seized.

The level of cooperation and coordination that was required among the various agencies in the United States and the other five countries was immense, and it is a credit to all involved that so many of the participants were successfully prosecuted. One of the issues that increasingly affects investigations was highlighted in this case. Certainly, in the case of the two individuals who were convicted in the UK in 2005 (other members of the group had previously pled guilty), much of the evidence against them had been recovered from systems based in the United States. It is an indication of how far international collaboration has developed that the information could be recovered and stored in one country under one set of laws and be used in another country under entirely different laws.

CASE STUDY 2

Another example of a large and complex investigation that took place in 1998 was given the nickname "solar sunrise." This incident took place at a time when the US Air Force was mobilizing for action in the Gulf, and the initial analysis indicated that the attack was being perpetrated by agents hostile to the coalition forces. After considerable investigation by five different federal agencies and more than 30 FBI agents, the perpetrators were eventually found to be two youths from Cloverdale, California, and a third youth that was based in Israel. During the attack, the youths gained access to computers at MIT, Harvard and Yale universities, and systems on at least 14 different Air Force bases.

SUMMARY

This chapter provides the investigator with an introduction to the whole of the forensic process for investigations that involve computer-based evidence. It covered a range of the issues that must be addressed if an investigation is to be successful, and provided some more detailed guidance in some of the areas.

Always remember that even if you have done everything correctly and the evidence is irrefutable, the defense will attack your processes and procedures in court in an attempt to cast doubt in the eyes of the judge and jury.

REFERENCES

1. Information Security and Forensics Society. (April 2004). *Draft Computer Forensics, Part 1: An Introduction to Computer Forensics.*
2. www.byte.com/art/9511/sec3/art11.htm
3. www.sptimes.ru/secur1/141/guilty.html
4. www.isfs.org.hk/
5. (January 14, 2002). *U.S. Nabs 30 Suspects in Antipiracy "DrinkOrDie" Raids.*
6. www.techdirt.com/articles/20040325/1722257.shtml
7. www.sans.org/resources/idfaq/solar_sunrise.php

10

Establishing and Managing a Computer Forensics Laboratory

This chapter discusses how to get started and set up a computer forensics laboratory, provides advice on the issues that you will need to consider when you decide to establish a computer forensic laboratory, and details how to manage it after it has been set up.

INTRODUCTION

Establishing and managing a state-of-the-art computer forensics laboratory may be a worthy endeavor for a large, high-technology-dependent international corporation, and it is undoubtedly so for government investigative agencies. Government agencies can also pool their resources and allocate them to establish and manage a computer forensics laboratory that can be used by all government agencies.

In the United Kingdom there is now a government home office document called the *ACPO Advice and Good Practice Guide for Managers of Hi-Tech/Computer Crime Units*[1] that provides guidance and advice on the creation of a computer forensics laboratory for a law enforcement organization. After all, if you don't set up the laboratory correctly in the first place or fail to manage it effectively from the time you set it up, anything that is processed in the laboratory may be contaminated or tainted and could be challenged in a criminal or civil proceeding, which relies on evidence that the laboratory subsequently produces.

ESTABLISHING THE LABORATORY

Before you rush out and buy all of the latest and "sexiest" kits and software, be warned: Someone in the management chain who wields the checkbook is probably going to want to see a comprehensive business case for what you are proposing. Therefore, the starting point is researching and making a business case for setting up the laboratory. The justification should include answers to the following questions:

- What is it going to be used for?
- Why is it needed?
- What is the business case for changing from the arrangements that you currently have?
- What is the budget that is required?
- What is the budget that is available?

If you do not have answers to these questions, then you have not done your homework and will probably fail in any bid for the funds and resources to establish your computer forensics laboratory. The creation of a computer forensics laboratory is not a trivial undertaking and without a clear understanding of the rationale for developing it, it will probably fail to achieve its potential.

The budget that is required will be determined by the answers to the first three questions. The budget that you are allocated will depend on the strength of the business case that you put forward and the amount that the organization can afford. If the amount that the organization can afford is not as high as the level of funding that the business case requires, you will either have to modify the level of capability and service you can deliver or you will have to reapply with a more persuasive case.

When you have the answers to these questions, then you can start to prepare for setting up the laboratory. Considerations such as the size and type of laboratory will depend on some of the answers that you obtained to the previous questions, but some of the things that you need to address will be common throughout.

The first action you need to take is to develop the terms of reference for the laboratory. This will be derived from the rationale that was used for the business case and will outline the customer base to be supported by the laboratory, the roles of management and assigned individuals, as well as identifying (in writing) their job descriptions and responsibilities. The terms of reference will also provide guidance on the scope of activities that the laboratory will carry out.

Once you have developed the terms of reference for the laboratory, you will be able to identify the duties and responsibilities of the laboratory manager and the members of staff. Examples of the types of duties that should be considered for the respective roles are detailed by professional organizations such as the American Society of Crime Laboratory Directors (www.ascld.org) and the UK ACPO good practice guide.[1] The laboratory manager will be responsible for such issues as the selection and training of staff, the financing of the laboratory, staff mentoring, counseling and ethical guidance, and the day-to-day running of the laboratory.

COMPUTER FORENSICS LABORATORY MANAGEMENT AND STAFF

The staff members, depending on the size of the laboratory and the purpose for which it was set up, and depending on their individual skills and levels of experience, may have individual roles and responsibilities. Documenting roles and responsibilities from the start will ensure that people are clear regarding their role in the laboratory and the organization.

Some of the roles that you may consider for the laboratory include:

- *A reception officer,* who will be responsible for managing the external interface with the customers and with any external representatives who may require access to specific elements of the evidence (a defense expert or legal representative). It is essential that, whenever possible, there is one person that acts as the focal point for the customer and external contacts. This will help ensure a consistency of approach through this central, recognized point of contact within the laboratory.
- *A triage officer,* who will be responsible for determining whether tasks are accepted into the laboratory and, if they are, for determining the priority in which cases are to be dealt with. It is essential that the person nominated is mature and has the experience to be able to provide strong management and leadership when dealing with potential customers who will have their own priorities.
- *An imaging officer,* who will be responsible for creating the copy (image) of the seized material and ensuring that the image is created in a forensically sound manner. There may be a multiplatform, trained imaging officer or several people, each of whom may specialize in specific platforms and software products. The imaging officer may also be responsible for the coordination and collection of relevant information from external sources and for ensuring that this information has also been collected in an appropriate manner. The imaging officer will need to be well trained and experienced in the imaging of all types of media and will have to have a good knowledge of the relevant legislation and points of contact in other countries where evidence may be located.
- *An analyst,* who will be responsible for the analysis of the available material and for ensuring that any findings of the forensic evidence that are to be presented are in a clear and understandable form and can be reproduced by anyone else who needs to do so. The analyst, with training and experience, should be able to inform management, and possibly customers, of the progress of an investigation. They may find useful information or evidence that relates to the current investigation and potentially to other incidents or crimes that were not known at the time that the material was seized.

> It is vital that you understand that one of the most important issues to be dealt with will be the selection of staff for the forensic laboratory. You must have a clear idea of the purpose and function of the laboratory and the roles that have been identified to be able to select staff with the right mix of skills and experience to meet the needs of the laboratory.

When the staff have been recruited, the combined staff will need a mix of skills that will include:

- Understanding of the relevant legal processes
- IT knowledge
- Communications, both oral and written
- Administration
- Investigation
- Analyses

It is worth investing significant effort in this aspect, because the right mixture of staff who can work effectively as a team will be crucial in the effectiveness and success of the laboratory. Also, the retention of the individual members in whom you will have had to invest a significant level of funding in both education and training is an important issue for management to address.

COMPUTER FORENSICS LABORATORY: PHYSICAL SIZE

Another important issue that you need to address is the physical size of the laboratory. How big a laboratory will you need to meet the terms of reference, and what can you afford? You will need to take into account that the facility should be in a secure location and ideally it should not be on a ground floor (to reduce the likelihood of flood damage and to make break-ins more difficult). You will need to consider where you are going to locate the laboratory. The location of the staff that you are going to utilize in the laboratory may influence this decision, but you must also consider that situating the laboratory in a "remote outpost" of your organization may not be effective or optimal.

Other issues that must be considered and that will affect the size of the laboratory will be how many of the staff are likely to be employed in the laboratory and the types of procedures that are expected to be carried out within it. You will need enough space for each staff member and for work areas to allow for the dismantling of systems and for the storage of equipment and evidence.

Also, potentially, you will need accommodations to allow visitors a work area to view information that has been discovered during the course of the analysis of systems, although this area should be separate from the main area of the laboratory. If the laboratory is likely to deal with cases that may be of a sensitive nature, you may need an area that can be segregated from the main laboratory to minimize the number of people who have access to the information that is revealed as a result of your investigations.

The type of information that may constitute "sensitive information" could include state or corporate classified or sensitive material, or sexually explicit material. One interesting issue that you may have to deal with is that, if there is a likelihood that the information will be particularly sensitive, it may be necessary to introduce a "two-person-present" rule to ensure that the material is handled in accordance with specific rules for the type of information.

The facility will need to have adequate security, and you will need space for a reception area where nonlaboratory staff can be dealt with, without having access to the processing area of the laboratory. Depending on the type of organization that you belong to, some of these issues may already be addressed by the wider organization. Many organizations already have facilities that have some level of security that, if available, can be modified to meet the requirements of the laboratory. There will also need to be space within the facility for office accommodation for staff and for a relaxation and refreshments area. This may be a facility where there is intense pressure and where there is a need to work unsociable hours. One final thought on the size of the laboratory is that, if possible, you should ensure that you have sufficient room to allow for future expansion, and also to address any TEMPEST needs or issues.[2]

AN EXAMPLE OF A COMPUTER FORENSICS LABORATORY

The figures in the following pages depict a reasonably sized, commercially based computer forensics laboratory. The laboratory belongs to the University of Glamorgan in the UK and is used for both research and commercial forensic work.

Figure 10-1 shows a typical forensic analysis workstation. Note the number of power points that are available, the number of network ports, and the lack of clutter. The small device on the top of the CPU is a portable storage media device. At the end of the desk is a cross-cut paper shredder.

Figure 10-2 shows two of the four forensic analysis workstations and gives some idea of the space required. Note the separation of the cubicles with privacy screens to prevent inadvertent visibility of material on the screen of one workstation by anyone using the others. All the monitors face away from the access point to the laboratory for two reasons. The first is to prevent anyone entering the lab from having a view of material on the analysis workstation monitors and the second is that the analyst can see anyone who enters the laboratory.

Figure 10-3 shows the workstation for the disassembly of computers or for any custom building and maintenance of equipment that is required. On the floor is a small fire-proof safe for the short-term storage of material. Long-term storage is at an off-site location. Under the work surface are stored all the spare components that may be required, such as cables, connectors, specific function boards, and so forth.

Figure 10-1 A typical forensic analysis workstation.

Figure 10-2 Two of the four forensic analysis workstations showing space considerations.

Figure 10-3   Workstation for the disassembly of computers.

Figure 10-4 shows a hard disk being removed from a desktop computer. Note the use of an antistatic mat under the chassis of the computer being worked on. The flooring in the laboratory is also made of an antistatic material.

Figure 10-5 shows the dedicated and separate Internet-connected computer for the laboratory. Just visible under the cable duct is the cable to connect the system to the Internet, which is color-coded red. This system is used to check information that is found on systems under investigation and to gain access to information that is relevant and useful to any investigation. All activity on this system is recorded and regularly audited. The system uses a fixed IP address that has been made known to the local law enforcement agencies, so that if it should cause any interest as a result of the subjects that are being checked out

Figure 10-4 A hard disk is being removed from a desktop computer.

Figure 10-5 A dedicated and separate Internet-connected computer for the laboratory.

or the sites that are being accessed, they will be able to contact the head of the laboratory.

Figure 10-6 shows the storage area within the laboratory for documents and clean disks, all of which are individually labeled and can be identified by unique labels. The cabinet is for the short-term storage of equipment.

Figure 10-7 shows the data storage and server rack for the laboratory network. This network is isolated from the rest of the organization and all data stored on the server are encrypted for additional security. The rack contains 8 TB of data storage in a RAID array, which is expandable as required. The door of the rack in Figure 10-7 has been removed to allow for the photographs to be taken; the door is normally in place and secured.

Figure 10-6   Storage area within the laboratory.

Figure 10-7   The data storage and server rack for the laboratory network.

This is a typical laboratory that would be suitable for a small to medium-size organization. This particular laboratory was the second attempt by the university, which initially built a laboratory that was less than half the size of the current facility. This laboratory is fully alarmed and has internal motion sensors. There are no windows in the laboratory because the site that was selected for the laboratory is at the core of the building to gain additional security.

WHO WILL BE YOUR CUSTOMERS?

Other issues that will have to be addressed is who the customers that the forensic laboratory will serve are and how the staff will interact with them? In reality, in most cases, the high-technology crime investigators are your customers, but there must be a clear understanding of the boundaries of responsibilities between the different roles.

It would be wise to place the laboratory directly under the manager of the high-technology crime investigative unit or the chief of security. It would be unwise to place the laboratory under the management of the IT department or the audit department for the same reasons that you would not want them conducting high-technology crime investigations (e.g., lack of knowledge of laws and evidence collection and preservation and interview and interrogation techniques).

If the "rules" are not sorted out from the start (your terms of reference), there will be an inevitable expansion of the role or "task creep" of the forensic lab. After all, you will have highly trained staff who are extremely technically competent, and there will always be a call for their skills to "help out" on system and network problems.

CASE PRIORITY

Another issue that must be sorted out in advance is the priority that different types of cases will be given. If priorities are set and incorporated into the procedures from the start, it will prevent arguments and undue pressure from being placed on the staff by investigators who want their job done first. This is one of the factors that will have to be regularly reviewed and adjusted as necessary. The role of the triage officer or unit manager, if it is adopted, will handle the day-to-day prioritization and any conflicts in requirements.

ALLOCATION OF DUTIES

If there are a number of members of staff in the lab, make sure that duties are allocated equitably, taking account of their individual levels of expertise. Also, make sure that there is sufficient overlap in their skill sets to allow for absences and for peaks and troughs in workloads.

STAFF TRAINING AND EXPERIENCE

Depending on the software that is to be used for the forensic examination of the evidence in cases, ensure that staff members have received appropriate training and have sufficient experience in using it. They should not be put in the position of having to stand by the results of investigations and attest to the "facts" if they have not had the appropriate training on the use of the software and are not experienced in its use. It would also be sensible to investigate professionally recognized certification or accreditation for any staff working in the laboratory.

Training is not a once-only event. If staff members are to operate effectively, they must have access to an ongoing program of training that will take account of the changes in technologies and developments in the tools available. This will be expensive to maintain, but must be supported because any failure to maintain the currency of staff training will lead to disillusioned staff who are not properly skilled to carry out the tasks required of them.

STAFF AND LABORATORY PRODUCTIVITY

When you put together your business case for funding to develop a laboratory, assumptions must have been made with regard to the level of investigations that could be supported by the number of staff you identified. After the lab is fully operational and the staff have settled into routines and gained experience, this should be reviewed and adjusted. Also remember that the laboratory would be more cost-effective if it could also support other types of inquiries or investigations, not just those of high-technology crimes.

PROCEDURES FOR QUALITY REVIEW

Procedures for quality review need to be established from the start, so that a level of service quality can be established and maintained and so the procedures are understood by the staff working in the lab and by management. The procedures will have to be agreed upon with the relevant authorities.

EQUIPMENT TESTING

All laboratory equipment must be regularly tested to ensure electrical safety, that it is sterile, and that it carries out its function as expected. Tests should be carried out at scheduled periods or when there is any doubt about any functional or secure aspects of the equipment. Within the laboratory there may also be equipment that requires regular calibration.

STANDARDS

Depending on the type of organization that you belong to, there may be a range of standards that need to be adhered to. There may well be national standards as well as local and organizational standards to achieve and maintain. If they are addressed from the start, this will give your staff confidence and pride in working for an organization that aspires to the standards. Two of the best known standards that should be considered are ISO 9000, which is a set of quality management standards, and ISO 17799, which is a comprehensive set of controls comprising best practices in information security.

POLICY ON OUTSOURCING

Work out in advance what your policy will be on outsourcing if there is an excess of work to be carried out. If you think that there will be a requirement to outsource, line up your candidates in advance and make sure that you have checked them out before you entrust your "crown jewels" to them.

Furthermore, if you decide to outsource the entire forensics function, you should be sure your contract specification meets at least the minimal information presented in this chapter, and you can inspect the site at will.

POLICY ON USE OF EXTERNAL EXPERTS

As with the outsourcing of excess workload, it may be necessary to identify people outside the organization who have specific knowledge and expertise that is not available from your own resources. The policy for who can be called upon, when, and under what conditions they can be engaged must be defined in advance. To do this you will have to have a good understanding of the skills held by your staff and who the domain experts are.

One word of caution about hiring "ex-hackers"—we highly recommend that any hackers, phreakers, or other miscreants who have been involved in illegal activities not be hired, regardless of their expertise. After all, the risk of trustworthiness will always be questioned and questionable.

COUNSELING

Computer forensics can be an extremely stressful occupation, especially when dealing with cases of pornography and pedophilia. It is essential that you have the procedures and arrangements in place for staff to have access to counseling services at predetermined periods and whenever they feel it is necessary. Staff should not be given the option on counseling; there is no place for "macho" acts of bravado. A regular, well-considered program should be adhered to.

EQUIPMENT AND SOFTWARE

Now that you have worked out what you are going to be doing, the customers that the work will be done for, and how you are going to approach the problems, it is time to work out what equipment and software you will need.

Equipment Selection*

In general this will, in part, depend on whether you are a law enforcement or a business organization. The reason for this is that law enforcement organizations will often have access to equipment and tools that are not available to other organizations. As a basic rule, each analyst will need a workstation (and they will need enough elbow room to work comfortably for considerable periods of time).

There will also need to be at least one terminal available in the lab that can be dedicated to Internet searches. The staff will need an area to strip and rebuild computers, and they will also need a very efficient air-conditioning system. Depending on the way that you organize the laboratory, you will also have to decide whether you are going to need the workstations to be networked together and have a server to store the data. When deciding on your hardware requirements you should consider that the systems you create will probably need to:

- Have swappable bays
- Support fast imaging of the evidence disks
- Support IDE, SCSI, laptop, and micro drives
- Support a range of removable storage media, including tape drives, zip drives, LS120 drives, and jazz drives, either through external drives or in the swappable bays
- Have a DVD writer
- Have a reader for flash media storage devices
- Be capable of supporting PCMCIA drives and devices

You will also need to decide on a write protection system for use in your imaging of the systems to ensure there is no possibility of contaminating the evidence from the system being used to create the image. There are a number of hardware and software systems available to ensure the write protection of the material being imaged. Some of the more commonly used hardware and software write blockers are:

- Guidance Software Fastbloc FE
- Paralan SCSI Write Blocker
- MyKey Techlogy Inc. NoWrite
- WiebeTECH Forensic Drivedock
- LCTechnology International Firewire Second Generation Read-Only Removable IDE Bay
- Royal Canadian Mounted Police Hard-Disk Write Lock V0.8

---

*Remember high technology rapidly changes, and you must have a process in place to update your equipment when needed.

Please note that we do not recommend any specific product, but only provide such lists to help you get started at determining the equipment and software that is right for your environment.

You will need to consider how you are going to store your backups and to arrange for an off-site backup location that can protect them to the same level of security as the laboratory. You will need to decide what equipment is required for "crime scene" forensic work. What type of portable workstations and imaging equipment will you need? You must also decide the quantity and type of equipment you need to hold (and store) for the seizure of systems at the scene of the crime.

You will need storage space for the crime scene equipment and you will need to arrange secure storage space for seized equipment. You may need to hold equipment for a considerable period of time, and as a result, you may have to allow quite a bit of space. Also as you process more and more cases, the volume of data you will need to store will grow rapidly.

Software*

When you have decided on the software that you are going to use in the laboratory, purchased it, and installed it, you must also test it to make sure that it works on the systems as you have configured them and works in the manner advertised, because this may become an issue in any disciplinary or judicial proceedings.

Inevitably, with the wide range of crimes you will investigate, you are going to require a wide range of software tools to look at different aspects of the data that you find. Take advice from the professional and forensic associations and self-help groups that are available to find the tools that have gained peer approval and are accepted in cases that have already been taken to court.

A word of caution—be scrupulous in ensuring that any licenses for software that you use or hold in the lab are valid and up to date. It would be unethical and negligent to use software that was not properly licensed, and it could prejudice any cases for which the software was used. It would also be a huge waste of effort and make the laboratory unworkable if it loses its reputation through the use of such software.

INFORMATION RESOURCES

There will always be a requirement to maintain and increase knowledge to address issues that have not been encountered before. This can be achieved through subscriptions to journals and magazines, the purchase of books and subscriptions to online list servers, and so on.

---

*Remember, high technology rapidly changes, and you must have a process in place to update your equipment when needed.

Another invaluable source of information can be peer organizations—other computer forensic laboratories and associations. Other sources of information are organizations such as the National Institute for Standards and Technology (www.nist.gov/), the National White Collar Crime Center (www.nw3c.com/board_contact.html), the FBI (www.fbi.gov/), the UK NHTCU (www.nhtcu.org/), and the sites of forensic equipment manufacturers or service providers. As the disciplines become more accepted, the number of repositories of information will continue to increase.

HEALTH AND SAFETY

The issue of the availability of counseling was addressed earlier in this chapter, but the wider issue of health and safety must be addressed as well. A computer forensic laboratory with a lot of electrical devices—some of which will be in the process of being dismantled and reassembled—is a potentially hazardous zone. The materials being brought into service may also be contaminated. Staff should be briefed on health and safety measures, and this type of education should be reinforced at regular intervals. There should also be a strict regimen of electrical and chemical safety testing within the laboratory.

DATA RETENTION POLICY

A computer forensics laboratory that does not have a well-defined data retention policy will very quickly run out of storage space. There is also a likelihood that the unnecessary retention of data will be illegal in the majority of jurisdictions. Therefore, the policy for the retention of data should be thought out in advance and validated with the legal department. It should then be rigorously applied with periodic checks made to ensure that the laboratory is compliant.

REPORTING OF FINDINGS

Decisions must be made on the types of reports that are to be produced, who they are to be supplied to, and the time frame for their production. This policy must be a "living" document, as experience is gained and as the pressure of work and tasking develop.

Also, plans such as contingency, emergency, disaster recovery, and operational must be established and kept current to ensure an effective and efficient computer forensics laboratory.

COMMUNICATIONS

Because the forensics laboratory works for its customers, there must be a dialogue and a procedure for ensuring that the needs of both parties are recognized and satisfied whenever possible. If the investigators do not understand the capabilities and limitations of the forensics laboratory, they will not be able to work effectively. The last thing that anybody working in a forensic lab needs is to be asked to "tell me what is on the disk," without being given some indication of the type of crime that is suspected and some guidance with regard to what the investigator is hoping to find.

Conversely, if the investigator, who may not understand what it is possible for the forensic laboratory to achieve, is not informed and educated regarding capabilities of the laboratory, he/she will not know what to ask for. As a result, it is essential that there is a regular dialogue between the "customer" and the "service provider." There should also be clearly defined and understood protocols for the tasking of the laboratory, with established procedures for the hand-over of material and acceptance of tasking into the laboratory.

SUMMARY

This chapter looked at the issues that you have to take into account to obtain funding for and then establish a computer forensics laboratory. The issue of the recruitment of and allocation of duties to the staff, and their subsequent training and welfare need to be considered before the laboratory is created.

REFERENCES

1. www.nhtcu.org
2. en.wikipedia.org/wiki/TEMPEST

11

High-Technology Crimes: Case Summaries

The purpose of this chapter is to provide a range of summaries of high-technology crimes and related issues that illustrate the types of incidents that may be encountered under the general grouping of high-technology crimes. In addition, the information provided will give the high-technology crime investigator a basic understanding of the high-technology working environment and will provide a sense of the many challenges that face high-technology crime investigators in both the public and private sectors.

INTRODUCTION

Throughout Parts I and II we discussed some basic ideas, definitions, and methodologies used for high-technology crime investigations, as well as basic techniques used by miscreants. If you recall, we identified some basic malicious threat categories in Chapter 1. They were:

- Criminals
- Terrorists
- State sponsored agents
- Disaffected employees
- Hackers
- Pressure groups
- Commercial groups

As you read through the high-technology crime case summaries and related topics, identify them as they relate to these categories. We hope that understanding a range of actual high-technology crimes or incidents will provide some awareness regarding what you may be facing when you are called in to investigate a high-technology crime or incident. It may also help you when developing your investigative plan (e.g., which steps and in which order you will use to investigate the incident). We have added a commentary to each case that we hope will provide some insight to help you understand this environment. Please note that the quoted text has been edited for clarity (see http://www.isfs.org.hk).

THE DRINKORDIE GROUP

This was a copyright infringement and software piracy case. DrinkOrDie was an underground warez (software cracking and trading) network that operated during the last decade of the 20th century and into the start of the 21st century. It was finally shut down as a result of a major series of raids in 2001, which went under the name of Operation Buccaneer. According to FBI reports, the DrinkOrDie network was started in 1993 by a Russian with the handle "deviator" and a friend who went by the name of CyberAngel. By 1995, when the group was at its peak, their network had spread worldwide. One of its earliest exploits of note was the release of the Microsoft Windows 95 operating system a full two weeks before the official Microsoft release. Other software that the group obtained included business software and multimedia files, including a number of films. One of the authors witnessed the scale of the operation when he visited the UK National High-technology crime Unit after raids carried out in the UK. The quantity of media, mainly CDs, that was confiscated as a result of the raids in the UK covered the whole of the floor of one of the operations rooms. The activity of the group gradually slowed, and by the year 2000 they were not considered to be major players in the warez scene. When shut down in December 2001, the group was reputed to have had two leaders—one based in the United States and another in Australia.

The Australian leader, Hew Raymond Griffiths, who used the handle Bandido, was subsequently involved in legal action in Australia involving possible extradition to the United States. The Operation Buccaneer raids were part of a coordinated international operation that involved law enforcement agents in six countries and targeted 62 people, and there were leads in an additional 20 countries. In the United States, the law enforcement effort was led by the US Customs Service, and resulted in raids on MIT (in the in the economics department), the University of California at Los Angeles, the University of Oregon (at an off-campus location), Duke (at the campus dormitory of a male undergraduate), and Purdue, and a number of software companies. This effort required 56 search warrants and resulted in 130 computers being seized, each holding an average of a terabyte of data. Raids were also carried out in Australia and in Europe in Britain, Finland, Norway, and Sweden.[1,2]

Commentary: This was a mammoth investigation that took place over a number of years. The coordination alone for the raids that took place on December 11, 2001, was an immense undertaking (trying to coordinate a number of agencies in the United States and law enforcement from a number of other countries to try and ensure that the raids took place at the same time and that none of the suspects received warning from activity in another part of the world). Imagine the level of effort that had to be invested in this investigation to ensure that sufficient evidence was secured from the immense amount of data recovered to ensure the convictions that were achieved.

The vast amount of data, from sources in a number of countries and seized under a range of national laws had to be collected and stored (in some cases for years) in a manner that meant that it remained evidentially sound. In the case that took place in the Old Bailey in the United Kingdom, evidence was used that had been recovered from servers located in the United States to prove that one of the individuals had carried out the actions for which he was charged.

This operation is at the top end of anything that you may ever be involved in, but it clearly shows what it is possible to achieve when the right procedures and resources are applied.

OLDIE BUT GOODIE HACKER CASE

The most famous and extremely well-documented case is the one reported by Cliff Stoll in the book the *Cuckoo's Egg*.[3] A group of German hackers allegedly were being paid by the KGB to hack US computers.

Commentary: This case, which took place in the Lawrence Berkeley Laboratory, had it all: the hacking, the international espionage, and the investigation. It should be remembered that this took place in the days before computer forensics existed, and remains, even today, one of the most famous and best-documented cases of a computer investigation.

MILITARY HACKER FREED ON BAIL

Gary McKinnon, from London in the United Kingdom, was indicted in the United States for seven counts of computer fraud and abuse for the unauthorized access and damage to a total of 92 computers that belonged to the US Army, Navy, and Air Force; the Department of Defense, including a computer classified as "used by the military for national defense and security"; and the National Aeronautics and Space Administration (NASA); and six computers belonging to a number of private businesses.

The indictment alleged that Gary McKinnon had scanned a large number of computers in the .mil network domain. It said he managed to access the computers and gain administrative privileges and then installed a remote administration tool and a range of hacker tools, copied passwords and other files, and deleted user accounts and critical system files. Once inside a network, he used the hacked computer to find other military and NASA victims. As a result of his activities, McKinnon caused a network in the Washington, DC, area to be shut down, resulting in the total loss of Internet access and e-mail service to approximately

2000 users for 3 days. It is estimated that the losses to the various military organizations, NASA, and private businesses was approximately $900,000.

The indictment in this case came about as the result of a 17-month-long investigation that involved the US Army Criminal Investigation Command's Computer Crime Investigative Unit, the NASA Office of the Inspector General, Naval Criminal Investigative Service, the 902nd Military Intelligence Group-Information Warfare Branch, the Defense Criminal Investigative Service, the Air Force Office of Special Investigations, and the United Kingdom's NHTCU. Also assisting in the investigation were the US Army CERT located at Fort Belvoir, Virginia; the Army Regional CERT at Fort Huachuca; the Naval Computer Incident Response Team; and the Department of Defense CERT.[4]

Commentary: Once again the international nature of the case, the number of computers involved, and the range of agencies that had an interest and an input to this case give an indication of the complexity of the investigation. If you do not have your communications sorted out and do not have acceptable procedures in place, it is likely that the case will collapse before it goes to court. In this case, at least 11 different agencies were involved. The ability to transfer information and evidence between these agencies in such a way that it remains usable comes as a result of agreed and accepted practices.

WORM STRIKES DOWN WINDOWS 2000 SYSTEMS

"Microsoft in 'emergency response' as worm reported on three continents: ...A fast-moving computer worm...attacked computer systems using Microsoft operating systems, shutting down computers in the United States, Germany, and Asia. Among those hit were offices on Capitol Hill, which is in the midst of August recess, and media organizations, including CNN, ABC, and the *New York Times*. The Caterpillar Co. in Peoria, Illinois, reportedly also had problems. A small number of computers in an administrative office at San Francisco International Airport also crashed, but these computers were not essential to the airport's operation, spokesman Mike McCarron said. The FBI said the computer problems did not appear to be part of any widespread attack."[5]

Commentary: The days of viruses have turned into the days of worms. Because they are rather easy to write and distribute through networks, they will undoubtedly be around for many years to come because various miscreants will use them for meeting their own goals. Such goals may be for "fun" by some juvenile delinquent to corporations trying to shutdown a competitor's network to assist in gaining a competitive advantage. It may also be done by government information warfare agents to test their newest offensive information warfare software weapons, such as a worm, to determine the affect of their worm. Later this "weapon" could be modified if needed and then added to their information warfare weapons arsenal.

If the major operating systems (e.g., Microsoft) ever provide automatic defenses against them, they will no longer be a problem. However, we do not ever expect to see that day in our lifetime. Therefore, one must continually rely on third-party sources for the latest antiworm software.

The problem with investigating such matters is that they generally must be investigated by government agencies such as the FBI, because this malicious type of software is often developed and sent from nations where many high-technology crime investigators lack jurisdiction.

The best way to defend against such attacks is to install and maintain up-to-date antiworm software set at a highly defensive setting. However, many, if not most, IT personnel rationalize not using the highest setting possible; thus, worms find their way into the networks of corporations, government agencies, and individual systems. As a high-technology crime investigator, your excellent liaison contacts with government agencies and others may help you keep abreast of their latest worm attack investigations.

As a high-technology crime investigator for a corporation, your investigation may center on how such an attack was able to be successful against the corporate networks. Therefore, your investigation may focus more on how the attack occurred, negligence on the part of those with protection responsibility, as well as whether proper procedures were followed and, if so, whether those procedures are sufficient.

FBI AGENTS BUST "BOTMASTER": LOS ANGELES, CALIFORNIA (REUTERS)

"A 20-year-old man accused of using thousands of hijacked computers, or "bot nets," to damage systems and send massive amounts of spam across the Internet was arrested...called the first such prosecution of its kind...well-known member of the "Botmaster Underground"—or the secret network of computer hackers skilled at bot attacks—was taken into custody.... A bot is a program that surreptitiously installs itself on a computer and allows the hacker to control the computer. A bot net is a network of such robot computers, which can harness their collective power to do considerable damage or send out huge quantities of spam."[6]

Commentary: Miscreants seem to be continually finding ways to take advantage of the vulnerabilities of computer systems. Spam has been another phenomenon that has been used by anyone from juvenile delinquents to businesses. These miscreants have spawned a new business—antispam software products. Such products, like antivirus and antiworm software, should be installed and constantly maintained to ensure the best protection possible.

One can easily imagine the uses that a bot can offer a miscreant. After a miscreant controls your system, he or she can use system power to attack other systems. Once found out, it may be that the corporate system that was taken over will be identified as the one doing the attacking, and thus the corporation may be liable for any damages to other systems. Furthermore, after the system is taken over, any proprietary information can be easily stolen without the owner even knowing it was taken.

As a high-technology crime investigator, you will run into the same problems investigating these attacks as with other types of attacks noted in the previous commentary concerning worm attacks. In fact, because of the global nature of networks, the miscreants may be out of the jurisdiction of the investigator. In those cases, one must rely on the national investigative agencies to investigate and identify the miscreants. The victim corporation may seek civil damage remedies from the courts in the nation where the miscreant is a citizen. Such matters are not only costly, but in some instances the penalties for such offenses make a mockery out of the judicial systems.

RESEARCHERS SNOOP ON KEYBOARD SOUNDS

"Computer eavesdropping yields 96% accuracy rate.... If spyware and key-logging software weren't a big enough threat to privacy, researchers have figured out a way to eavesdrop on your computer simply by listening to the clicks and clacks of the keyboard. Those seemingly random noises, when processed by a computer, were translated with up to 96% accuracy, according to researchers at the University of California, Berkeley. "It's a form of acoustical spying that should raise red flags among computer security and privacy experts," said Doug Tygar, a Berkeley computer science professor and the study's principal investigator. Researchers used several 10-minute audio recordings of people typing away at their keyboards. They fed the recordings into a computer that used an algorithm to detect subtle differences in the sound as each letter is struck."[7]

Commentary: This type of spyware has been known for some time in the government's world of classified matters. However, it has recently become common knowledge and, as expected, it can be a great tool for a miscreant seeking a competitor's information, passwords, and the like.

SPAMMERS FACE JAIL IN NIGERIA

"Nigeria, home to some of the world's most notorious cyber crimes, has proposed a law making spamming a criminal offense for which senders of unsolicited e-mail could be jailed for at least 3 years. The draft law identifies the use of computers for fraud, spamming, identity theft, child pornography, and terrorism as criminal offenses punishable by jail terms of between 6 months and 5 years, and fines of 10,000 naira ($77) to 1 million naira ($7700). Under the bill, which has to be approved by the National Assembly to become law, convicted spammers face jail terms of 3 to 5 years and could also be made to hand the proceeds of crime to the government. 'Any person spamming electronic messages to recipients with whom he has no previous relationship commits an offense.' ...The draft law empowers law enforcement agents to enter and search any premises or computer and arrest any person in connection with an offense."[8]

Commentary: Nigeria is a known haven for many of the scams found on the Internet (e.g., a solicitation to contact someone in Nigeria to help get money out of the country). For that country to propose a law concerning spamming leads one to believe that they have had enough, or are at least trying to pacify other nations because of possibly many complaints concerning miscreants operating in their country. Nigeria is typical of the international problem—how to identify a miscreant operating out of Nigeria and have him prosecuted. This problem may be complicated by the lack of a nation's laws that would even allow such prosecution.

STOLEN UC-BERKELEY LAPTOP RECOVERED

"Computer had personal information on 98,000 students. A stolen laptop computer holding personal information of more than 98,000 California university students and applicants has been recovered, but is uncertain whether the information had been tapped, the University of California, Berkeley said.... The laptop, which stored names and social security numbers, disappeared in March from a restricted area of the university's graduate division offices, forcing the university to alert more than 98,000 students and applicants of the theft. The university said in a statement that a San Francisco man has been arrested and charged by the Alameda County district attorney with possession of stolen property after investigators discovered the laptop had been bought over the Internet by a man in South Carolina."[9]

Commentary: Identity theft is a major concern these days. When such a crime is committed, it is important to determine whether the person stole the computer for resale only or for use by the miscreant or others for identity theft uses. As an investigator, besides the normal theft-of-property investigative approach, one must be sure to include an analysis of the physical security processes that allowed the theft to take place.

THREE JAILED IN GLOBAL EBAY SCAM

"A British judge jailed three Romanians Friday for tricking thousands of eBay customers around the world into paying for nonexistent goods advertised on the Internet auction site.... [They] pleaded guilty to conspiracy to obtain property by deception and money laundering.... More than half of the 3000 victims were from the United States and they paid more than £250,000—about $450,000 or 370,000 Euros—for advertised goods including cars, binoculars, parachute trousers, and tickets to sporting events between July 2003 and May 2005. Payment was sent by instant money transfer via Western Union, but none of the goods existed and the buyers were left empty-handed. eBay advises customers against using instant money transfers when paying for goods because of the risk of fraud.... During the trial, prosecutors told the court that the three defendants transferred most of the stolen money to a criminal network in Romania, and spent the rest on their lifestyles."[10]

Commentary: This type of crime is a common fraud perpetrated in a new environment. Therefore, the basic investigative techniques of such a fraud should be incorporated into the investigative processes that are part of Internet-related investigative techniques. As a high-technology crime investigator, remember that many of today's high-technology crimes are old crimes, but they are being perpetrated in a new environment—a high-technology environment. Therefore, basic investigative techniques still apply.

BLOGGERS LEARN THE PRICE OF TELLING TOO MUCH

"Blogs are everywhere, increasingly, the place where young people go to bare their souls, to vent, to gossip. And often they do so with unabashed fervor and little self-editing, posting their innermost thoughts for any number of Web surfers to see.... 'Since the people who read my blog are friends or acquaintances of mine, my philosophy is to be totally honest—whether it's about how uncomfortable my panty hose are or my opinions about First Amendment law'.... Some are, however, finding that putting one's life online can have a price. A few bloggers, for instance, have been fired for writing about work on personal online journals.... Some also speculate that more scandalous blog entries—especially those about partying and dating exploits—will have ramifications down the road.[11]

Commentary: The "baring of one's soul" through blogs and e-mail can cause subsequent liable suits, and may be the reason for miscreants to blackmail or become involved in extortion schemes. Such incidents are in their infancy, but it is expected that they too will soon be a cause for investigations. So as a high-technology crime investigator, are you prepared to conduct such investigations? Have you put together your basic investigative plan and identified the steps to be taken during such an investigation?

   If you are a high-technology crime investigator for a corporation and have been asked to investigate or look into the incident of an employee using blogs on corporate time or talking about the corporation and some of its employees, are you prepared for such an inquiry? As with the other types of incidents described in this chapter, you should have a basic plan of investigative steps for each example or groups of examples. This will save you time and effort, both of which will be valuable as executive management demands results and results now!

TWENTY ARRESTED IN CRACKDOWN ON INTERNET PHARMACIES

"Twenty people in the United States and abroad were arrested on charges they ran Internet pharmacies that illegally shipped narcotics, steroids, and amphetamines to teenagers and other buyers around the world.... The arrests were the result of a year-long investigation by six federal agencies of online pharmacies that often operate in the shadows of the Internet, with no fixed address and no way to track where they are located.... 'The Internet has become an open medicine cabinet....' 'Strangers are peddling drugs in your home and you don't even know it....' The drugs were shipped to buyers with little or no effort to verify ages or medical need, allowing teenagers or drug abusers easy access to addictive and dangerous drugs,...the pharmacies forfeited 41 bank accounts valued at more than $6 million. Among the organizations targeted was a Philadelphia-based Internet pharmacy that allegedly smuggled prescription painkillers, steroids, and amphetamines into the United States from India, Germany, Hungary, and elsewhere, and repackaged them and sold them throughout the world."[12]

Commentary: The Internet has made it much easier to commit certain types of crimes. This example is basically using the Internet and e-mail as tools to perpetrate a crime that otherwise would have been done, but by other means. If you are an investigator for a pharmaceutical company or other business who has an interest in drug distribution, such incidents are of interest because they are your corporation's illegal competitors.

ALLEGED HACKER IS MICROSOFT EMPLOYEE

"A man accused of hacking into search engine company AltaVista's computer systems about 2 years ago now works at Microsoft Corp., the company said Friday.... [He] hacked into AltaVista's computer system to obtain software blueprints called source code and recklessly caused damage to AltaVista's computers."[13]

Commentary: Such an incident makes a great case for corporations requiring background investigations on potential employees. Suppose this person decided to attack other companies' systems. Would Microsoft be viewed by the "victim" as liable for such attacks?

ANTIIDENTITY THEFT FREEZE GAINING MOMENTUM

"Credit companies resist measure.... Little by little, a weapon against identity theft is gaining currency—but few people know about it. It's called the security freeze, and it lets individuals block access to their credit reports until they personally unlock the files by contacting the credit bureaus and providing a PIN. The process is a bit of a hassle, and the credit-reporting industry believes it complicates things unnecessarily .... But identity theft watchdogs say usage is low simply because the credit bureaus don't publicize the option. With identity theft apparently growing, the advocates hope the freeze gains national momentum. Congress resisted calls for a freeze rule during debate over a major credit law last year" (place and date of source unknown).

Commentary: Sometimes individuals' high-technology safety and security depend on their seeking answers on how best to maintain that safety and security, because one cannot always rely on those that play an integral role in causing the problem to be part of the solution. As a high-technology crime investigator involved in such cases as identity theft, this type of information would be worth knowing when conducting your investigation.

E-MAIL RECEIVED BY ONE OF THE AUTHORS

"**From:** customercare@bankofthewest.com
Sent: Tuesday, June 28, 2005 10:20 AM
Subject: BANK OF THE WEST NOTICE

Dear Bank of the West customer,

We recently noticed one or more attempts to log in to your Bank of the West account from a foreign IP address and we have reasons to believe that your account was hijacked by a third party without your authorization. If you recently accessed your account while traveling, the unusual login attempts may have initiated by you. However, if you are the rightful holder of the account, click on the link below and submit, as we try to verify your account. (In case you are not enrolled use your social security number as User Name and first six digits of your social security number as Password).... The log in attempt was made from: ...If you choose to ignore our request, you leave us no choice but to suspend your account temporarily. We ask that you allow at least 48 hours for the case to be investigated and we strongly recommend not making any changes to your account in that time. If you received this notice and you are not the authorized account holder, please be aware that is in violation of Bank of the West policy to represent oneself as another Bank of the West account owner. Such action may also be in violation of local, national, and/or international law. Bank of the

West is committed to assist law enforcement with any inquires related to attempts to misappropriate personal information with the Internet to commit fraud or theft.

Information will be provided at the request of law enforcement agencies to ensure that perpetrators are prosecuted to the fullest extent of the law. Please do not respond to this e-mail as your reply will not be received. For assistance, log in to your Bank of the West account and choose the 'HELP' link. Thanks for your patience as we work together to protect your account."

Commentary: Such unsolicited e-mail should always be brought to the attention of the business allegedly involved. This e-mail message is asking for information of a personal nature. If you are not a customer of the institution, you would generally just delete the e-mail or, better yet, notify the institution involved by other means than answering this e-mail. For example, such e-mail is often a solicitation for information so that one can perpetrate identity theft–related crimes. In this case, the financial institution involved advised (when contacted) that they did not and do not send out such e-mail. One may wonder why a miscreant would send out such blanket e-mail. Once in awhile, someone receiving the e-mail may be a customer of the financial institution and may respond as requested. As an investigator for the financial institution, how would you go about investigating this matter? Would the financial institution be liable for any damage done to the e-mail receiver even though there was no financial connection other than the use of its name, which it cannot control? Such information is useful because it is related to elements of proof and violations of laws or regulations.

BARRED NO MORE

"Inmates use intermediaries to escape into Internet...jail cells are roomier than most. Must be all that cyber space. State and federal prisons don't let inmates use Internet computers behind bars—and the Allegheny County Jail doesn't either. Yet...has answered a reporter's e-mail from the Pittsburgh jail, and later an Ohio lockup, while he awaits sentencing for violating probation on a 900-number phone scam that cost AT&T $550,000. Thousands of other inmates access the Internet indirectly using inmate telephone and mail privileges, and a network of family, friends, or activists. Once on the Web, they enlist celebrities like Susan Sarandon to plead their case, pillory the prosecutors who imprisoned them, or simply find pen pals."[14]

Commentary: "Where there's a will there's a way" as the old saying goes. It just goes to show you how difficult it is to stop some types of high-technology-related crimes.

PERSON USING AN ALIAS AND REPRESENTING A FICTITIOUS ISP INSTALLED SIX TOLL-FREE 800 NUMBERS FOR A TELEMARKETING COMPANY

"There was no written contract and the 800 numbers were subleased to other ISP companies.... Seven weeks later, all numbers were deactivated for nonpayment, leaving an outstanding debt of $1,514,985.03. Investigative Services contacted the FBI.... The subject served time in federal prison...and was subsequently ordered to pay $1.5M upon his release" (source wished to remain anonymous).

Commentary: Such a crime being investigated by a federal investigative agency would leave little for the corporation (of one of the victim ISPs) to do except, through good liaison with the FBI, obtain details of the investigation, support the special agents doing the investigation, and determine what action was taken by the business' employees that helped this crime to occur.

A NETWORK SECURITY OPERATIONS CENTER RECEIVED A CATASTROPHIC OUTAGE NOTIFICATION FROM THEIR NETWORK MANAGEMENT CENTER INDICATING A FIBER OUTAGE HAD OCCURRED

"Interviews conducted and evidence obtained at the outage site disclosed that personnel...severed both the local and long-distance cables while conducting an underground bore.... The underground cables were snagged and twisted around the reamer head until they were severed by the tension.... Witness statements and evidence indicated that the area immediately surrounding the cut site prior to the outage had been properly marked" (source wished to remain anonymous).

Commentary: Such matters are often classified as accidents but still must be investigated and documented so that liability issues can be resolved and compensation received for such damages. Furthermore, such incidents, which are numerous, point to a vulnerability that others can take advantage of (e.g., terrorists).

TELECOMMUNICATIONS CABLES VULNERABLE TO TERRORISTS' ATTACKS

An employee of a large telecommunications corporation was working in a desert area in the southwestern United States when he was approached by three young Middle Eastern men who began asking very detailed questions about the underground telecommunications cable. The employee was suspicious and gave vague answers. The three subsequently left the area, and the employee reported the matter to the corporate investigative department, which subsequently reported it to the FBI. The individuals allegedly were stopped prior to boarding a flight and detained. No further information was available (source wished to remain anonymous).

Commentary: Such incidents are rare but point out how vulnerable some telecommunications cables are. These cables carry the vital information that allows networks to transmit information on a global basis for corporations and government agencies.

SO YOUR EMPLOYER "LOST" YOUR INFORMATION

"Millions of employees and consumers have gotten some unwelcome news in 2005. They were told that their personal information was lost or had been stolen. That personal information included names, social security numbers, and other valuable identifiers. The breaches may have been the result of human error or, more troubling, a heist by identity thieves or other criminally minded menaces. If you find an e-mail from your company telling you that there's been a security breach of employee information, chances are you won't know for a while whether theft was the cause."[15]

Commentary: Such incidents are no longer rare, it seems. As a high-technology crime investigator, you must determine whether the incident was human error or at least a violation of corporate policy and, at most, a crime, which may have been perpetrated by a company employee. Would such an incident violate any government laws or regulations? You should determine this as part of your planned investigative steps because it affects your plan relative to identifying elements of proof.

CALIFORNIA TO BAN HUNTING OVER INTERNET

"Wildlife regulators took the first step Tuesday to bar hunters from using the Internet to shoot animals, responding to a Texas Web site that planned to let users fire at real game with the click of a mouse. The Fish and Game Commission ordered wildlife officials to prepare emergency regulations to ban the practice. A period of public comment will follow. 'We don't think Californians should be able to hunt sitting at their computers at home,' said Steve Martarano, a spokesman for the state Department of Fish and Game. A bill passed by the state Senate 2 weeks earlier would prohibit use of computer-assisted hunting sites and ban the import or export of any animal killed using computer-assisted hunting. The measure now moves to the state assembly. At least 14 other states and Congress are considering similar bills.... Supporters have suggested the remote hunting could be beneficial for hunters with disabilities and questioned why Californians should be barred from patronizing a legitimate Texas business."

Commentary: It seems there is no end to the uses of the Internet and the associated controversies surrounding how it can be used. If such a law were enacted, what investigative steps can you identify if asked to investigate a violation of such "hunting" laws?

E-MAIL RECEIVED BY ONE OF THE AUTHORS

"My Greetings to you,

I am [name withheld] from Libya. I am married to Late [name withheld] of blessed memory who was an oil explorer in Libya and Kuwait for 12 years; before he died in the year 2000. We were married for 12 years without a child. My husband died after a brief illness that lasted for only four nights. Since his death I too have been battling with both cancer and fibroid problems. When my late husband was alive he deposited a substantial amount of money in millions of dollars with a finance firm overseas.

Recently, my doctor told me that I have only 6 months to live in this world due to cancer problem. Though what disturbs me most is my stroke sickness.

Having known my condition I decided to donate this fund to either a charity/orphanage home or devoted God-fearing individual/company that will utilize this money the way I am going to instruct herein. I want this organization or individual to use this money in all sincerity to fund charity homes (motherless homes), orphanages, and widows.

Although, I took this decision because I don't have any child that will inherit this money and my husband's relatives are into radical organization and I don't want a situation where this money will be used in an unholy manner. Hence the reasons for this bold decision. Please, pray for me to recover as your prayers will go a long way in uplifting my spirit. I don't need any telephone communication in this regard, because of the presence of my husband's relatives around me always and my doctor has advised me not to speak on phone because of my health.

I don't want them to know about this development. As soon as I receive your reply I shall give you further directives on what to do and how to go about actualizing this project. I will also issue a letter of authorization to the finance company authorizing them that the said fund is being willed to you and a copy of such authorization will be forwarded to you. I want you to always pray for me. However, any delay in your reply will give room in sourcing for an organization or a devoted individual for this same purpose. Until I hear from you by e-mail and you can as well reply to this e-mail address [address withheld], my dreams will rest squarely on your shoulders.

Remain Blessed,
[name withheld]"

Commentary: This seems to be a variation on a theme based on the old Nigerian-based letter, fax, and, subsequently, e-mail scams. Obviously, anytime someone wants to give you, a complete stranger, a great deal of money, there is something wrong. However, it is amazing how many people fall for such a scheme and reply to the sender. As an investigator, and as part of a corporate awareness program, you should ensure such techniques are brought to the attention of the company employees and any such e-mail received at work should be reported to you. As an investigator, an initial first step would be to trace the e-mail back to its originator.

The results will, in all probability, lead to the sender residing in a country other than where they say they are or one known for such types of scams. You may want to investigate such matters out of curiosity, ignore it, or report it to some government agency. The simplest method is to ensure that employees report these e-mail messages and not answer them. Also, coordinate the matter with the IT personnel responsible for filtering spam and other unwanted e-mail and have the miscreant's address added to the blocked list.

NINE OF ISRAEL'S TOP BUSINESS EXECUTIVES AND 11 HEADS OF 3 LEADING INQUIRY COMPANIES—INCLUDING MODIIN EZRAHI—ARE IN CUSTODY SUSPECTED OF COMPLICITY IN A MASSIVE COMPUTERIZED COMMERCIAL ESPIONAGE CONSPIRACY

"Suspected of designing the illegal raider software called Trojan Horse for the three inquiry firms.... They offered clients business intelligence on their rivals, some of whom trade on the stock exchange, by illegally planting spy software in the targeted computers and downloading their classified data. Clients under suspicion of accepting the offer include Volvo Motors importers, Yes satellite TV, and Pelephone and Cellcom cell phone license holders. Their senior officers are in custody. Their victims included Orange (Partner) cell phones, Hot cable TV, Strauss-Elite, Champion Motors, Mei Eden mineral water, Ace DIY, and Zoglobek sausages."

Commentary: Earlier, DEBKA*file*[16] reported the following: In professional intelligence literature, this locution usually refers to industrial espionage by the illegal invasion of computers. The offense most often takes the form of an unauthorized "mirror" planted in a target's computer to download its contents to another computer. The kind of software used is not new; it derives from the PROMIS program developed in the United States in the 1980s to help the US Justice Department and the FBI crack financial crime cases. The targets of PROMIS and its offspring never know they are raided, their firewalls penetrated, and their passwords cracked.

Throughout the years, many intelligence agencies, including Israel's, upgraded the earlier version of PROMIS and developed better protective software against these silent invaders. Some of their experts ended up on the world market, notably in the United States, India, Russia, and probably Israel too. They can be found selling their expertise to security and financial companies or even to organized crime. The illegal practitioners are known in professional parlance as *black hat hackers.*

Corporate America has suffered vast losses, estimated in many billions of dollars, from such hackers, who are contracted by rival businesses to lift customer lists, the contents of contracts, marketing strategy, and financial situation. It is believed that most victims decide not to complain to the police for fear of publicity that would ruin their business and undermine their stocks. The soundless black hat hackers often as not get away with their crime. Indeed, many are hired by victimized business to trace the intruders and strengthen its security. The underground hacker will then come in from the cold and become a *white hat hacker.*

"BLASTER" TEEN SENTENCED TO 1½ YEARS

"A teenager was sentenced Friday to 1½ years in prison for unleashing a variant of the 'Blaster' Internet worm that crippled 48,000 computers in 2003."[17]

Commentary: This punishment seems somewhat unusual, but we are not complaining, because most punishments include a fine that the miscreant does not have the ability to pay and a suspended sentence, probation, and such. However, usually the damages incurred by the victim business can never be recouped. As an investigator, it is usually depressing to identify a miscreant, have the miscreant prosecuted and then given a light sentence, especially after the chaos and damages the miscreant has caused and the amount of time you took to investigate the crime successfully.

INFO ON 3.9M CITIGROUP CUSTOMERS LOST

"Computer tapes with information about consumer lending lost by UPS in transit to credit bureau.... Citigroup said...that personal information on 3.9 million consumer lending customers was lost by UPS while in transit to a credit bureau—the biggest breach of customer or employee data reported so far."[18]

Commentary: This is another case of all too many cases of lost information that can ruin millions of people's lives through identity theft, spamming, and so forth. Corporations should be held liable and aggressively prosecuted when such incidents occur, and individuals are the victims of identify theft and other forms of privacy loss. Only then will this type of problem be minimized. As an investigator for such a corporation, you should do your best not only to resolve the matter, but also to be in a position to, in coordination with the corporate auditors, legal staff, and security specialists, recommend changes to processes that will prevent future occurrences.

WORLDPAY STRUGGLES UNDER DDOS ATTACK (AGAIN)

"The Royal Bank of Scotland's Internet payment transaction outfit is continuing to fight a sustained Internet attack that has left its services largely unavailable for a third successive day.... WorldPay's online payment and administration system has been reduced to a crawl, as a result of a malicious distributed denial-of-service attack by unidentified computer criminals. A spokesman for the company stressed that although it is fighting a serious denial-of-service attack, its system is uncompromised and customer data remain secure. 'We are processing transactions securely but the attack is blocking our ability to operate normally.... Our payment and administration systems are working, safe and secure, but the networks around them are being flooded with requests on a huge scale, causing 'service denials.' We are processing payments, but far slower and fewer than we normally would. We are executing our contingency plans to move to full restoration of the service.'"[19]

Commentary: Such attacks can be devastating to a business. These attacks may be investigated internally or by a government investigative agency. While the attacks are occurring, it is important to be working continually with the IT staff and to collect volatile evidence.

DENIAL-OF-SERVICE ATTACK VICTIM SPEAKS OUT

"The founder of an online payment system has spoken to silicon.com about his experience of being targeted by Russian gangsters who threatened to destroy his Web site and his business if he didn't pay them $10,000 to leave him alone. To this day his Web site is under continual attack.... Such an attack, often generated by a network of compromised machines all directing traffic at a particular server or Web site, will overload and bring down a Web site.... Many other victims of such attacks, most commonly targeted at businesses such as on-line casinos, bookmakers, and payment services, whose businesses are very time sensitive, have also spoken out about their problems.... Paul King, chief security architect at Cisco, told silicon.com: 'Criminals aren't looking for a sophisticated challenge. They just want to make money. If somebody thinks they can bring your site down and can ask for money, then you need protection.' According to John Whitty, CTO of Pipex, those committing denial-of-service attacks can now launch around 500 Mb of data at a Web site at any one time. There are very few companies, if any, in the world whose Web site would withstand such a barrage undefended."[20]

Commentary: This is an other example of how easy it is to threaten today's high-technology-dependent businesses. As an investigator for such a business, are you prepared to conduct such an investigation? This case also shows the global reach of miscreants.

NEW VIRUS USES SONY BMG SOFTWARE

"A computer security firm said Thursday it had discovered the first virus that uses music publisher Sony BMG's controversial CD copy protection software to hide on PCs and wreak havoc. Under a subject line containing the words 'Photo approval,' a hacker has mass mailed the so-called Stinx-E Trojan virus to British e-mail addresses, said British anti-virus firm Sophos.... Later on Thursday, security software firm Symantec Corp. also discovered the first Trojans to abuse the security flaw in Sony BMG's copy protection software. A Trojan is a program that appears desirable but actually contains something harmful. When the CD is played on a Windows personal computer, the software first installs itself and then limits the usage rights of a consumer. It only allows playback with Sony software."[21]

Commentary: All new high-technology devices seem to have vulnerabilities and, because of that, eventually they are the targets of attacks by miscreants. As an investigator, remember to begin now to plan for future attacks and develop additional investigative techniques to be used as you see new high-technology devices coming to market.

DUMPSTER DIVING FOR IDS

"CNN's Keith Oppenheim joins a private detective on a tour of trash bins in Chicago, Illinois, to show how easy it is to obtain personal information from documents thrown out as garbage. Bank account number, name, birth, and social security numbers.... Done in Chicago, IL on public property, pay stubs, 15 documents with 19 names.... Medical and car facilities show others don't safeguard your info. Only one from home garbage..."[22]

Commentary: If you want to be proactive as a high-technology crime investigator, you should help defend against such crimes by conducting high-technology anticrime surveys. This can be done by being part of an assets protection security team or as part of your corporate duties and responsibilities, depending on your working environment. Eliminating such vulnerabilities for the corporation may help prevent future lawsuits by those victimized by the corporation not adequately safeguarding their personal information.

FIVE ARRESTED OVER PHISHING FRAUD

"German police have arrested five men in Bonn on suspicion of stealing 30,000 Euros through phishing fraud and Trojan horse attacks. A sixth man associated with the group, which is suspected of targeting Postbank online account holders, is said to be on the run. More than 12 million people hold Postbank accounts.... Trojan horse and phishing attacks... attempting to steal passwords and login information.... 'We are increasingly seeing organized criminals writing Trojan horses to monitor the activity of innocent computer users,' said Graham Cluley, senior technology consultant for Sophos. 'They wait for them to visit a legitimate banking Web site before stealing their essential login information.' Former White House cyber security advisors Richard Clarke and Howard Schmidt have called for banks to implement two-factor authentication, such as RSA's SecureID, in a bid to halt phishing attacks. Clarke added that online transactions cost half of 1% of a physical banking transaction. Microsoft has backed the call. The Association of Payment and Clearing Houses said that it was looking into using the technology, but had made no decisions yet. Russian antivirus company Kaspersky Labs recently said that 90% of malware is created and sent by criminals looking to steal money."[23]

Commentary: Another example of criminals using high technology. And why? Well, as the old bank robber Willy Sutton reportedly said when asked why he robbed banks, "That's where the money is." It also points out the globalization of crime due to high-technology more than ever before and its adoption by organized crime groups, as well as terrorists, to gain financially.

GEEKFATHERS: CYBER CRIME MOBS REVEALED

"Crime is now organized on the Internet. Operating in the anonymity of cyber space, Web mobs with names like Shadowcrew and Stealthdivision are building networks that help crackers and phishers, money launderers and fences skim off some of the billions that travel through the Web every day. The players and their games change so quickly it's hard to piece together who they are and how they work together. But that picture's becoming more clear, as the US Secret Service, the FBI, and other law enforcement agencies crack open the networks and prosecute those that run them."[24]

Commentary: This is another example that points to this new high-technology crime environment, which is getting more sophisticated with each passing day. As a high-technology crime investigator, are you prepared to investigate such crimes?

HACKER HELPS WANNABE BIZ STUDENTS

"A computer hacker helped applicants break into records at some of the most prestigious US business schools to see if they were accepted weeks before official offers were sent out, officials said Friday. A person who applied to Harvard Business School posted instructions on how to check the application status at several business schools, including Stanford, Duke, and Dartmouth, on *Business Week's* online technology forum this week. Roughly 100 people who applied to Harvard followed the directions, but many did not learn their fate because decisions had not been entered into the computer yet. Harvard's next batch of acceptances will be sent out later this month."[25]

Commentary: Hackers ply their trade for many reasons, some of which may be wrong, but are not as bad as some others. This is an example of a typical hacker ploy to get information.

HACKERS BATTER CRITICAL UK INFRASTRUCTURE

"Three hundred UK government departments and businesses are being targeted by specifically engineered viral attacks. A report from the National Infrastructure Security Co-ordination Centre (NISCC) suggests the bodies, critical to the country's infrastructure, have been the subject of attacks mainly originating from the Far East. 'The provenance goes back a number of months,' said Roger Cumming, director at NISCC. 'Over the last few months we've seen consistent attacks against the UK critical national infrastructure. What characterizes it is the scale rather than anything else.' According to NISCC, the attacks take the form of Trojan viruses intended to steal information specific to the UK national infrastructure, including information about trade and commerce. Cumming said NISCC is working with foreign Computer Emergency Response Team agencies to shut down the virus-writing operations.... 'Finally the NISCC has awoken to the serious issue of cyber crime and is actively tackling the problem. Businesses that have been lagging behind in getting the right security protection in place need to sit up and listen to the NISCC's warning against this new onslaught of cyber attacks,' said Bob Jones, of Internet security company Equiinet. 'Whilst antivirus software and firewalls are critical components of any security infrastructure, the NISCC is right in its statement that companies need to go beyond these traditional defenses.'"[26]

Commentary: As Asia grows in high technology, the number of attacks by Asian miscreants continues to increase as well. In this case, are the attacks by hackers who operate in their nation with impunity or is this an orchestrated series of attacks to gain information for eventual use during a war in which information warfare plays an integral role? Could the attacks be coming from terrorists who are preparing for what some have long warned about—the "Pearl Harbor" of cyber space attacks?

HACKER INFILTRATED GOVERNMENT COMPUTERS, US MILITARY INSTALLATIONS, LABORATORIES, AND NASA

"The FBI confirmed Tuesday the accuracy of a *New York Times* report that software on routers, computers that control the Internet, was compromised last year by a hacker who claimed that he had infiltrated systems serving US military installations, research laboratories, and NASA. The *Times* reported, and the FBI confirmed, that the focus of the investigation is a youth in Uppsala, Sweden, who has been charged as a juvenile. The FBI said it is unclear to US authorities what, if anything, can be done to prosecute the youth for violating US laws. The *Times* reported that the youth did not devise a new kind of attack but cleverly organized computers, automating the theft of computer logins and passwords."[27]

Commentary: The summary speaks for itself. A hacker in a foreign country, a juvenile, may not be prosecuted but illegally accessed systems. This is typical of the matters that will continue to frustrate high-technology crime investigators around the world.

HACKERS TAKE A CRACK AT CISCO FLAW

"Computer hackers worked through the weekend to expose a flaw that could allow an attacker to take control of the Cisco Systems routers that direct traffic across much of the Internet. Angered and inspired by Cisco's attempts to suppress news of the flaw earlier in the week, several computer security experts at the Defcon computer security conference worked past midnight Saturday to discover and map out the vulnerability. 'The reason we're doing this is because someone said you can't,' said one hacker, who, like others, spoke on condition of anonymity. Cisco's routers direct traffic across at least 60% of the Internet, and the security hole has dominated a pair of conferences that draw thousands of security researchers, US government employees, and teenage troublemakers to Las Vegas each summer. The hackers said they had no intention of hijacking e-commerce payments, reading private e-mail, or launching any of the other malicious attacks that could be possible by exploiting the flaw. Rather, they said they wanted to illustrate the need for Cisco customers to update their software to defend against such possibilities. Many Cisco customers have postponed the difficult process because it could require them to unplug entirely from the Internet."[28]

Commentary: This is another typical hacker technique. Many hackers are just curious about systems and want to identify their vulnerabilities and bring them to the attention of the vendor. For many it is like working a crossword puzzle, but better! Unfortunately, most vendors are still as they were in the 1980s and do not want vulnerabilities looked for or exposed to others. They should, of course, be constantly "stress testing" their new products to identify vulnerabilities before the products are released to customers. Their actions make the job of the high-technology crime investigator much more difficult.

HOME PCS HARNESSED TO SOLVE GLOBAL PROBLEMS

"IBM and top scientific research organizations are joining forces in a humanitarian effort to tap the unused power of millions of computers and help solve complex social problems. The World Community Grid will seek to tap the vast underutilized power of computers belonging to individuals and businesses worldwide and channel it into selected medical and environmental research programs. Volunteers will be asked to download a program to their computers that runs when the machine is idle and reaches out to request data to contribute to ongoing research projects."[29]

Commentary: This is a good idea that can be the target of massive abuse. Can you imagine what would happen if an attacker successfully accessed and took over this network? Would you put your corporation's systems or even your own home computer at risk by allowing others to use it? Often good intentions look good on paper, but turn out to be a terribly poor idea when looked at from the eyes of a high-technology crime investigator. How would you like to be called in to investigate a breach of such a network with millions of computers that are part of the crime scene?

INTERNET CRASHES IN PAKISTAN

"An undersea cable carrying data between Pakistan and the outside world has developed a serious fault, virtually crippling data feeds, including the Internet, telecommunications officials said.... Many offices across the country ground to a halt as people realized it was not one of Pakistan's regular, but usually brief, technical hitches. 'It's a worst-case scenario. We are literally blank,' said a senior foreign banker who declined to be identified. Airlines and credit card companies were among the businesses hit by the crash. 'It's a total disaster,' said Nasir Ali, commercial director of the private Air Blue airline. 'We have a Web-based booking system which has totally collapsed.'"[30]

Commentary: Even if this were an accident, it points out the extreme dependency government agencies and businesses have on their telecommunications systems and how vulnerable they are. Even third world countries like Pakistan, which is not as high tech as many nations, can be devastated by such incidents. As a high-technology crime investigator you should ask: Was this an accident? Human error? How could this happen? How would I go about investigating such an incident?

IPOD BLAMED FOR SPIKE IN SUBWAY CRIME

"The iPod craze has spawned a crime wave in city subways. Police told the city transportation board on Wednesday that 50 iPods have been reported stolen on the subways so far this year, compared to none during the same period last year. Cell phone thefts have more than doubled to 165 from 82 last year. The thefts fueled a 20% spike in robberies last month on the subway, officials said. Most thieves are believed to keep the devices, which can retail for $100 to $500. 'It usually has to do with young people taking them from young people,' said police.... Thieves spot people with the telltale white earphones, then snatch the devices and run out train doors. On Web sites, iPod devotees suggest keeping the devices concealed and switching to cheaper looking earphones. An average of 9 to 10 serious crimes occur daily on the city's subway system, officials said. Kelly called that number 'remarkably low' and attributed it to extra police patrols."[31]

Commentary: This points out that high-technology theft is not sophisticated, but happens often. The theft will become more of an issue as your cell phone and iPod turn more into multimedia devices storing personal information that can be used for identity theft, possibly blackmail, extortion, and so forth.

"MEDICA IGNORED WARNINGS," SAYS EX-EMPLOYEE

"The former manager of computer security for Medica Health Plans said the company ignored repeated warnings that its information system was vulnerable to attack and abuse. The health plan's security engineer until early 2004, said Medica didn't act on his recommendation to "lock down" the computer system and protect sensitive information, including personal information about Medica's 1.2 million members. That and other measures could have prevented two Medica computer administrators from allegedly sabotaging the company's computers and downloading data earlier this year."

Commentary: The high-technology crime investigator will continue to find that basic security measures are not put in place, and often the advice of these professionals is ignored by executive management. When conducting a high-technology crime investigation, security professionals such as the chief information security officer can provide support and insight regarding how and why such crimes occurred.

WEB SITE OWNER DEFIES JUDGE'S ORDERS

"Four days after a federal judge shut down a lucrative Internet pharmacy in Burnsville in May and ordered owner Christopher William Smith to refrain from selling drugs, Smith boarded a plane to the Dominican Republic and opened a new online pharmacy, authorities said Tuesday. To do so, an FBI affidavit says, Smith traveled abroad under a false passport, used a cash card to obtain money from a bank account after it had been seized by the court, and had his wife, his girlfriend, and others bring him thousands of dollars in cash (source information unknown, other than Warren Wolfe, *Star Tribune*)."

Commentary: This case points out one of the global problems of high-technology crimes—lack of jurisdiction. A person can operate with impunity in some countries, whereas in others the miscreant would be arrested. Solving a high-technology crime is only half the battle. Getting the miscreant prosecuted is the other half.

PHISHERS ADOPT SCAM TRICKS FROM VIRUS WRITERS

"Dangerous new ways to try to steal your money are in progress. You know all about phishing scams, right? You know better than to click on a Web link embedded in an e-mail that purports to be from your bank, or to reply to messages requesting your user name and password. But if you think that's enough to protect yourself, think again. A phishing scam currently spreading online works without your ever having to click on a link. All that's required to activate the scam is for you to open an e-mail. And, many security experts warn, this threat may be a sign of things to come. 'This style of attack is new and old at the same time. It's a common approach that virus writers take, but it's new with regard to phishing attacks,' says Jim McGrath, senior director of security management products for NetIQ. "Phishers are trying to use the techniques that have been very successful for virus writers. It's a new and dangerous trend." The current phishing scam, which has been labeled JS/QHosts21-A by antivirus vendor Sophos, is an example of this kind of blended threat. In this case, the scam involves a Trojan horse that combines with an ActiveX vulnerability in Windows to install itself on your machine invisibly, without warning."[32]

Commentary: This case is another phishing example. Miscreants continue to become more sophisticated in their attacks, and security and investigative professionals are slow to react and learn.

LEXISNEXIS: HACKERS ACCESSED 32,000 IDS

"Hackers commandeered a database owned by information industry giant LexisNexis, gaining access to the personal files of as many as 32,000 people, company officials said Wednesday. Federal and company investigators were looking into the breach at Seisint, which was recently acquired by LexisNexis and includes millions of personal files for use by such customers as police and legal professionals. Information accessed included names, addresses, social security and driver's license numbers.... It is the second such infiltration at a large database provider in recent months. Rival ChoicePoint Inc. said last month that the personal information of 145,000 Americans may have been compromised by thieves posing as small business customers."

Commentary: An information systems security consultant had this to say about the attacks: "I know for a fact that LexisNexis has been continuously hacked for at least the last 10 years. Some of the hackers I've run into showed me how they were accessing it about 8 years ago. LexisNexis is the tool of choice for hackers because it has a wealth of knowledge that you can use to leverage an attack against an organization, not just an individual. A few days ago I got an e-mail message from a company I use for background checks...saying that they acknowledge the recent hack of ChoicePoint and telling me not to worry because it won't happen to them. It seems like its time for all of these data mining companies to get serious about security."

TELEPHONE SCAM

"I received a telephone call last evening from an individual identifying himself as an AT&T service technician who was conducting a test on telephone lines. He stated that to complete the test I should touch nine, zero, the pound sign, and then hang up. Luckily, I was suspicious and refused. Upon contacting the telephone company, I was informed that by pushing 90#, you give the requesting individual full access to your telephone line, which enables them to place long-distance calls billed to your home phone number. I was further informed that this scam has been originating from many local jails/prisons. I have also verified this information with UCB Telecom, Pacific Bell, MCI, Bell Atlantic, and GTE" (received from a source who wished to remain anonymous).

Commentary: The key is not to do what strangers tell you to do without verifying the information. In this case, don't press 90# for anyone. As an investigator in this case, how would you go about capturing this miscreant?

E-MAIL RECEIVED BY ONE OF THE AUTHORS

"Dear eBay customer: Need Help? We regret to inform you that the primary e-mail for your eBay account was changed on April 10, 2005. If you did not authorize this change, please contact us using the link below. Click here and reenter your account information. Please do not reply to this e-mail. This mailbox is not monitored and you will not receive a response. For assistance, log in to your eBay account and click the Help link located in the top right corner of any eBay page. Regards, Safeharbor Department eBay, Inc. The eBay team. This is an automatic message. Please do not reply."

Commentary: A security officer for eBay said, "It is like playing whack-a-mole. We normally get them down in about 3 hours." One important sign is asking for personal information, while another is "Do not reply to this e-mail." As an investigator, this happens often, so an inquiry may truly be like a whack-a-mole game. An awareness bulletin to customers and posted on the Web site is one way to help others not become victims by advising them of this scam and may help minimize the number of investigations required in such cases.

E-MAIL MESSAGE RECEIVED BY ONE OF THE AUTHORS: ANOTHER VARIATION ON THE THEME

"Subject: ITS REAL LETS DO IT

Hello Friend, Hope you are doing great and sound? I am...at law and attorney to late...a Greek Merchant otherwise known as my client who was based in the United Kingdom and died of complications from injuries sustained after a ghastly motor accident. As the attorney to...I was his confidant as he shared with me virtually everything about himself, his business, and family. I was his attorney for 15 years and during that period I wrote his will and was also named as the executor, which has since been fulfilled. I am also aware, due to my closeness to him, that the amount of 22 Million Euros he deposited with a bank in Europe was not willed out. He told me about this on his sick bed and even instructed that I should prepare a codicil to that effect; however, before I could finish my work he had died. After his death, funeral, and subsequent execution of his will, I went into action to ascertain the information passed unto me by my client. My investigation conformed to the information; at that point I knew I had to do something to move the funds out of the bank and, knowing that I cannot do this alone, I have decided to contact you and seek your assistance and acceptance to be the next of kin to the estate. It is necessary for us to move the money out of the bank now because if we do not do this within the next 2 years, the bank would regard the money as sundry funds, which becomes as good as their own money.

I cannot move the money in my name because he was my client, for it could arouse suspicion, thus the importance of your assistance. Have my assurance that there is nothing to fear about, as I also need your assurance that you would work with me without fear or favor to achieve our desired objective. The legal backup is no problem for I would be responsible. Since the codicil was not ready before his death, Letters of Administration without Will would be secured from the probate office, with this document granting probate rights in your favor. I would personally apply to the bank for the release of the funds to you on your behalf. What I require from you to enable us achieve the above are your: full and official names; address; date of birth; telephone and fax numbers. Upon receipt of a confirmation of acceptance from you, a sharing ratio would be worked out between us on the most liberal and magnanimous terms. Take care and have a nice day. Reply me at MOST SECURE AND PRIVATE E-MAIL ADDRESS."

Commentary: What can we say? Such e-mail is running wild on the Internet. The best thing to do is provide awareness to customers and employees to report them and then block their recurrence.

TIME WARNER ALERTS STAFF TO LOST DATA FILES FOR 600,000 WORKERS

"Time Warner Inc. said that a cooler-size container of computer tapes containing personal information about 600,000 current and former employees was lost, apparently during a truck ride to a data storage facility in March. The computer tapes contained the names, social security numbers, and other data pertaining to the media conglomerate's 85,000 current employees as well as former employees dating to 1986. The tapes didn't contain data on customers. The loss of another large trove of personal data, which follows security breaches at ChoicePoint Inc., Bank of America Corp., and the DSW subsidiary of Retail Ventures Inc., among others, highlights the concern about the increasing value to criminals of illegally obtained personal information in the digital age. The Internet hosts a thriving black market in social security, credit card, and driver's license numbers, with each such data "element" fetching as much as $100, experts say. The breach also exposes the vulnerability of data-handling procedures—online and off."[33]

Commentary: This is yet another case of human error or deliberate highjacking and theft. As an investigator, such incidents will be common occurrences that will require you to investigate.

FEDERAL AGENTS HAVE CARRIED OUT SEARCHES IN AT LEAST TWO STATES AS PART OF THE INVESTIGATION INTO THE THEFT OF SOCIAL SECURITY NUMBERS AND OTHER PERSONAL INFORMATION FROM DATABASE GIANT LEXISNEXIS INC.

"Secret Service and FBI agents executed a search warrant in Minnesota, while FBI agents conducted 10 searches in northern California, federal law enforcement officials said Thursday. The search in Minnesota is 'definitely the LexisNexis case,' said Mike Brooks, an FBI spokesman in Ohio. No arrests have been made in connection with the searches, which were carried out in recent days.... LexisNexis disclosed in March that hackers had commandeered a database and gained access to the personal files of as many as 32,000 people. The company has since increased its estimate of the people affected to 310,000.

The breaches were uncovered during a review and integration of the systems of Seisint Inc. shortly after LexisNexis bought the Boca Raton, Florida-based unit for $775 million in August. Seisint's databases store millions of personal records including individuals' addresses and social security numbers. Customers include police and legal professionals and public and private sector organizations. Information accessed included names, addresses, social security and driver's license numbers, but not credit history, medical records, or financial information, corporate parent Reed Elsevier Group PLC said in a statement. It was the second such infiltration at a large database provider in recent months. Rival ChoicePoint Inc. said in February that the personal information of 145,000 Americans may have been compromised by thieves posing as small business customers."[34]

Commentary: This case is included to give you some idea of what investigators are attempting to do in such cases of information thefts. The number of searches at the various locations shows how widespread such crimes can be.

HACKERS TARGET ITUNES, ANTIVIRUS WARE

"Survey shows that online criminals are also attacking antivirus software, media players like iTunes.... Online criminals turned their attention to antivirus software and media players like Apple Computer's iTunes in the first 3 months of 2005 as they sought new ways to take control of users' computers, according to a survey released Monday. While hackers continued to poke new holes in Microsoft's popular Windows operating system, they increasingly exploited flaws in software made by other companies as well, the nonprofit SANS Institute found."[35]

Commentary: Nothing is immune from high-technology miscreant attacks.

JUDGE DISMISSES SPAM CONVICTION

"A judge dismissed a felony spamming conviction that had been called one of the first of its kind, saying he found no "rational basis" for the verdict and wondering if jurors were confused by technical evidence. Ruling Tuesday, Judge...also said jurors may have gotten "lost" when navigating Virginia's new antispam law in the case...upheld the conviction of her brother,...who prosecutors said led the operation from his...area home... were each convicted in November for using false Internet addresses to send mass e-mail ads through an AOL server.... The jury recommended that...spend 9 years in prison and that...pay $7,500 in fines."[36]

Commentary: After all long, hard investigative work, this happens much too often. A judge accusing the jury of "being confused" is insulting and indicates some trends in our judicial system today, in which judges overrule jury's decisions.

MASTERCARD SECURITY ALERT—MORE THAN 40 MILLION CREDIT CARDS MAY HAVE BEEN BREACHED; WARNING TO MEMBER BANKS ISSUED

"MasterCard International said on Friday it was alerting member financial institutions of a security breach that could affect over 40 million credit cards, of which nearly 14 million are MasterCard branded. The breach took place at CardSystems Solutions in Tucson, which processes transactions on behalf of financial institutions and merchants. MasterCard said it is giving member financial institutions the specific card account numbers that may have been compromised. MasterCard-brand cards include MasterCard, Maestro, and Cirrus."[37]

Commentary: Another example of incidents that lead to identity theft.

SASSER AUTHOR GETS SUSPENDED TERM

"A German court has convicted the teenager who created the Sasser worm that snarled tens of thousands of computers last year and sentenced him to 21 months' probation...could have faced 5 years in prison as an adult but was tried as a minor because the court determined he created the virus when he was 17."[38]

Commentary: This case is another example of attacks against systems, causing multimillions of dollars in lost productivity, damage, and the like. Then, after successfully identifying the attacker, the judicial system failed to look at the crime as a serious one based on the lenient sentencing.

A FEDERAL JUDGE HAS AWARDED AN INTERNET SERVICE PROVIDER MORE THAN $1 BILLION IN WHAT IS BELIEVED TO BE THE LARGEST JUDGMENT EVER AGAINST SPAMMERS

"Company provides e-mail service for about 5000 subscribers in eastern Iowa, filed suit against 300 spammers after his inbound mail servers received up to 10 million spam e-mail a day in 2000, according to court documents. US District Judge...filed default judgments Friday against three of the defendants under the Federal Racketeer Influenced and Corrupt Organizations Act and the Iowa Ongoing Criminal Conduct Act."[39]

Commentary: What is of interest in this case is the number of spams received and the penalty imposed by the judge. Whether that decision stays, it does help send a message to spammers; however, it only works if there is not a jurisdiction issue.

TEEN SENTENCED FOR "BLASTER" WORM VARIANT

"A teenager was sentenced Friday to 1½ years in prison for unleashing a variant of the "Blaster" Internet worm that crippled 48,000 computers in 2003...will serve his time at a low-security prison and must perform 10 months of community service. He had faced up to 10 years in prison, but the judge took pity on the teen, saying his neglectful parents were to blame for the psychological troubles that led to his actions. '[The Internet] has created a dark hole, a dungeon if you will, for people who have mental illnesses or people who are lonely,' US District Judge Marsha Pechman said. 'I didn't see any parent standing there saying, "It's not a healthy thing to lock yourself in a room and create your own reality."' Defense lawyers said Parson feared leaving the house and his parents provided little support. He pleaded guilty last summer to one count of intentionally causing or attempting to cause damage to a protected computer."[40]

Commentary: Lack of jurisdiction and lenient sentences, we believe, help encourage miscreants to continue to commit their crime undeterred. As a high-technology crime investigator, it is often difficult to see the results of one's investigation go for naught.

SUMMARY

High-technology crimes of various types continue to grow, supported by lax protection of these valuable high-technology assets, lack of jurisdiction, and lenient sentencing. Loss of personal data seems to be growing exponentially, with the keepers of the data not being held accountable and punished for their lack of adequate security. High-technology crimes continue to grow in sophistication, with new type of attacks happening on a regular basis, providing the high-technology crime investigator with many challenges.

REFERENCES

1. www.infoworld.com/article/03/03/13/HNpiracyring_1.html

2. www.computerworld.com.au/index.php/id;598535608;fp;512;fpid;600923431
3. Stoll, C. (1990). *The Cuckoo's Egg*. The Bodley Head.
4. www.nydailynews.com/front/story/317389p-271379c.html
5. www.cnn.com/2005/TECH/internet/08/16/computer.worm/index.html
6. http://edition.cnn.com/2005/TECH/11/04/crime.botmaster.reut/index.html
7. http://us.cnn.com/2005/TECH/internet/09/21/keyboard.sniffing.ap/index.html
8. http://edition.cnn.com/2005/TECH/internet/10/19/nigeria.crime.reut/index.html
9. http://edition.cnn.com/2005/TECH/ptech/09/15/berkeley.id.theft.reut/index.html
10. http://edition.cnn.com/2005/WORLD/europe/10/28/ebay.scam.ap/index.html
11. www.cnn.com/2005/TECH/internet/07/11/tell.all.blogs.ap/index.html
12. www.cnn.com/2005/LAW/04/20/internet.drugs.ap/index.html
13. (2004, July 12).
14. www.cnn.com/2005/TECH/internet/05/02/internet.inmates.ap/index.html
15. http://money.cnn.com/2005/05/03/pf/security_employees/index.htm
16. (2005, May 29). *Two Suspected Israeli Computer Hackers Face Extradition from London. DEBKAfile special update.*
17. www.foxnews.com/printer_friendly_story/0,3566,145730,00.html
18. http://money.cnn.com/2005/06/06/news/fortune500/security_citigroup/index.htm?cnn=yes
19. www.theregister.co.uk/2004/10/04/worldpay_ddos/
20. http://management.silicon.com/smedirector/0,39024679,39130810,00.htm
21. http://us.cnn.com/2005/TECH/internet/11/10/sony.hack.reut/index.html
22. www.CNN.com
23. www.zdnet.com.au/news/security/0,2000061744,39174828,00.htm
24. www.baselinemag.com/print_article2/0,2533,a=147696,00.asp
25. www.cnn.com/2005/TECH/internet/03/07/hacker.biz.schools.reut/index.html
26. www.scmagazine.com/news/index.cfm?fuseaction=newsDetails&newsUID=5c2c2ef7-72d9-48fa-922b-6eb346d7e522&newsType=Latest%20News&s=n)
27. www.cnn.com/2005/TECH/05/10/govt.computer.hacker/ index.html
28. www.cnn.com/2005/TECH/08/01/defcon.hackers.reut/index.html
29. www.cnn.com/2004/TECH/internet/11/16/science.ibm.grid.reut/index.html
30. www.cnn.com/2005/WORLD/asiapcf/06/28/pakistan.internet.reut/index.html
31. www.cnn.com/2005/TECH/ptech/04/28/subway.crime.ipod.ap/index.html
32. Cassavoy, L., and Brandt, A. (2004, November 5). *PC World*.
33. Angwin, J., and Bank, D. *The Wall Street Journal*.
34. www.cnn.com/2005/US/05/19/lexisnexis.hack.ap/index.html
35. http://money.cnn.com/2005/05/02/technology/microsoft.reut/index.htm?cnn=yes
36. www.cnn.com/2005/LAW/03/02/spam.trial.ap/index.html
37. http://money.cnn.com/2005/06/17/news/master_card/index.htm?cnn=yes
38. www.cnn.com/2005/LAW/07/08/sasser.suspended/index.html
39. www.cnn.com/2004/LAW/12/18/spam.lawsuit.ap/index.html
40. www.cnn.com/2005/TECH/internet/01/28/internet.attack.ap/index.html

PART III

Overview of the High-Technology Crime Investigation Profession and Unit

The high-technology crime investigation profession is often one of
frustration as well as challenges.

The objective of this section is to provide the information needed for the
reader to establish and manage a corporate high-technology crime investigative unit using a fictional corporation as the model on which to build
such a program.

Chapter 12 describes a fictional company in which the high-technology
crime investigator and high-technology crime investigative manager will work.

This approach will provide you with a practical baseline model on which to build a company's high-technology anticrime or crime prevention program. If you don't work for such a company, pretend you do, and build your high-technology crime investigative unit and high-technology crime program.

Chapter 13 defines the role that the high-technology crime investigator will play in a corporation or government agency. In this case, it is the role of the high-technology crime investigator for the Global Enterprise Corporation (or GEC). The duties and responsibilities of a high-technology crime investigator vary, depending on the place of employment. However, in this case, we are assuming the high-technology crime investigator has the "perfect" position.

The objective of Chapter 14 is to establish the plans for the high-technology anticrime organization that provide the subsets of the GEC strategic, tactical, and annual plans. These plans will set the direction for GEC's high-technology anticrime program while integrating the plans into GEC's plans, thus indicating that the high-technology anticrime program is an integral part of GEC.

The objective of Chapter 15 is to describe and discuss the establishment and management of the organization chartered with the responsibility to lead the high-technology anticrime effort for GEC, including structuring the organization, and describing the organization and the job descriptions of the personnel to be hired to fill the positions within the high-technology anticrime organization.

The objective of Chapter 16 is to describe and discuss the major high-technology crime investigative functions that are to be performed by the high-technology crime investigative unit. We also describe the flow processes that can be used to establish the baseline in performing the functions.

The objective of Chapter 17 is to identify, describe, and discuss sources of various types, networking, and liaisons with outside agencies.

The objective of Chapter 18 is to describe and discuss the identification, development, and use of metrics charts to assist in managing a high-technology crime investigative unit and high-technology crime prevention program (HTCPP).

Outsourcing is a management tool used today to help save corporations and government agencies money. Chapter 19 looks at the possibilities of outsourcing the high-technology crime investigative function and a process that can be used to make that determination.

This section is the heart of the book in that, unlike other books relative to high-technology crime or computer crime investigations, which delve into the details of how to investigate such offenses, this book provides that information more as related background information so that the high-technology crime investigator can better understand this "crime scene" environment. Our use of the term *high-technology crime investigator* in general throughout Part III means one who is also the leader and manager of an HTCPP and organization.

In this way, the security professional, consultant, or private investigative firm has the basic understanding on which to build a high-technology crime investigative unit for a corporation, as a business, or, at the very least, to add this function to the other security (asset protection) functions of the security department.

Part III focuses on the individual CSO, or similar individual, who must build such a unit or function for a major international corporation. It is approached from a management perspective of one responsible for such a unit using basic management and business philosophies.

12

The Global Enterprise Corporation

This chapter describes a fictional company in which the high-technology crime investigative manager will establish and manage a high-technology crime investigative unit. This approach provides the reader with a practical baseline model on which to build a corporate high-technology crime prevention program (HTCPP) as part of a corporate asset protection program.

INTRODUCTION

We encourage you to develop a plan and then build an HTCPP based on GEC. This practice not only assists in focusing on the "how-to's," but it can be used as a model on which to build such a program when the opportunities arises, as part of your career development and advancement program, which is addressed in Part IV of this book.

One word of caution. The approach used is provided in a simplistic form, and often, unfortunately, things are more complex. However, we believe that the basics provided will assist the high-technology crime investigator manager in developing a foundation, an outline, for a more complex environment.

GEC BACKGROUND INFORMATION

The high-technology crime investigator must understand the business and processes of GEC if a quality, cost-effective HTCPP unit and/or function is to be developed for GEC. Part of this process requires the high-technology crime investigator to identify those key elements of GEC's history and business that must be considered in developing the GEC HTCPP and high-technology crime investigative unit.

The following is a summary of GEC's business environment. Italics have been added to identify the key phrases, which are important elements the high-technology crime investigator must take into consideration when building the HTCPP. The high-technology crime investigative unit is part of that program.

GEC is a high-technology corporation that *makes a high-technology widget*. To make these widgets, it uses a *proprietary process* that has evolved during the last 7 years that GEC has been in business.

The *proprietary process is the key to GEC's success* as a leading manufacturer of high-technology widgets. The process costs million of dollars to develop. The protection of the high-technology widget process is *vital to company survival*.

GEC is in an *extremely competitive business* environment. Based on changes in high technology, which allow for a more efficient and effective operation through telecommunications and networks, it has found that it must *network with its customers and subcontractors*.

To provide for maximization of the high-technology widget process, it shares its networks with its *subcontractors, who must also use GEC's proprietary process*. The subcontractors, *under contractual agreements*, have promised not to use or share GEC's proprietary information with anyone. They have also agreed to protect that information in accordance with the security requirements, for example, information systems security (Info Sec), of their contract with GEC.

GEC has a European distribution office in London; a components manufacturing plant in Jakarta, Indonesia; and a components manufacturing plant and Asian distribution center in Hsinchu, Taiwan. The employees at all locations use state-of-the art high technology to support their jobs (e.g., cell phones, notebook computers, working-from-home concepts).

KEY ELEMENTS FOR THE HIGH-TECHNOLOGY CRIME INVESTIGATOR TO CONSIDER

From the background information about GEC, the GEC high-technology crime investigator should remember some key elements:

1. *GEC is a high-technology corporation.* This means that it uses and is dependent on state-of-the-art high-technology equipment and systems—a key factor that makes the HTCPP of vital importance.
2. *It uses a proprietary process.* This means that information relative to the proprietary process is the most valuable information within GEC, and it probably resides on one or more of GEC's information systems that are integrated and interface with the Internet, the GII, and portions of the NII of the United States, Europe, and Asian nation–states (e.g., telecommunications, water, power, and emergency systems).
3. *The proprietary process is the key to GEC's success and vital to company survival.* The number one priority of the HTCPP must be proactive. Any breach of ethics, security, or other significant policies and procedures that adversely affect GEC's business must be quickly and aggressively investigated and resolved.

4. *GEC is in an extremely competitive business environment.* To the high-technology crime investigator, this means that the potential for industrial and economic espionage is a factor to consider in establishing the HTCPP.
5. *GEC is networked with its customers and subcontractors; subcontractors, must also use GEC's proprietary process, under contractual agreements.* When the high-technology crime investigator builds the GEC HTCPP, the customers and subcontractors must be prepared to assist and support any high-technology crime investigation.

If necessary, the high-technology crime investigator must request additional provisions be made to the contract relative to liability issues and the GEC high-technology crime investigator's authority to conduct inquiries and investigations within customers and subcontractors facilities. This is a major challenge, but if presented in the proper way, it may be welcomed by the subcontractors and/or customers.

GETTING TO KNOW GEC

Once hired, the new high-technology crime investigator should walk around the entire company, see how widgets are made and see what processes are used to make the widgets—in other words, watch the process from beginning to end to understand the business completely. The high-technology crime investigator should know as much as possible about the company. It is very important that the high-technology crime investigator understand the inner workings of the company, asset controls, and applicable policies, procedures, and processes.

It is unfortunate, but true, that many new high-technology crime investigators sit through the general in-briefing given to new employees and learn some general information about the company. They then go to their office. They start working and may not see how the company actually operates or makes widgets. They never meet the other people who have a major support role to play in any HTCPP—the employees. These personnel include the people using automated systems on the factory floor, human resources personnel, quality control personnel, auditors, procurement personnel, contracts personnel, in-house subcontractors, and other non-GEC employees. The reality is that, almost inevitably, the way things are actually done is different from the way it was planned and from the way that the people who manage the processes believe they are being done. Speak to the people who are doing the work to find out how it is actually done.

It is important to gauge the climate of the corporation and the morale of the employees. This helps to gauge potential high-technology crime issues that may arise. Employees who like working for the corporation and have high morale are less likely to commit any high-technology-related crimes. The reverse is also true, especially in times of layoffs.

When high-technology crime investigators are asked why they don't walk around the plant or understand the company processes, their usual reply is, "I don't have the time. I just got here. I'm under pressure to develop this program." The answer to this dilemma is: Take a time-management course, manage your time better, and make the time! A high-technology crime investigator can't provide a service and support-oriented HTCPP if there is no understanding of the company, its culture, and how its products are made. The high-technology crime investigator should know how the manufacturing process takes place, how manufacturing is supported by other company elements, how (and if) employees follow the policies and procedures in place, and how they use the high-technology systems.

All the high-technology crime prevention policies and procedures (neatly typed and placed in binders) are ignored if they get in the way of employees doing their primary functions. High-technology crime investigators can't see this from the office or cubicle. They can only find this out by walking around the areas where the people are working and actually using information systems.

GEC'S STRATEGIC BUSINESS PLAN

GEC has developed a proprietary strategic business plan. The plan describes GEC's strategy for maintaining its competitive edge in the manufacturing of high-technology widgets. That plan sets the baseline and the direction that GEC will follow for the next 7 years. It is considered GEC's long-range plan. It was decided that any plan longer than 7 years was not feasible because of the rapidly changing environment brought on by technology and GEC's competitive business environment. This is not unusual, and most organizations have plans that range from 5 to 10 years.

GEC'S TACTICAL BUSINESS PLAN

GEC also has a proprietary tactical business plan. The tactical business plan, which is a 3-year plan, sets more definitive goals, objectives, and tasks. This is the short-range plan that is used to support GEC's strategic business plan. GEC's successful implementation and completion of its projects is a critical element in meeting GEC's goals and objectives.

The tactical business plan also calls for the completion of an HTCPP. If violations occur that meet the requirements for an inquiry or investigation, then one can be conducted professionally, aggressively, and quickly.

GEC'S ANNUAL BUSINESS PLAN

GEC also has a proprietary annual plan that sets forth its goals and objectives for the year. This plan defines the specific projects to be implemented and completed by the end of the year. The successful completion of these projects will contribute to the success of GEC's tactical business and strategic business plans. GEC's annual plan calls for the hiring of a high-technology crime investigator to establish an HTCPP that can provide the high-technology crime investigative support for GEC on a global basis.

High-technology crime investigators will also be responsible for forming and managing a high-technology crime prevention organization. They will report to the director of security, who reports to the vice-president of human resources.

It should be noted that GEC's executive management agreed that a high-technology crime investigator position and the high-technology crime investigator hired should establish GEC's HTCPP, and establish and manage the high-technology crime prevention organization. However, there was not complete agreement regarding to whom the high-technology crime investigator reported. Some members of GEC's executive management suggested that, because the position is related to high technology, it should report to the vice-president of IT, whereas others suggested that the high-technology crime investigator report to the vice-president of the legal department.

Other members of executive management recommended that the high-technology crime investigator report to the director of auditing. However, the director of auditing advised that the auditing department was strictly responsible for determining GEC's compliance with applicable state, federal, and international laws, and company policies and procedures. The director felt that the auditor's limited scope and functions would adversely limit the high-technology crime investigator in establishing and managing an HTCPP. The director of auditing also argued that it may be a conflict of interest for the high-technology crime investigator to establish high-technology crime prevention policies and procedures, albeit with management support and approval, while at the same time having another part of that organization (the audit group) determine not only compliance with the high-technology crime prevention policies and procedures, but also adequacy.

The director of security advised that having the high-technology crime investigator and the high-technology crime prevention organization in his department was the only logical choice, because the high-technology crime prevention organization related to assets protection—a security responsibility. Eventually, a consensus was reached. It was decided that the high-technology crime investigator position and organization should be established within the GEC security department.

The new high-technology crime investigator's understanding of how this position ended up where it did provides some clues regarding the feelings and inner workings of GEC's management vis-à-vis the high-technology crime investigator and the HTCPP. This information will be useful when the high-technology crime investigator begins to establish GEC's HTCPP, and when the high-technology crime investigator requests support from these directors. It also provides the high-technology crime investigators some insight regarding the type of support they may receive from these directors.

Newly hired high-technology crime investigators should know the corporation, its workings, as well as why their position was established, and why they report to whom.

It is clear that the director of auditing would support the HTCPP from a compliance audit standpoint, but would probably not want to join a GEC team that has the responsibility for writing the new high-technology crime prevention policies and procedures. High-technology crime investigators must keep this in mind when they decide how to establish high-technology crime prevention policies and procedures, how to determine which departments should be involved in some part of that development process, and so on.

HIGH-TECHNOLOGY CRIME PREVENTION PROGRAM PLANNING

The main philosophy running through the previous paragraphs should be obvious: As a service and support organization, the GEC HTCPP must include plans that support the business plans of the company. The high-technology crime investigator should be able to map each major business goal and objective of each plan to key security department and high-technology crime prevention projects and functions. When writing the applicable high-technology crime prevention plans, the high-technology crime investigator will also be able to see which functions are not being supported. This may not be a problem. However, the mapping will allow the high-technology crime investigator to identify areas where required support to the plans has not been identified in the high-technology crime investigator's plans. The high-technology crime investigator can then add additional tasks where increased HTCPP support is needed.

The HTCPP must focus on meeting the company goals as stated by executive management. All policies, procedures, processes, plans, and projects must support the security department's as well as the company's strategic, tactical, and annual business plans.

An additional benefit of following this procedure is to be able to show management how the HTCPP is supporting the business. When mapping the high-technology crime prevention plans to the security and business plans, summarize the goals, because they will be easier to map.

SUMMARY

GEC, our fictitious corporation, can be used by the reader to build an HTCPP that can be used as part of an interview portfolio (see Part IV) and to build or improve an HTCPP for a corporation.

Most corporations set their goals and objectives in planning documents such as strategic, tactical, and annual business plans. These plans are key documents for the high-technology crime investigator to use to determine the corporation's future directions. These plans are also key documents that the high-technology crime investigator may be able to use to determine what is expected from the high-technology crime investigator and the HTCPP. The plans should also be used as the basis for writing service and support high-technology crime prevention plans, as separate documents or as sections that are integrated into the identified security and/or corporate planning documents.

The decision process of GEC executive management in determining in which department the high-technology crime investigator and the high-technology crime prevention organization belong provides some key information that should be used by the high-technology crime investigator in establishing the HTCPP and high-technology crime organization.

13

Understanding the Role of the High-Technology Crime Investigator and a Crime Prevention Unit in the Business and Management Environment

The objective of this chapter is to define the role that the high-technology crime investigator will play in a corporation or government agency. In this case, it is the role of the high-technology crime investigator for GEC, our fictitious company. The duties and responsibilities of a high-technology crime investigator vary depending on the place of employment. However, in this case, we are assuming the high-technology crime investigator has the *perfect* position when it comes to scope of the job, budget, authority, and responsibilities.

INTRODUCTION

The high-technology crime investigator position is extremely important because that person is the in-house consultant on high-technology crime investigations and prevention matters. The high-technology crime investigator also represents GEC to the *outside world* on high-technology crime prevention matters.

If you are chosen as the new high-technology crime investigator, you should have determined the history of that position:

- When was it established?
- Why?
- What is expected of the high-technology crime investigator?
- What happened to the last one? (You want to know so you can understand the political environment in which you will be working.)

These questions should have been asked and answered during the interview process. If not, get them answered now.

As you begin your new job as the GEC high-technology crime investigator, you must clearly determine what is expected of you. What are your responsibilities and duties? What are you accountable for? Again, this information should have been asked during your interview process for two reasons: First, so you know what you are getting into by accepting the high-technology crime investigator position with GEC and, second, so you could better prepare for the position with a more detailed HTCPP prior to beginning your first day at work.

The reason that you need a detailed plan prior to beginning your employment at GEC is because you will be behind from the moment you walk into GEC. This is because putting together an HTCPP from the start is a tremendous project.

The high-technology crime investigator's biggest challenge is not being looked upon as the "cop." For those retiring from law enforcement or the military, you may have to change how you conduct yourself and investigations. You no longer have a position of authority backed by the law, badge, and gun. You have your authority just as long as management and the employees are willing to give it to you, and that can change quickly. It is a different world with different attitudes. There are no interrogations as you may have come to know them. In addition, if you are dealing with a company that has a strong "rights-oriented" human resources group and/or unions, you most definitely must change your tactics.

This change from a law enforcement profession to a corporate security or high-technology investigative position may cause you untold hours of frustration if you let it get to you. Don't! If it does, your employment longevity will come to an abrupt end—either by the actions of GEC or your ulcer, high blood pressure, or heart attack. So, do your job professionally, but remember that the decisions as far as what to do, how to do it, and when to do it, are ultimately those of GEC management. Don't let it get to you, which of course is easier said than done.

In your new position, you must also determine how many high-technology investigators, if any, you will need. You must determine the qualifications for each position, the tasks to be performed, and so forth. In addition to this are your responsibilities for learning about GEC, the culture, normal corporate policies and procedures, and all the other learning experiences that come with joining a new company.

As the new GEC high-technology crime investigator, you can't afford to waste any time in your 12- to 14-hour, time-consuming day. You must understand and learn your new environment, the key players, and the issues that must be addressed first.

The GEC high-technology crime investigator must eventually get into a proactive mode to be successful. That is, you must identify problems and solutions *before* they come to the attention of management, which happens when the problem adversely affects costs and/or schedules.

> Adverse effects to costs and schedules run contrary to a company's business plans and negatively affect that company's globally competitive position.

When a high-technology crime investigator is in the position of constantly putting out fires, the proactive high-technology crime prevention battle is lost. If that battle is lost, the results are adverse impacts on costs and schedules. Thus, the goal of your cost-effective HTCPP probably was not attained. You must lead an effort to be cost-effective! When you first start, you will have to work hard to balance the time you spend fighting fires with the time spent on the development of the HTCPP.

WHAT IS EXPECTED OF YOU?

At GEC, you are told that you are expected to establish and manage an HTCPP that works and is not a burden on GEC. You are told to establish a program that you believe is necessary to get the job done. You have the full support of management, because they have come to realize how important high technology is to GEC maintaining its competitive advantage in the marketplace.

This "honeymoon" may last as long as 6 months. So, take advantage of it. To do so, you must have a fast start, and then pick up speed! After your honeymoon period, you better have a cost-effective HTCPP in place, or at least well on the way to having one, with plans showing how and when you will have completed the initial program and when it will be in "maintenance mode." By "maintenance mode," we mean that the baseline has been established. Now you are constantly updating the policies, procedures, and functions and finding more efficient and effective methods to doing your job and the jobs of those in your unit.

Based on the "blank management check" and your prior experience (or for the inexperienced high-technology crime investigator, the information gained reading this book), you evaluate the GEC environment and decide that the overall goal of GEC's HTCPP is to *administer an innovative HTCPP that mitigates crime at least impact to costs and schedules, while meeting all of GEC's and its customers' reasonable expectations.*

If this is what is expected of you, then it is your primary goal. Everything you do as the GEC high-technology crime investigator should be directed toward meeting this goal. This includes

- The high-technology crime prevention strategic plan
- The high-technology crime prevention tactical plan

- The high-technology crime prevention annual plan
- The organization of the high-technology crime prevention program and unit
- The functions to be established
- The process flow of those functions

GEC HIGH-TECHNOLOGY CRIME INVESTIGATOR RESPONSIBILITIES

As GEC's high-technology crime investigator, you have certain duties and responsibilities. These include the following:

1. *Managing people,* which includes
   - Building a reputation of professional integrity
   - Maintaining excellent business relationships
   - Dealing with changes
   - Communicating
   - Supporting staff and career development
   - Developing people through performance management (e.g., direct and help high-technology crime prevention staff to be results oriented)
   - Influencing people in a positive way
   - Building a team environment
2. *Managing the business of high-technology crime prevention,* which consists of
   - Demonstrating a commitment to results
   - Being customer/supplier focused
   - Taking responsibility for making decisions
   - Developing and managing resource allocations
   - Planning and organizing
   - Being a problem solver
   - Thinking strategically
   - Using sound business judgment
   - Accepting personal accountability and ownership
3. *Managing high-technology crime prevention processes,* which includes
   - Planning and implementing projects
   - Ensuring quality in everything
   - Maintaining a systems perspective
   - Maintaining current job knowledge

GOALS AND OBJECTIVES

Remember, your primary goal is to administer *an innovative HTCPP that mitigates crimes with least impact to costs and schedules, while meeting all of GEC's and its customers' reasonable expectations.* At the very least, you must have the following objectives:

- Enhancing the quality, efficiency, and effectiveness of the high-technology crime prevention organization
- Identifying potential problem areas and striving to mitigate them before GEC management and/or customers identify them
- Enhancing the company's ability to attract customers because of your ability to conduct high-technology crime investigations and inquiries efficiently, effectively, and discreetly
- Establishing the high-technology crime prevention organization as the high-technology crime prevention leader in the widget industry

LEADERSHIP POSITION

As the high-technology crime investigator and unit manager, you will be in a leadership position. In that position, it is extremely important that you understand what a leader is and how a leader acts. According to the definition of leaders and leadership found in numerous dictionaries and management books, it is basically the ability to lead, the leader of a group; a person who leads; directing, commanding, or guiding head, as of a group or activity.

As a *leader*, you must set the example. Create and foster an ethical and crime prevention consciousness within the company:

- As a *corporate leader* you must communicate the company's community involvement, eliminate unnecessary expenses, inspire corporate pride, and find ways to increase profitability.
- As a *team leader* you must encourage teamwork, communicate clear direction, create a high-technology crime prevention environment conducive to working as a team, and treat others as peers and team members—not as competitors, or worse yet, suspects.
- As a *personal leader* you must improve your leadership skills, accept and learn from constructive criticism, take ownership and responsibility for decisions, make decisions in a timely manner, and demonstrate self-confidence.

PROVIDING HIGH-TECHNOLOGY CRIME PREVENTION SERVICE AND SUPPORT

As the high-technology crime investigator and leader of a high-technology crime prevention service and support organization, you must be especially tuned to the needs, wants, and desires of your customers: those within the company, your boss, executive management, GEC managers, GEC employees (your internal customers), and your external customers (those who are not paid by GEC, such as suppliers and those who purchase GEC products). To provide service and support to your external customers, you must:

- Identify their high-technology crime prevention needs.
- Meet their reasonable expectations.
- Show by example that you can meet their expectations.
- Treat customer satisfaction as priority number one.
- Encourage feedback and listen.
- Understand customer needs and expectations.
- Treat customer requirements as an important part of the job.
- Establish measures to ensure customer satisfaction.
- Provide honest feedback to customers.

To provide service and support to your internal customers, you must:

- Support their business needs.
- Add value to their services.
- Minimize investigative and crime prevention program impact on current processes.
- Follow the same guidelines as for external customers.

The GEC high-technology crime investigator will also be dealing with suppliers of high-technology crime prevention products. These suppliers are a valuable ally because they can explain to you what's new in the area of high-technology crime and how their products mitigate those crimes. Generally, they can keep you up to date on the latest news within the high-technology crime investigator profession.

In dealing with suppliers of high-technology crime prevention-related products, you should:

- Advise them of your needs and the types of products that can help you.
- Assist them in understanding your requirements and the types of products that you want from them, including what modifications they must make to their products before you are willing to purchase them.
- Direct them in the support and assistance they are to provide you.
- Respect them as team members.
- Value their contributions.
- Require quality products and high standards of performance from them.
- Recognize their needs as well.

USE TEAM CONCEPTS

It is important that the GEC high-technology crime investigator understand that GEC's HTCPP is a company program. To be successful, the high-technology crime investigator cannot operate independently but must work as a team leader with a team of others who also have a vested interest in the mitigation of high-technology crime through an excellent HTCPP.

It is important to remember that a good HTCPP and functions will place responsibility on everyone to support the program and get involved in making it a success. This will require the high-technology crime investigator to improve and use the most important tool available—constant communication. The high-technology crime investigator must be sensitive to the division of functions, "turf," and office politics; and must ensure that even more communication and coordination occurs between all departments concerned.

The program must be sold to the management and staff of GEC. If it is presented as a law that must be followed "or else," then it will be doomed to failure. Everyone must understand why the program is necessary, be willing to abide by it, and see a personal need to support the HTCPP because they know it is the best way and in their own interests, as well as in the interest of GEC.

In GEC, as in many companies today, success can only be achieved through continuous interdepartmental communication, cooperation, and integrated project teams composed of specialists from various organizations for solving company problems. The high-technology crime investigator should keep in mind that teaming and success go together in today's modern corporations.

VISION, MISSION, AND QUALITY STATEMENTS

Many of today's modern corporations have developed vision, mission, and quality statements using a hierarchical process. The statements, if used, should link all levels in the management and organizational chain. The statements of the lower levels should be written and used to support the upper levels and vice versa.

Most employees seem to look at such "statements" as just another management task that is somehow supposed to help all employees understand their jobs. However, these statements are often developed in employee team meetings, get printed, placed on walls, and are soon forgotten. Confidentially, many managers do not place a high value on vision, mission, and quality statements either, and that is probably why they are presented by managers as nothing more than another task to be performed by or with employees.

This is unfortunate, since the concept of vision, mission, and quality statements is a good one. If the idea is presented with the right attitude and is used to focus on objectives employees as a team, it can help them to get a better understanding of why they are there doing what they are doing.

The following examples can be used by the high-technology crime investigator to develop such statements, if they are necessary. And, as you can already guess, they are required at GEC.

Vision Statements

In many of today's businesses, management develops a vision statement. The vision statement is usually a short paragraph that attempts to set the strategic goal, objective, or direction of the company. GEC has a vision statement and requires all organizations to have statements based on the GEC corporate statements.

What Is a Vision Statement?

A vision statement is a short statement that:

- Is clear, concise, and understandable by the employees
- Connects to ethics, values, and behaviors
- States where GEC wants to be (long term)
- Sets the tone
- Sets the direction for GEC

GEC Vision Statement

Design, produce, and sell a high-quality widget and thus expand market shares while continuing to improve processes to manage cost and meet customers' expectations.

GEC's Security Department Vision Statement

In partnership with our customers, provide a competitive advantage for the GEC widget by continuous protection of all GEC's assets without hindering productivity and support increased production of GEC widgets in a cost-effective manner.

High-Technology Crime Prevention Vision Statement

Provide the most efficient and effective high-technology crime prevention program for GEC, which adds value to GEC products and services as a recognized leader in the widget industry.

Mission Statements

Mission statements are declarations regarding the purpose of a business or government agency.

GEC Mission Statement

GEC's mission is to maintain its competitive advantage in the market place by providing widgets to our customers when they want them, where they want them, and at a fair price.

GEC's Security Department Mission Statement

The mission of GEC's security department is to provide low-cost, productivity-enhanced, technology-based assets protection services and support that will assist GEC in maintaining its competitive advantage in the marketplace.

High-Technology Crime Prevention Mission Statement

Administer an innovative HTCPP that assists in deterring or minimizing high-technology crime risks at least impact to cost and schedule, while meeting all the company's and customers' high-technology crime prevention requirements.

Quality Statements

Quality is what adds value to your company's products and services. It is what your internal and external customers expect from you.

GEC's Quality Statement

To provide quality widgets to our customers with zero defects by building it right the first time.

GEC's Security Department Quality Statement

To provide quality security support and services while enhancing the productivity opportunities of the GEC workforce.

High-Technology Crime Prevention Quality Statement

To provide quality high-technology crime prevention and investigative professional services and support that meet the customers' requirements and reasonable expectations, in concert with good business practices and company guidelines. (You may have noticed that the themes of service, support, cost-effectiveness, customer expectations, and so forth, run throughout this book. We hope their constant reinforcement will cause you to think of them when establishing and managing an HTCPP.)

HIGH-TECHNOLOGY CRIME PREVENTION PRINCIPLES

The high-technology crime investigator's duties and responsibilities are many and sometimes are quite complex and conflicting. However, as the GEC high-technology crime investigator, you must never lose sight of the four basic high-technology crime prevention principles:

1. Develop and support the development of policies, procedures, and processes that mitigate the motive, rationalization, and/or opportunity to violate GEC rules, policies, procedures, controls, and local, state, and federal laws.
2. Conduct statistical analyses and provide feedback to management relative to high-technology crime prevention investigations, threats, vulnerabilities, profiles of offenders, and preventive measures.
3. Conduct professional, efficient, and discreet high-technology crime investigations, inquiries, and surveys, and provide investigative reports to management.
4. Provide education and awareness training to staff.

These four high-technology crime prevention principles must be incorporated into the GEC HTCPP.

PROJECT AND RISK MANAGEMENT PROCESSES

Two basic processes that are an integral part of a HTCPP are project management and risk management.

Project Management

As the high-technology crime prevention manager and leader for GEC you will also provide oversight on high-technology crime prevention-related projects that are being worked by members of your staff. The criteria for a project are as follows. Formal projects, along with project management charts, will be initiated where improvements or other changes need to be accomplished and where that effort has an objective, beginning and ending dates, and a completion schedule greater than 30 days.

If the project will be accomplished in less than 30 days, a formal project management process is not needed. The rationale for this is that projects of short duration are not worth the effort (costs in terms of hours to complete the project plan, charts, and so on) of such a formal process.

Risk Management

To be cost-effective, the high-technology crime investigator must apply risk management concepts and identify:

- Threats to GEC assets, including personnel
- Vulnerabilities that some internal or external threat may use to its advantage
- Risks to GEC assets through analyses of the results of inquiries, investigations, and surveys
- The countermeasures to mitigate those risks in a cost-effective way

HIGH-TECHNOLOGY CRIME PREVENTION ORGANIZATIONAL RESPONSIBILITIES

As the GEC high-technology crime investigator, you will be managing and leading a high-technology crime prevention organization. You will be responsible for developing, implementing, maintaining, and administering a companywide HTCPP.

You have evaluated the GEC environment and found that a centralized HTCPP would not work at GEC. However, you do believe that leading a team of representatives from selected departments can cost-effectively jump-start the HTCPP and its associated processes.

GEC HIGH-TECHNOLOGY CRIME INVESTIGATOR FORMAL DUTIES AND RESPONSIBILITIES

In concert with executive management of GEC, the high-technology crime investigator has developed and received approval for formally establishing the following charter of the GEC high-technology crime investigator responsibilities. *The high-technology crime investigator manager is responsible for leading the development, implementation, maintenance, and administration of an overall, GEC-wide HTCPP and unit, including all plans, policies, procedures, and processes necessary to mitigate high-technology crime and to conduct applicable inquiries, surveys, and investigations effectively, efficiently, and discreetly.*

As the high-technology crime investigator manager, you are responsible for performing certain functions. At GEC these are as follows:

- Identify all government, customer, and GEC high-technology crime prevention requirements necessary for the mitigation of high-technology crime; interpret these requirements; and develop and lead the implementation and administration of GEC plans, policies, and procedures necessary to ensure compliance.
- Identify high-technology business practices and security violations/infractions, conduct inquiries, assess potential damage, direct and monitor GEC management's corrective action, and implement and recommend corrective/preventive action.
- Establish and direct a GEC-wide HTCPP.
- Develop, implement, and administer a proactive crime survey and inquiry program, provide analyses to management, and modify GEC and subcontractor requirements accordingly to ensure a minimal-cost HTCPP.
- Establish and administer a high-technology crime prevention awareness program for all GEC employees, customers, and subcontractors as part of the security department's security awareness program. Ensure attendees are cognizant of high-technology crime threats and preventive measures.
- Direct the development, acquisition, implementation, and administration of high-technology crime prevention software systems.
- Represent GEC on all high-technology crime prevention matters with customers, government agencies, suppliers, and other outside entities.
- Provide advice, guidance, and assistance to GEC management relative to high-technology crime prevention matters.
- Perform common management accountabilities in accordance with GEC's management policies and procedures.

SUMMARY

The high-technology crime investigator position is a leadership position within a company or organization. The recently hired high-technology crime investigator manager must know what is expected as GEC's new high-technology crime investigator and unit manager and should have a clear understanding of these expectations before taking the position.

The three primary responsibilities of a high-technology crime investigator are:

1. Managing people
2. Managing the high-technology crime prevention business
3. Managing high-technology crime investigation processes

The high-technology crime investigator must:

- Set forth clear goals and objectives.
- Be a company leader, team leader, and personal leader.
- Provide a high-technology crime prevention service and support using team concepts.
- Develop vision, mission, and quality statements as guides to developing a successful HTCPP.
- Strive to lead the administration of an HTCPP.

14

The High-Technology Crime Investigation Unit's Strategic, Tactical, and Annual Plans

The objective of this chapter is to establish the plans for the high-technology crime prevention organization that provides the GEC security department's strategic, tactical, and annual plans, as well as those of GEC overall. These plans will set the direction for GEC's HTCPP, and their integration will indicate that the HTCPP is an integral part of both the GEC security department and GEC itself.

INTRODUCTION

To be successful, the GEC high-technology crime investigator must have a high-technology crime prevention strategic plan. That plan should be integrated or at least compatible with GEC's security department and overall GEC strategic business plan (the 7-year plan). It is this plan that sets the long-term direction, goals, and objectives for the HTCPP. The GEC high-technology crime prevention strategic plan is the basic document on which to build the overall GEC HTCPP, with a goal of building a comprehensive high-technology crime prevention environment at least cost and impact to GEC.

When developing the high-technology crime prevention strategic plan, the high-technology crime investigator manager must ensure that the following basic high-technology crime prevention principles are included, either specifically or in principle (because it is part of the high-technology crime prevention strategy):

- Minimize the probability of a high-technology crime.
- Conduct professional, effective, efficient, and discreet inquiries or investigations if allegations of high-technology crimes are reported.

- Report the investigative findings to management (including an analysis of each investigation), coordinate the results with other security functions, and make recommendations to minimize the probability of recurrence.

The High-Technology Crime Prevention Strategic Plan Objective

The objectives of the high-technology crime prevention strategic plan are to:

- Minimize the probability of a high-technology crime.
- Minimize impact to costs.
- Minimize impact to schedules.
- Assist in meeting contractual requirements.
- Assist in meeting noncontractual requirements.
- Build a comprehensive high-technology crime-free and crime prevention environment.
- Be flexible to respond to changing needs.
- Support multiple customers' high-technology crime investigative needs.
- Incorporate new high technology and related investigative techniques as soon as needed.
- Assist in attracting new customers.
- Maximize the use of available resources.

The High-Technology Crime Prevention Strategic Plan and Team Concepts, Communication, and Coordination

To have a successful HTCPP, the strategy calls for one that also deals with the office politics aspects of the GEC environment. A key element is to remember that the information and information systems belong to GEC, not the security department or the high-technology crime investigator manager. Therefore, cooperation and coordination with all levels of GEC management and employees are a must.

Many functional organizations have an interest in the high-technology crime prevention strategic plan and other high-technology crime prevention-related plans; therefore, the plans should be discussed with other team members, such as auditors, security personnel, human resources personnel, legal staff, and so forth.

The high-technology crime prevention strategic plan should be discussed, and input should be requested from employees. After all, what *you* do affects what *they* do. It is a great way to get communication and interaction going. This will lead to a better plan and one that has a broad base of support.

The input and understanding by GEC management and employees of what the GEC high-technology crime investigator is trying to accomplish will assist in ensuring GEC-wide support for the high-technology crime prevention plans. For only by helping each other can the high-technology crime investigator's GEC's HTCPP succeed.

High-Technology Crime Prevention Strategic Plan Planning Considerations

The high-technology crime prevention strategic plan planning considerations must also include:

- Good business practices
- Quality management
- Innovative ideas
- Risk management philosophy and techniques
- High-technology crime prevention vision statement
- High-technology crime prevention mission statement
- High-technology crime prevention quality statement
- Channels of open communication with others such as the employees, auditors, systems personnel, security personnel, users, management, and so forth

All these factors must be considered when developing a high-technology crime prevention strategy and documenting that strategy in the GEC high-technology crime prevention strategic plan.

The GEC process flow of plans begins with the GEC strategic business plan through the GEC tactical business plan and GEC annual business plan. Each plan's goals and objectives must be able to support each other from the top down and the bottom up. After this process is understood, the next step is to map the GEC high-technology crime prevention strategic plan to the GEC security department's strategic business plan goals and objectives.

Mapping GEC's High-Technology Crime Prevention Strategic Plan to the GEC Security Department and GEC Strategic Business Plan

GEC's strategic business plan identifies the annual earnings for the next 7 years as well as market share percentage goals. This clearly underscores the need for an HTCPP that is cost effective. Furthermore, any high-technology crime investigation must also have as one of its goals the recuperation of any financial losses. This could be accomplished through such processes as recovery or supporting legal action against the violators.

Any overhead program, one that is not directly related to building the widget (e.g., the HTCPP) is a "parasite" on the profits of GEC if it cannot be shown to be a value-added function (i.e., needed to support the bottom line). Therefore, the high-technology crime prevention strategy must be efficient (cheap) and effective (good). If that can be accomplished, then the HTCPP will be in a position to support GEC's strategy relative to earnings and market share.

Mapping these points (e.g., visually tying plans together using flowcharts or organization chart formats) can help the high-technology crime investigator visualize a strategy prior to documenting that strategy in the high-technology crime prevention strategic plan. The mapping will also assist the high-technology crime investigator in focusing on the strategies that support the GEC strategies. Of course, it also must be integrated into the overall GEC security department's plans. For example:

- GEC strategic goal #1: Increase employee productivity.
- Security department's supporting goal #1: Minimize the adverse impact of assets protection on the productivity of employees while maintaining an acceptable level of risk relative to the misappropriation, destruction, modification, and theft of GEC assets.
- High-technology crime prevention strategic plan goal #1: Coordinate with employees' managers prior to interviewing employees and, when possible, establish a time for the interview that will not adversely affect or will minimize the impact, of employees' work schedules.

Writing the High-Technology Crime Prevention Strategic Plan

Writing the high-technology crime prevention strategic plan will be much easier when the mapping is completed. After that is accomplished, the high-technology crime investigator will write the high-technology crime prevention strategic plan following the standard GEC format for plan writing.

The GEC format is as follows:

1. Executive summary
2. Table of contents
3. Introduction
4. Vision statement
5. Mission statement
6. Quality statement

7. High-technology crime prevention strategic goals
8. How the high-technology crime prevention strategies support GEC strategies
9. Mapping charts
10. Conclusion

GEC'S HIGH-TECHNOLOGY CRIME PREVENTION TACTICAL PLAN

A tactical plan is a short-range (3-year) plan that supports the GEC high-technology crime prevention strategic plan goals and objectives. The high-technology crime prevention tactical plan should:

- Identify and define, in more detail, the vision of a comprehensive high-technology crime prevention environment, as stated in the high-technology crime prevention strategic plan.
- Identify and define the current GEC high-technology crime prevention environment.
- Identify the process to be used to determine the differences between the two.

After this is accomplished, the high-technology crime investigator can identify projects to progress from the current GEC high-technology crime prevention environment to where they should be, as stated in the high-technology crime prevention strategic plan. In the high-technology crime prevention tactical plan, it is also important to keep in mind GEC's:

- Business direction
- Customers' direction
- Direction of high technology

After that is established, the individual projects can be identified and implemented, beginning with the high-technology crime prevention annual plan.

The GEC tactical business plan states that *it is expected to be able to integrate new high-technology hardware, software, networks, and devices with minimum impact to schedules or costs.* The GEC security department's tactical business plan, which supports the GEC plan, is to *provide adequate protection to the new high-technology equipment and devices at least impact to GEC schedules and costs.* Therefore, it will be necessary to establish a project with the objective of training all high-technology crime investigators on the new technologies prior to or soon after their arrival. After all, the location of the new technologies will be the potential new crime scene.

The high-technology crime investigator must then also consider that the GEC HTCPP must contain processes to upgrade high-technology crime investigative methodologies that will be used in conducting investigations in the new environment. Therefore, a project must be established to accomplish that goal.

The GEC tactical business plan also called for the *completion* of an HTCPP within 3 years. Therefore, another project that must be developed is one that can accomplish this goal.

Writing the High-Technology Crime Prevention Tactical Plan

Writing the high-technology crime prevention tactical plan should be somewhat easier based on the experience gained in mapping the goals for the high-technology crime prevention strategic and tactical plans and writing the high-technology crime prevention strategic plan. Only after these tasks are completed can the high-technology crime investigator manager write the high-technology crime prevention tactical plan following the standard GEC format for plan writing.

The GEC format is as follows:

1. Executive summary
2. Table of contents
3. Introduction
4. High-technology crime prevention strategic goals
5. How the high-technology crime prevention tactics support the high-technology crime prevention strategic plan
6. How the high-technology crime prevention tactics support GEC tactics
7. Mapping charts
8. Conclusion

GEC'S HIGH-TECHNOLOGY CRIME PREVENTION ANNUAL PLAN

The high-technology crime investigator manager must also develop a high-technology crime prevention annual plan to support the GEC security department and overall GEC high-technology crime prevention strategic and tactical plans. The plan must include goals, objectives, and projects that will support the goals and objectives of both GEC's and the security department's annual business plans.

GEC's and the security department's high-technology crime prevention annual plan is used to identify and implement projects to accomplish the annual goals and objectives stated in the high-technology crime prevention strategic and tactical plans. These projects are the "building blocks" of the HTCPP.

The HTCPP requires the following:

- Project management techniques
- Gantt charts (schedule)
- Identified beginning date for each project
- Identified ending date for each project
- An objective for each project
- Costs tracking and budget
- Identification of the responsible project lead

High-Technology Crime Prevention Annual Plan Projects

The initial and major project of the GEC high-technology crime investigator's first high-technology crime prevention annual plan is to begin to identify the current GEC high-technology crime prevention environment. To gain an understanding of the current GEC environment, culture, and philosophy, the following projects are to be established:

Project 1

Project title: GEC high-technology crime prevention organization
Project lead: High-technology crime investigator
Objective: Establish a high-technology crime prevention organization.
Start date: June 15, 2006
End date: December 1, 2006

Project 2

Project title: High-technology crime prevention policies and procedures review
Project lead: High-technology crime investigator
Objective: Identify and review all high-technology crime prevention-related GEC documentation, and establish a process to ensure applicability and currency.
Start date: February 1, 2006
End date: April 1, 2006

Project 3

Project title: High-technology crime prevention team
Project lead: High-technology crime investigator

Objective: Establish a GEC high-technology crime prevention work-
ing group to assist in establishing and supporting an HTCPP.
Start date: June 1, 2006
End date: July 1, 2006

Project 4

Project title: High-technology crime prevention organizational functions
Project lead: High-technology crime investigator
Objective: Identify and establish high-technology crime prevention
organizational functions and their associated processes and work
instructions.
Start date: June 15, 2006
End date: December 15, 2006

Mapping the GEC High-Technology Crime Prevention Annual Plan to the GEC Security Department and Overall GEC Annual Business Plan

As was done with the other plan (Figure 14-1), the GEC high-technology
crime prevention annual plan to the GEC annual business plan can be easily accomplished.

Writing the High-Technology Crime Prevention Annual Plan

As noted earlier, writing of the plans must follow the GEC format. The
GEC high-technology crime prevention annual plan is no exception, and
the following format is required:

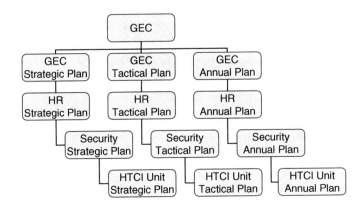

Figure 14-1   Mapping of plans up and down the oranizational structure.

1. Executive summary
2. Table of contents
3. Introduction
4. High-technology crime prevention annual goals
5. High-technology crime prevention projects
6. How the high-technology crime prevention projects support GEC's annual plan goals
7. Mapping charts
8. Conclusion

Mapping High-Technology Crime Prevention Strategic, Tactical, and Annual Plans to Projects Using a Matrix

Another approach to mapping is to use a matrix. This method can be used in a number of ways, and at various levels (e.g., GEC Strategic business plan to high-technology crime prevention strategic plan). It can identify "holes" in your plans that must be addressed.

SUMMARY

When it comes to high-technology crime prevention planning, the high-technology crime investigator manager must integrate the plans with those of the GEC security department and GEC overall. Remember that:

- The GEC HTCPP strategic, tactical, and annual plans must be mapped and integrated into the GEC strategic, tactical, and annual business plans.
- The high-technology crime prevention plans must incorporate the high-technology crime prevention vision, mission, and quality statements, and their philosophies and concepts.
- The high-technology crime prevention plans must identify strategies, goals, objectives, and projects that support each other and the GEC plans.
- By mapping the goals of the GEC plans with those of the high-technology crime prevention plans, the required information fusion can take place and can be graphically represented.
- Mapping will make it easier for the high-technology crime investigator to write the applicable high-technology crime prevention plans.
- The high-technology crime prevention annual plan generally consists of projects that are the building blocks of the HTCPP, following the strategies and tactics of the high-technology crime prevention strategic and tactical plans.

15

High-Technology Crime Investigation Program and Organization

The objective of this chapter is to describe and discuss the establishment and management of the organization chartered with the responsibility to lead the high-technology crime prevention effort for GEC, including describing the organization, structuring the organization, and detailing the job descriptions of the personnel to be hired to fill the positions within the high-technology crime prevention organization.

INTRODUCTION

Although the vast majority of corporations are not large enough or have that many incidents (hopefully) to establish a separate high-technology crime investigations unit, in this case we will assume it does as a sub-organization of the GEC security department (Fig. 15-1) This has several advantages in that the information provided can be:

- Incorporated into a corporate investigation unit as part of a security department
- Established as a separate organization under the corporate security department or other department when necessary
- Established as a function in a separate company that provides security services and support for those corporations who outsource their investigative function
- Established into a separate law enforcement investigative bureau unit, with some modifications resulting from the difference in managing a law enforcement function and a corporate security-related function

Thus, the information provided allows for some flexibility in meeting your various objectives for applying this information in a range of

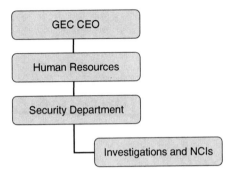

Figure 15-1   GEC's security department organizational chart (NCI: noncompliance inquiry).

environments. In some cases, the unit may be a subset of the investigation and noncompliance inquiry (NCI) organization. An NCI is considered an investigation but is related to violations of corporate policies, whereas an investigation is conducted when there is a violation of external regulations or laws. Generally, these are conducted by outside law enforcement agencies; however, GEC investigators may conduct a preliminary investigation to determine the validity of the allegation. Furthermore, using the term *NCI* instead of *investigation* gives the impression the incident is less serious (which in fact it is) and thus there will hopefully be less talk or rumors spreading about the "investigations being conducted at GEC."

When establishing such an investigative unit you can, and probably should, use the same processes as you would in setting up any other security department unit and its various functions. This means that the processes used to establish the personnel security, administrative security, operational security, and other security organizations or functions can be applied to establishing and managing the high-technology crime investigation organization.

HIGH-TECHNOTLOGY CRIME INVESTIGATION UNIT DRIVERS

Why has the CSO of GEC decided to form a high-technology crime investigations unit? Hopefully, it was not based on a perceived need to expand the bureaucracy for personal gain (e.g., more staff, higher management position). So, why would such a unit be formed? Something must have driven the CSO to make such a decision; these things are called *drivers* (Fig. 15-2). All security functions should be established and managed based on drivers. The drivers include:

- Numerous violations of corporate policies; in general, assets protection policies related to high technology
- Numerous violations of regulations and laws related to high technology

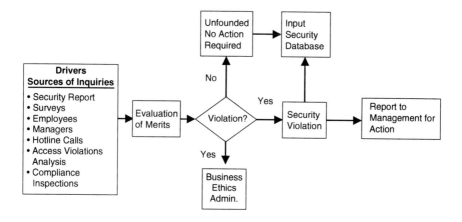

Figure 15-2 Items that drive high-technology crime investigations.

- GEC is a high-technology corporation that is based on high technology; therefore, all violations of any kind are likely to be related to high technology.
- Risk management studies have found the need for such a unit and it should develop and manage an HTCPP.
- The CSO, supported by GEC executive management, has decided such a unit was necessary to minimize the loss of high technology and thus GEC's competitive edge in the global marketplace.

> The unit should be established based on some needs, some requirements, which we call *drivers*. These drivers are what make the establishment of a high-technology crime investigative unit necessary.

HIGH-TECHNOLOGY CRIME INVESTIGATOR MANAGER THOUGHT PROCESS IN ESTABLISHING THE HTCPP AND INVESTIGATION ORGANIZATION

The GEC high-technology crime investigator manager must now begin the arduous task of establishing a high-technology crime prevention and investigation program and organization. In doing so, the high-technology crime investigator must understand:

- The extent and limits of authority
- The amount of budget available

- The impact of establishing an HTCPP on GEC (e.g., the culture change)
- The overall functional process, at least in summary form, to begin with

SECURITY FUNCTIONAL PROCESS SUMMARY

1. *Process name:* High-Technology Crime Investigations and NCIs
2. *Process description:* Provide professional high-technology investigative and NCI support to all corporate sites
3. *Supplier:* Customers and GEC employees
4. *Input:* Complaints, allegations, requests for assistance, and asset protection requirements
5. *Subprocesses:* High-technology-related investigations, NCIs, high-technology crime prevention surveys and programs
6. *Customers:* GEC management, GEC employees, and customers
7. *Output:* Investigative reports, security assessment reports, briefings, survey reports, testimony
8. *Requirements and directives that govern the process (drivers):* Corporate assets protection program (CAPP) and GEC policies, laws, regulations, and management decisions

The high-technology crime investigator manager must also determine how to find qualified people who can build and maintain a cost-effective HTCPP. The staff must also be able to develop into a high-technology crime prevention team in which everyone acts and is treated as a professional. They must form a group of high-technology crime prevention investigative professionals who are talented and yet leave their egos at the door when they come to work (not an easy task for very talented people!).

The high-technology crime investigator manager must also consider that building an empire and a massive, bureaucratic organization will not only give the wrong impression to GEC management, but also will be costly. Furthermore, the manager must build an efficient and effective high-technology crime prevention organization, as required by GEC and as stated in the numerous plans. After all, wasn't that one of the implied conditions of employment?

Building a bureaucracy leads to cumbersome processes, which leads to slow decision cycles, which causes high-technology crime prevention to have an adverse impact on costs and schedules for GEC, which leads to an HTCPP that does not provide the services and support needed by GEC. This snowballing effect, once started, will be difficult to stop. And if stopped, it requires twice as long to rebuild the service and support reputation of the manager, high-technology crime investigators, organization, and the HTCPP.

When developing the high-technology crime prevention organization, the manager must also bear in mind all that has been discussed with GEC management, including:

- GEC's history, business, and the competitive environment
- Mission, vision, and quality statements
- GEC and high-technology crime prevention plans
- Need for developing an HTCPP as quickly as possible because the work will not wait until the manager is fully prepared

HIGH-TECHNOLOGY CRIME INVESTIGATIVE ORGANIZATION

The high-technology crime investigator manager was hired as an investigator and manager of the new organization to be formed. However, little did he know that the only guidance given was to follow the GEC format and to develop a charter that would be approved through the GEC process for approving new organizations. He quickly found that the paperwork, meetings, and various bureaucratic requirements were not only more than he expected, but they were also taking up the majority of his workday. After researching the GEC files and reviewing other organizational charters and talking to other managers, human resources personnel, the legal staff, security personnel, audit managers, and, of course, the director of security, the following charter was submitted for approval.

High-Technology Crime Prevention and Investigation Organization Charter

Purpose of the organization: Lead a GEC-wide effort to mitigate high-technology criminal activities and, when identified, to investigate such incidents thoroughly.

Responsibilities:

- Develop and manage an HTCPP as an integral part of the security department's asset protection program.
- Conduct high-technology crime investigations and report the results to applicable management when there are allegations of unlawful activity.
- Conduct high-technology crime inquiries and report the results to appropriate management when there are indications of violations of GEC policies and/or procedures that adversely affect GEC.

- Conduct proactive high-technology crime prevention surveys upon management request and report the results to management.
- Represent GEC as the focal point for all high-technology crime investigation coordination with local, state, federal, and foreign investigative agencies; other members of the criminal justice system; and other authorities as required.
- Serve as GEC liaison with customers, subcontractors, government agencies, suppliers, and other non-GEC agencies with regard to high-technology crime prevention and investigative matters.
- Provide the ability to conduct high-technology forensic support for all investigations.

After gaining the approval of the director of security, the manager submitted the document to the organizational development focal point in the human resources department and hoped for the best. After all, nothing should really go wrong because the director of security already signed off on it.

DETERMINING THE NEED FOR HIGH-TECHNOLOGY CRIME INVESTIGATION SUBORDINATE ORGANIZATIONS

The human resources manager who reviewed the draft organizational charter was told that all charters were considered to be in the draft stage and were stamped accordingly until they had been sent through the formal approval process—estimated time until completion: unknown, of course. However, the CSO could not wait until final approval was given, so assuming approval, he gave the go-ahead to put together the organizational structure.

> The manager must determine whether subordinate organizations are needed. If so, a functional work breakdown structure must be developed to determine how many subordinate organizations are needed and which functions should be integrated into which subordinate organizations.

The high-technology crime investigative manager discussed the current and potential workload with the boss (CSO), audit manager, and the legal staff. They subsequently determined that there was not enough money nor was there enough of an investigative workload at this time to warrant developing subordinate organizations.

HIGH-TECHNOLOGY CRIME INVESTIGATION JOB DESCRIPTIONS FOR THE UNIT

The following detailed high-technology crime investigation functional descriptions were developed and approved by the applicable GEC departments.

High-Technology Crime Investigative Administrative Support

Position summary: Provide all technical administrative support for the high-technology crime investigation organization, including filing, typing reports, word processing, and developing related spreadsheets, databases, and text/graphic presentations.

Qualifications: This position requires a high school diploma, 1 year of security administration or 2 years of clerical experience. Must be computer literate in word processing, spreadsheet and database creation, and able to type at least 60 words per minute.

High-Technology Crime Investigator Associate

Position summary: Assist and support high-technology crime investigative staff in conducting administrative inquiries and surveys.

Duties and responsibilities:

1. Support the implementation and administration of high-technology crime investigation software support systems.
2. Provide advice, guidance, and assistance to employees relative to high-technology crime prevention matters.
3. Identify current high-technology crime prevention functional processes and assist in the development of automated tools to support those functions.
4. Assist in the analysis of manual high-technology crime prevention functions, and provide input to recommendations and reports of the analyses to high-technology crime investigative management.
5. Collect, compile, and generate high-technology functional informational reports and briefing packages for presentation to customers and management.
6. Perform other functions as assigned by high-technology crime investigation management.

Qualifications: This position requires a bachelor's degree in a high-technology, business, security, criminal justice, or social science profession.

High-Technology Crime Analyst

Position summary: Identify, schedule, administer, and perform assigned technical high-technology crime analysis functions.

Duties and responsibilities:

1. Represent GEC's high-technology crime investigation organization to other organizations on select high-technology crime and crime prevention-related matters.
2. Provide advice, guidance, and assistance to managers, employees, and guests relative to high-technology crime and crime prevention matters.
3. Provide general advice and assistance in the interpretation of high-technology crime prevention requirements.
4. Identify high-technology crime prevention requirements necessary for the mitigation and deterrence of unlawful conduct.
5. Identify current high-technology crime prevention functional processes and develop or acquire automated tools to support those functions.
6. Analyze manual high-technology crime prevention functions, and provide recommendations and reports of the analyses to high-technology crime prevention management.
7. Maintain, modify, and enhance automated high-technology crime prevention functional systems and processes.
8. Collect, compile, and generate high-technology crime and crime prevention functional informational reports and briefing packages for presentation to customers and management.
9. Perform other functions as assigned by high-technology crime investigation management.
10. Conduct NCIs, including identifying and analyzing high-technology crime prevention business practice irregularities and high-technology crime prevention violations/infractions; conduct detailed inquiries; assess potential damage; monitor corrective action; and recommend preventive, cost-effective measures to preclude recurrences.
11. Perform limited risk assessments of high-technology crime prevention systems and processes; determine their threats, vulnerabilities, and risks; and recommend cost-effective risk mitigation solutions.
12. Plan, conduct, and lead high-technology crime surveys.

Qualifications: This position requires a bachelor's degree in a high-technology, business, social science, security, or criminal justice profession and at least 2 years of relevant practical experience.

High-Technology Crime Analyst Senior

Position summary: Identify, evaluate, conduct, schedule, and lead technical high-technology crime and crime prevention analysis functions, inquiries, surveys, and investigations.

Duties and responsibilities:

1. Provide technical analysis of high-technology crime prevention requirements necessary for the protection of all high-technology assets; interpret those requirements; and implement and administer GEC plans, policies, and procedures.
2. Represent high-technology crime and crime prevention investigative matters with other entities as assigned.
3. Provide advice, guidance, and assistance to senior management, system managers, system users, and system custodians relative to high-technology crime and crime prevention matters.
4. Perform other functions as assigned by high-technology crime investigation management.
5. Conduct NCIs, including identifying and conducting technical analyses of high-technology crime prevention business practices and violations/infractions; plan, coordinate, and conduct detailed inquiries; assess potential damage; and develop and implement corrective action plans.
6. Conduct proactive high-technology crime surveys and investigations, and prepare reports of the results for presentation to management.
7. Support high-technology investigations through the use of high-technology devices and equipment.

Qualifications: This position requires a bachelor's degree in a high-technology, business, criminal justice, security, or social science profession and 4 years of practical, related experience.

High-Technology Crime Analyst Specialist

Position summary: Act as technical high-technology crime prevention advisor, focal point, and leader to ensure all high-technology crime prevention functions and investigations meet GEC requirements; and conduct computer forensics examinations.

Duties and responsibilities:

1. Act as technical advisor for complex high-technology crime investigations.

2. Represent the high-technology crime investigation organization with other entities as assigned.
3. Provide advice, guidance, and assistance to senior management, IT managers, system users, and system custodians relative to high-technology crime and crime prevention matters.
4. Perform other functions as assigned by high-technology crime prevention management.

Qualifications: This position requires a bachelor's degree in a high-technology profession and 6 years of high-technology crime prevention experience.

High-Technology Crime Systems Engineer

Position summary: Act as a technical systems management consultant, focal point, and project leader for high-technology crime investigations and crime prevention functions and programs developed to ensure GEC requirements are met; and conduct compute forensics examinations.

Duties and responsibilities:

1. Act as a lead in the identification of government, customer, and GEC high-technology crime investigations and meet crime prevention requirements; interpret those requirements and develop, implement, and administer GEC high-technology crime prevention plans, policies, and procedures.
2. Represent the high-technology crime investigation organization, when applicable, on high-technology crime and crime prevention matters and serve as GEC's liaison with customers, government agencies, suppliers, and other outside entities.
3. Provide advice, guidance, and assistance to senior and executive management, GEC subcontractors, and government entities relative to high-technology crime and crime prevention matters.
4. Provide technical consultation, guidance, and assistance to all GEC management, and system users; and high-technology crime prevention software systems by providing controls, processes, and procedures.
5. Establish, direct, coordinate, and maintain high-technology crime investigation and crime prevention processes.
6. Act as lead for the technical evaluation and testing of crime prevention and crime investigation hardware, firmware, and software.
7. Develop or direct the development of original techniques, procedures, and utilities for conducting high-technology crime prevention risk assessments and schedules.

8. Direct and/or lead others in conducting technical high-technology crime investigations and crime prevention countermeasure surveys to support high-technology crime prevention requirements and report findings.
9. Investigate methods and procedures related to the high-technology crime prevention aspects of microcomputers, LANs, WANs, Internet, GII, and NII networks, and their associated connectivity and communications.
10. Develop and maintain high-technology crime prevention-related databases.
11. Recommend and obtain approval for procedural changes to effect high-technology crime prevention implementations with emphasis on least-cost/minimum risk.
12. Lead and direct high-technology crime investigations and crime prevention personnel in the conduct of investigations, surveys, and inquiries.
13. Participate in the development and promulgation of high-technology crime prevention information for general awareness.
14. Perform other functions as assigned by the high-technology crime prevention manager.

Qualifications: This position requires a bachelor's degree or higher in a high-technology, security, criminal justice, social science, or psychology profession and a minimum of 10 years of high-technology crime prevention-related experience.

RECRUITING HIGH-TECHNOLOGY CRIME PREVENTION PROFESSIONALS

After the manager has gotten the high-technology crime investigation and crime prevention organizational structure, and the high-technology crime prevention functional job descriptions approved through the human resource process, the next task is to begin recruiting and hiring qualified high-technology crime prevention professionals. To do so, the manager should first determine the following:

- How many high-technology crime investigators are needed and at what level?
- What functions will they perform?
- How many are needed in each function?
- How many are needed in what pay grade?

The high-technology crime investigator manager must plan for the gradual hiring of personnel to meet the high-technology crime investigations needs based on a prioritized listing of functions. Obviously, a mixture of personnel should be considered. One or two high-level personnel should be hired to begin establishing the basic high-technology crime investigations. In addition, these more experienced investigators are capable of handling a greater range of functions and investigations. A less experienced person would be limited in skills and could very well damage the fledgling organization's reputation by actually conducting an inadequate investigation.

Personnel who meet the qualifications of a high-technology crime investigator engineer should be hired immediately. At least two should be hired. One would be the project lead to begin the process of assisting the manager in establishing the formal functions of the HTCPP. The other would begin the process of assisting the manager in formalizing the high-technology crime investigative processes.

For the high-technology crime investigator manager who is quickly trying to build an HTCPP and high-technology crime prevention organization, compromises on staff selection may come into play because very few ideal candidates are usually found. In either case, it is important to quickly begin the hiring process.

IDENTIFYING IN-HOUSE HIGH-TECHNOLOGY CRIME INVESTIGATOR CANDIDATES

Those individuals within the GEC organization who have been providing the audit function, security duties, and information systems security functions may be good job candidates because they know the GEC culture, processes, and people. They have talents that, with some training, can probably make them into good or excellent investigators. In addition, because these potential candidates already work for GEC, their transfer to the new organization would be faster than locating and hiring those candidates from outside GEC. Furthermore, the in-house training time would be faster because outsiders would have to learn the GEC processes, culture, contacts, and so forth. Insiders should already be aware of them. Members of the IT department may also be a place to recruit high-technology crime investigators.

> When hiring personnel, you may have to decide which is the best course: teach someone with a technical background the necessary investigative skills or teach an investigator the relevant aspects of technology?

A word of caution to the manager is needed. Most managers do not take kindly to you recruiting their employees because it means they will be short-handed until they can find replacements. In addition, the high-technology crime investigator manager should beware of individuals who managers recommend. These may just be the people that the manager has been trying to find some way to get rid of for some time. The high-technology crime investigator manager has enough problems building a high-technology crime investigative unit and crime prevention program, establishing and managing a high-technology crime prevention organization, handling the day-to-day high-technology crime prevention problems, attending endless meetings, hiring professional high-technology crime prevention staff, transferring personnel who don't meet the high-technology crime investigator's ideal expectations, never mind being saddled with a manager-recommended employee who turns out to be a *difficult* employee. A difficult employee will occupy the manager's time more than three other staff members combined! So, *beware of geeks bearing gifts!*

IDENTIFYING OUTSIDE HIGH-TECHNOLOGY CRIME INVESTIGATOR CANDIDATES

There are many sources that can be used to recruit talented high-technology crime investigators, many limited only by imagination and budget (especially budget). Regardless of how or where you recruit, the recruitment must be coordinated with the human resources staff.

To recruit high-technology crime investigators, there is a process that must be gone through to validate the position opening, budget, and so forth. This process normally does not work quickly. The manager must be prepared for this gap between identification of a candidate, interview, selection, approval, and hiring and start date. It is not unusual for such recruitment to take several months, sometimes as long as six or more.

> The newly hired, optimistic, and enthusiastic high-technology crime investigator manager usually soon begins to realize that building and managing an outstanding, state-of-the-art high-technology crime investigation and crime prevention unit staffed by talented high-technology crime prevention professionals may become more of a dream than a reality!

The usual way to recruit high-technology crime investigators, along with the support of the human resources department, is to:

- Place local advertisement in trade journals, newspapers, and so forth.
- Hire a consulting firm to find the right people.
- Pass the word among colleagues.

- Ask the High-Technology Crime Investigation Association to pass the word.
- Use your own network of friends and associates.
- Advise the local law enforcement agencies, because they may have investigators who will soon be retiring and who have done some high-technology crime investigative work.
- Use the Internet to advertise the position.

With a few high-technology crime investigators onboard, the manager and staff can begin to work on:

- Establishing the high-technology crime investigative processes
- Conducting inquiries, investigations, and surveys
- Beginning the process of establishing an HTCPP

SUMMARY

In summary, you should remember that:

- Establishing an effective and efficient high-technology crime investigative unit and crime prevention program requires a detailed analysis and integration of all the information that has been learned.
- Determining the need for a high-technology crime investigative subordinate unit requires detailed analysis of company environment, budget, and an understanding of how to apply resource allocation techniques successfully to the high-technology crime investigative and crime prevention functions.
- After the need for a high-technology crime prevention subordinate organization is determined, then the high-technology crime investigator must determine what functions must be performed and in what priority.
- Establishing a formal high-technology crime investigative unit and high-technology crime investigator job "family" requires cooperation with the human resource department and others; patience and understanding are mandatory.
- A high-technology crime investigator manager who establishes a new organization for a corporation will be compelled to work within a less than ideal corporate world where forms and bureaucracies rule the day. To survive, the high-technology crime investigator manager must understand how to use those processes efficiently and effectively. This is where the skills of being people oriented, being experienced in working sources, and having contacts can help smooth the way.
- In most corporations, currently employed personnel who desire a high-technology crime investigative position and who meet the

minimum requirements must be hired before hiring an individual from the outside.

- Recruiting qualified professionals can only be accomplished through widespread recruitment effort, using many marketing media; successful advertisement is sometimes a factor of how much recruitment budget is available.

16

High-Technology Crime Investigative Functions

The objective of this chapter is to describe and discuss the major high-technology crime investigative functions that are to be performed by the high-technology crime investigation unit and to describe the flow of processes that can be used to establish the baseline in performing the functions.

INTRODUCION

When determining what functions are to be performed by the high-technology crime investigative unit, it is important to go back to the charter of duties and responsibilities assigned to the unit. Based on that charter, as noted in Chapter 15, specific functions can be identified. In this way, the drivers for each high-technology investigative function are tied directly to the charter of duties and responsibilities, which has been approved by the CSO and other necessary layers of management.

DETERMINING MAJOR HIGH-TECHNOLOGY CRIME INVESTIGATIVE FUNCTIONS

High-technology crime investigative functions may be defined in numerous ways. However, the manager of the high-technology crime investigation unit, after careful analysis and coordination, established five basic functions to be performed by the unit:

- Awareness program
- Surveys
- Risk management studies
- Investigations
- NCIs

The analysis of GEC's culture, environment, and the unit charter was conducted because the establishment of a high-technology crime unit is a very sensitive matter. This is especially true in high-technology-related corporations—and GEC is no exception—because GEC management seem to have more of a "college campus" atmosphere and are often called a "campus." Therefore, they often treat security, controls, and investigative matters as something that is hopefully unneeded and unwarranted. However, management has no recourse but to have such functions to safeguard the interest of the shareholders, especially as required by current laws and regulations for publically held corporations.

The high-technology crime investigation unit manager has coordinated his ideas about the functional breakdown, obviously with the boss, but also with the audit manager, InfoSec manager, and the legal staff. This was done because the manager knew that their support is needed if the unit is to be successful. In addition, their experience and advice will assist in ensuring that the functions are not only supported, but that the functions do not overlap, contradict, or interfere with functions in any other of GEC's organizations.

Furthermore, the coordination effort was another indication of the manager trying to do the right thing and be a team player. The worst thing, the manager knew, would be to develop and implement such functions in a vacuum, because it may be the wrong thing to do or the manager may have had to reword or drop some functions altogether if they were not properly perceived or structured, or conflicted with others' functions. In addition, the manager would then look bad, be embarrassed, and "lose face." Because many others in GEC were watching and hoping for the unit's failure, the manager didn't want to give them any excuses to say "I told you so."

The first function that the high-technology crime unit was to perform was to support the security department by integrating high-technology anticrime policies, procedures, and awareness information into those processes already established by and operational within the security department. The unit manager enthusiastically agreed with this approach because it saved the unit in terms of budget and other resources, because it was easier to add documents, slides, and other high-technology crime and anticrime media than to establish an entire program (with additional personnel and other resources). Thus, GEC would save money because of the efficiency gains of an integrated program. It was also another good indication of being a team player and gaining the manager "points" in the office politics arena.

The second function that the high-technology crime unit was to perform was to conduct high-technology crime investigations. These investigations were only to be related to those matters that were in violation of local, state, federal, or international laws. Allegations of criminal conduct by an employee were to be evaluated regarding their merit and coordinated with the legal staff and others as appropriate. A decision would then be reached regarding whether to conduct the investigation, refer it immediately to the appropriate law enforcement office, or classify it as an inquiry for the purpose of determining whether there was sufficient evidence to refer it to a law enforcement agency.

GEC management was always hesitant to refer matters to the local law enforcement authorities for the following reasons:

- Such allegations normally caused the employee in question to sue GEC, costing a great deal of money in legal fees, regardless of whether they won.
- The bad publicity and poor public image caused by allegations of high-technology fraud and other crimes by employees always concerned stockholders and was bad for business.

In addition, the law enforcement investigators were often not competent in handling such investigations, they took a great deal of the employees' time for interviews, other employees had to be dedicated to supporting their requests for assistance, computers were sometimes taken off-line to search for evidence during peak operational hours, the investigation tended to drag on or get buried by higher priorities of the law enforcement investigator, and in the end the cases were dropped or prosecution was declined by the prosecutor. If the matter did go to a trial, more bad publicity followed and the defendants were often found not guilty by the jury or judge. In most cases, it appeared to be the result of their lack of understanding of what the defendant had done and how. Also, it appeared that "not guilty" verdicts of the past were, in some cases, the result of poor investigations.

In fact, because the high-technology crime investigations conducted by law enforcement ended up including most of the issues identified earlier, the idea of a GEC high-technology crime investigative unit was born. GEC executive management believed that such a unit would cost little compared with the benefits of having such a unit in house. If it could save GEC the legal costs of even one employee's lawsuit that was settled out of court, it could pay for the unit's budget costs for several years!

The third function that the high-technology crime unit was to perform was to conduct NCIs at the request of management. The NCIs would be either a "preliminary" high-technology crime investigation or an inquiry into a violation of GEC policies, procedures, or rules. It was decided to differentiate between a criminal investigation and an NCI, because even if the allegations were of a criminal nature, obviously some GEC policies or procedures would have been violated. Therefore, these investigations were considered to be violations of GEC rules. If the NCI determined that a criminal act had occurred, then management would be in a better position to look at the options of internal, nontermination disciplinary action against the employee, termination for cause, allowing the employee to resign, or referring the matter to law enforcement authorities. In other words, it gave GEC management options.

The fourth function that the high-technology crime unit was to perform was to conduct crime prevention surveys. These surveys were used to indicate areas in which the potential for high-technology crime might be high and to determine whether there were any indications that crimes were being committed. They were also to be conducted as a form of risk management to determine whether there were external or internal threats and GEC vulnerabilities that would cause GEC to take unacceptable risks.

The fifth function that the high-technology crime unit was to perform was to establish and lead a high-technology anticrime (or crime prevention) program, with the objective of being a deterrent especially to those within GEC who would contemplate the commission of a high-technology crime either against GEC or through the use of GEC resources. It was hoped that this program would lessen the motivation of an employee to commit such a crime; as well as eliminate the opportunity. The unit manager believed that if the employees knew that controls were in place, proactive crime prevention surveys were being conducted, and a professional investigative unit was available to assist GEC in investigating and supporting GEC, then they might perceive that they would get caught. Thus the "opportunity" portion of the triad of opportunity, motive, and rationale would "prevent" a crime from occurring.

HIGH-TECHNOLOGY CRIME INVESTIGATION POLICY

Based on the GEC assets protection requirements and high-technology crime investigation drivers, the high-technology crime investigation manager must take the next step, which is to develop a high-technology crime investigation policy, coordinate that policy with relevant department managers, and gain executive management approval for the GEC high-technology crime investigation policy to be incorporated into the GEC security policy.

The high-technology crime investigation policy should be clear, concise, and written at somewhat of a high level, and it must conform to the GEC policy format. The GEC high-technology crime investigation policy should not get bogged down in details, but should set the guidelines for high-technology crime investigations for GEC.

Once integrated in the GEC security policy document, the high-technology crime investigation policy should be distributed to all department managers. This distribution should be accompanied by a cover letter signed by the CEO, president, and/or chairman of the board. The letter should state that GEC's high technology and information are important to GEC's well-being and competitive edge. The new security policy incorporating the high-technology crime investigations policy, which alludes to the HTCPP, provides the overall policy for protecting that competitive edge and obligates all GEC employees to support that policy.

A sample cover letter is included here:

To: All GEC Employees
Subject: Protecting GEC's Information, High Technology, and Competitive Edge

The advances in the technology of computers and telecommunications and our use of them have provided us with the opportunity to gain a competitive advantage. Therefore, they are, aside from you, some of our most vital assets. They are vital because they are used to run our business by transmitting, processing, and storing our information.

All of us at GEC have derived great benefit from being able to use our state-of-the-art high-technology equipment and devices, not the least of which includes our access to our systems and our ability to communicate across the corporation as well as with our customers, suppliers, and subcontractors. At the same time, GEC systems contain vital information that, if destroyed, modified, or disclosed to outsiders, would be harmful to the corporation and would adversely affect our competitive edge. If this happens, it is in the interest of all of us to report such incidents to the security department's high-technology crime investigation unit.

We must be able to use our high technology, our systems, devices, and information, but in a secure manner. It is imperative that these vital GEC resources be protected to the maximum extent possible, but consistent with cost-effective operations.

The protection of our systems and information can only be accomplished through an effective and efficient information systems security program coupled with a professional high-technology crime prevention program. We have begun an aggressive effort to build such programs.

This directive is the road map to our high-technology protection and anticrime programs. They are needed to help ensure the continued success of GEC. In order for these programs to be successful, you must give them your full support. Your support is vital to ensure that GEC continues to grow and maintain its leadership role in the global widget industry.

(Signed by the GEC president and CEO)

GEC'S HIGH-TECHNOLOGY CRIME INVESTIGATION REQUIREMENTS AND POLICY DIRECTIVE (IRPD)

The GEC high-technology crime investigation policy is set forth in the GEC high-technology crime IRPD. This directive follows the standard format for GEC policies and includes the following:

> *Introduction*—includes some history regarding the need for a high-technology crime investigation unit at GEC
> *Purpose*—describes why the document exists
> *Scope*—defines the breadth of the directive

Responsibilities—defines and identifies the responsibilities at all levels including executive management, organizational managers, and all users of the high-technology equipment and devices

Requirements—includes the requirements for

- Customer, subcontractor, and vendor access to GEC's high-technology equipment
- Identifying the value of the high technology assets
- Access to the GEC systems
- Access to specific applications and files
- Audit trails and their review
- Reporting responsibilities and action to be taken in the event of an indication of a possible violation
- Minimum protection requirements for the hardware, firmware and software. (The physical security aspects of the requirements were coordinated with the applicable security department and InfoSec managers, because they have the responsibility for the security of GEC assets.)
- Requirements for reporting high-technology crimes at a GEC department and lower level

HIGH-TECHNOLOGY CRIME INVESTIGATION PROCEDURES

Based on the GEC high-technology crime investigation policy, and as stated in the IRPD, each department must establish procedures for reporting high-technology crime and related incidents to the high-technology crime investigation unit.

GEC culture is such that the protection of the information systems and the information that they store, process, and transmit is the obligation of every GEC employee. The managers of GEC are required, based on their management positions, to protect the assets of GEC. Thus, the high-technology crime investigator reasoned, and executive management agreed, that each department should comply with the IRPD based on each department's unique position with GEC. Thus they were to document the procedures and processes that they would use to comply with the reporting and other requirements of the high-technology crime investigation procedural directive. This has several advantages, including:

- GEC management was in a better position to write the document and develop cost-effective procedures that worked for them
- It made the department, especially managers, responsible for compliance with the IRPD
- It negated the managers' complaints that their situation was unique and thus they could not comply with all aspects of a high-technology crime investigation procedure (one written by the high-technology crime investigator) as written. It took this level of detail for high-technology crime investigation responsibility to be taken off the shoul-

ders of the high-technology crime investigator and placed it squarely where it belonged: on the managers.

AWARENESS PROGRAM

The GEC high-technology crime investigator manager decided to concentrate, as a high priority, on incorporating the high-technology crime awareness information into the security department's security awareness program. This was done to "get the word out" and to gain the support of managers and employees in identifying and reporting incidents that fell under the purview of the high-technology crime investigation unit.

The high-technology crime investigator manager reasoned that after the GEC high-technology crime investigation policies and baseline procedures were developed and published, the employees must be made aware of them and why they were necessary. Only with the full support and cooperation of GEC employees can a successful HTCPP be established and maintained.

The high-technology crime prevention and investigation portion of the security department's awareness program was patterned and developed in accordance with the format being used by security. This approach ensured a smooth, quick integration of the material. The awareness program was broken into two parts: awareness briefings and continuous awareness material.

Awareness Briefings

The awareness briefings included the security department's information relative to the need for high-technology protection, controls, and for reporting violations of rules, policies, procedures, and laws. The impact of not doing so and an explanation of the GEC security program that included that high-technology crime prevention and investigations program would be detrimental to the protection of the GEC assets.

The high-technology crime investigator manager was informed by the manager responsible for the awareness program that the awareness material and briefings, when given as a general briefing, could only be used for new employees. The general briefings failed to provide the specific information required by various groups. Thus, the awareness briefings were subsequently tailored to specific audiences as follows:

- All new hires, regardless of whether they use high technology systems. The rationale was that they all handle information and come in contact with computer and telecommunication systems in one form or another.
- Managers
- System users
- IT department personnel
- Engineers
- Manufacturers

- Accounting and finance personnel
- Procurement personnel
- Human resource personnel
- Security and audit personnel
- The system security custodians (those who are given day-to-day responsibility to ensure that the systems and information are protected in accordance with the information systems security policy and procedures)

A process was established to identify these personnel, input their profile information into a database and, using a standard format, track their awareness briefing attendance, both their initial briefings and annual rebriefings. This information would also be used to provide them, through the GEC mail system, with awareness material.

The high-technology crime investigator manager determined that the current awareness program was perfect and met the needs of the unit. Therefore, his staff would provide specific information concerning high-technology crimes and their prevention to the awareness program manager for incorporation into the current program. This is another example of saving money by not reinventing the wheel and using other organizations' resources to meet the goals of the unit.

Awareness Material

The high-technology crime investigator manager, in concert with the human resource and training staff, decided that ensuring that employees were aware of their high-technology crime reporting responsibilities and crime prevention techniques would require constant reminders. After all, high-technology crime prevention is not the major function of most GEC employees; however, a way had to be found to remind the employees that it is a *part* of their duties at the company.

It was decided that awareness material could be cost-effectively provided to the employees by providing high-technology crime investigation material to the employees through the following:

- Annual calendars
- Posters
- Labels for systems and diskettes
- Articles published in GEC publications, such as the weekly newsletter
- Logon notices and system broadcast messages, especially of high-technology crime investigation changes

Although not all inclusive, the high-technology crime investigator manager believed that this was a good start and could be analyzed for cost-effective improvements at the end of the calendar year.

PROACTIVE HIGH-TECHNOLOGY CRIME PREVENTION SURVEYS AND RISK MANAGEMENT

The high-technology crime investigator manager believed that an integral part of an HTCPP, aside from the policies, procedures, and awareness program, was the need to assess the threats, vulnerabilities, and risks that affect the potential for high-technology crimes. He reasoned that it was always more cost-effective to prevent crimes than to investigate them. Besides, an aggressive, proactive position is always more effective than reacting to crimes that have already occurred.

The high-technology crime investigator manager coordinated the survey process with the audit manager to ensure there was no duplication of effort. The audit manager noted that their audits focused primarily on compliance with GEC controls through GEC policies and procedures, as well as government rules and regulations. Therefore, the audit manager did not see any redundancies or conflicts with audit processes and goals.

To ensure that everyone was working together in the best interest of GEC and communicating and sharing information, the unit manager advised that a copy of each survey be forwarded to the audit manager for her use. The audit manager thought that such information would be very beneficial and indicated that the annual audit schedule would be provided to the unit manager so there would not be a scheduling conflict between organizations.

They both discussed each other's work and decided to establish a process to share information, including:

- Planned and posted audit meetings to discuss targets and results
- Current investigations
- Discussions of deficiencies and findings found during investigations that point to a lack of controls and/or inadequate procedures
- Discussions of audit findings that may be indicators of fraud, waste, abuse, some type of GEC policy violation, or other forms of criminal activity

Both managers believed that by working together they could work "smarter" and maximize the use of resources at least impact to their budgets, thus meeting their charter obligations and benefiting GEC. In addition, they agreed that the investigation unit manager would conduct a series of fraud, waste, and abuse awareness briefings at the auditor's staff meetings so company auditors would be more knowledgeable concerning fraud indicators when they conducted their audits.

WHAT IS RISK MANAGEMENT?

To understand the high-technology crime prevention survey approach, one should have a basic understanding of risk management methodology. To do this, one must first understand what risk management means. Risk management is defined as the total process of identifying, controlling, eliminating, or minimizing uncertain events that may affect system resources. It includes risk assessments; risk analyses, including cost–benefit analyses; target selection; implementation and testing; security evaluation of safeguards; and an overall high-technology crime investigation review.

Risk Assessments

The process of identifying high-technology crime risks, determining their magnitude, and identifying areas needing safeguards is called *risk assessment*. In other words, you are assessing the risk of a particular target (e.g., the potential for overhearing cellular phone conversations of the GEC's CEO).

The risk assessment process is subdivided into threats, vulnerabilities, and risks. Threats are man-made or natural occurrences that can cause adverse affects to systems and information when combined with specific vulnerabilities. For example, natural threats include such things as fire, floods, hurricanes, and earthquakes. Man-made threats or threat-related matters include such things as unauthorized system access, hacker/cracker/phreaker programs, the perpetrators themselves, theft of systems or services, denial of services, and destruction of systems or information.

Vulnerabilities are weaknesses that allow specific threats to cause adverse effects to systems and information. They include, for example:

- Lack of audit trails
- Lack of information backups
- Lack of access controls
- Anything that weakens the security of GEC's high technology (i.e., the systems and the information they process, store, and transmit)

Risks are the chances that a specific threat can take advantage of a specific vulnerability to cause adverse effects to systems and information. For example, if you live in an area prone to earthquakes, chances are that your systems will be damaged in the event of a strong earthquake. Another example is: What if you do not have audit trails on your system and the system contains company information that would be of value to others? What are the chances that someone would try to steal that information? Without the audit trail logs, you would not know if someone had tried to penetrate your system or, worse yet, whether they succeeded!

Assessments are an evaluation of the threats and vulnerabilities to determine the level of risk to your systems or information that the systems store, process, and transmit. Assessments are usually done via a qualitative analysis, a quantitative analysis, or a combination of the two. They measure risk.

Qualitative analyses usually use the three categories of risk: high, medium, and low. These levels are assigned by an "educated best guess," based primarily on the opinions of others "in the know" gathered through interviews, history, tests, and the experience of the person doing the assessment. Quantitative analyses usually use statistical sampling based on mathematical computations to determine the probability of an adverse occurrence based on historical data. The results are still an "educated best guess," but they are based primarily on statistical results.

Risk Analysis

Analysis of the risks, the countermeasures to mitigate those risks, the cost benefits associated with those risks, and countermeasures make up the risk analysis process. Basically, risk analysis is risk assessments with the cost and benefit factors added.

Risk Management Process Goals

The goal of the risk management process is to provide the best protection of high technology and the information stored, processed, and transmitted at least cost, consistent with the value of the devices and the information. For the high-technology crime prevention surveys, the goals would be to identify the threats, vulnerabilities, and risks that would allow the commission of a high-technology crime.

Risk Management Process

Remember that the high-technology crime investigation program is a company program made up of professionals who provide service and support to their company. Therefore, the combination of a proactive survey and risk management processes must be based on the needs of GEC customers.

Also, be sure that the survey and risk management concepts, programs, and processes are informally and formally used in all aspects of the high-technology crime prevention and investigation program.

The following steps should be considered in the HTCPP:

- *Management interest*—Identify areas that are of major interest to executive management and customers, and approach them from a business point of view. The process should begin with interviews of your internal customers to determine what high-technology areas can be adversely affected by noncompliance and crime. Then, target those areas first as the starting point for the surveys.
- *Specific targets*—Identify specific targets such as the servers or the PBX.
- *Input sources*—Users, system administrators, auditors, security officers, managers, technical journals, technical bulletins, CERT alerts (Internet), risk assessment, application programs, and so forth
- *Survey format*—Conduct the survey using a standard high-technology crime prevention survey format.

RECOMMENDATIONS TO MANAGEMENT

When the high-technology crime prevention survey is complete, the high-technology crime investigator must make recommendations to management. Remember that when making recommendations, think from a business point of view and address cost, benefits, profits, PR, and so forth.

RISK MANAGEMENT REPORTS

A briefing that includes a formal, written report is the vehicle used to bring the results of the survey to management's attention. The report should include identifying areas that need improvement, areas that are performing well, and recommended actions for improvement, including costs and benefits as applicable.

Remember that it is management's decision to accept the risk or mitigate the risk, and how much to spend to do so. The high-technology crime investigator is the specialist, the in-house consultant on high-technology crime and crime prevention. It is management's responsibility to decide what to do. They may follow your recommendations, ignore them, or take some other action. In any case, you have provided the service and support required.

If the decision is made that no action will be taken, there is still a benefit to conducting the analyses. The high-technology crime investigator now has a better understanding of the potential high-technology crime scene environment, as well as an understanding of some of its vulnerabilities. This information will help investigators in the event a high-technology-related crime is reported in that specific high-technology environment.

HIGH-TECHNOLOGY CRIME PREVENTION SURVEYS

The following survey standard was developed to assist in successfully meeting the goals and objectives of the strategic, tactical, and annual plans of GEC and the high-technology crime investigation unit. The objective of the high-technology crime prevention survey is to determine proactively the potential for an individual or individuals to attack or otherwise take advantage of a GEC high-technology vulnerability for unauthorized and/or illegal purposes. In addition, the survey is to be used to provide information necessary for management to assist them in deciding the potential for unauthorized conduct and/or criminal risk within their high-technology environment and to assist them in making cost-effective decisions based on the results of the survey.

Survey Report Format

The following standard format was developed to meet the needs of GEC management:

- Title page
- Table of contents
- Executive summary—a summary of the report that is clear and concise (not more than one page in length)
- Body of the report—five sections
  - *Purpose*—a sentence or two to describe the reason/objective of the survey. For example: This high-technology crime prevention survey was conducted to determine the potential misuse, abuse, and theft of hardware, software, and information possible by the introduction of notebook computers into the workforce.
  - *Background information*—not more than one page of information explaining the rationale for the survey
  - *Methodology*—the philosophy and approach used in conducting the survey (not more than one page in length)
  - *Findings*—a list of the discrepancies, deficiencies, and/or noteworthy (good) items discovered during the survey (not more than two pages in length)

○ *Recommendations*—recommendations for corrective action to mitigate the potential for crime or violation of GEC rules. These recommendations must be clear, concise, and written based on the professional expertise of the investigator and agreed to by the manager. They must also include considerations of costs and productivity impact.
- Appreciation—a list of the people, their titles, and their organization that assisted the investigator in successfully accomplishing the survey.
- Attachments
  ○ *Attachment 1*—glossary
  ○ *Attachment 2*—the operational plan used to conduct the survey
  ○ *Attachment 3*—supporting documents deemed appropriate (e.g., audit reports, prior investigations related to that high technology, news items relative to the high technology in question, hacker site comments, CERT announcements)
- Audience—GEC management. The investigator is to assume that the reader does not have any knowledge of surveys, high-technology crimes, or crime prevention.

Cellular Telephone High-Technology Crime Prevention Survey

Once the high-technology crime investigator manager was prepared, the manager sent e-mail to GEC managers advising them of the unit's capability to conduct surveys. The manager responsible for the GEC cellular telephone immediately contacted the unit manager regarding her concerns about cellular phone fraud. She had read about some recent cellular phone frauds in the newspaper and was concerned about the more than 200 GEC cellular phones that were being used by GEC employees that might become "victims" of fraudsters.

A survey was conducted using the following operational plan outline:

Introduction: Cellular phones are continuing to proliferate in our society as a common business communications tool. In addition, they have become an object for instigating fraud and other crimes. GEC has procured cellular phones for GEC personnel to use in the furtherance of GEC business. The potential for exploitation of GEC cellular phones by unauthorized users is no less that that for other corporations.

Purpose: The purpose of this Cellular Phone Crime Prevention Survey is to determine whether any of GEC cellular phones or related services are being misused, abused, or used for criminal activities or other unauthorized activities.

Objective: To identify the processes being used to procure, distribute, use, and control GEC cellular phones that may lead to their theft or use for criminal or unauthorized activities

Resources: One senior high-technology crime investigator to be used for 32 hours per week for a period of 5 weeks

Target: GEC cellular phone use and processes

Target Plan:

- Identify the process used to request a cellular phone.
- Identify the process to monitor cellular phone usage.
- Identify the focal points in the processes.
- Identify the cellular phone tracking processes.
- Identify the process used by the provider to bill and safeguard GEC cellular phones.
- Identify the process used to install cellular phones in GEC vehicles.
- Identify all directives and rules that apply to the cellular phone processes.
- Locate and interview the GEC cellular phone focal points.
- Conduct applicable interviews.
- Interview a statistical sampling of GEC cellular phone users.
- Review and analyze a statistical sampling of cellular phone bills.
- Compare the cellular phone database inventory files with the current record of employees.
- Set up a controlled test of the processes by making up an identity of a nonexistent person and, using the current process, request a cellular phone. If it is received, make several calls that should stand out (e.g., calls to a foreign country). Then, report the cellular phone missing, by memo, to the focal point for the cellular phones.
- Document the results.

Results: The survey determined that

- Monthly billing statements were paid without verification by those responsible for the individual cellular phones that the charges were for valid GEC business.
- The cellular phone database inventory was out of date.
- Some employees had taken their GEC cellular phone with them when they left GEC's employment and GEC was still paying for their monthly calls.
- The policy and procedures governing the entire cellular phone process was more than 6 years old—very outdated.
- All cellular phones included call features such as call forwarding, three-way conference calling, and STAR* services (STAR JAM, STAR FIND, STAR SORT, and START WAITING) that were an additional cost, but there was no justification for these features.

- Anyone could request a cellular phone as long as any level of management approved it; however, no one questioned the justification, use, or even the manager's signature on the request.

Recommendations: Recommendations included

- That GEC employee records be cross-referenced against those in receipt of cellular phones
- That those cellular phones that could not be identified to current employees have their service immediately terminated
- That those individuals who were no longer employees be sent a registered letter billing them for past calls and requesting an appointment for picking up the phone. If the letter went unanswered, a second registered letter would be sent advising the former employee that further use of the phone could possibly constitute fraudulent, criminal conduct. It was decided that to pursue the issue further and confiscate the phones from former employees would not be cost-effective based on the price of replacement. In addition, it would be an embarrassment to GEC to pursue the matter further with former employees, some of whom had moved to another state.
- That all call features be eliminated on all cellular phones until such features could be shown and endorsed by *executive* management to be in the best interest of GEC
- That all cellular phones users receive an acknowledgment statement to sign and return, stating they would safeguard the cellular phone, use it only for GEC business, and reimburse GEC for any unauthorized (e.g., personal, nonemergency) calls. Furthermore, they were responsible for reimbursing GEC in the event the phone was stolen.
- That the cellular phone policy be immediately updated
- That the monthly bills be sent to the manager of the employee's organization and the employee and the manager both sign and date the bill, verifying its accuracy and that the calls were made in furtherance of GEC business

Results of the Survey

Executive management and others were extremely pleased with the results of this "quick-and-dirty" survey because it:

- Pointed to potential cellular fraud problems
- Helped to prevent future occurrences
- Saved GEC hundreds of thousands of "future" dollars as a result of closer monitoring of the monthly bills, elimination of a justified need for some phones, and the elimination of most of the STAR features

• Allowed GEC to recoup thousands of dollars from employees and some former employees for unauthorized calls

Such surveys can have a positive effect on profits and costs, and it is an excellent PR tool for the high-technology crime investigator. (A sample PBX survey is provided in Appendix 16-1.)

SUMMARY

It is important to establish properly the needed functions to support the high-technology crime investigation unit's charter of duties and responsibilities. They include the following:

• Establishing the proper high-technology crime investigation functions in correct priority order is vital to establishing the high-technology crime investigation program baseline.
• The high-technology crime investigation functional processes should generally follow the function descriptions noted in the high-technology crime investigator's charter of responsibilities.
• The functions and processes that should be developed first are high-technology crime investigation policies and procedures documentation, a high-technology crime investigation and prevention awareness function, an investigative function, and an NCI function.
• High-technology crime prevention surveys are much like risk assessments. However, the survey should concentrate exclusively on potential criminal activities.

APPENDIX 16-1

Private Branch Exchange (PBX) Survey

The following is a "sanitized" version of a survey operations plan and operation developed and used by Dr. Kovacich and an associate to conduct high-technology crime surveys. It can be used as a baseline by high-technology crime investigators for conducting PBX high-technology crime prevention surveys. Although somewhat dated, it provides a reasonable format, philosophy, and process, which can be used by today's high-technology crime investigative professionals.

I. INTRODUCTION

1.0 Purpose: The purpose of this survey is to identify the process of maintaining, configuring, receiving, storing, and transmitting phone calls using the site A telephone switch (also referred to as the PBX); the threats, vulnerabilities, and risks associated with that process; and recommend changes to mitigate the risks by threat agents. The survey will concentrate on external attempts to penetrate the Southern Phonecom Zenith PZ-2 system telephone switch and use it to perpetrate toll fraud or damage, destroy, modify, or read the switch or voice mail of others.

PBX penetration and long-distance toll fraud are increasing dramatically in both the number of occurrences and dollars lost. Toll fraud is a highly charged issue because long-distance carriers contend customers should pay for fraudulent calls.[1] The US Secret Service estimates companies in the United States lose about $2.23 billion each year in charges for fraudulent calls. Other experts claim the total is probably closer to $4 billion. In any case, the typical average "hit" today is worth $40,000.[2]

How do they do it? Phone phreaks and hackers gain access to company telephone systems in a variety of ways—by accessing the direct inward system access (DISA) function; by obtaining remote access telecom codes; by using "demon attack dialers" to penetrate a system; through underground "call–sell" operations, "shoulder surfers," "dumpster divers," and "phone phreakers"; or just by asking for it (social engineering).

2.0 **Scope:** The scope of this survey will address common penetration techniques used by hackers to gain access to company phone systems. Select use of certain techniques will determine company vulnerabilities. It will also identify the telephone system service process from initial installation and user training to the termination of user service. Each step in this process will be analyzed to determine threat, vulnerability, and risk potential. After the survey results are analyzed, recommendations will be made to mitigate risks. Recommendations will be based on a "least-cost" approach.

3.0 **Target:** For the purposes of this survey, the target will be the Southern Phonecom Zenith PZ-2 system currently in use at the XYZ Company's manufacturing facility, located at site A, Anytown, CA. The survey will also include the Zenith voice mail messaging option also in use at site A.

II.   OBJECTIVES

- Identify the common penetration techniques used by hackers to gain access to company phone systems.
- Under controlled test conditions, determine how vulnerable the site A Zenith PZ-2 system (with the Zenith mail option) is to penetration attempts by hackers from outside the facility.
- Ascertain what preventive steps can be taken to lessen exposure to this type of activity.
- Make recommendations to management.

III. OPERATIONAL STEPS

1.0 *Phase I (covert)*

1.1 Initially coordinate the survey with the system integrity (security) staff of NDI, a long-distance service provider. (NOTE: NDI offered their expertise in identifying system weaknesses and vulnerabilities, as well as their knowledge of techniques used to exploit them.)

1.2 Perform the following tests on the indicated systems to determine whether they can be penetrated from the outside. (NOTE: These tests may be performed off-site at the writer's home to preclude the compromise of any test that may result if done at the office, using an extension on the PZ-2 switch.)

Switch (Zenith PZ-2 PBX)

1.2.1 Is a remote maintenance access port available on the system? Can it be accessed? In other words, no password protection, use of a common number string (1111, 9999, 1234, 1993), and so forth. Is it adequately protected from outside penetration?

1.2.2 Can it be determined whether the modem supporting the remote maintenance access port is using an unpublished number with a prefix different from the system's voice telephones?

1.2.3 Can the system be penetrated through DISA?

1.2.4 Can any unused DISA numbers or unauthorized codes be located in the system?

1.2.5 Can it be determined whether DISA numbers have unrestricted or restricted trunk group access?

1.2.6 Are system administration accounts still in the original default condition or have they been customized by the administrator?

1.2.7 Can system administrator and/or user passwords be accessed and compromised through outside penetration?

1.2.8 Are vendor maintenance accounts in a default condition or have they been customized for specific system use?

1.2.9 Can install codes be determined? If so, are they in a default condition or have they been customized?

1.2.10 Can it be determined whether trunk tie-lines have been configured for restricted or unrestricted use?

1.2.11 Are tie-lines protected by class-of-service configuration?

1.2.12 Is the external access parameter set to disallow caller transfers to an outside line?

1.2.13 Is the system's international calling capability in use? Can it be accessed through penetration attempts?

1.2.14 Using social engineering techniques, can any restricted number be compromised by telecommunications or help desk personnel?

Voice Mail (Zenith Mail)

1.2.15 Has the voice mail capability been configured to facilitate trunk access? (This permits access to long-distance calling or through-dial capability.)

1.2.16 Are any controls in place to protect trunk access (i.e., voice mail software or PBX operating system)?

1.2.17 Can outbound international dialing be accessed or is it restricted in voice mail?

1.2.18 Can it be determined whether call blocking is in use through voice mail?

1.2.19 Have the restricted extension dialing access codes been adjusted to block dialing access to trunk lines from within the voice mail system?

1.3 Utilize techniques and support provided by NDI security representatives in testing the site A Zenith PZ-2 system against outside penetration.

1.4 Document test results.

1.5 Develop countermeasures matrix.

2.0 *Phase II (overt)*

2.1 Identify the processes for (a) acquiring and installing system hardware, (b) installing and maintaining software, (c) making system software modifications, (d) handling internal/external maintenance, (e) providing system physical security, (f) establishing and maintaining system operational safeguards, (g) maintaining and reviewing audit trails, (h) reporting lost/stolen company telephone credit cards, and (i) terminating user features/services.

2.2 Identify the requirements and directives that govern telephone operation at site A, and obtain and review copies of pertinent documentation.

2.3 Identify key vendor representatives (i.e., Telecom) and players who make up the overall site A telecommunication environment.

2.4 Locate and interview key vendor and Telecom personnel who have functional responsibility for (a) PZ-2 switch operations, (b) telephone installation/maintenance, (c) PZ-2 switch maintenance, and (d) telephone customer service. Locate and interview the site A Telecom management representative.

2.5 Interview key personnel to (a) develop a good understanding of the processes and system used to provide telecommunications support and (b) identify the various features and functions of the switch that may be susceptible to break-in and/or fraudulent use of the system.

Switch (Zenith PZ-2 PBX)

2.5.1 Are system administration accounts still in the original default condition or have they been customized by the administrator?

2.5.2 Can system administrator and/or user passwords be accessed and compromised through outside penetration?

2.5.3 Are vendor maintenance accounts in a default condition or have they been customized for specific system use?

2.5.4 How easy can system features be activated or disabled (especially at night and during the weekends? Are those features denied or disabled by default?

2.5.5 Are user-assigned features (i.e., remote access, weekend remote access, inbound 800 calls, outbound dialing, remote originating, and call forwarding) disabled when not required by a particular user?

2.5.6 Are default remote access codes limited to one per person?

2.5.7 Are trunk tie-lines configured for restricted or unrestricted use?

2.5.8 Are tie-lines protected by class-of-service configuration?

2.5.9 Can the system be penetrated through DISA?

2.5.10 Are unauthorized DISA numbers and codes disabled?

2.5.11 Is call blocking in use?

2.5.12 Can the system be penetrated through use of the system's 800 number?

2.5.13 Are calls to area codes 900 and 976 restricted?

2.5.14 Can area code 809 be accessed?

2.5.15 Is the external access parameter set to disallow caller transfers to an outside line?

2.5.16 Are credit cards used to facilitate long-distance calls? (The law limits victim liability to $50 per card for losses resulting from fraud.)

2.5.17 Is the system's international calling capability in use?

2.5.18 Have controls been established on remote maintenance access?

2.5.19 Is an unpublished number used for the modem port with a prefix different from those used for voice phone numbers?

Voice Mail (Zenith Mail)

2.5.20 Has the voice mail capability been configured to facilitate trunk access? (This permits access to long-distance calling or through-dial capability.)

2.5.21 Are any controls in place to protect trunk access (i.e., voice mail software or PBX operating system)?

2.5.22 Has outbound international dialing been restricted in voice mail?

2.5.23 Can it be determined whether call blocking is in use through voice mail?

2.5.24 Have the restricted extension dialing access codes been adjusted to block dialing access to trunk lines from within the voice mail system?

2.6   Document interview results.

3.0 *Phase III: Report Writing*

3.1 Compile survey and test data.

3.2 Prepare draft report.

3.3 Conduct management review and determine addressees.

3.4 Finalize survey report and disseminate to addressees.

IV. RESOURCES

1.0 *Labor*

1.1 The services of the project lead are required part-time (4 hours a day) for a period of 10 nonconsecutive days to (a) read and digest survey training material, (b) develop a security assessment survey operation plan and associated charts, (c) coordinate plan with and seek approval of investigations management, (d) coordinate with and obtain training from long-distance carrier security personnel, and (e) brief survey personnel on the operation plan. Subtotal: 40 hours

1.2 The services of the project lead and one investigator are required full-time (8 hours a day) for a period of 5 days to identify processes, requirements, and directives. Subtotal: 80 hours

1.3 The services of the project lead and one investigator are required full-time (8 hours per day) for a period of 5 days to identify key players, develop questions, interview personnel, and document results. Subtotal: 80 hours

1.4 The periodic, nonconsecutive support of key telecommunications personnel is required to identify and provide copies of applicable processes, requirements, and directives. Additionally, approximately 1 hour of interview time is required for each key representative. Subtotal: 15 hours

1.5 The services of long-distance carrier (NDI) security representatives are required to provide training and technical assistance in support of this survey. Subtotal: 10 hours

1.6 The services of the project lead and one investigator are required part-time (5 hours a day) for a period of 2 nonconsecutive days to conduct penetration testing and document results. Subtotal: 40 hours

1.7 The services of the project lead and one investigator are required part-time (4 hours a day) for a period of 5 nonconsecutive days to conduct analyses of all accumulated data to determine specific threats, vulnerabilities, and risks before documenting findings and recommendations. Subtotal: 40 hours

1.8 The services of the project lead are required full-time (6 hours a day) and one investigator is required part-time (2 hours a day) for a period of 7 nonconsecutive days to draft, coordinate, finalize, and disseminate the survey report. Subtotal: 56 hours

1.9 Grand Total of Hours: 361 hours
Local security staff time: 336 hours
Local Telecom staff time: 15 hours
NDI representative time: 10 hours

2.0 *Equipment*

2.1 XYZ Company security: use of off-site telephones, two personal computer systems equipped with modem and printer (one system on-site and one off-site), and specialized software

2.2 XYZ Telecomm staff: none

2.3 NDI: unknown

3.0 *Monetary Contingency:* Company reimbursement is required for (a) long-distance phone calls made from off-site location during test periods and (b) incidental expenses (e.g., purchase of special connectors, cabling, etc.).

V.   EZ GANTT CHART

Project management charts depict the plan schedule.

VI.   ANALYSES

This section details the general threat, vulnerability, and risk criteria to be used for this survey.

1.0 *Threats:* The Zenith PZ-2 system used at site A can be penetrated from the outside using a variety of previously proved hacker methods, some of which are described next.

1.1 Using a compromised DISA number to gain PBX access

1.2 Obtaining and using compromised user, system, and system administrator passwords exchanged through hacker bulletin boards

1.3 Acquiring and using a stolen or illegally acquired company phone credit card or credit cart information, including unique access code information

1.4 Obtaining and using illegally acquired remote access telecom codes

1.5 Dialing "800" numbers to gain access to the PBX-attached voice mail feature

1.6 Taking advantage of special phone system features to penetrate or manipulate the system

1.7 Using a "demon" or "war dialer" (automated attack dialer) that repeatedly calls a system and pumps in access codes until a valid one is found, allowing system penetration

1.8 Giving up company information to "dumpster divers" (people who dig through trash cans for discarded information)

1.9 Using a cover story to request system information from company employees, switchboard operators, switch maintenance personnel, management, and so on (i.e., social engineering)

2.0 *Vulnerabilities:* Listed here are general system vulnerabilities previously identified in other surveys, investigations, and audits.

2.1 The DISA number is listed, is in the incoming service group, is not deactivated when not in use or not required, and account codes are not changed on a regular basis.

2.2 User and system passwords are not adequately protected. They do not meet acceptable criteria for selection, minimum password length, or invalid password attempts. Allowable user access is not periodically reviewed and revalidated. Information regarding configuration, modem numbers, and passwords is not adequately safeguarded.

2.3 Procedures are in effect to notify the phone company immediately of lost, misplaced, or stolen company telephone credit, access, or calling cards. Cards may contain an access telephone number. Employees are not security conscious when using calling cards in public places.

2.4 Employees are not instructed to protect phone access numbers adequately, and authorization codes are changed infrequently.

2.5 Special parameters are not placed on the company "800" numbers (i.e., dialed from only those calling areas specified).

2.6 International calling (011) and area code 809 (the Caribbean) is accessible to all system users. Calls to the "900" and "976" prefixes are not restricted.

2.7 PBX remote maintenance ports are not disabled when service is not needed. System physical dial-in ports DISA ports are not monitored regularly.

2.8 Company phone books and system administrator manuals are not treated as sensitive material when discarded.

2.9 Switchboard operators, master console operators, system administrators, maintenance personnel, and other system support employees are not trained to be suspicious of telephone requests for system information, maintenance work, execution of programs, and so forth.

3.0 *Risks:* Risks will be classified as high, medium, or low based upon the severity of the threat/vulnerability. Recommendations will be developed using a "least-cost" approach.

EXCERPTS FROM A SAMPLE SURVEY ACTIVITY LOG

I. GENERAL AND TECHNICAL COMMENTS

- During the period March 2–3, 2006, received and installed a Hayes-compatible modem on the test PC.
- On March 3, 2006, installed RapidFAX, BitCom, and PC-Scan software.
- During the period March 3–5, 2006, encountered problems with setup and initial operation of PC-Scan software. During this same period, coordinated preparation of system Standard Practice Procedure with Eugene Holt and submitted same to Computer Security for approval.
- During the period March 9–10, 2006, continued having technical problems with the PC-Scan software. Spent a great deal of time troubleshooting over the phone with G. L. Kovacich. Even though modem and communications software reflected everything was installed correctly, kept getting an error code message (error code 24). According to the Microsoft *GW-BASIC User's Guide and Reference,* error code 24 is described as "DEVICE TIME OUT: GW-BASIC did not receive information from an I/O device within a predetermined amount of time." Several parameter changes were made to the PC-Scan program code but did not rectify the problem. Smythe suggested we attempt to get different software of this type from the NDI system integrity (security) staff.
- On April 11, 2006, met with Symthe and Jack Gray, NDI system integrity staff supervisor for this area, in Anytown, CA. Gray provided other hacker software previously acquired and used by his staff to determine telecommunications system vulnerabilities.
- On April 11, 2006, successfully installed software provided by Gray, using home PC; printed off and read software documentation (rather sparse).

- On April 11, 2006, rechecked modem settings and made necessary adjustments; began using hacker software.
- On April 12, 2006, was provided the name of Butch Sells (tel: 919-555-1212) as the NDI technical point of contact.
- On April 18, 2006, adjusted project management charts to reflect schedule slippage resulting from events identified in previous paragraphs.
- On April 22, 2006, Ron Roll, NDI System Integrity, Baltimore, MD, called and advised that Butch Sells was on vacation. A Rob Nilson would call in Sells' absence on Monday morning (4/23/93) and offer any assistance he could.
- On April 23, 2006, Rob Nilson, Technician, NDI System Integrity, Baltimore, MD, called. He was given an overview regarding the status of penetration tests to date. He answered several technical questions and advised we were doing all the right steps. He did suggest that we try a variety of modem parameters when attempting to penetrate the remote maintenance port modem number.
- On April 30, 2006, conducted in-briefing of key telecommunications personnel at site A. In attendance were Douglas Johnson, Jeannine Headington, Bernard Snow, and Will Fox regarding phase II of this survey.
- On May 15, 2006, Rob Nilson of NDI contacted the writer from Dallas, TX, while on business travel. We discussed how one could attempt to hack into voice mailboxes. Nilson said that, to his knowledge, there was no software available in the hacker community that would aid in this type penetration. He suggested using what he called "finger hacking" methods (accessing a mailbox and trying simple number sequences such as 1111111, 9999999, 1234567, spell out user's name, his home phone number, an employee number, etc.). Default passwords were normally a string of numeric characters designated by software houses. They generally weren't too elaborate (e.g., 22222, 33333, 99999, 098765). They were normally good for one-time use and then prompted the user to change the password to a unique sequence. Nilson said if entry was gained into a mailbox, one should immediately set up a unique password series and attempt to place a toll call from the box.

II.   SL-1 SWITCH (PBX) TEST RESULTS

1.0 *Test:* Attempt to identify any 800 numbers used by the company at either Palmdale or Pico Rivera.

Results: At 11:30 AM on July 26, 1993, contacted the Pacific Bell 800 assistance operator at 1-800-555-1212 from extension 7152 to determine whether there were any 800 numbers listed for the XYZ Company for any of their facility locations. According to the operator, there were none listed.

2.0 *Test:* Using hacker social engineering techniques, attempt to gain access to the PZ-2 switch using a suitable ruse.

Ruse: Cletus "Clete" Boyer, a Pacific Bell short-time maintenance employee, needs access to the site A PZ-2 remote maintenance port for repair work. To do this work, the maintenance port modem number is needed.

Results:

- On May 28, 2006, at 2:50 PM, the writer (using the identity of "Clete" Boyer) called 555-7659, a number listed for the site A Telephone Trouble Desk, from an outside number.
- An automated call attendant feature thanked the caller for contacting the XYZ Customer Assistance Center and requested an appropriate button be pushed, depending upon the type of assistance requested. "Telephones" (button 4) was selected.
- Mike Baylow answered and asked how he could help. The writer identified himself as "Clete" Boyer with Pacific Bell and said he needed assistance in repairing a telephone maintenance problem. Baylow advised he would put the caller in touch with Douglas Johnson and did. Johnson answered and the Boyer ruse was used again. Johnson acknowledged he understood the problem and would provide the requested number, but had to look it up. "Clete" advised he would call Johnson back in 5 minutes.
- At 3:05 PM, "Clete" contacted Johnson and was provided the number 555-0679. Johnson also complained he had just got back and noticed the system was "picking up a lot of hits, trunk error codes" or words to that affect. "Clete" told Johnson he would see what he could do and the conversation ended.
- On May 29, 2006, attempts to use the number 555-0679 were unsuccessful. When the number was dialed, there was a long carrier tone lasting approximately 2 seconds and then no sound.
- On May 29, 2006, the test results were coordinated with G. L. Kovacich. He suggested Johnson be contacted again and be told the problem may be with his equipment. Attempts should be made to determine whether Johnson would describe what kind of line 555-0679 was, or if he were willing to share further information on the type of switch he was running.

3.0 *Test:* Using a telephone, blindly hack at the XYZ Company site A home system in an attempt to determine type of system, size, features, and so on.

Results: Between 10:00 AM and 3:15 PM on July 28 and 29, a series of calls were placed through a standard off-site telephone, and they determined the following:

- The system used the following local phone prefixes:
  555-2xxx
  555-42 (tie-line); 555-7557 (the Telecommunications Customer Assistance Center, automated call attendant)
  555-5xxx (except 50xx and 51xx)
  555-6xxx
  555-7xxx
  555-8xxx
  555-9 (outside line)
  444-50xx
  444-51xx
  444-52xx
  444-53xx
  444-54xx
  444-55xx
- System has voice mail (several numbers called indicated the "voice mailbox of..." had been reached).
- System belongs to "XYZ Company...site A...Anytown," as evidenced by various voice mailbox massages.

4.0 *Test:* Using hacker techniques, attempt to identify all lines equipped with modems attached to the system as a potential means of external penetration.

Results: During the following periods, utilized the described hacker software to dial sequentially prefixes and numbers assigned to the XYZ Company at site A (lines equipped with modems are indicated by an asterisk).

DATE/INCLUSIVE TIME	TYPE DIALER	PREFIX/NUMBER SERIES
8/13/93 2:00–3:15 AM	WarDial 1.2 Sequential dialer	555-800 to 555-8099
8/13/93 3:15–4:15 AM	A-I-O Phone Hacker 5.0b	555-7900 to 555-7999 (*carrier @0679)
8/13/93 4:30–5:25 AM	A-I-O Phone Hacker 5.0b	555-2000 to 555-2099

5.0 *Test:* Using hacker techniques, attempt to identify authorization codes on those lines equipped with modems as a potential means of system penetration from the outside.

Results: During the following periods, utilized the described hacker software to enter randomly possible authorization codes on modem-equipped lines assigned to the XYZ Company at site A (successful entries are so noted):

DATE/INCLUSIVE TIMES	SOFTWARE USED	PHONE	MIN TRIED
5/12/06 3:25–10:30 AM Svc Code Finder Code Length: 5 First Digit: 1...9	WarDial 1.2 Selected	555-0679	45 each
5/13/06 5:25–9:00 AM Svc Code Finder Code Length: 6 First Digit: I...7	WarDial 1.2 Selected	555-0679	30 each
5/16/06 1:45–2:45 PM Svc Code Finder Code Length: 6 First Digit: 8...9	WarDial 1.2 Selected	555-0679	30 each
5/16/06 2:45–4:45 PM Code Length: 7 First Digit: 1...4			30 each
5/17/06 2:30–5:10 PM Svc Code Finder Code Length: 7 First Digit: 5...9	WarDial 1.2 Selected	555-0679	30 each
5/18/06 12:00–2:30 PM Svc Code Finder Code Length: 8 First Digit: 1...3	WarlDial 1.2 Selected	555-0679	45 each
5/18/06 5:45–8:50 PM Code Length: 8 First Digit: 4...7			45 each

III. VOICE MAIL TEST RESULTS

1.0 *Test:* Attempt to access an outside line using the "Dial Thru" feature on voice mail.

   Result: On July 26, 2006, tried to access an outside line and phone number from extension 7152 using the Zenith mail "Dial Thru" feature. The attempts were unsuccessful. Call block probably in use. Determined that only another internal extension number on the same PBX switch could be accessed on "Dial Thru" feature.

2.0 *Test:* Attempt to access an outside line through voice mail by dialing a voice mail extension and transferring to outside line ("9") or site B tie-line ("42").

   Results: On July 30, 2006, between the hours of 12:00–3:00 PM, the following attempts were made from an outside line (333-9587):

2.1 Dialed 555-8511 (extension of Pick Hayamashi at site A). Hayamashi answered and tried to transfer the call to a "9" (outside) line or a "42" tie-line. The transfer could not be completed. Apparently, call blocking is in place to prohibit this type activity.

2.2 Dialed 555-7152 (extension of Perry Garvin at site A). Voice mail message advised Garvin was not available and to leave a brief message. After the message tone activated, the receiver bar on the outside phone was quickly depressed and released to determine whether a dial tone could be achieved. It could not.

3.0 *Test:* Determine the process for issuing, monitoring, and terminating voice mailboxes.

Results: On August 9, 2006, Bernard Snow, Alternate Voice Mail Administrator, site A Telecommunications, provided the following information:

3.1 Site A had a maximum of 2000 voice mailboxes available for use. Currently, 1119 were in use. Snow ran a listing of all current mailbox users to acquire this information.

3.2 A site A employee desiring the voice mail feature on her telephone line initiated a request for this feature through company training, utilizing an XYZ Company Voice Mail Request Form. After the employee had been scheduled for and received voice mail training, conducted by Steve Trimble, Computer Systems Training, the request form was noted and sent to telecommunications for voice mail installation/setup.

3.3 When an employee no longer needed voice mail as a result of termination, transfer, and so on, telecommunications was notified in one of several ways: through the use of a Transfer/Termination Checklist, by the employee's departmental secretary, or by the employee's manager. The voice mail feature for that employee would be "pulled" (suspended) the following business day. The number could be rendered inactive or could stay active online, but was unused until someone else was given that phone number. According to Snow, the turnover and reassignment of numbers can be quite rapid (within a day to a week). A new user assigned that number would then have to initiate a voicemail request if he desired the voice mail feature.

3.4 On September 14, 2006, the listing previously run by Snow on September 9, 1993 was delivered to this office for review. This listing was to be compared with the XYZ Company personnel home address and telephone roster (dated September 5, 1993). Individuals on the mailbox list and not on the access roster were highlighted as potentially unauthorized users.

3.5 During the period September 15–23, 2006, a comparison of employee names on the personnel roster and listing of active voice mail users was conducted. The following was noted:

- Ninety-five entities on the listing of active voice mail users were not reflected on the personnel home address and telephone roster.
- Of that number, 36 users were reflected as subcontractors, vendors, or US government employees. Fifteen were organizational mailboxes not assigned to a specific individual (e.g., material handling, FOE line, help desk, radios and alarms, recreation club, etc.)
- The remaining 44 entities were allegedly current or previous company employees whose names did not appear on the XYZ Company personnel home address and telephone roster.
- Eighteen of those entities were further identified as XYZ Company employees using other than a given first name.
- Twelve of the remaining entities were possibly identified as a current company employee using a different name who had relocated to another department and/or site location.
- The final remaining 14 entities could not be further identified and remained as unknown entities, representing a 1.25% error rate. It is possible they are new employees not yet on the personnel roster or are terminated or transferred employees.

4.0 *Test:* Determine whether voice mailboxes can be penetrated from the outside by compromising the user's individual password.

Results: During the following periods, the site A voice mail telephone number (555-6565) was called repeatedly from an off-site telephone. Each time a mailbox number was requested, a known four-digit voice mail extension was entered (e.g., 7152, 8460, etc.). A password was then requested. The criteria for site A voice mail passwords is as follows: will be 6 to 16 digits, should be changed every 90 days, can be changed anytime, and the letter "O" should not be part of the password. For purposes of this test, two common digit sequences known to the individual mailbox owner were used (i.e., office phone number and home phone number).

DATE/TIME ACCESSED	STARTING NAME/ ENDING NAME	MAILBOXES TESTED
9/16/93 9:15 AM	D. Ablington/T. Armylield	23/0
9/16/93 10:45 AM	C. Armstrong/U. Balonfine	24/0
9/16/93 11:55 AM	W. Bankertein/E. Bums	94/0
9/17/93 11:00 AM	L Burnstem/P. Dinwiddle	111/0
9/23/93 3:45 PM	K. Dobbins/M. Finney	62/0

Communication provided the information contained in the Sample Survey Report.

Sample Survey Report

Contents

Executive Summary

A crime prevention survey was undertaken to determine how susceptible the XYZ Company site A facility telephone switch (PBX) was to penetration attempts from the outside. The survey was conducted in two phases—a covert phase, during which a series of tests were conducted to assimilate hacker penetrations and an overt phase, during which the telecommunications processes used were analyzed and compared with established threats and vulnerabilities.

The site A PBX was generally well protected from outside penetration. System security software features were installed and in use. Voice mail audit trails were reviewed regularly and discrepancies were identified to the appropriate authorities.

There were no current work instructions or written procedures for the basic processes that were surveyed. It is recommended these procedures be created and implemented as soon as possible. Regular updating and maintenance of these procedures is highly recommended. Any procedure developed should include information protection guidance (e.g., what to do if someone calls asking for an outside line, what to do when an individual calls stating he is with a local or long-distance phone company and asks for PBX access or information).

One local Telecom employee (formerly employed by Southern Phonecom) operates the SL-1 switch and is fully knowledgeable of its operation.

In the event of his absence, there did not appear to be sufficiently trained backup personnel available to assume his responsibilities.

I. INTRODUCTION

A security assessment survey was conducted of the Southern Phonecom Zenith PZ-2 system, in use at XYZ Company's manufacturing facility, located at site A, Anytown, CA. The survey also included the Zenith mail voice message option used at site A.

The purpose of the security assessment survey was to see how vulnerable site A is against external attempts to penetrate the Southern Phonecom Zenith PZ-2 system telephone switch (PBX) and to use it to perpetrate toll fraud, or damage, destroy, or modify the switch or voice mail. A secondary purpose was to ascertain and identify PBX system weaknesses that could affect site operations negatively.

PBX penetration and long-distance toll fraud are increasing dramatically, in both the number of occurrences and dollars lost. Toll fraud is a highly charged issue because long-distance carriers contend customers should pay for fraudulent calls.[1] A company in Sunnyvale, CA, first learned it had been victimized when it received a $42,000 phone bill. The company, which normally averaged about $1000 a month in toll calls, immediately contacted AT&T and PacBell. They tried to fix the problem but were unsuccessful. The next month's bill rose to $118,000. By the time the company was able to secure their system, they had lost $230,000 in fraudulent charges...and were liable for the entire bill.

The US Secret Service estimates companies in the United States lose about $2.23 billion each year in charges for fraudulent calls. Other experts claim the total is probably closer to $4 billion. In any case, the typical average "hit" today is worth $40,000.[2]

How do they do it? Phone phreaks and hackers gain access to company telephone systems in a variety of ways: by accessing the direct inward system access (DISA) function; by obtaining remote access telecom codes; by using "demon attack dialers" to penetrate a system; through underground "call–sell" operations, "shoulder surfers," "dumpster divers," and "phone phreakers"; or just by asking for it (social engineering).

The scope of this survey addressed common penetration techniques used by hackers to gain access to company phone systems. Certain select techniques were used to determine how vulnerable XYZ Company was and to identify our weaknesses specifically. The survey also identified the telephone system service process from initial installation and user training to the termination of user service. Each step in this process was analyzed to determine threat/vulnerability potential. After the survey results were analyzed, recommendations were made to mitigate risks, improve overall telephone system security, and reduce the company's potential exposure to this kind of penetration. Recommendations were based on a "least-cost" approach.

II.   OBJECTIVES

- To determine the susceptibility of the site A telephone system to penetration attempts from the outside
- To ascertain weaknesses in the system and voice mail capability processes that leave the system vulnerable to any potential fraud, waste, or abuse attempt from outside sources
- To identify other system weaknesses that could affect site operations

III.   CURRENT PBX/VOICE MAIL ENVIRONMENT

The Southern Phonecom Zenith PZ-2 is the system of choice for XYZ Company's facilities at Anytown (site A) and Anycity (site B). The PZ-2 was initially installed at site A when the facility was placed into operation in 1986, and has been in use at that location since that time. This system also supports XYZ's mountain test site (site C). In the beginning, the PZ-2 system provided service for less than 100 site users through 50 instruments. It has grown consistently since that time. At the time of the survey, the system supported 3350 users and 3200 telephone instruments. The local PZ-2 system administrator was identified as Douglas Johnson, Wide Area Networks Telecommunications. The manager of wide area networks is Ms. Linda Scott. She is located at Anycity (site B).

The Southern Phonecom Zenith 1 voice messaging option (commonly referred to as *voice mail*) was added to the PZ-2 system in January 1992. This option is available to all site A and site C phone users. At the time of the survey, more than 1350 system users had the voice mail option. The voice mail administrators were identified as Jeannine Headington and Bernard Snow, site A telecommunications services. They are supervised by manager Ted Wlliams, site A telecommunications.

IV.   PBX/VOICE MAIL PROCESS DESCRIPTIONS

1.0   *Process for Physical Safeguarding of the SL-1 switch:*

    1.1 The Southern Phonecom PZ-2 system is located at site A, building 101, in a secure room located at the southwest corner of the building.

1.2 The switch and frame room has only one entry door. It is secured with the following:
- A Unicom-brand 10-button touch keypad, requiring a combination of three numbers to enter
- A High Tek-brand three-position spin-dial-type high-security lock
- A BMT alarm system that utilizes motion detection sensors and balanced magnetic switches

1.3 During normal working hours, the spin-dial lock is unlocked and the BMT alarm system is deactivated. The Unicom lock is the only active security device. Access to the area is granted to authorized personnel only.

1.4 After normal hours, all locking devices are used, and the alarm is set.

2.0 *Process for Safeguarding SL-1 Software:*

2.1 After initial installation of the software, the following security measures were implemented:
- Password protection was initiated for authorized telecommunication personnel accessed to the switch.
- There are two master passwords. Master password 1 (the "grand master") permits access and allows master password 2 to be changed. Master password 2 allows assignment of new passwords or changing of existing passwords as the need arises.
- Master password 1 is known to two authorized employees—the PBX switch system administrator and a second individual who is a backup in case of emergency.
- Three copies of system software were originally supplied by the system vendor. Two sets are maintained in a locked safe inside a room-size vault, located in building 105 at site A, whereas the third set is installed with the PZ-2 switch. The three copies are rotated through the PZ-2 switch on a monthly basis.
- Only specifically authorized telecommunications personnel are permitted to remove the system software from the secured storage area. After installation is complete, the replaced software is returned to the storage location and secured.

3.0 *Process for Safeguarding the Voice Mail Software:*

3.1 The original voice mail software was furnished in three sets. The operating system is the PZ-2 switch. Original software is secured with the PZ-2 software in a safe inside a vault, in building 105.

3.2 Access and removal of the software are permitted by authorized telecommunications personnel only.

3.3 Operation of the voice mail option is controlled by a grand master password and a secondary master password, similar to the PZ-2 switch system.

3.4 There are two employees who operate the voice mail system on a daily basis. They access new employees, modify and change user information, assign new phone numbers, and so forth. Only users who have been briefed, trained, and issued password protection are allowed access to the system.

V. SPECIFIC TEST THREATS, VULNERABILITIES, RISKS, AND RECOMMENDATIONS

1.0 *PBX Penetration Tests*

1.1 *Test 1:* Try to gain information about site A PBX using "social engineering" skills. (NOTE: Hackers typically use cover stories to request system information from company employees.)

Result: During this test, the caller (a survey team member) used the ruse of a local telephone company repairman who needed system access to check out line interference problems. A potentially sensitive number was divulged to the caller without challenging the authenticity of the caller. A callback procedure was not used to verify the "repairman's" identity with telecommunication supervisory personnel.

Threats: Hackers frequently use a cover story to request system information from company employees, switchboard operators, switch maintenance personnel, management, and others.

Vulnerabilities: A hacker could gain system access without his identity being questioned. Divulging sensitive system phone numbers, or authentication or access codes without verifying a legitimate need for the information places the entire system at risk to penetration from the outside.

Risks: High

Comments: There is no documented company telecommunications policy that sets forth clear guidance on handling outside requests for telecommunications information.

Recommendations:

- Train help desk operators, master console operators, system administrators, maintenance personnel, and other system support employees to be suspicious of telephone requests for system information, maintenance work, execution of programs, and so on.
- Develop a written policy and specific instructions that tell system personnel how to challenge any request for information, and how to report such requests if they are not valid.

- Instruct employees that any telephone company representative requesting privileged system information should be
identified in person and questioned regarding his need-to-
know. Their identity should be further verified with telecommunications supervisory personnel before allowing
access to the desired information.

1.2 *Test 2:* Attempt to penetrate the system and gain information
about the site A phone system (e.g., type of system in use, size,
features, etc.).

Results: Using a regular telephone from outside the facility,
several phone calls were placed to numbers suspected of being
assigned to site A. The calls produced information that identified who the system belonged to and reflected it had a voice mail
feature. The caller (a survey team member) was able to determine
what phone number prefixes were used, what number was used
as a tie-line to the facility, and what number served as the automated call attendant (part of the Telecommunications Customer
Assistance Center). This is significant, because it would provide
a hacker with information he could use to test other hacking
techniques based on known system weaknesses.

Threats: Information given out about a phone system can be
extremely sensitive. Hackers take advantage of special phone
system features to penetrate or manipulate. Often, this information is provided online to help the caller interact with the phone
system. Divulging too much information can compromise the
integrity of the system.

Vulnerabilities: Should too much information about a particular system be divulged, it can provide hackers with information
that better aids their penetration of the system. International calling (011) and company PBX service to area code 809 (the Caribbean) should be limited to only those who require it. Calls to
"900" and "976" prefixes should be restricted or disconnected.

Risk: Low

Comments: All information disclosed during this test was
considered public knowledge and did not compromise the
overall PBX environment. System safeguards were in place to
prohibit intentional or accidental access to a tie-line from a
phone outside the switch. The automated call attendant provided a clearly defined assistance path to the caller without
compromising system integrity.

Recommendations:

- Educate users adequately to protect phone access numbers
and voice mail passwords.

- Treat company phone directories and system administrator manuals as sensitive, need-to-know material and place them in burn barrels when they are no longer needed.
- Safeguard information regarding configuration, modem numbers, and passwords.

1.3 *Test 3:* Employ hacker techniques in an attempt to gain system access for the purpose of placing unauthorized long-distance phone calls. Attempt to access an outside line after dialing a company extension.

Result: It was determined that an outside caller could not gain access to a system through which a call could be placed outside the facility.

Threats: If system access was gained, a hacker could place a number of long-distance calls that would be charged back to the company. Depending upon the system audit trails, these calls could go undetected from hours to days. A system is under a constant external threat as hackers and phreakers attempt to access and penetrate a system for personal financial gain, to disrupt the normal operations of such a system, or to gain access to sensitive company information. Compromised system information can often end up on a hacker bulletin boards.

Vulnerabilities: System misuse or abuse caused by unauthorized individuals (hackers/phreakers) who place illegal long-distance calls throughout the United States and to foreign countries. If safeguards and audit trails are not functional, an illegally penetrated system could be exploited by many unauthorized users and cost the company thousands of dollars over a short time period.

Risk: Low

Comments: All system security safeguards appeared to be functioning properly.

Recommendations:

- Continue to watch for unauthorized system usage by monitoring system audit trails and activity records on a daily basis.
- Report any such activity immediately to investigations.

1.4 *Test 4:* Try to identify system phone lines equipped with external modems by using hacker software.

Result: A total of 3487 numbers maintained by the PBX were accessed using this software. Only two numbers were identified with a carrier tone indicative of a modem. One number was subsequently identified as a remote maintenance port to the PBX. The other number was assigned to a facsimile modem used by a company subcontractor (Smith & Burns) who is located in a trailer outside the company parameter.

Threats: The modem represents an external portal to the PBX system. Once located, the hacker can use a variety of specialized software programs (commonly referred to as *demon dialers* or *war dialers*) to dial the number repeatedly and search for a valid authority code. He can "attack" the number at his leisure, in the hope of gaining system access.

Vulnerabilities: External gateways to the PBX (i.e., remote maintenance ports, DISA numbers) are accessible when not in use. This alerts the hacker to an avenue for system penetration. If the authorization code is compromised, the hacker has gained system access for personal financial gain (through unauthorized long-distance calls), to disrupt the normal operations of such a system, or to gain access to sensitive company information. Compromised authorization codes can be exchanged through hacker bulletin boards and shared with others. The system then becomes vulnerable to attack from more than one source. At that point, it is only a matter of time until the authorization code is compromised and access is gained.

Risk: Low

Comments: Repeated attempts to gain system access through the maintenance port by compromising the authorization code were not successful. The system administrator later advised that maintenance ports were routinely disabled when not in use.

Recommendations:

- Disable PBX remote maintenance ports when service is not needed, and keep records of when they are activated, including who made the request and when (date/time), as well as the purpose of the request.
- Limit external modems on the system to reduce the potential for penetration from the outside.
- Monitor physical dial-in ports (i.e., DISA ports) on a regular basis.
- Continue to watch for unauthorized system usage by reviewing system audit trails and activity records on a daily basis. Report any such activity immediately to the investigation unit.

1.5 ***Test 5:*** Attempt to gain system access by using specialized hacker software programs to search randomly for valid authorization codes on modem-equipped phone lines attached to the PBX.

Result: The specialized software repeatedly dialed the one modem-equipped number of the PBX remote maintenance port, "attacking" it with a series of randomly generated authorization codes ranging from 5 to 15 characters in length. The software was not able to identify the authorization code in use.

Threats: After a modem-equipped line is located, the hacker can use his specialized programs to "attack" (meaning, dial the number repeatedly in the search for a valid authorization code). If the authorization code is compromised, the hacker has gained system access for personal financial gain (through unauthorized long-distance calls), to disrupt the normal operations of such a system, or to gain access to sensitive company information.

Vulnerabilities: After a modem tone is identified to the hacker, he can "attack" the number many times over, at his leisure, in the hope of gaining system access. A hacker often will publicize the number within the hacker community on bulletin boards. The system then becomes vulnerable to attack from more than one source. It is then only a matter of time until the authorization code is compromised and access is gained. By dialing once every 30 seconds, a hacker can log more than 2800 calls in a 24-hour period. If an authorization code is created that is convenient for users, it is convenient for hackers as well.

Risk: Low

Comments: The system could not be penetrated, although repeated attempts were made at all hours over a prolonged period of time (70 hours over a 3-week period).

Recommendations:

- Make the authorization code as long as possible and change it frequently.
- Control who has access to authorization codes within the organization.
- Avoid activating authorization codes until they are actually needed and assigned to an actual user; assign actual authorization codes randomly.
- Avoid repeating digits (keeping the same digits in the same position in your authorization codes); avoid using "O" at the beginning of an authorization code.
- Notify company authorities (investigations, computer security, and telecommunications management) immediately whenever it is suspected that an authorization code has been compromised.

2.0 *Voice Mail Penetration Tests*

2.1 *Test 1:* Attempt to access an outside line and phone number using the Zenith mail "Dial Thru" feature.

Result: This test did not work. It was determined that only another internal extension number on the same PBX switch can be accessed.

Threats: System penetration by surreptitious means.

Vulnerabilities: Not using built-in system security features (e.g., call blocking, limiting switches, etc.) would allow a hacker the ability to penetrate a system and make numerous toll calls at the company's expense, damage or delete information in individual user mailboxes, or disrupt normal system operation.

Risk: Low

Comments: The Zenith PZ-2 and Zenith voice mail option have system safeguards in place to prohibit access to the "Dial Thru" feature from outside the system itself.

Recommendations:

- Verify periodically that security features are in place and validate that they are working properly

2.2 ***Test 2:*** Try to reach a voice mail extension from a local outside line and have the call transferred to a tie-line or outside line with long distance capability.

Result: This test was not successful. Apparently, call blocking is in place.

Threats: System penetration by surreptitious means.

Vulnerabilities: A lack of adequate system security safeguards (e.g., call blocking, limiting switches, etc.) would allow a hacker the ability to penetrate a system and make numerous toll calls at the company's expense, damage or delete information in individual user mailboxes, or disrupt normal system operation.

Risk: Low

Comments: The Zenith PZ-2 and Zenith voice mail feature have system safeguards in place to prohibit access to the "Dial Thru" feature from outside the system itself.

Recommendations:

- Monitor system audit trails on a regular basis and report any indication of suspicious activity to appropriate company authorities immediately.
- Control assignment of system features to users, and limit long-distance capability only to those who have a requirement for it in their jobs.

2.3 ***Test 3:*** Try to determine whether voice mailboxes of transferred or terminated employees are still active and accessible from external phones.

Result: Repeated attempts to access were unsuccessful.

Threats: If a hacker can penetrate a PBX with a voice mail feature, he will attempt to locate a voice mailbox to establish a "legitimate" individual user presence. He then will have access to voice mail features, such as tie-lines to other areas, long-distance calling, and so forth.

Vulnerabilities: Leaving unused, inactive voice mailboxes on the active system creates the potential for misuse. Once established within the PBX, hackers can use the system to their advantage at the company's expense. Hackers can use the system for their own purposes or to sell toll calls through the system to others.

Risk: Low

Comments: Because of the limited number of available voice mailboxes, turnover and assignment to new users is rapid—generally within several days to a week.

Recommendations:

- Immediately deactivate all unused voice mailboxes.
- Develop a policy and implement a procedure to close out this feature on numbers assigned to transferring or terminating company employees, subcontractor personnel, or resident government representatives.

2.4 ***Test 4:*** Try to determine whether access can be gained to voice mailboxes from an outside phone by guessing potential passwords. For the purposes of this test, two common digit sequences known to the individual mailbox owner were used—their home phone number and office phone number. (NOTE: The passwords used met the acceptable password criteria.)

Result: Attempts to access 815 user voice mailboxes were made over a 2-week period without success.

Threats: Hackers can obtain and use compromised user, system, and system administrator passwords. They can also acquire and use stolen or illegally obtained company phone credit cards or credit card information. Stolen phone card information is often used in "call–sell" operations, during which the phone card information (i.e., phone card account numbers, access/authorization codes) is obtained from unsuspecting individuals and is shared with others for the purpose of making unauthorized toll calls at the owner's expense, be it an individual or a business.

Vulnerabilities: Active passwords give the hacker immediate and unchallenged access to the PBX and system features (i.e., voice mail). Likewise, phone cards and/or illegally obtained phone card information can give them ready access. Once access is achieved, hackers can use the system at will for their own purposes. Any expense caused by misuse or abuse is borne by the company.

Risk: Low

Comments: There has been no local indication or report of phone card misuse or abuse.

Recommendations:

- Ensure new employees who are issued phone cards receive training in developing passwords that meet acceptable criteria; they should not be used as a form of identification.
- Educate users about safeguarding their individual passwords and changing them periodically; always check surroundings for suspicious individuals.
- Ensure users know who to contact within company channels if a password is lost or compromised (telecommunications and investigations).
- Advocate that all passwords be randomly generated. The use of birth dates, anniversaries, and other commonly known events should be avoided. Also, the user should be educated not to use a recurring letter and/or number sequence if the pattern can be easily identified.
- Advertise that extra steps should be taken to protect company phone cards while traveling or when they are being used.

2.5 *Test 5:* Test system audit trails by determining what steps are taken by system administrators to report system irregularities.

Result: A number of voice mail users were revoked, using hacker techniques in attempting to compromise passwords. Voice mail administrators reported "possible hacking activity" on their system within 24 hours of the attempts. Review of audit trails for that period confirmed the suspect activity by date, time, and phone extension involved.

Threats: Systems without adequate audit trails are extremely vulnerable to external misuse. Systems with inoperative audit trails are equally susceptible to fraud and abuse.

Vulnerabilities: Systems with no audit trails or a failure to utilize installed audit trails are susceptible to serious ramifications (i.e., undetected misuse or abuse). Audit trails are necessary to collect historical information regarding system/user activity. Audit trails are also installed to highlight or flag suspicious activity. To be effective, they must be utilized to their fullest extent.

Risk: Low

Comments: System audit trails are in place and utilized.

Recommendations:

- Review audit trails on at least a weekly basis to ensure system faults, discrepancies, shortcomings, and performance are being tracked.
- Ensure all system audit trails are used on a regular basis. Sometimes, audit trails are intentionally turned off because they allegedly affect system performance or generate too much work for someone. Although this is rarely true, it is important to use this feature because these records identify system problems, weaknesses, and performance issues.
- Ensure all system administrators are aware of the proper reporting procedures for identifying system irregularities or weaknesses. Depending upon the type of problem, this information should be reported to telecommunications management, computer security, security inspections, or investigations.

3.0 *PBX Processes*
3.1 *Process for Physically Safeguarding the PZ-2 Switch*

This is the physical safeguarding process for the Southern Phonecom Zenith PZ-2 system located at XYZ Company's site A.

Threats: Access to the equipment room by unauthorized personnel. Damage to the hardware/software equipment by unauthorized employees.

Vulnerabilities: During the workday, the equipment room is secured by the Unicom lock only. Often the adjacent outer offices are vacant during the workday. When the offices are vacant, the outer office perimeter doors are not secured to prevent entry and possible tampering with the safeguard systems by unauthorized personnel. One perimeter office door stands open during normal working hours regardless of whether the offices are occupied.

Risks: Low

Comments: As of this date, there have been no incidents reporting unauthorized entry into the equipment room containing the PZ-2 switch, and there have been no reports of damage, destroyed, or stolen equipment.

Recommendations:

- Close and secure (lock set only) the perimeter doors to the outer offices to prevent random entry into the office area by unauthorized personnel when the outer offices are not occupied.

3.2 *Process for Safeguarding the PZ-2 Software*
This is the process for safeguarding the PZ-2 switch software, an integral part of the Southern Phonecom Zenith PZ-2 system.

Threats: Tampering of software by individuals with or without authorized access.

Vulnerabilities: Lack of good physical security controls, no process in place that identifies employees who have access to storage areas for the PZ-2 software in the event it had been tampered with. At the time of the audit, there was only one employee at site A with the knowledge and expertise to handle the maintenance, modification changes, and updates to the PZ-2 switch software. If unforeseen circumstances prevented the employee from performing his duties, serious situations could develop. There were no written procedural work instructions for safeguarding the PZ-2 software.

Risks: Low

Comments: As of this date, there has been no failure, no unauthorized tampering, or damage incurred to the PZ-2 switch software.

Recommendations:

- Establish sign-in/sign-out sheets for employees who remove or return the PZ-2 software.
- Review the need to train another employee as a backup to the primary employee responsible for the PZ-2 switch duties in the event the primary employee is unable to perform such duties.
- Create written procedural work instructions for this segment.

4.0 *Voice Mail Processes*
4.1 *Process for Safeguarding the Voice Mail Software*
This is the process used to safeguard voice mail software on the PZ-2 system.

Threats: The possibility of tampering or adding hidden passwords exists if outside vendor personnel are summoned to troubleshoot problems that exceed the expertise of company personnel.

Vulnerabilities: Company personnel do not watch work being done by contracted vendor maintenance personnel. Vendor personnel have free, unmonitored access to system hardware and software.

Risks: Low

Comments: There has been no indication of tampering and no interruption of service to date.

Recommendations:

- Develop a security procedure to ensure vendors are closely supervised during visits to avoid accidental or unauthorized changes or modifications to the software.
- Develop a written work procedure to verify physically all work accomplished by contracted maintenance personnel.

REFERENCES

1. Dodd, A. (April 12, 1993). When Going the Extra Mile Is Not Enough. *NETWORK WORLD.*
2. Quinn, B. (May 1993). Dialing for Dollars. CORPORATE COMPUTING.

17

Sources, Networking, and Liaison

The objective of this chapter is to identify, describe, and discuss sources of various types, networking, and liaison with outside agencies. We will continue to use the fictitious corporation, GEC, to facilitate discussing this topic in a "real-world" environment.

INTRODUCTION

It is imperative that the chief of security and the submanagers of the various security organizations maintain good working relationships with those inside and outside the corporation. This includes the appropriate security managers maintaining good relationships with the local community and their applicable counterparts outside the corporation. It is especially and vitally important for the CSO and the manager of the high-technology crime investigation unit to maintain a good working relationship with the local, state/province, and federal intelligence, security, and law enforcement agencies where the corporation's facilities are located, regardless of where in the world they may be.

In today's world of global competition, the theft of high-technology equipment and devices that the corporation has classified and is trying to protect as proprietary or trade secrets, along with their related information, can be the difference between maintaining a global competitive advantage and the acquisition of the corporation by a competitor. In addition, because of the global reach of terrorism, many corporations of some nation-states are their targets. Liaison and networking with the local government intelligence and security agencies' personnel may mean the difference between the loss of valuable corporate assets (people, information, and physical entities—such as facilities) and the safeguarding of those assets. Therefore, it is necessary that the high-technology crime investigator manager, supported by the CSO and the corporation's executive management, spend time networking and interacting with applicable government and other corporate security and intelligence professionals (Fig. 17-1).

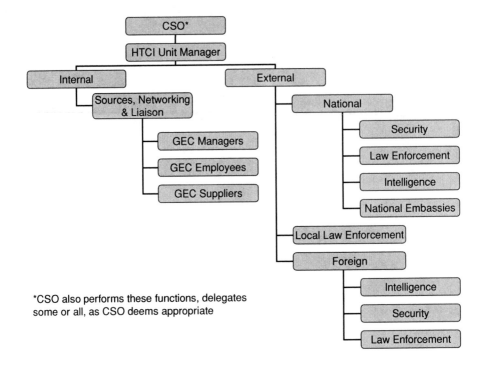

Figure 17-1 The relationship between the CSO and high-technology crime investigation (HTCI) unit manager, and their associated liaison, networking, and sourcing functions.

COLLECTING INFORMATION

As any good investigator knows, when it comes to getting information, you are usually only as good as your sources. In government agencies at the local, state, and federal levels, the use of sources (also known by some as spies, informants, rats, finks) is not only practiced, it is usually encouraged. Law enforcement officers and investigators often receive extensive training in handling sources. The sources that work for local, state, or federal government agencies can usually be "leveraged" to assist investigators by providing information relevant to an ongoing investigation.

In the business world, the use of sources (covert) within a corporation is generally not only not condoned—it may even be prohibited. However, some corporations require that all employees always cooperate and be truthful to those individuals conducting an inquiry or investigation. The high-technology crime investigator manager found that this was the policy at GEC. He also determined that the following other "pro investigation" policies were in effect at GEC:

- If a person refuses to cooperate, that is usually grounds for immediate termination of employment.
- If the employee lies to an investigator conducting a formal corporate investigation and those lies are subsequently verified, that is also grounds for immediate termination. Such a policy is quite logical when considering that a corporation wants to employ honest people. If a person would lie during a formal corporate investigation, always considered a very serious matter, the corporation reasons that he probably would lie about other work-related matters that affect the quality of the products, or commit other dishonest acts.
- All GEC property, high technology, and other assets are only to be used for corporate business. Therefore, GEC advises all new employees in writing that their e-mail, desks, and office areas are subject to search. Employees must acknowledge this in writing on a document that is maintained in each employee's personnel record. One main reason for security officers to conduct such searches is to assist in ensuring that sensitive corporate documents are properly secured.

One other advantage that high-technology crime investigators have at GEC, and in most businesses, is the fact that they do not have police powers. Therefore, no employee or any other person being interviewed by the investigator has any Fifth Amendment rights to self-incrimination. So the investigator does not have to inform the interviewee or suspect that he may retain a lawyer, may refuse to answer if that answer may incriminate him, and so forth.

However, once a public law enforcement officer or investigator is involved in the investigation and that investigator asks you to find out certain information from a suspect or others, you may be considered by the courts as acting in behalf of the law enforcement officer, and therefore, the interviewee's Fifth Amendment rights would apply. We recommend that the corporate investigator coordinate with the legal staff because a court decision may change this process. However, as good as that sounds to an investigator, in most corporations, human resource personnel and/or union representatives may impede the conduct of your investigation.

SOURCES

The use of the word *sources* has a more politically correct connotation than the word *informants* or other similar words one can think of to describe someone who provides information. There are two primary types of sources: overt and covert. Overt sources are people who openly provide information to an investigator, newspapers, journals, radio, television, or generally any source of information that is available to the public. Covert sources are those people who provide information or other sources (spy satellites) whose identity is protected.

In GEC and most corporations, the use of people as covert sources is generally either prohibited or not condoned except under special circumstances. This also applies to the use of hidden cameras and microphones.

Internal Sources

Internal sources at GEC must be overt sources unless someone contacts a member of the high-technology crime investigation unit and requests that their name not be used. Those GEC overt sources that would be of use should first be identified by their positions. This is because it does not matter who is in that position, that person has access to information that is beneficial to conducting high-technology crime investigations, NCIs, and surveys. Positions would include at least the following:

- Manager of the audit organization
- Manager of the employment organization
- Manager of each major security organization
- Security guards at specific posts
- Manager of employee relations
- Manager of the legal department
- Manager of the accounting and finance organization
- Manager of the procurement and purchasing organization
- Manager of each information technology organization, specifically the manager of the InfoSec organization

You can probably add others to this list. As the manager of the high-technology crime investigation unit, you should make it a point to:

- Meet these people.
- Get to know them.
- Learn what they do.
- Become familiar with their duties and responsibilities (e.g., obtain copies of their organizational charts.
- Identify how they can help your unit.
- Identify ways that your unit can help them.

As your unit matures and you have a few more high-technology crime investigators, they should each be assigned specific organizations to visit regularly when they are not conducting investigation, inquiries, briefings, surveys, and the like.

At the same time, as the unit manager, some overt sources must be handled personally because of their positions. In fact, some managers who have a high opinion of themselves may not have time in their schedules for one of your investigators, but they always seem to find time for you. As the CSO or unit manager, if that occurs, then bringing a specific investigator along for several visits may help build a relationship between the source and the investigator, and your visits can then be reduced (but never eliminated). That your visits will never be eliminated may be too obvious, and it may adversely affect any relationship that you have built over the past months or years.

As you receive information from other individuals who appear to be helpful and willing to assist at times, you need to determine the type of information this person has access to. Again, you must be careful to not appear to be recruiting "informants." The purpose of identifying these individuals is not to task them to "spy" on others. However, if you were conducting an investigation in an organization or pertaining to a matter to which the employee may have knowledge, that person would logically be the first or one of the first that you, the investigator, would interview.

When someone does contact or has been contacted by the investigator and does not want their name used for fear of reprisals, there should be a process to accommodate that. However, that accommodation should be coordinated with a member of the legal staff so that this protection can be properly handled. This process should be developed as one of the first coordination meetings held between the unit manager and the manager of the legal department. In this way, the investigator would be able to explain to the source exactly what protection can be ensured under what circumstances.

External Sources

External sources may be anyone outside GEC or anyone in GEC who is not considered a GEC employee (e.g., a consultant, subcontractor working in a GEC facility). One should be very cautious when dealing with such sources. If they are overt sources, then there is less concern that someone may look upon your activities as covertly recruiting informants. If the source wants his identity protected, one should be cautious not to be tainted by accusations of source recruitment against employees of another company. Again, a process for handling these types of sources should have already been developed with the coordination of the legal department manager.

"CARDING" SOURCES

Those individuals who provide high-technology crime–related information should be identified for future reference. In the "old days," source information was kept on index cards. In the information age, this information is better kept on the unit's source database. Searches and queries can easily be conducted to find sources who have provided information in the past and who work in the organization or may have knowledge of an incident being investigated. These sources are also good contacts to talk to before conducting a survey because they can provide information regarding how the processes in place work, how information flows, and so on. Some of the basic information that should be placed in the database on a source is:

- Name
- Employee number or other identification numbers
- Organization
- Address
- Telephone number
- Fax number
- E-mail address
- Time, date, and location of first contact
- Purpose of the contact
- Results of the first contact
- Details of subsequent contacts
- Name of investigator providing this input

The information can be expanded and can include more details, such as social security number, date and place of birth, home address, and so forth. However, caution must be used to ensure that this information can be shown to be necessary in the event it becomes known to others outside the unit. Additionally, such information should have a short expiration date. If there isn't any contact with the source in a year, then the information should be deleted. However, such decisions are based on the culture and working environment within a business. They are judgment calls made by the unit manager.

The database should also have fields for input each time source contact is made and information is provided. The fields should include basically the same information noted earlier: time, date, and place of contact; information provided; and which investigator was contacted. Also, all inquiries and high-technology crime investigation suspects, crimes, and so forth, should be entered in the database. Later, this will provide an excellent tool for doing searches relative to unsolved crimes in which commonalties, patterns, and trends can be seen.

CLASSIFYING THE RELIABILITY OF SOURCES AND THE ACCURACY OF THEIR INFORMATION

Sources of all kinds each have a motive for providing information and cooperating with investigators. A "track record" of source contacts maintained in the database provides that information. However, what is lacking is anything indicating the importance and validity of the information and the reliability of the source to provide reliable information.

At GEC, the unit manager decided to include two fields in the record of each database that would assist in evaluating the source and the information provided by the source. The unit manager devised the following two fields: Reliability of Source and Reliability of Source's Information. Investigators who had significant contact (when a source provided meaningful information) would be required to update the database with this information, but they also had to "code" the source and information. The following codes were used.

Source Reliability

- Code 1: Always reliable
- Code 2: Usually reliable
- Code 3: Sometimes reliable
- Code 4: Questionable reliability
- Code 5: Has never been reliable
- Code 6: Reliability unknown at this time

Source Information Reliability

- Code A: Always accurate
- Code B: Usually accurate
- Code C: Sometimes accurate
- Code D: Accuracy always questionable
- Code E: Never accurate
- Code F: Accuracy of information unknown at this time

By keeping the source database up to date, the investigators can have a ready source of reference to the source's reliability and be in a better position to judge the accuracy of the information they are providing based on past information. This database will be a good reference point for investigators, and it should be queried prior to any interview with individuals to determine whether they have previously provided information and whether their information was useful.

> Caution must always be used in talking to sources, and constant questioning of their motives is necessary.

Here is an example of an ulterior motive. During a period of downsizing at GEC, several individuals made anonymous calls to the investigation unit and advised that an employee in a certain department was using the computer to operate a personal tax service.

Should an investigator, having received such information, immediately open an investigation? It is a difficult decision. If ignored, it may continue indefinitely—if it were true. If an investigation is opened, it may be based on a false accusation. The person calling may have done so to make a peer look bad. The reason for the doubt is that because downsizing occurred, a person under investigation would be a more likely candidate for layoff than one who was not under investigation. During downsizing, desperate measures are sometimes taken by desperate people.

NETWORKING

It is imperative that the investigator continuously network with peers met at conferences and association meetings. These individuals should also be identified in a database or their business cards should be placed in a file and categorized by their line of business (e.g., computer consultant, vendor, government employee).

In today's information environment, one can obtain a great deal of free information, advice, and warnings of various types of high-technology crimes and criminals through contacts. Most of these individuals will have e-mail addresses. Contacting them periodically via e-mail and telephone calls is a very cost-effective way to gather information and keep abreast in your profession.

It is recommended that periodically these individuals be contacted to determine "what's new." It is surprising how much relevant information can be gathered using this cost-effective method. Often, the information gathered could provide the source and an indication that may call for a high-technology crime prevention survey targeting a particular process on high-technology device or other actions.

For example, if a new social engineering technique were being used by phreakers to gain access to a corporation's PBX, that information could be sent out immediately in a GEC e-mail message. The message would warn the employees of such a technique and would advise the employees to report any such attempts but not to provide the information or action that the phreaker has requested. In fact, this happened at GEC and also was the basis for a new checklist to be given to employees.

The unit investigators devised a short checklist similar to the one provided by the security department and used in the event a caller made a bomb threat. The checklist included similar information as on the bomb checklist about the person calling being male, female, background noises, and so on. This one provided not only a list of some of the social engineering techniques used to obtain user IDs, passwords, and PBX access, but also reporting procedures. It also called for the person receiving the call to transfer the call to the high-technology crime investigation unit under one of several ruses, but the phreaker would think that the call was being transferred to allow accesses per the phreaker's request. The high-technology crime investigator then has several options: gather more details to identify the phreaker, determine the phreaker's objective, and so forth.

This checklist and the information provided was expanded and included in the updated awareness briefings given employees. Subsequently, the investigators conducted a survey by making social engineering calls to selected organizations as a quality check. When conducting such a test, the objective is not to embarrass anyone but to ensure that a high-technology crime prevention process is in place and working. Therefore, any report should not include the names of individuals contacted. One of the fastest ways to lose the respect and support of employees is to conduct such a covert test and then place the names of those who fail in the report. The manager would then, in all probability, contact that employee and counsel him or her.

However, if this survey was done again after 6 months or a year, and the same person provided the information in violation of the policy, then the employee should be contacted. The employee's manager should be advised. With the employee's manager present, the issue should be discussed using a briefing and teaching method in lieu of a counseling method. For those that object to this "soft" approach, remember in the business world you succeed by gaining the trust and support of the employees. After all, you don't have a badge and a gun to provide that support.

LIAISON

According to the Franklin Language Master Dictionary and Thesaurus, the word *liaison* means "close bond; communication between groups." For GEC's high-technology crime investigation unit it means just that: communicating between the unit and local, state, and federal criminal justice agencies. Such a liaison is always in the best interest of GEC as part of their involvement in the community. In addition, the sharing of information with law enforcement agencies on high-technology crime and crime prevention matters will be of mutual benefit to both groups.

Membership and active support of your local high-technology crime investigation association will provide the opportunity to build a relationship of trust and support.

As with other sources of information, the individuals with whom you come in contact should be entered into the database. Another advantage of such a database is that the source is not lost if an investigator leaves the unit.

SUMMARY

Contacting sources of all types, networking, and creating a liaison with outside groups and government agencies are all excellent ways to

- Help solve crime cases
- Obtain the necessary information to keep up with the latest events in the profession
- Share information with peers
- Provide a community service by supporting the local law enforcement agencies and others

Caution should always be used when dealing with sources because of the potentially adverse political and legal ramifications. If done properly, a database is an excellent method of maintaining a "source file" of sources.

18

High-Technology Crime Investigation Unit Metrics Management System[*]

This chapter addresses the use of security metrics as a tool for managing investigative and NCI security functions. Process analysis will be discussed along with the use of metrics to assess the effectiveness, costs, benefits, successes, and failures.

INTRODUCTION

Investigations and NCIs are security functions that, at some corporations, may be candidates for outsourcing. At this time, both are internal functions at GEC, and these two functions are much alike. However, the primary difference is scope and magnitude. That is to say, the term *NCI* is used to describe an investigation that is conducted as a result of a violation of corporate policy or procedure, in which there has not been a violation of law. At GEC an investigation is generally a much more complex process associated with a more serious situation and may involve a violation of the law or a regulation external to the corporation.

One primary reason for the differentiation is for PR purposes. When one hears that an investigation is being conducted, it sounds more serious than if one hears that an NCI is being conducted. In addition, an NCI may be used as a preliminary inquiry to assess whether something is wrong and whether it requires a full investigation.

---

[*]The information provided in this chapter was excerpted with permission from *Security Metrics Management: How to Manage the Costs of an Assets Protection Program*: December 2005, ISBN 10: 0-7506-7899-2; coauthored by Dr. Gerald L. Kovacich and Edward P. Halibozek; published by Butterworth-Heinemann.

An NCI may be conducted by almost any security professional or member of management. An investigation requires someone skilled in the techniques and processes of investigations; that person will need to have a working relationship with different governmental investigative organizations (local, state, and federal).

INVESTIGATIONS

The investigation and NCI organization (Fig. 18-1) falls under the direct management of the CSO. As depicted in Figure 18-1, the organization consists of much more than the investigative and NCI functions. It is particularly important for the investigative element of this organization to report directly to the CSO. This function may handle some of the most sensitive issues within the company, sometimes involving the sensitive issue of employee misbehavior.

Extra layers of oversight and management between the CSO and the investigative function are generally problematic.

Risk assessments are conducted in coordination with other applicable security functions and are carried out after an investigation or NCI indi-

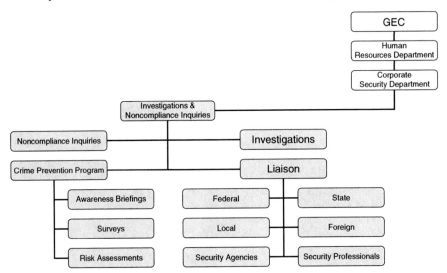

Figure 18-1   The organizational location of the investigations and NCI function.

cates that some corporate assets have been determined to be vulnerable and at risk. This function is a proactive process used primarily to mitigate risks to assets and to minimize the number of times there will be need for an NCI or investigation.

The liaison function is carried out by both the CSO and the investigation and NCI organization manager. Liaisons occur with local, state, federal, and foreign law enforcement, criminal justice, and security officers; and with intelligence offers as appropriate. The awareness function is accomplished as a standalone process used when management requires special information such as a "crime prevention" briefing. Other forms of investigations and NCI-related briefings are coordinated with the administrative security functional lead for security awareness briefings and training.

Investigation Drivers and Flowcharts

After the organizational structure of the investigations and NCI function is identified and charted, its primary drivers are identified and graphically depicted. As shown in Figures 18-2 and 18-3, complaints and allegations from various sources are considered the security drivers.

An important driver for the Investigations and NCI process is the total number of GEC employees: The more employees, the more potential employees who will violate GEC rules or federal laws. Another driver is the number of requests for support from other organizations (such as the legal and ethics staffs and their need to have investigators support their processes). Remember that the Investigations and NCI organization is also a service and support organization and as such must provide professional support to other GEC organizations when that service and support is requested and determined to be warranted.

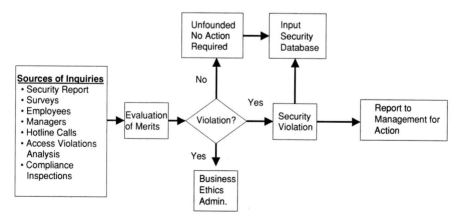

Figure 18-2   Overall flowchart of the drivers of investigations and NCIs.

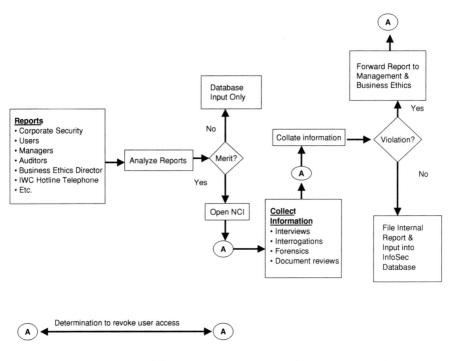

Figure 18-3 Depiction of the investigation or NCI of a system user where continued access is periodically being evaluated as part of the InfoSec function.

Examples of Investigations Metrics

There are many different security metrics that a CSO or unit manager can use to help understand, assess, and manage the investigations and NCI processes. A problem that the CSO may face, as with all other security metrics, is determining the most useful metrics.

When in doubt regarding the most valuable metrics, the CSO or unit manager can start by identifying as many as possible and then sort through them to determine which offer the most utility.

The CSO may first want to develop a process flow diagram depicting the macroprocess and then develop flow diagrams for the investigative subprocesses or microprocesses. After that is accomplished, the CSO can begin to develop points for different process measures. An example of such a data collection list and its associated charts for investigations may look like the following (and one for the NCI function would be almost identical):

- Number of investigations opened per month
- Number of investigations closed per month
- Number of investigations pending per month
- Average time used to conduct an investigation
- Average cost in terms of investigator's time, GEC employees' time, administrative time, and cost of resources used
- All previous information, but categorized by type of investigation
- All previous information, but categorized by quarter, year, and multiple years
- Identification of the GEC department in which the incident took place
- Identification of the GEC department in which the subject (employee) of the investigation was assigned
- Number of allegations proved correct
- Number of allegations proved wrong
- Subject's position and job code
- Type of investigations categorized by department
- Department information categorized monthly, quarterly, annually, and by multiple years
- Associate a cost chart with each of the above charts

By using the previously described approach, one can begin to get a sense of the type of information that offers potential for developing useful metrics. Furthermore, the CSO can relate the potential data points to what he or she needs to know. For example, if the CSO is attempting to determine the average time to conduct an investigation, tracking the time taken to complete all steps from the opening of an investigation to the closing of an investigation will provide that data. The CSO can further analyze that information by sorting investigations by type. An investigation into the theft of a physical asset, on average, may require less time than an investigation into misuse of information systems.

Metrics developed and used in the investigations and NCI process may provide value beyond the investigative processes itself. Trend data may be developed and used to drive changes in other routine security policies, procedures, and processes. For example, if investigative trend data reveal thefts to be occurring during a specific time frame, additional protective measures may be implemented during that vulnerable period to prevent the thefts or catch those committing the thefts.

The information gathered may be used proactively to reduce the number of incidents requiring investigations, thus reducing the overall workload for security investigators. Learning from security incidents helps prevent their occurrence in the future.

Figures 18-4 through 18-9 are just a few examples of graphically depicted security metrics charts that a CSO may find useful in assessing effectiveness of the investigations and NCI process and in managing the organization.

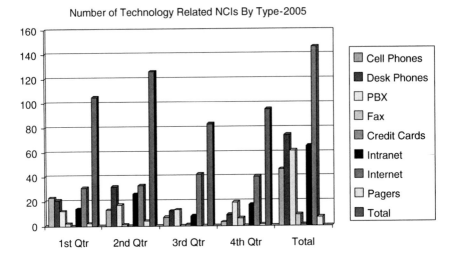

Figure 18-4   The number of technology-related NCIs conducted in 2005 broken down by type.

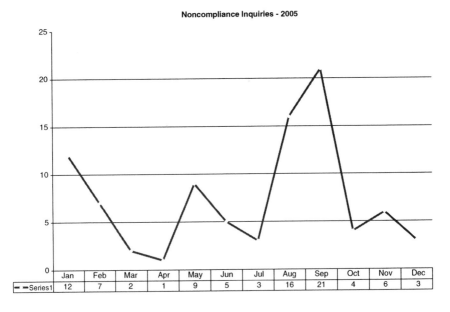

	Jan	Feb	Mar	Apr	May	Jun	Jul	Aug	Sep	Oct	Nov	Dec
Series1	12	7	2	1	9	5	3	16	21	4	6	3

Figure 18-5   The number of NCIs conducted in 2005 broken down by month. This is an important depiction to establish a trend.

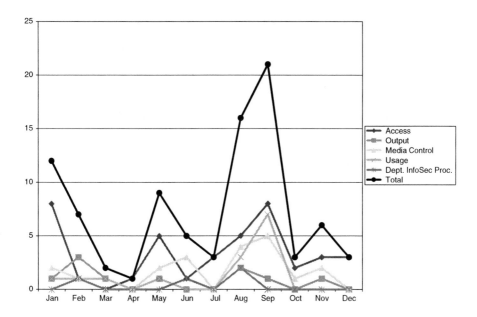

Figure 18-6   The number of InfoSec-related NCIs in 2005 broken
down by type per month.

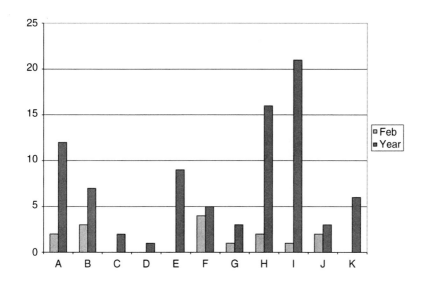

Figure 18-7   The number of NCIs conducted broken down by department for the
past month and the past year.

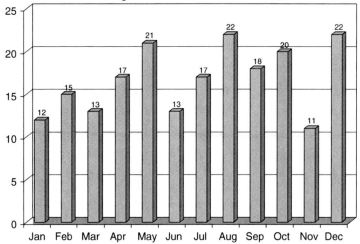

Average Time Per NCI Per Month—2005

Figure 18-8 The number of investigations conducted per month for a 1-year period for US-only facilities.

Investigations and NCI Resource Allocation's Drivers

- The number of IWC employees have increased based on IWC's need to rapidly build up the workforce to handle the new contract work.

- The number of noncompliance inquiries have increased during that same time period.

- The number of investigations have increased during that same period of time.

- This increased workload has caused some delays in completing the inquiries and investigations in the 30-day period that was set as the goal.

- The ratio of incidents compared to the total number of employees indicates:
  - Personnel may not be getting sufficient information during their new-hire briefings
  - The personnel being hired may not be thoroughly screened prior to hiring

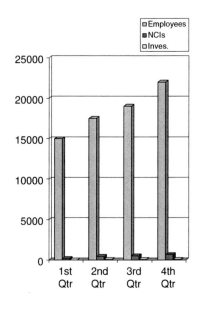

Figure 18-9 Different drivers of the investigations and NCI process. The number of IWC employees has increased based on IWC's need to rapidly build up the workforce to handle the new contract work. The number of noncompliance inquiries has increased during that same time period. The number of investigations has increased during that same period of time. This increased workload has caused some delays in completing the inquiries and investigations in the 30-day period that was set as the goal. The ratio of incidents compared to the total number of employees indicates that personnel may not be getting sufficient information during their new-hire briefings and that the personnel being hired may not be thoroughly screened prior to hiring.

Remember that as the employee population increases, so does investigative and NCI activity (Fig. 18-10). This in turn drives the need for additional supporting resources.

Figure 18-11 is an important chart in that it depicts a trend. From this graphic depiction, the CSO* can conclude a continuous yearly increase in the number of investigations. This trend should drive the CSO to analyze the investigative data to determine why. Action taken or not taken will be influenced by the results of the analysis.

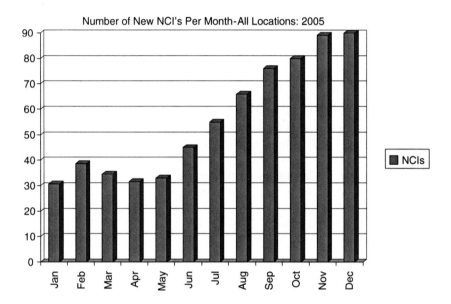

Figure 18-10   The total number of NCIs per month at all GEC locations.

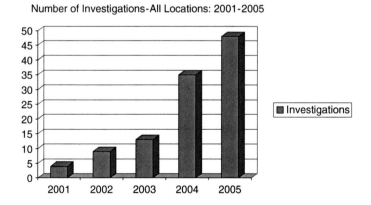

Figure 18-11   The total number of investigations at all locations from 2001 to 2005.

---

*The information provided primarily relates to the CSO, but the unit manager should also approach the metrics like the CSO.

The figures in this chapter offer a few examples of the many security metrics a CSO may find useful in the effort to understand process performance and manage an investigations and NCI function.

Process measurements can tell much about a process. The type of measures used should correlate to what the CSO wants or needs to track and understand. For example, if it is important to the CSO to know what percent of cases are closed each month, then Figure 18-12 may be of value. The ultimate goal for the CSO should be to understand what is occurring that drives the need for investigations. Can those drivers be changed to such a degree as to eliminate or reduce the need for investigations? Measuring will also tell the CSO if the changes made had any effect on the process. Of course, cost issues must always be considered.

INVESTIGATION CASE STUDY

As a CSO, you decided that it would be a good idea to use the security driver's metrics, which is used for tracking the number of employees, the number of inquiries, and the number of investigations conducted over time. You have gone through the analytical process to make that decision based on answering the following how, what, why, when, who, and where questions.

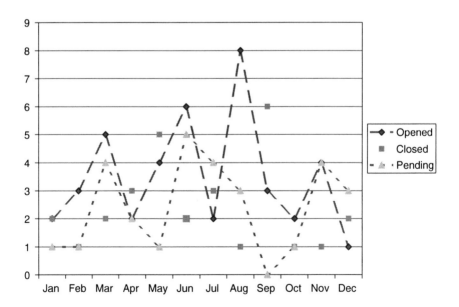

Figure 18-12   The percentage of NCIs opened, closed, and pending per month.

1. Why should this data be collected? To determine the ratio of employees to the workload. In this way, manpower requirements can be forecasted over time.
2. What specific data will be collected?
   * Total number of GEC employees
   * Total number of NCIs
   * Total number of investigations
3. How will these data be collected?
   * Total employees—The collection will be accomplished by taking the total number of paid employees from the human resource department's master personnel database file.
   * Total number of NCIs—This information will be gathered by the unit coordinator from the unit's NCI database file.
   * Total number of investigations—The unit coordinator will also gather this information from the unit's investigation database file.
4. When will these data be collected? The data from each of the previous months will be compiled on the first business day of each of the following months and incorporated into the crime investigation drivers' graph, maintained on the investigation and NCI administrative information system.
5. Who will collect these data? The data will be collected, input, and maintained by the unit coordinator.
6. Where (at what point in the function's process) will these data be collected? The collection of data will be based on the information available and on file in the investigation and NCI database at the close of business on the last business day of the month.

The CSO and organizational manager will analyze the NCI data, for example, to determine:

* The reason for each employee's noncompliance
* The position and organization of the employee
* The employee's hire date
* Identification of patterns
* Main offenses

This information will then be provided to the project team assigned to the goal of decreasing the need for NCIs and investigations. Based on this information, briefings would be updated and more emphasis placed in those areas that caused the majority of problems.

Remember, there are numerous types of graphic depictions of data that can be a great tool for management. They include bar charts, pie charts, and line charts. The charts can be monthly, quarterly, weekly, or annually. The timeliness of the charts should be dependent on the manager's need for the information.

The key to data collection and related graphic depiction is to look more at trends than monthly numbers. The goal is to continue to maintain and improve on positive trends. Negative trends should be analyzed for systemic causes, and project plans should be implemented to reverse the negative trends. The metrics could then be used to monitor the process and to determine whether process changes actually cause the reversal of the negative trends. If not, then new analyses and rethinking of the problem are called for.

The organizational manager, in coordination with the CSO, began this process by identifying the drivers requiring the functions to be performed. Then the processes were flowcharted, and a process analysis summary was developed to help provide a high-level view of the process.

That process summary included the following information:

- Security department—investigations and NCIs
- Process definition—professional investigative services in support of GEC and its customers
- Subprocesses
  - Conduct investigations
  - Conduct NCIs
  - Conduct crime prevention surveys
  - Conduct crime prevention special briefings
- Requirements and directives that govern the process
  - Corporate Assets Protection Program (CAPP)
  - Contractual security requirements
  - Position descriptions
  - Corporate policies
- Suppliers
  - GEC employees
  - Customers
  - GEC management
- Input
  - Complaints
  - Allegations
  - Requests for assistance
  - Security requirements
- Output
  - Investigative reports
  - NCI reports
  - Inspection reports
  - Security assessment reports
  - Briefings
  - Testimony

- Key metrics
  - Subprocess 1—case totals year to date and 5-year trends, case-aging charts
  - Subprocess 2—crime prevention surveys completed, results, and cost–benefit charts
  - Subprocess 3—number of NCIs completed each year, costs, and GEC departments where conducted
  - Subprocess 4—number of investigations completed each year, costs, and GEC departments where conducted
- Customer and expectations
  - GEC management (internal customers)—timely and complete investigative and NCI reports
  - GEC customers—timely and complete investigative and NCI reports as applicable to external customers

Using this identification process, the GEC CSO can view a summary of not only investigative and NCI organizational security metrics and process-related information, but the CSO can establish a form or format for such summaries and require its use throughout the security department.

SUMMARY

The investigations and NCI organization is a highly visible and important function within the GEC security department. Using a security metrics management program to assess effectiveness of the function is critical to a CSO. The information collected and analyzed can be used to improve the process and help mitigate risks and thus better protect GEC assets.

19

*Outsource or Proprietary?**

This chapter discusses whether to outsource or keep in-house the high-technology crime investigation function. Remember that the high-technology crime investigative function and unit is an overhead cost, as are all the GEC security department functions. Therefore, the CSO should always be analyzing the department's organizations and functions to determine whether they can be accomplished more effectively (better) and efficiently (cheaper). One way of meeting this objective is to look at outsourcing the high-technology crime investigative function.

INTRODUCTION

GEC, like most corporations, is in business to produce and sell goods, products, and services, most of which are not security products or services. GEC is in the business of designing, manufacturing, producing, and selling high-technology widgets. It is not in the business of selling security or assets protection services. GEC does provide security services for itself. It does so to meet the security and assets protection needs of the company and employees, which includes the high-technology crime investigative function. In this context, the high-technology crime investigative function is a subset of the security department as a cost center. Security services are not sold to others and, therefore, do not bring in revenue. For GEC, security functions are not a core competency, and, therefore, all security functions are candidates for outsourcing (Fig. 19-1).

Within the GEC security department there are a range of services provided. Some of the services are simple transactional services, such as employee identification badge making. Others are much more complicated, such as the contingency planning process and the CAPP.

*This information is primarily taken with permission from or based on the book *Security Metrics Management: How to Measure the Costs and Benefits of Security*: December 2005, ISBN 10: 0-7506-7899-2; coauthored by Dr. Gerald L. Kovacich and Edward P. Halibozek; published by Butterworth-Heinemann.

Figure 19-1   The location of an investigative function in the relationship to other potential outsourcing of security functions.

Like other managers, the GEC CSO has limited resources available to provide security services to the company. The CSO is very interested in being able to provide the best possible services at the lowest cost. To do this, the CSO is considering outsourcing some assets protection functions and this includes the high-technology crime investigative function. To begin the process of outsourcing, there are actions the CSO must take and information needed that will assist in conducting a comprehensive analysis. This analysis will take two parts. First, an initial assessment must be made to determine whether outsourcing the high-technology crime investigative function is a viable option. Second, a detailed analysis must be made to determine whether it is actually more cost-effective to outsource.

OUTSOURCING: A DEFINITION

Outsourcing is defined as contracting for outside services that are a necessary part of doing business but are not core functions or core competencies. A core competency is a service, activity, or process that adds strategic value to GEC. It contributes to the strategic direction and success of GEC. Core competencies are not candidates for outsourcing. They differentiate GEC from other companies and add strategic value, supporting the competitive advantage of GEC.

Outsourcing is a tool, not a cure.

Outsourcing allows GEC to focus on its core functions and to let other companies assist by providing the services they perform best. Outsourcing converts an in-house cost center into a customer-focused service operation, with the GEC CSO as the customer for outsourced security functions or projects. In general, transactional and occasional or one-time activities lend themselves to outsourcing. Intellectual functions, functions that have strong governmental oversight, and functions for which success relies on management's trusted relationships are not ideal for outsourcing.

THE ADVANTAGES AND DISADVANTAGES OF A PROPRIETARY HIGH-TECHNOLOGY CRIME INVESTIGATIVE UNIT

With any activity there are reasons to perform that activity and reasons not to perform that activity. Depending upon conditions and circumstances, every activity has its advantages and disadvantages. This is true of both proprietary and outsourced security service providers. Before considering outsourcing the high-technology crime investigative function as an option to perform and deliver services, it is essential to know and understand the advantages and disadvantages of outsourcing this function. It is just as essential to know and understand the advantages and disadvantages of providing high-technology investigative support through GEC's proprietary security organization.

Proprietary Pros

The following is a list of reasons for maintaining the proprietary high-technology crime investigative function:

- *Staffing continuity*—Turnover of investigative personnel within a proprietary security force is generally less frequent than turnover of investigative personnel with an outsource provider. Because proprietary investigators are generally paid better and have better employee benefits, they move on less frequently.
- *Loyalty*—There is a perception that proprietary employees exhibit more loyalty toward their employer than contract or outsource personnel do. This is difficult to assess and may be best accomplished through a customer survey.
- *Tighter management controls*—Proprietary investigators, as GEC employees, work for the CSO and GEC. This arrangement provides direct control over performance and career opportunities.
- *Familiarity with company and company history*—Because proprietary employees stay with companies longer, they have a greater opportunity to learn more about the company they work for and the

people they work with and serve. Thus, leading (hopefully) to a more "team-oriented" workforce.

- *Maintenance of functional expertise*—Having proprietary investigators allows you to use them to meet GEC's security statement of work and company needs. Those particularly skilled employees are available for use in many ways. Having them as employees allows the CSO to keep that functional expertise within the company and under CSO control. If the most skilled investigators are employees of an outsource provider, that provider has the option to use their expertise elsewhere.

Proprietary Cons

The following is a list of reasons for not maintaining proprietary security functions:

- *Higher costs*—Because proprietary employees generally cost more than outsourced employees, a proprietary high-technology crime investigative unit generally costs more than an outsourced one. Moreover, there are hidden costs associated with proprietary employees that are not associated with outsourced employees. Costs include things such as occasional perks provided to employees or the associated costs of facility usage, which are not easily identified and are often overlooked when making a comparison or assessment (e.g., benefits, time spent on performance reviews, discipline).
- *Lack of flexibility*—With a proprietary investigative force, the CSO has available a limited number of employees. When a situation occurs when an unplanned or even a planned event requires additional support, having a limited number of employees inhibits the CSO's ability to fully staff it. No surge capability exists. Therefore, it may be necessary to hire temporary or part-time personnel or expand the use of overtime. Any of these options can be costly.

THE ADVANTAGES AND DISADVANTAGES OF AN OUTSOURCED HIGH-TECHNOLOGY CRIME INVESTIGATIVE UNIT

> Outsourcing should always be viewed as a serious option for delivering security services.

At the very least, outsourcing will provide for a capability to augment existing services or provide necessary resources during surge periods.

Some may find that outsourcing, when a carefully selected provider is used and the relationship is more of a partnership as opposed to a customer/supplier relationship, meets all their high-technology crime investigative needs. Others seek a mix, attempting to achieve a balance between cost and flexibility. Others prefer not to outsource at all, for a variety of reasons. Some of these issues will be addressed here. Outsourcing is not an activity that can be turned on and walked away from. It requires a dedication to results, regular oversight, and active management. Furthermore, outsourcing must be a win–win situation. There will be no long-term value derived from an outsourcing relationship if the relationship is one sided. If the relationship is not mutually beneficial, it will be unproductive and ultimately a failure. Both parties must have an interest in a successful relationship and no interest in the exploitation of the other.

Outsourcing Pros

The following is a list of reasons for outsourcing proprietary security functions:

- *Cost savings*—Reducing costs is the primary reason for outsourcing. Although outsourcing has other benefits, reducing cost is its largest advantage. As mentioned earlier, the GEC security department and all its subunits and functions are a cost center. Security contributes to the continuity and viability of the business but does not generate revenue. Reducing costs is the way the CSO can contribute to the bottom-line profitability of GEC.
- *Mobility of people*—Outsourcing can provide greater flexibility for investigative staffing than having a proprietary investigative unit. It is much easier to move or replace an investigator of an outsource provider than it is to move or replace one who is an employee. Employees of an outsource provider are not on your payroll. That condition alone affords you more flexibility in making changes.
- *Surge capability*—Special events or unforeseen activities can place a heavy burden on staffing. With a proprietary high-technology crime investigative unit and employees, the short-term option is to use overtime to meet surge requirements, but sometimes this is not enough. The longer-term options are hiring additional part-time or full-time investigative personnel to support the need. Outsourcing better addresses this problem in two ways: First, outsource providers have a larger cadre of personnel to draw from, which makes it easier for them to meet your surge needs. Second, contractual arrangements may be made during contract negotiations establishing parameters for surge support to keep unexpected costs to a minimum. If the CSO does not use an outsource provider for high-technology crime

investigative services, he may be valuable to contract one for special circumstances. In this way, outsourcing becomes an augmentation to the proprietary high-technology crime investigative unit.

- *Indirect management; maintenance of control and contract administration*—Outsourcing to a high-technology crime investigative service provider brings more to GEC than just investigative professionals. It also brings supervision and management. As a customer to the outsource provider, the role of GEC's CSO shifts from the management of daily personnel and related investigative issues to that of an administrator managing the provisions of a contract. More of the CSO's time and effort will focus on ensuring the outsource provider fulfills the obligations of the contract. The outsource provider's managers will handle the daily personnel issues and security tasks.

Outsourcing Cons

The following is a list of reasons for not outsourcing the proprietary high-technology crime investigative function:

- *Perceived decrease in company loyalty by customers*—It has been the experience of the GEC CSO that management and employees perceive proprietary high-technology crime investigative personnel to be more loyal to the interest of the company than contract or outsourced security personnel. In a large part, this is just that—a perception. Experience indicates this is not the case. If the relationship between the outsource provider and the customer security organization is that of a partnership, a well-defined and mutually beneficial relationship, loyalty is not an issue. Furthermore, a long-term relationship between the customer (GEC CSO) and service provider will provide a basis to develop loyalty toward each other.
- *Quality of personnel*—There is an old adage that states "you get what you pay for." Any consumer will support this claim. If you buy cheap, you get cheap. On the other hand, getting quality personnel does not mean you must pay the highest price. Getting quality high-technology crime investigative personnel to perform investigative duties is as much related to having a well-defined statement of work as it is to understanding the market you operate within and offering a competitive wage. A clear and well-defined statement of work will tell you what investigative skills are necessary to fulfill the needs of GEC. An understanding of the local geographic market will enable you to establish competitive wages—wages that will be attractive to the caliber of personnel you are seeking. Failure to establish a competitive wage and having an ill-defined statement of work will lead to unfulfilled expectations and high turnover. This will satisfy no one.

- *Cultural change*—Changing from a proprietary security force to a contract service is a significant change in culture. Security management, company management, and employees have been used to conduct business in an established way. Changes are generally not well received. Even positive changes sometimes meet resistance. To deal effectively with the negative aspects of change, a PR and employee awareness campaign should be used. Once a decision has been made to outsource the high-technology crime investigative function, and all involved parties have been notified, a positive internal media campaign should begin. Keeping management and employees as well informed as possible, in advance of all changes, will be valuable in eliminating potential resistance and conflict. Management and employees want to feel that they are part of the process, if not part of the decision. Clear and regular communications regarding why and how changes will occur can reduce resistance, anxiety, and the all-too-familiar second-guessing.

CANDIDATE SECURITY FUNCTIONS FOR OUTSOURCING: HIGH-TECHNOLOGY CRIME INVESTIGATION

It is possible to outsource the high-technology crime investigative function. There are companies that provide a broad spectrum of investigative services. There are also many other companies that specialize in a limited number of high-technology crime investigative services. Some companies offer a wide range of investigative services. Some offer more sophisticated high-technology crime investigative services than others. Others have a more specialized approach, offering international investigative consulting services. Their services may range from crime prevention surveys and intelligence assessments of international locations to kidnapping and ransom negotiations.

> There is no shortage of companies offering to sell investigative services. The difficult task is finding the right one.

Finding the right high-technology crime investigative service provider is a product of analysis. Part of that analysis is determining just what investigative services or processes you as the GEC CSO intend to outsource. Many companies offer high-technology crime-related investigative services and have proven track records of good performance. Some offer the most basic investigative functions nearly every security organization handles. Others offer more specialized and sophisticated services needed only on an occasional basis. Services of this type are difficult to maintain as a proprietary expertise as a result of the high cost to maintain and low frequency of use.

Investigative Services

Some offer nationwide or international services and are nationally and internationally recognized whereas others perform on a local basis only. The types of investigations available cover the full spectrum—from pre-employment investigations to security incident and due diligence assessments. An outsource provider can be found for all of them. There are also high-technology crime-related investigative services.

Consulting Services

High-technology crime investigative consulting services differ, as do the skills and expertise of the various consulting firms and companies. Generally, consulting services are needed on an occasional basis, rather than on a regular basis. Before seeking consulting services, understand what capabilities are available within GEC and the security organization. All too often, professional advice is sought and received, but ends up only validating what is already known or recommended. There are times when this "second opinion" or "validation" is necessary. However, some of the time it is money unnecessarily spent. After you define the need, seek a company with a track record in providing that service, and ask the customer about their support.

Due Diligence Services

These services are not used often. When necessary, it is essential they be performed thoroughly and effectively. If a proprietary capability does not exist, due diligence services should be outsourced to a skilled provider. If an internal capability does exist, use it. In some cases, the due diligence effort may take place internationally. In this event, it is best to seek support from a company capable of conducting due diligence efforts that has a presence in the geographic area of your interest.

SAMPLE OUTSOURCING ANALYSIS

The rest of the chapter is an example of an outsourcing analysis conducted by GEC's CSO. It includes a detailed analysis and considerations of costs, quality of services to be provided, and expenses.

Initial Analysis

Outsourcing is done for a reason. For example, cost reduction, higher quality of service, or gaining a competitive advantage are good reasons to outsource. The GEC CSO has determined that more time should be spent focusing on core competencies that add value to GEC and less time should be spent on support functions such as the high-technology crime investigative function. Because support work is capital intensive and because there is no competition, outsourcing seems to make sense. The GEC CSO recognizes this and is prepared to conduct an outsourcing analysis.

> If a process falls into the category of one of the corporation's core competencies, then it is not a candidate for outsourcing. If a process does not fall into the category of a core competency, it is a candidate for outsourcing.

When it has been determined that a process is not a core competency, it is essential to assess the proprietary nature of that process before proceeding further with outsourcing considerations. To do this, the CSO must first determine answers to the following questions:

- Is the process a proprietary process?
- Is the information proprietary?
- Is the process a strategic or competitive activity?

If the answer to each question is no, then the CSO will be ready to proceed with the analysis. If the answer to any of the three questions is yes, consideration must be made regarding whether the GEC assets (e.g., information) can be adequately protected through confidentiality agreements and proprietary processes. Nevertheless, it may not be prudent to share GEC-sensitive information with more people than necessary. The good news is that the CSO determined that most security processes are not proprietary processes, so they lend themselves to the next step in the outsourcing analysis.

After conducting the initial analysis, the GEC CSO decides to proceed to the next step—a more detailed analysis. In essence, it is time to build a case to outsource or not to outsource. As part of that detailed assessment, the CSO must consider the culture of GEC. What impact will the GEC culture have on a decision to outsource the high-technology crime investigative function? Even though a detailed analysis indicates that outsourcing is the right course of action, there may be cultural issues requiring further assessment. For example, outsourcing a process in a union environment may be problematic. If the process is one staffed with and performed by union personnel, then a review of the union agreement may be necessary.

There may be provisions in the union contract that prohibit outsourcing or make it problematic to outsource. Furthermore, the impact of outsourcing a nonunion process may lead to or create resistance from unions in other areas. Examining the bigger picture early on usually helps prevent potential problems from developing. If no unions are involved, the decision to outsource is usually easier.

> Clearly define the work to be outsourced. This is critical to successful outsourcing.

To ensure the potential outsource provider meets all expectations and the GEC CSO becomes a satisfied customer, each party must have a clear understanding of what work needs to be accomplished, for whom, in what time period, and at what cost. Operating within the same well-defined parameters is the baseline for success.

The GEC CSO decides that an important component of assessing the initial prospects for outsourcing the high-technology crime investigative function is to seek out like companies and see what they have done. The CSO will determine whether any similar security organizations outsourced the high-technology crime investigative processes that he is considering to outsource. It should not be difficult to obtain the information needed to help make good decisions. The CSO will contact security colleagues from other companies and talk to them. More than likely, they can offer assistance. If not, they may know someone who can. If the CSO does not have any luck working through colleagues and their contacts, assistance may be obtained from any of the major professional security associations, such as the American Society for Industrial Security. The CSO is considering contacting their headquarters in Arlington, Virginia, and asking them if they can put him in contact with a company willing to benchmark. When he or she finds another CSO who has outsourced and who will share his data, the following questions should be answered:

- Did they outsource their investigative or high-technology crime investigative function?
- What outsource provider did they use?
- What others were considered or not considered and why?
- Were their expected cost savings achieved?
- If not, did they achieve any cost savings at all?
- Was there a degradation in service?
- What other benefits did they derive from outsourcing?
- What pitfalls were encountered?
- Are they a satisfied customer?

The information the CSO obtains from this process will be useful in setting him on a successful path. Learning from the experience, successes, and failures of others can save considerable time and money. At this point the GEC CSO has determined candidate processes for outsourcing and concludes the following:

- The high-technology crime investigative processes considered for outsourcing are not core competencies.
- There are no proprietary issues to be concerned with.
- Company culture or union issues don't exist (or have been reasonably addressed and will not prevent the firm from proceeding).

The CSO then determines that it is time to proceed further with the analysis: finding a capable provider of high-technology crime investigative services. He also figures that the GEC procurement office may be of assistance in identifying potential suppliers. It is necessary to identify a sufficient number of suppliers to hold a competitive bid process. Usually this means soliciting three to five potential providers, depending upon availability.

> The more potential suppliers included, the better the competition.

The competitive bid process is the best way to ensure the CSO and GEC get the best results. The competitive bid process should provide for a fair assessment of each company's capabilities and ability to perform. This process should assess the following:

- Supplier experience
- Contact references
- Response to CSO's statement of work
- Cost and affordability
- Availability for service (time and location limitations if any)
- Responsiveness and flexibility
- Available resources to perform the work
- Quality and metrics program

The competitive bid process should also give each potential outsource provider an opportunity to view GEC's high-technology crime investigation statement of work or charter. The bid process should also include developing a transition plan—one that addresses how the outsource provider will transition, for example, from a proprietary high-technology crime investigation team to the contract team.

Detailed Analysis

Now it is time for the CSO to perform a detailed analysis of cost, quality, and experience to make a final determination regarding the value of outsourcing. Remember, if outsourcing costs more or causes GEC to experience a significant degradation in the quality of service, then outsourcing should not be done. The following paragraphs contain guidelines for assessing cost, quality, and experience. Following these guidelines will enable the CSO to develop sufficient detail to make a good comparison between a proprietary process and an outsource process.

Cost + Quality + Experience = Outsourcing

Cost

The CSO must know the current high-technology crime investigation and unit costs. These will then be compared with what the supplier thinks it will cost to provide the CSO with the services needed. Through the competitive bid process, suppliers will provide the CSO with cost information. As the customer, the CSO can play a major role in establishing and managing asset protection costs.

It may be best to allow the outsource provider to use the marketplace and market conditions for determining high-technology crime investigator wages. The outsource provider will add to that wage the cost of employee benefits and other associated costs. The provider will also add a profit margin as a percentage of the total cost. You must expect this because they are in business to make a profit. As the CSO proceeds with the cost analysis, the following data will be collected from the proprietary operation for comparison with data provided by potential outsource providers:

1. Budget
   - Total high-technology crime investigation unit salary by employee
   - Total bonus costs
   - Cost of benefit package for all employees (current and future)
   - Cost per employee (current and future)
   - Costs by posts to be filled
2. Facilities
   - Office space (square footage) occupied by the unit
   - Cost of that space for the unit
   - Cost of unit equipment
   - Cost of common use equipment
3. Travel
   - Cost of all business travel and associated expenses

4. Training/development
   - Cost for seminars/courses
   - Cost for internal meetings
   - Cost for other activities
5. Oversight obligations
   - Cost of time demands placed on line units
   - Development and maintenance of performance measures
   - Cost of reports
6. Other
   - Legal (factor in claims of various types)
   - Administrative support
7. Subcontractor (if applicable)
   - Total cost of subcontractors, including labor, materials, and so forth

A comparison of the data collected from the proprietary operation with data provided by a potential outsource provider should provide an immediate indication regarding any cost differences.

Quality

Unlike costs, quality is a bit more subjective to assess. Perhaps the best way to assess quality is to conduct a customer survey. Through a customer survey, the CSO can establish a baseline of quality.

In essence, determine the quality of high-technology crime investigative services provided as assessed by the actual customers, those who receive the service.

Once determined, the survey results will serve as the baseline of quality that can be used to measure against future performance by the outsource provider. To conduct a quality survey, the CSO first decides to identify the following:

- What high-technology crime investigation-related services are provided?
- What processes are performed?
- For whom are they performed?
- What are the customer expectations?

Then the CSO designs a sample to send to selected or random employees. It should be a sizable representation of the customer population for input to be statistically accurate in representing the entire population. If the internal customer community is small, it may be practical to survey all employees. Complicated and long surveys will generally not get a response. Brief and to-the-point surveys will get a response. Never expect a 100% response to any survey. A 50% response is considered an excellent representation of respondents. More than likely, you will receive a 25 to 50% response rate.

In a full survey, all responses can be scored and averaged, and a baseline established. This baseline should be identified as the level of service provided going into an outsource condition. If the service was poor, the CSO's expectation may be for the outsource provider to deliver better service. If the baseline is high (very satisfied), for the sake of keeping costs low, the CSO may be satisfied with a lower level of service (satisfied).

Experience

The purposes of assessing experience of any outsource provider are to determine the probability of failure should the CSO hire them to provide high-technology crime investigative services and to compare that probability with the consequence of failure. For example, if the probability of failure is high on the part of any outsource provider in performing one of the critical processes, and the consequence of failure is also high, outsourcing that process becomes a risky proposition. On the other hand, if the probability of failure for a particular outsourced process is low and the consequence of failure is low, the risk for outsourcing that process is low. Proceeding is prudent. However, a thorough assessment of the probability of failure should be undertaken.

PROBABILITY OF FAILURE

Assessing the probability of failure must take into consideration three factors:

1. The maturity of the process
2. The complexity of the process
3. Any process-related dependency factors

How each factor is weighed is up to the CSO and the specific needs and conditions of the operating environment.

Maturity Factor

The more mature a process, the greater the likelihood of success. Success is most likely when a proprietary process is mature and it is outsourced to a provider that has performed that process before. For example, outsourcing an internal investigation process to an investigative company has a high probability of success.

- Exact service exists and has been done before—probability of failure, low
- Similar service exists and has been done before—probability of failure, medium
- No service exists—probability of failure, high

There is also the sensitivity issue relating to investigations (e.g., privacy, PR if information were to be leaked to the news media).

Complexity Factor

How complex is the high-technology crime investigative process to be outsourced? Simple processes have a greater probability of success when outsourced. The more complex a process, the greater potential for things to go wrong and for failure to occur.

- Simple changeover— probability of failure, low
- Moderate increase in complexity—probability of failure, medium
- Complex—probability of failure, high

Dependency Factor

The less dependent a process is on other factors, the higher the likelihood of success. Conversely, the more dependencies a high-technology crime investigative process has, the greater the likelihood of something going wrong. This leads to failure.

- Independent of existing process, systems, or suppliers—probability of failure low
- Performance dependent on existing processes, system, facility, or supplier—probability of failure medium
- Performance dependent on new systems, schedules, processes, or suppliers—probability of failure high

CONSEQUENCE OF FAILURE

Performance Factor

How important is it that the outsource provider perform as well as or better than the proprietary operation? If maintaining a similar level of performance is important, then performance degradation can be critical.

- No change in performance—very low probability of adverse impact
- Small reduction in performance—relatively low probability of adverse impact
- Significant degradation in performance—likely probability of adverse impact
- Goals cannot be achieved—high probability of adverse impact

Cost Factor

The CSO decides, with management support, to choose to outsource to reduce GEC costs. If outsourcing the high-technology crime investigative function increases costs, other factors must be significantly improved or it is not worth outsourcing.

- Budget estimates not exceeded—no adverse impact
- Cost estimates exceed budget by less than 10%—may not be a problem if performance is significantly improved
- Cost estimates exceed budget by more than 10%—a problem
- Cost estimates exceed budget by more than 25%—failed effort unless mitigated by a significant factor

Schedule Factor

As with any process or service, on-time delivery is important. The axiom "faster, cheaper, and better" fits the expectations of the CSO. The following schedule impacts must be considered in outsourcing:

- No change in schedule—not an issue
- Minor slip in schedule—may not be a problem, considering other factors
- Small slip in schedule—may be a problem if costs have not been reduced
- Major slip in schedule—a problem regardless of cost savings

FINAL OUTSOURCING DECISION

After completing the analysis, a decision to outsource the high-technology crime investigative function must be made. If the analysis shows an experienced outsource provider can be found, costs can be reduced, performance will improve or at least not be degraded, and the likelihood of success is high, the decision has been made. It is time to outsource the process.

If the analysis shows costs will increase or performance will be significantly degraded or the effort is highly likely to fail, outsourcing should not be pursued. Anything in between these two assessments will require a risk management decision by the CSO and concurrence by GEC's executive management. However, having gone through an assessment considering all factors mentioned earlier, the GEC CSO will be well prepared to make a risk management decision. Not conducting a thorough analysis before proceeding is the riskiest of all propositions.

After the CSO has made the decision to outsource and has awarded a contract to a selected provider, there are still a few factors that should be mutually agreed to, enabling complete success. Doing this will ensure both parties—the customer (GEC) and the provider—benefit from the relationship.

1. *Identify critical success factors*—Critical success factors are those that must be fully achieved for the effort to be considered a success. For example, if the reason for outsourcing is to reduce cost by 10% or more, then achieving that 10% cost reduction is a critical success factor.
2. *Establish goals*—Clearly defined goals are a means of defining expectations.
3. *Measure performance to goals*—How well the provider performs to established goals is a measurement of success. Moreover, it is a futile effort if goals are established but performance to them is not measured
4. *Improve performance*—Performance measurement is a management tool. It establishes where GEC is as compared with where it should expect to be. If performance is below expectations, improvements must be made.
5. *Conduct periodic reevaluations*—All relationships require periodic reevaluation. Neither customer nor supplier should assume all is well unless that is validated through some established means. For example, after doing business with a single supplier for several years the CSO decides to recompete a contract let to that supplier years earlier. Through a competitive bid process, the CSO can validate that the current supplier offers the best deal, or he can select another supplier who does.

SUMMARY

Never forget that corporate security is part of the business enterprise. Corporate security adds value to a corporation in many ways, but does not usually generate revenue. Therefore, corporate security is a cost center. Keeping costs under control and as low as possible are essential.

Outsourcing provides an effective avenue for the CSO to reduce costs or keep them under control. In today's business environment, there are many providers of a broad range of security services. These providers range from local companies providing few specialized services to international companies offering security services from the simple to the very complex. A skilled CSO will recognize this and use outsourcing as a tool to help manage the security organization effectively and efficiently.

PART IV

High-Technology Crime Investigation Challenges of the 21st Century

A high-technology crime investigator must be able to do many things
well—often all at once!

The objective of the last section of this book is to look into a crystal ball
and predict what it will be like to work in the global information environment for the 21st-century high-technology crime investigator and how to
prepare to work in that environment.

In Chapter 20 we discuss the future impact of technology on individuals, nations, societies, business, and government agencies based on current trends and some "best guesses."

The objective of Chapter 21 is to discuss the future of high-technology crimes, security, and the criminal justice system based on the global information environment.

Chapter 22 deals with today's old but new threats to corporate and government assets through high-technology means.

The objective of Chapter 23 is to discuss the future of the high-technology crime investigator.

Chapter 24 provides the high-technology crime investigator with a career development plan outline to be used in developing a career as a high-technology crime investigator.

The objective of Chapter 25 is to explain some of the more unique methods to prepare for a high-technology crime investigation job and the "interview by portfolio" method to get that investigative position you've been looking for.

Chapter 26 discusses the option of the high-technology crime investigator moving from a corporation or government agency environment to that of an independent high-technology crimes investigative consultant.

Chapter 27 includes a summary and some random thoughts.

20

The Future of High Technology and Its Impact on Working in a Global Information Environment

The objective of this chapter is to discuss the future impact of high technology on individuals, nations, societies, business, and government agencies based on current trends and some "best guesses."

INTRODUCTION

We have defined high technology as that technology based on the microprocessor. Microprocessors are the heart of our technological progress and the high-technology miscreant's "weapon of choice." There is no turning back the hands of time, so the more one knows about high technology and its strengths, weaknesses, and trends into the future, the more prepared a high-technology crime investigator can be to meet the investigative challenges of the future.

MICROPROCESSORS

The microprocessor is the heart of the computer, network, and a large number of other less obvious devices that run and support the processes of our government agencies, businesses, and, increasingly, our lives. This little silicon chip is the CPU of "all computer life as we know it." It has grown almost exponentially (for the purist, see Moore's Law) in power and flexibility, while at the same time it has decreased in size, power consumption, and price.

This trend is expected to continue for the foreseeable future. Pundits have said and continue to say that this little silicon chip will soon be reaching its physical limits. They say that miniaturization can only go so far and that eventually heat and other factors known only to God and physics majors will cause the chip to hit a technological advancement brick wall. Such may be the case. Yeah, right, and people aren't supposed to fly, and humans can't go to the moon or survive in space. These experts' great-grandparents are probably also the ones who thought the stock market in the early 1900s was a great place to put your money. The next generation, the quantum computer, is already here. There is now serious talk about computers that use light rather than electricity to run the processor.

As with any topic, there are always different, and usually opposing, opinions. If this pessimistic view is believed, then we will shortly be reaching that brick wall. If this happens, what is the worst-case scenario? The power of the chip would not stop the further development of the "sugar cube" and other storage devices, more memory, faster telecommunications, and continuously declining prices. So, progress would continue. We have already moved into the era of the disposable computer and storage devices that are so small that they can be carried in the pocket but can store gigabytes of data.

Maybe such a "breather" in this fast-paced development would be a good deal for all of us. Time could be taken to make the computers we use more user friendly. We could take time to concentrate on putting them to better use in a more focused effort to relieve people of more of life's burdens while increasing everyone's quality of life. Is this realistic? No, because the technology industry, to survive, must continue to improve. The chip race between the leading chip makers is similar to a space race or a drag race. Both sides are looking for more speed and, as "Tim the Tool Man" says (a US comedian who loves adding power to power tools), "More power!"

PESSIMISM VERSUS OPTIMISM

Even the most pessimistic view has acknowledged that current technologies are facilitating the convergence of telecommunications and computing, and that this, in itself, is allowing for the development of a whole range of services and a huge potential for more. On the optimistic side of the brick wall are those who continue to find innovative ways to get more speed and power out of those little chips. However, if such a brick wall were hit, would high technology progress stop? No, it wouldn't even slow down, because as chip makers are cranking out those little beasts, their research and development folks, coupled with university laboratories, think tanks, and the like, are looking for new materials to replace silicon.

ELECTRICALLY CHARGED AMOEBAE?

One such replacement vehicle may be the electrically charged amoeba. If you remember from your biology classes, these are little one-celled organisms that like to hang out in water. Even as long ago as the 1970s, some have thought of electrically charging them—a positive charge for the binary "1" and a negative charge for the binary "0" digit. Is this truth or fiction? We won't know until it happens. Whether it is the amoeba or some other form of organic medium, there is certainly huge potential in this area. However, in the United States, this may not be possible because these little buggers may fall under the umbrella of some law or animal rights activists who make it their personal objective to protect these "sweet little creatures" from the evil of the humans trying to use them as "slaves." Sound far-fetched? Think about it.

> Regardless of the physical properties of the microprocessor that we use, there is no doubt that any brick wall or other barrier will eventually be overcome. Assuming this is true, what will these new and innovative technologies bring to the global information environment?

HIGH-TECHNOLOGY DEVICE INTEGRATIONS AND TRENDS TOWARD THE FUTURE

Many of the current high-technology device integrations have been alluded to throughout much of this book. When discussing integrations, one can look back and see that they have been logical steps in the evolution of high technology. It seems that it is almost inevitable that these high-technology devices would expand their scope of options as microprocessors became more powerful, smaller, and cheaper.

The entire business of high technology fueling the fire that created the GII, Internet, NII, intranets, cellular telephones, pagers, PBXs was, is, and will be done for one very simple reason: to communicate information in one form or another. By "one form or another" we mean transmitting information in the form of voice, video, and data. In the future, this will all be merged into one as technology improves the bandwidth and corrects other deficiencies that limit our ability to share information in a totally integrated form at high speeds.

> We are in the "crawling stages" of this integration, but the next century will see us quickly move from crawling to walking, jogging, and then running at speeds only talked about in science fiction novels.

In the United Kingdom, the major telecommunications service provider will be converting its core network to an IP base in 2007. So it is fair to say that tomorrow is nearly here. The same service provider is already providing home and mobile communications from the same handset.

When you are in the area of your house, it connects to the land line, but when you move away from your base location, it seeks the favored mobile service provider and connects using the cell phone network. Imagine the impact this is going to have. No need for two separate phone numbers, no need for two-line rental agreements.

We see the hints of major communications changes coming now in the form of integration of services from several devices into one. It is normal now for people to wear a watch, carry a pager, a cellular telephone, a PDA, and a Blackberry. It comes as no surprise that many of these devices are now multifunctional and that their capabilities are interchangeable.

The Blackberry is capable of e-mail, Web browsing, text messages, and SMS and voice messaging, and the PDA can do very much the same. The new cellular phones are now digital, the size of the old pagers. As more of the global personal communications services have come online and their costs have come down to those of today's "normal" cellular phone service costs, there has been a tremendous increase in their use by the ordinary citizens of the world.

We already are beginning to see this new cellular phone–pager be incorporated into watches and similar-size items. In the not too distant future, watches as we know them will not exist. They will be information devices that provide satellite-supported voice, video, and data capabilities from any where in the world to any place in the world. Such devices will also include mini screens and cameras for teleconferencing and geographic positioning features and will no longer need batteries. Sure, in the interim, these systems may have their batteries charged at the same time that we are using infrared or Bluetooth signals to upload and download the updated information from our other high-technology devices, such as notebook computers, PDAs, desktops, intranets, and the Internet.

The "new" devices will be solar or perhaps kinetically powered (why not utilize the energy that is wasted as we move around?) with the ability to store that power for extended periods of time. So when you are sitting outside eating lunch, your "wrist information system" will be getting its "food" for the next several hours or days.

While all this is going on, our cable televisions will be sold as a completely integrated unit with built-in intranets and Internet accesses (actually, GII accesses to include telephones). After all, we can now make telephone calls via the Internet, albeit not as clear or "user friendly" as we would like, but the technology is getting there. If we look back at the computers of the 1940s to the 1970s, they weren't even close to being user friendly. So when you are shopping online at the various information stores and you purchase your home information system—television, telephone, GII access, video conferencing, and, oh yes, home computer, you may ask, "But how many remote devices, mice, and keyboards will we need to operate it?" The answer is none—well, maybe one. The input device for the next generation will probably be your voice. Is this more science fiction than science fact? Not at all. In fact voice-operated "mice" are being researched, developed, prototyped, and sold right now, but they are not yet fully developed. You can already get voice-activated systems and voice-operated word processing systems, but currently you have to "educate" the system to recognize each individual voice.

You won't have to reprogram or make any changes to your home information and entertainment system to get the information you want access to while you continue to deny that same access to your children. This future system will "scan" you and, perhaps based on specific biometrics, including your physical profile and voice identification, it will automatically configure itself according to your previous instructions. This is in total contrast to current video recorders that very few adults can operate effectively, but that a child can, apparently intuitively, set up correctly every time.

Just as we now have PDAs, notebook computers, desktop systems, workstations tied to servers, WANs, and the like, the new integrated devices will have us rethinking what we actually need that we currently use, such as pagers, computers, cellular phones, and watches. Those will be old, outdated terms for our information wrist device or whatever name the manufacturers dream up. Usually, the first to market sets the naming standards. For example, do we say we will copy a document or do we say we will Xerox it? Do we use a PC or a standalone microcomputer?

Miniaturization will continue, as well as mobility, flexibility, integration, lower costs, and increased communication bandwidth and information collection. This will all lead to one of the most important decisions that mankind will ever make in the next century, second only to whether we should clone humans. Although such decisions are made possible by the advances in high technology, they are also the tools that are, and will be, used.

The decision will be whether we will want to have this microprocessor embedded in our body and totally integrated with our brain. The advanced high technology that will do this is being researched today. These sugar cube–sized storage devices are already large in comparison with many of the current storage devices and those of the future.

These devices will allow us to access or possibly intuitively know all the information that's stored in all the libraries of the world. Instead of developing software that will automatically translate various languages to our own, we will be able to speak those languages. Thus a true one-on-one form of human communication can take place unhindered by the language barrier. The meaning of what is being said won't be lost in translation.

POWER TO THE PEOPLE?

Because information is power, who will decide:

- What goes in those possibly brain-attached storage devices full of information?
- Who will be able afford them?
- Whether only the rich and powerful be able to have these devices?
- What will they do to our social structure?
- Whether children, prior to leaving the hospital or laboratory after being born, will have a microprocessor embedded in their body and surgically connected to their brain?
- Whether this, at birth, will then give our children "total knowledge" as we know it, with their only learning challenge being how to use and access the information properly?

Imagine the new knowledge that can come from starting off at birth and then expanding from there.

> In the United States, we are quickly reaching the point that not having access to a computer connected to the Internet, NII, and GII immediately places an individual at such a basic disadvantage that it might be seen as a violation of one's civil rights.

Even though it is now estimated that more than 63% of the population in the United States has regular access to a computer, that number is still rising. As the disadvantage of not having regular access to a computer grows, a computer with appropriate accesses may be dispensed to those who cannot afford one. In the United Kingdom and in other parts of Europe, governments have recognized the importance of access to information and are developing social programs to ensure that the entire population has access through the placement of Internet-connected computers in libraries, social centers, and schools.

SUMMARY

In the future, the access to the GII, Internet, and NII will be an increasing necessity for working in the global information environment. It is no longer possible for governments or business to operate without the availability of this infrastructure and this, coupled with the potential damage that we have seen can be caused, even accidentally, may make it necessary for users to be required to attend a class and get a "license" to operate a computer on the "I-Way."

Those of us who are optimistic about the advances in technology that will occur in the future do not see any problem that cannot be overcome—only huge potential advantages. Maybe this optimism is based on the faith in the collective mind of mankind. But whatever it is, it is driving all of us into the future at the speed of light, and there are no brakes. Based on these ruminations, do you think you will prepared to conduct high-technology crime investigations in this new environment?

21

The Future of High-Technology Crimes, Security, and the Criminal Justice System

The objective of this chapter is to discuss the future of high-technology crimes, security, and the criminal justice system based on the global information environment.

INTRODUCTION

After reading the first three sections of this book, one has a fairly good overview of the types of high-technology crimes being perpetrated in the global information environment and what can be done about them. These crimes have increased in number as the numbers of individuals, networks, corporate intranets, the Internet, NII, and GII accesses have grown. So, more networks mean that more people have access to more networks and information.

As you know, the price and power of cellular phones, computers, and many other high-technology devices have made them more accessible to an increasing number of people on a global basis. This has occurred because the communications infrastructure has increased. Nations have adopted the Information Age to the point where the technologies are almost ubiquitous in many regions, with children as young as six having cellular phones and computers.

As with any industry, technology, or other asset that has a real or perceived value, there are those who want to take what others have; however, they neither want to pay for nor work for what they take. This has been the case since the beginning of the human race, with no end in sight.

So, high-technology crime is expected to continue to increase in the number of incidents and the impact they have. However, it is also expected that the level of sophistication will increase as the technology itself becomes more sophisticated. Because the global accessibility of networks, computers, and information provides mass communications, the miscreants and juvenile delinquents who use these devices for illegal acts also share their techniques with others around the world. This provides those "hacker wannabe's" and others with the ability to download attack tools and execute them with little knowledge of how they operate and what systems they are attacking.

Communications and computers have created another change. In the past, for these miscreants to "get together" and exchange knowledge and tools, they had to meet physically, which restricted the number of people that the information was passed on to. After all, they would only pass it on to people they knew and trusted. Now, with the removal of the need to meet, the information spreads much more rapidly. These types of attacks will continue to increase in the foreseeable future because very little technical knowledge is required to carry them out.

It should be remembered that although the Internet originated in the West, the countries that are now joining the Internet are some of the most populated regions of the world (Table 21-1). As people in countries such as China, India, and Pakistan are given access to the Internet, the impact will inevitably be a huge shift in the culture.

According to an online source,[1] the online users' language by population has reached more than 801.4 million as of September 2004. The languages were broken down as follows:

- Dutch, 1.7%
- Portuguese, 3.1%
- Italian, 3.8%
- Korean, 3.9%
- French, 4.2%
- German, 6.9%
- Japanese, 8.4%
- Spanish, 9%
- Chinese, 13.7%
- English, 35.2%

Those of us in the West will suddenly find ourselves in the minority, and the values that we subscribe to will not be those that are understood by the majority of the users of the Internet. Furthermore, the miscreants in these countries may use sophisticated attack programs that have been developed in their regions before they had access to the latest technologies and that have not been found on the Internet before. These and others will continue to find an increasingly more profitable job market. They

Table 21-1 World Internet Usage and Population Statistics

World Regions	Population (2005 est.)	World Population, %	Internet Usage Latest Data	% Population Penetration	Usage % of World	Usage Growth 2000–2005
Africa	896,721,874	14.0	23,917,500	2.7	2.5	429.8
Asia	3,622,994,130	56.4	332,590,713	9.2	34.2	191.0
Europe	804,574,696	12.5	285,408,118	35.5	29.3	171.6
North America	328,387,059	5.1	224,103,811	68.2	23.0	107.3
Latin America/ Caribbean	546,723,509	8.5	72,953,597	13.3	7.5	303.8
Oceania/Australia	33,443,448	0.5	17,690,762	52.9	1.8	132.2
WORLD TOTAL	6,420,102,722	100	972,828,001	15.2	100	169.5

NOTES: (1) Internet Usage and World Population Statistics were updated on November 21, 2005. (2) Demographic (Population) numbers are based on data contained in the world-gazetteer Web site. (3) Internet usage information comes from data published by *Nielsen//NetRatings*, by the International Telecommunications Union, by local NICs, and by other reliable sources. (4) For definitions, disclaimer, and navigation help, see the *Site Surfing Guide*. (5) Information from this site may be cited, giving due credit and establishing an active link back to www.internetworldstats.com. Copyright 2005, Miniwatts International, Ltd. All rights reserved.

will be the new "hired killers" of the global organized crime rings, and drug cartels; or terrorists, governments, and espionage agents. They will be hired to infiltrate systems, steal information, and prevent access to systems through denial-of-service attacks and destruction of information.

With the increased dependency of businesses and government agencies on the Internet, NII, and GII, there will be more and more lucrative targets for these miscreants. This high-technology global increase in crime will be fueled by the exponentially increasing e-commerce and electronic online banking. Crime will always follow the money, and the penalties for online crimes are much lower than those for the equivalent physical crime.

There were justifiable concerns that highly skilled Russian, Bulgarian, and other computer scientists who have been having a difficult time finding work and getting paid might be recruited to work for other nations and organized crime. The next area of concern must be countries such as China and India, where there are large numbers of highly skilled but very poorly paid individuals. Do you recall the discussion earlier in the book about motive, opportunity, and rationalization? When you are out of work, have a family, and are hungry, being convinced to work for miscreants may not take much convincing. After all, you're going after foreign corporations and governments who you have been told your whole life are the "evil enemy"; it is easy to convince yourself that your actions are reasonable.

> The future will continue to see major increases in industrial and economic espionage (Netspionage) as more and more global businesses and government agencies become more reliant on the Internet.

There are many documented cases of the use of networks to steal private and sensitive information having already occurred. An indication of this was the expulsion of several Russians from a nation for soliciting one or more government employees to spy for them. That's not unusual. What *is* unusual is that they had also asked for the user IDs and passwords to some government databases. The Cold War has ended?

Let us not forget the efforts of the Chinese. In 1999 a report to the US Congress known as the *Cox Report* indicated that the United States had gathered intelligence that China has obtained secrets about seven US nuclear weapons, including the W-56, W-62, W-76, W-78, and W-87 nuclear warheads. More recently, in 2000, Los Alamos nuclear scientist Wen Ho Lee was held on espionage charges and eventually pled guilty to a charge of improperly handling sensitive data. More indications can be gathered from a 2005 speech delivered by FBI assistant director for counterintelligence David Szady[2] in 2005 in which he named Russia, Iran,

Cuba, and North Korea among the countries that he said were engaged in espionage against the United States, but he highlighted the activities of China. He went on to state: "There are 150,000 students from China. Some of those are sent here to work their way up into the corporations." He then noted that there are about 300,000 Chinese visitors to the United States each year, as well as 15,000 Chinese delegations, of which 3500 were in the New York area.

> Thus far, high-technology terrorists have been predicted, but little has happened to indicate that any terrorist groups have been involved or are planning to conduct high-technology terrorist acts using the Internet or the national or global networks.

There are few who doubt that eventually the terrorists of the world will take advantage of system vulnerabilities to successfully attack the networks of corporations and governments. This will happen when their priorities change from the wanton destruction of innocent people for the fear effect to the destruction of the economic power of a nation-state.

In the Information Age of nations' dependencies on the GII, NII, Internet, and intranets, attacks on the networks of corporations and governments would be too important and too easy targets for someone who wants to damage an information-dependent nation to ignore. The power of a global nation in this new century will continue to be economic power. That is the real influence in the world.

HIGH-TECHNOLOGY SECURITY

In the area of physical security, high technology will continue to provide the tools to monitor anything from streets, building, and rooms to individual people. In the 21st century, security will come nearer to mirroring completely the fears of Big Brother that were first expressed in the book *1984*. Some idea of the level to which an individual can be monitored can be gained when you think of the following, which is only a small sample of possible methods. Your location and activity can be determined from any one of any combination of the following:

- Your cell phone, which can locate you by the local cell from which you are operating and can also be tracked as it moves from cell to cell
- Your car, which can be located through the use of automatic number plate readers (ANPRs)

- Your credit card, which records time, date, and location each time it is used
- Closed-circuit television, which can track your movements in real time or recreate them from the recordings that are maintained
- Access control systems in buildings
- The developing technology of radiofrequency identification, which allows tags to be embedded in almost any article so that they can be uniquely identified and can be passively detected or can be actively transmitting information
- An antitheft tracking device on your vehicle
- Your Internet activity, which monitors your interests and actions as well as the location of the system you used
- Your purchasing habits when you use your store cards or credit cards (which can be collected and analyzed)

As high-technology crimes become likely to affect the individual, and the crimes' costs continue to increase, government agencies such as the FBI and US National Security Agency (NSA), who are probably lobbying for more intrusive measures in the name of protection and investigations, will be able to use new, sophisticated high-technology investigative and security-related tools. These tools will be used to monitor individuals and their actions on a global scale that was previously feared only in science fiction novels. People will continue to vote for fewer liberties in favor of improved security, particularly in the post-9/11 environment.

> The excuse for more authority to protect people must be balanced with the seriousness of the threat and the less freedom that it causes.

We are already seeing the uses of such high-technology tools to monitor prisoners and to track vehicles and people. One of the newest is a camera device installed on public streets that can compare a database of digitized faces of criminals or others and match them with people walking on the street. Although this technology is still immature and has not reached its full potential, it is improving all the time.

> WASHINGTON (Reuters)—US officials are opening personal mail that arrives from abroad when they deem it necessary to protect the country from terrorism, a Customs and Border Protection spokeswoman said.[3]

In London (the financial district), systems were installed in the aftermath of an IRA bombing that included an ANPR system that also included a camera that captured a photograph of the driver. One of the unanticipated benefits of this counterterrorist system was that there was an increase in the number of criminals that were arrested! When a car entered London and was captured by the ANPR system, it was routinely checked against the criminal databases as well as those on terrorists. If the vehicle was registered to a known and wanted criminal, the police had time to check the photograph to make sure that the criminal they were after was actually driving the car. They could react in sufficient time to enable them to arrest him before he could leave the area.

This and other high-technology devices will increase the debate on privacy and individual freedoms. Those on the "other side" will argue that if you don't do anything wrong, you have no reason to fear these new high-technology security measures. That debate over the use of sophisticated high-technology devices will intensify in the future. Who will win the argument is anybody's guess. However, as stated before, most people, who do see themselves as doing nothing wrong and are persuaded that they have nothing to fear, are willing to give up more freedoms for more security.

WASHINGTON (CNN)—President Bush on Sunday defended his administration's use of wiretaps on US citizens without a court order, saying comments he made in 2004 that "nothing has changed" in the use of wiretaps were not misleading.[4]

INFORMATION SYSTEM SECURITY

InfoSec will continue to increase in its complexity and sophistication. In the future, the gap between the sophisticated attacks on systems, PBXs, cellular phones, and other devices, and defenses will close, but the reality is that improvements in security will never catch up. New attacks will still hold the edge; however, the future will find quicker recoveries, countermeasures, counterattacks, and new defenses. They will work together to provide a "layered defense" approach.

The impetus and support for InfoSec will continue to grow, with the profession eventually achieving recognition and being considered one of the most important functions of a business or government agency.

The increase in InfoSec will occur because corporations and nation-states that are already almost totally dependent on access to the GII, Internet, and NII will start to understand the importance of this resource to their effective functioning. As greater dependence on the networks is acknowledged, there will be attacks detected. It will be absolutely crucial that any attacks be immediately addressed and that the lessons learned by attacks be shared.

The InfoSec profession will become one of the most important and dominant professions in the 21st century, gaining executive management recognition, support, and authority. This will be coupled with more aggressive defense and HTCPPs that will include tracing the sources of the attacks and, potentially, counterattacking. This aggressive approach by businesses and government agencies will be the result of the continuing inability of law enforcement agencies to identify, apprehend, and prosecute these miscreants.

Law enforcement agencies will become serious targets of the global high-technology criminal.

As law enforcement officers become more and more dependent on high technology to pursue criminals and gather intelligence, they will inevitably increase their presence on the GII, NII, and Internet, providing the miscreants with the opportunity to attack their systems, disrupt their efforts, and cause embarrassment. The majority of attacks will be to deny use of the systems; however, these systems will also be attacked to steal or destroy information related to informants, investigations, criminal records, and such, and finally to cause embarrassment and reduce public confidence in their competence.

When these attacks come to light, the public will demand, and eventually get, increased protection of the systems and any sensitive information. This will be accomplished by the hiring of InfoSec professionals, either on a contract basis or as employees. These individuals will eventually also be trained at the police academies and become sworn police officers. They will also conduct and assist in high-technology crime investigations, including arresting the high-technology suspects. This could be the beginning of a new aspect of the information security profession in that a law enforcement investigator is also the departments' information systems security officer. When you think about it, who is likely to have the best understanding of where, on a computer, a miscreant may have stored information or where evidence is likely to be held?

Because of the increased threats to information-dependent nations by other nations, there will continue to be an increase in the risk for information warfare.

Information warfare weapons, now highly classified, will be used as a deterrent to high-technology warfare using the same approach and philosophy as the use of nuclear weapons during the Cold War. In this global information environment, such offensive, high-technology information warfare weapons truly are potentially equivalent in power and impact to nuclear weapons with regard to the impact that their use would have on a nation's well-being. They will be treated as such. To counter these weapons, new, sophisticated defensive weapons will be developed. These will include the automatic analyses of threats, systems that will adapt to changing environments by reconfiguring themselves, automated defensive shields, automatically and rapidly disseminated warnings, and the use of counteroffensive weapons.

CRIMINAL JUSTICE SYSTEMS

As is now the case, the future will continue to see all major branches of the criminal justice system continuing to play catch-up in this global information environment. The use of high technology will continue to be done in piecemeal fashion, but through associations and networking, other criminal justice agencies will be quicker to adopt the high technology used by others. In time, this will evolve into online informal and formal groups within the global criminal justice systems that will develop cooperative, online processes to share information about new high-technology techniques, tools, and other methods to provide for more effective and efficient processes. Examples of this can already be seen in groups such as the High-Tech Crime Consortium (www.hightechcrimecops.org/), which runs a Web site and a bulletin board where high-tech crime investigators can ask for advice on specific topics or share their experience and knowledge. Another good example is the High-Tech-Crime Investigators Association, which has a good bulletin board and a repository of useful investigative tools. These Web sites, which limit access and membership to legitimate law enforcement and other investigators, are the bright hope for the future. When the good guys can share information as well as the bad guys, we all stand a better chance of preventing and detecting crimes.

As microprocessors and new uses for them in support of criminal justice systems begin to emerge, local, state, and federal governments will begin more concerted efforts to integrate this high technology into their processes. This will drive down costs of trials and help reduce backlog.

Effective and efficient use of high technology will result in the delivery of more timely justice, and in so doing may even reduce the amount of crime. This is because there are a number of indications that some crimes are committed because criminals believe the criminal justice system is so slow and backlogged, that even if they got caught, they will be given a suspended sentence or released from prison or jail early because of over-crowding. The overcrowding problem will be overcome by more use of technology to monitor better those who serve time in places other than jail or prison (e.g., house arrest while wearing an "ankle bracelet").

In the future, secure local, national, and global links will be estab-lished to track criminals regardless of their location. This high technology will also assist in the investigation of high-technology crimes. However, after the criminal is apprehended, anywhere in the world, production and delivery of evidence, and prosecution and incarceration will be done on a global scale using means such as teleconferencing. Therefore, because of the global dependence on the Internet and the GII, the United Nations and organizations such as the European Union will support international global high-technology crime laws that will allow for the investigation, apprehension, and prosecution of these offenders. All or most of the infor-mation-dependent nations will support such processes, because they all will be the main victims of these global attackers.

As a high-technology crime investigator, look at current and future high technologies and think of ways they can be put to good use in sup-porting the criminal justice processes and investigations.

SUMMARY

The future, based on today's trends, continues to indicate that we will be getting more of the same—more crime, with security lagging behind the criminals and their techniques used to attack computer networks around the globe successfully. High technology will allow for more invasive tools, taking away our freedom bit by bit in the name of security. The crimi-nal justice systems of nation-states will continue to adopt and adapt high technology to provide for more effective and efficient criminal justice systems.

REFERENCES

1. *Global Reach.* http://globalreach.biz/globstats/index.php3
2. (February 11, 2005). *FBI Spy Chief Asks Private Sector for Help: Szady Highlights Threat of Chinese Espionage.*
3. http://edition.cnn.com/2006/US/01/09/terrorism.mail.reut/index.html
4. http://edition.cnn.com/2006/POLITICS/01/001/nsa.spying/

22

Terrorism—Crime or War? Its Impact on the High-Technology Crime Investigator and the Profession

This chapter deals with today's old (yet in some ways new) threats to corporate and government assets through high-technology means.

INTRODUCTION

In the United States and other nations, there has been some debate regarding whether terrorism is a law enforcement or military matter. In the United States under the Clinton administration it was handled as more of a law enforcement matter, with the FBI leading most of the investigations. Under the Bush administration it has been deemed a military matter, with the US Department of Defense leading the effort generally outside the United States. Homeland Security generally takes the lead within the United States. However, this may have changed somewhat as we hear more and more about the NSA becoming more involved in domestic monitoring of potential terrorists.

> Terrorism: A law enforcement or military matter or both? We leave it up to you to decide where you see such investigations of terrorist activities taking place.

When the first edition of this book was published in 2000, we predicted that it was only a matter of time before we saw the events listed here. Rather than update the book with a new list, we thought it more sensible to review the list and see which of the predictions had come to pass.

1. Terrorists, using a computer, penetrate a control tower computer system and send false signals to aircraft, causing them to crash in midair or into the ground.

   Comment: Not yet seen, at least not publicly known, but an example of the potential was clearly depicted in the Bruce Willis film *Die Hard 2.*

2. Terrorists use fraudulent credit cards to finance their operations.

   Comment: There is some evidence that this is taking place, but its extent is unknown. It is being heavily exploited by organized crime. In the United Kingdom, cardholder not present fraud is reported to have risen from £2.5 million in 1994 to £116.4 million in 2003, and all types of credit card fraud had risen to £420 Million. The global figure for credit card fraud losses in 2000 were estimated to be in the region of $4 billion.

3. Terrorists penetrate a financial computer system and divert millions of dollars to finance their activities

   Comment: No public evidence to date; however, when such attacks occur and the miscreants are not identified, one does not know if the attacks were perpetrated by hackers, organized crime techies, or terrorists. Furthermore, such attacks would be held as closely guarded secrets as much as possible by financial institutions. As many of the nations of the world begin to close down terrorists' financial support networks, terrorists must find other avenues for funding. This approach is a likely one.

4. Terrorists bleach US $1 bills and, using a color copier, reproduce them as $100 bills and flood the market with them to try to destabilize the dollar.

   Comment: No evidence to date; however, in the past, it was rumored that at least one Middle Eastern nation was counterfeiting US currency for the purpose of either destabilizing the currency or for funding some of its activities.

5. Terrorists use cloned cellular phones and computers over the Internet to communicate using encryption to protect their transmissions.

   Comment: No firm evidence to date, but terrorists have used Web sites, e-mail, and "throwaway" cell phones to communicate. There were numerous reports in 2001, none publicly substantiated, of Al-Qaeda using steganography to exchange messages. Prior to that, organizations such as the IRA, the Basque Separatist Movement (ETA), and a number of other terrorist organizations all have very effective Web presences to put out their messages. It is highly probable that they will also be using the Web to communicate in either IRC channels or on peer-to-peer networks. The Zapatista movement in Mexico used the Internet very effectively to get its message out to the world and to bring pressure to bear on the Mexican government. Also, in Japan, the Aum Shinrikyo cult, the group that launched the sarin gas attack in the Tokyo subway in 1995 that killed 12 people was subsequently suspected of having up to 40 members who were running five software companies, among whose clients were the defense, construction, education, post, and telecommunications ministries of the Japanese government. The fear was that cult members may have installed backdoors, logic bombs, or bugs into these systems, although there has been no evidence that this did occur. With easy availability of pay-for-use phones in many parts of the world, and with the move from analogue to digital cell phone systems, the likelihood of terrorists using cloned mobile phones has diminished.

6. Terrorists use virus and worm programs to shut down vital government computer systems.

   Comment: No public evidence to date, but then again, if the attacker's identity is not known, it is possible that a terrorist may be involved. Is this likely? Who knows?

7. Terrorists change hospital records causing patients to die because of an overdose of medicine or the wrong medicine caused by changing computerized test and analysis results.

   Comment: No public evidence of terrorist use thus far.

8. Terrorists penetrate a government computer and cause it to issue checks to all its citizens, thus destabilizing the economy.

   Comment: No public evidence to date; however, in the United Kingdom, a new government social benefit system that was introduced to pay family credit to families was so badly implemented that many families did not receive what they were due or were paid far in excess of what they were due. The families that were overpaid subsequently received bills, in some cases for many thousands of dollars. The social impact of this badly implemented system was huge and caused significant hardship to what became a very vocal section of the community. Although this was an unintentional impact, it demonstrated the potential effects this type of attack would have.

9. Terrorists destroy critical government computer systems processing tax returns.

   Comment: No public evidence to date of such attempts.

10. Terrorists penetrate computerized train routing systems, causing passenger trains to collide.

    Comment: No public evidence to date; however, when train accidents do occur, do the investigators even look at terrorism being the cause? Sometimes such attacks may be made to look like accidents. Furthermore, to help assure the public, officials may hide the true cause of such collisions, derailments, and such. Based on the terrorist attacks against the rail systems in Spain and in the United Kingdom, we do know that the rail systems are considered a good target by terrorists.

11. Terrorists take over telecommunications links or shut them down.

    Comment: No public evidence to date, but as we said before, if the attackers are not identified, one does not know if they are terrorists.

12. Terrorists take over satellite links to broadcast their messages over televisions and radios.

   Comment: No evidence to date. However, since 9/11 and the Gulf War, there has been a significant increase in the number of anti-Western Web sites and radio stations in the Middle East.

THE CURRENT ENVIRONMENT

In the past few years, particularly since 9/11, terrorism has had a significant impact on the lives of all people in the developed world, but none more so than in the United States and the United Kingdom. You may ask yourself, why is this relevant to me as a high-technology crime investigator? Well, when you think about it, it has affected all other aspects of our lives, so it is not too surprising that it will have some bearing when you are carrying out high-technology investigations.

Since the mid 1990s, it has been accepted that with the increased use of computers and other high-technology devices, there are now critical national infrastructures (CNIs) that, as their name indicates, are crucial to the effective and efficient running of a country. Although there is some debate regarding what types of organizations and systems are included in the CNI, it is generally accepted that, as a minimum, it includes:

- Communications
- Emergency services
- Energy
- Finance
- Food
- Government and public service
- Health
- Public safety
- Transportation
- Water

> With the recognition that there was a CNI, came the inevitable realization that this represented a potential vulnerability for a nation.

If terrorists should attack a part of the CNI, they could cause significant damage to the interests of the nation. It also became clear that the systems that were identified as a part of the CNI were largely not owned by the respective governments, but were in fact in the ownership of corporations. For example, very few countries still have nationalized communications or utilities (gas, electric, fuel). These are mostly in the ownership of local, national, or inter- or multinational corporations.

This means that the target of a high-technology terrorist attack is at least as likely to be the systems of a corporation rather than a government. The effect of this on the high-technology crime investigator in any organization that might be considered a part of the CNI is that any attack on the systems must be viewed in the light that it may not be an attack in which the aim is, specifically, to cause damage to the interests of the organization. It may be a part of a wider attack on national interests.

Given the way in which we normally conduct an investigation, probably the last thing that the high-technology crime investigator will think of doing is to ask other organizations in the same sector whether they are having similar problems. (We don't like to air our dirty laundry in public, particularly when it might give a competitor an advantage.)

> The governments in the United States and most European countries have recognized that there may be problems and have set up infrastructures to allow for the exchange of information and the alerting of organizations in the CNI when they think that an attack on the infrastructure is taking place.

A good example of this was the alert that was put out by the National Infrastructure Security Co-ordination Centre (NISCC) in the United Kingdom in June 2005.[1] They warned that although the potential for a serious security breach of the UK CNI was still remote, it had becoming increasingly probable as a result of the standardization of IT systems. NISCC issued a statement that 300 government departments and businesses had been the victims, since the start of the year, of an ongoing series of malicious software (Trojan-based) attacks that appeared to have originated in the Far East. This was the first time the organization has given such a high-profile warning.

> "Parts of the UK's critical national infrastructure are being targeted by an ongoing series of e-mail-borne electronic attacks. While the majority of the observed attacks have been against central government, other UK organizations, companies, and individuals are also at risk."[1]

In the United Kingdom, the NISCC has established a system that is known as WARP (Warning, Advice, and Reporting Point; www.warp. gov.uk) to help organizations in the United Kingdom support themselves and to collaborate with others in their sector or region. WARP service provides:

- A filtered warning service to provide members with only the security information relevant to their needs
- An advice brokering service from which members have the chance to learn from other members' initiatives/experience using a bulletin board messaging service restricted to WARP members
- A trusted sharing service from which reports from members have been made anonymous so that members can learn from each other's incidents without fear of embarrassment

This system provides the infrastructure to allow for collaborative help and offers the potential for the high-tech investigator to find out whether the attack on the system that he is investigating is an isolated event or part of a much wider attack. How useful it will be is still to be tested, but it offers some potential.

In the United States, the Department of Homeland Security (www. dhs.gov/dhspublic/) offers advice on threat and protection through the Homeland Security Advisory System. A scheme similar to the UK's WARP scheme has been developed and is known as the National Cyber Security Partnership (NCSP; www.cyberpartnership.org/about-overview.html.) This initiative is led by the Business Software Alliance, the Information Technology Association of America, the US Chamber of Commerce, and TechNet, in partnership with federal government agencies, academics, CEOs of a range of organizations, and industry experts. The partnership is described as having been created to develop shared strategies and programs to secure and enhance America's CNI.

One of the five task forces set up by the NCSP is the Cyber Security Early Warning Task Force, which was set up to improve the sharing, integrating, and disseminating of information about vulnerabilities, threats, and incidents through the range of distributed information systems.

> The aim of the NCSP task force is "to build a system in which critical information is distributed in a timely way before an incident occurs." (www. cyberpartnership.org/about-overview.html)

CURRENT TERRORIST USE

To date there has been no evidence of the use of the Internet to carry out destructive attacks on a nation, but there is already considerable evidence of terrorist groups using the Internet to spread their message. This type of activity has been in place since the Web became popular, and illicit organizations were among the early adopters.

Good examples of this are the Web pages that advocate the IRA in Ireland, such as Sinn Fein Online (www.sinnfein.org/), Ireland's OWN:

Óglaigh na hÉireann (irelandsown.net/IRA.htm), or the Irish Republican Army (irishrepublicanarmy.info/Home.html). Other good examples are the Web pages that advocate ETA, the Basque terrorist organization such as Euskalinfo—Information on the Basque Conflict in English (www.euskalinfo.org.uk/otherpress/index.php) and, from Indonesia, the East Timor and Indonesia Action Network (www.etan.org/). A final example is that of the Zapatista guerillas from the Chiapas region of Mexico at Chiapas Para el Mundo (Intercontinental Encuentro; http://planet.com.mx/~chiapas) or Comite Civil de Dialogo Utopia del FZLN (www.geocities.com/Athens/Troy/8864/).

> There has been speculation that terrorists have used the Internet for communicating with each other, but again there is no clear evidence. However, given the potential, it would be naive to presume that they have not and will not.

There were rumors in May 2003 that Al-Qaeda had used steganography to hide messages, but these were debunked shortly after. If you are to be a good high-technology crime investigator, you have to retain an awareness at all times of the cases that you will possibly have to investigate. If you work in the government or a defense department, you should have the potential use of the Internet by terrorists in mind, but it should also be borne in mind if you work in the commercial sector because, increasingly, your organization's systems will be the target.

Remember that terrorists will potentially want to try to use computers for a range of purposes. At one end of the scale, they will want to use them to transmit their propaganda or for fund-raising and money laundering. At the other end of the scale, they may use them to communicate among themselves and ultimately to launch an attack on an infrastructure. We have already seen hackers and organized crime using computer systems for all of these purposes, so it is not difficult to predict that when terrorists believe they can achieve their aims using this type of technology, they will.

An indication of the possible use of the Internet to finance terrorism can be found in a 2004 report from the Computer Crime Research Center. It stated that the French police had arrested Mustafa Baachi, a high-tech expert of Al-Qaeda who had allegedly committed numerous e-frauds and, assisted by his brother, had organized a number of attacks on a French financial institution. The report went on to quote Dale Watson, the FBI's former counterterrorism chief, as stating that "thefts of data on debit/credit cards allow criminals and terrorists to steal money. A number of Islamic organizations (like Al-Qaeda) use this method to replenish their cash. Terrorist organizations Al-Qaeda, Hezbollah, HAMAS, and Abu

Nidal actively use the Internet and newest achievements of high technologies for teaching their thoughts, recruiting new members, planning and committing terrorist attacks."

As a result of the arrests and subsequent investigation, French officers discovered that units of Al-Qaeda responsible for recent terrorist acts in Spain were financed by bank robberies and forged credit card activities in France. The investigators were reported to have said that "Moroccan extremists, which form the majority of Spanish cells of Al-Qaeda, received hundreds of thousands of dollars from their French 'colleagues' at the stage of preparation of large-scale terrorist acts."

Law enforcement or defense high-technology investigators may well find themselves investigating computers that have been recovered and that are known to have come from terrorist organizations or individuals (a number of computers were recovered in Afghanistan from Al-Qaeda). It is reported that a number of these contained significant quantities of information that was of use to Western security forces.

Another indication of the current use of high technology by terrorists can be found in the reports of the arrests that took place as a result of raids in the Pakistani city of Guirat in July 2004. A Tanzanian national, Ahmed Khalfan Ghailani, who was suspected of being a member of Al-Qaeda and was also involved in the 1998 US embassy bombings in East Africa, was captured.[2]

The reports of the arrests stated that e-mail had been found on the computer of the arrested man that outlined plans for a new series of terrorist attacks against Britain and the United States. The same reports quoted the Pakistani information minister, Sheikh Rashid Ahmed, as saying that the (Pakistani) authorities had also arrested in Lahore, in a separate raid, Muhammad Naeem Noor Khan, a 25-year-old computer and communications expert, who was thought to be another top Al-Qaeda suspect.

Shortly after the arrests, a warning was issued to financial institutions including Citicorp and the New York Stock Exchange in New York, World Bank buildings in Washington, and the Prudential building in New Jersey of a possible attack.

Another indication can be found in the reports[3] of the trial of an Algerian Islamist terrorist suspect, Abbas Boutrab, which started in September 2005 at Belfast Crown Court, Northern Ireland. Boutrab, age 27, initially arrested in 2003, was also prosecuted under three other names that he was suspected of using as aliases. He was accused of possessing articles for a purpose connected with terrorism under the UK Terrorism Act 2000. Among the evidence against him were 25 computer disks on which Islamist instruction manuals on how to construct bombs suitable for smuggling on to airplanes had been downloaded from the Internet.

> In the commercial sector, the investigator should bear in mind that it will be the systems in their organizations that terrorists are most likely to attack either to damage the CNI or to hide and store information. After all, although terrorists may seek to attack military systems, they will gain the greatest effect by attacking the civil infrastructure.

What is the future of terrorism in high-technology crime likely to be? There is no doubt that terrorists have understood and gained knowledge of the CNIs in Western nations. To date there are no reports that they have successfully attacked them, and, in truth, it is not likely that the new fundamentalist terrorists will use this type of attack. What must not be forgotten is that although we may have our focus on this new form of terrorism, there are lots of the old type of terrorists still around.

INTELLIGENCE GATHERING

In preparing for terrorist attacks on our countries, terrorists of today will need, as they have in the past, to gather intelligence on potential targets. Because we have moved so much of our information online, this is now a very rich area for this activity.

> In the old days, when we stored our information on paper, access to information was severely limited. Only so many copies would be produced and you had to go somewhere to read them, thus potentially leaving a trail. Now, the information is online and widely accessible.

The range of information that we have made available is staggering. Not only can we find out addresses and a great deal of information about people and organizations, but we can find maps, building plans, power network diagrams, pipeline routes, and just about anything that you can think of. In the past, it would have taken considerable effort and probably a visit to the location to discover. The modern-day terrorist can gain significant information on prospective targets over the Internet. During a high-tech investigation, take time to think about where the attackers gained the information they needed to initiate the attack on your systems. If possible, look through the audit trails of the systems, and see if there are any patterns of activity that may give a clue regarding how the reconnaissance was carried out.

DIRECT ATTACKS

As we all know, the world is rapidly becoming a more dangerous place. This is particularly true for Western companies doing business in Asia, the Middle East, and Africa. In April 2004, the US State Department released a report on patterns of global terrorism characterizing the global threat to US citizens and US interests. Some of the highlights of the statistics include the following:

- One hundred ninety international terrorist attacks occurred in 2003, based on the US definition of a terrorist attack.
- Three hundred seven people were killed in the attacks; of those, 35 US citizens were killed.
- One thousand five hundred ninety-three people were wounded in the attacks.
- The highest number of attacks and the highest casualty rates occurred in Asia. There were 70 attacks resulting in 159 dead and 951 injured.
- Sixteen US citizens were killed as a result of Palestinian attacks in Israel.
- Nine US citizens were killed in the May 12 attacks on expatriate housing in Riyadh, Saudi Arabia.

Although these statistics only include attacks on US interests, the threat to all Westerners and Western interests is expanding. This is particularly true in predominantly Islamic countries.

Terrorist attacks. They are a warning, loud and clear, indicating that if a company or government is doing business in certain parts of the world, there are more issues to be concerned about than just protecting information from competitors and foreign governments.

Terrorism is a real and present concern. Terrorists target US and other interests. These interests may be institutions of government, symbolic institutions, or economic institutions. Economic institutions include US and primarily Western companies. The suicide car bombing at the J.W. Marriott hotel on August 5, 2003, in Jakarta, Indonesia, serves as strong reminder of the vulnerability of such Western targets. This particular hotel was a location regularly used by Western business people. The hotel was an intended target and not a coincidental victim. Understanding that the world is a dangerous place is particularly important to companies doing international business.

Of the top 500 global companies, more that 75% are from Western countries. Understanding world security conditions, particularly in countries with strong anti-Western sentiments, is essential for the safety of personnel and success of the enterprise.

The potential effect that a direct terrorist attack might have on the infrastructure can be seen in a number of incidents that have occurred, none of which have been the result of malicious intent to date, rather as the result of accidents and errors. The first of these was on December 19, 1978, when approximately 80% of France was affected by a major power blackout. The next was in California in 2001 when there were regular blackouts and brownouts as a result of energy shortages and market manipulation that resulted from deregulation. The third, and one of the most memorable incidents, occurred on August 14, 2003, when there was a power failure that affected 50 million people in the northeastern United States and central Canada. In August of the same year, London, England, suffered from a major power cut, but this was small by comparison and affected half a million people. The following month, power failures affected nearly 40% of Malaysia and nearly five million people in Denmark and Sweden. At the end of that month, a massive power failure that was reported to have been caused by an uprooted tree in the Swiss Alps pulling a power line down affected 57 million people in Italy and some parts of Switzerland. Two years later, in May 2005, 10 million people in the Moscow area suffered a power failure that lasted up to 24 hours, and in August, 100 million people in Indonesia experienced a power failure.

All these incidents were power failures, but they are very visible demonstrations that critical infrastructures are fragile at the best of times without attempts to attack them by those with malicious intent. Imagine the impact that an attack on air traffic control systems would have, not only on the airport and the airlines, but also on the traveling public. Look what happened to airline travel in the United States after 9/11. It stopped, including no flights into the United States from other nations.

We have so far seen significant attacks on the financial sector by organized crime gangs, but we know that many terrorist organizations partially or fully finance their terrorist activities through the same type of criminal acts. Whether any of the attacks on the financial sector have resulted from fund-raising attempts by terrorist groups, is (as we stated earlier) unknown.

What we must assume is that at some point in the future, terrorists will use the Internet to carry out attacks. At the moment we think that it is not possible to terrorize the populace through the use of computers. Society is not yet sufficiently dependent on them to allow for the removal or corruption of the services that we gain from them to cause terror. Unfortunately, as the West continues its headlong rush to adopt new technologies in the drive to improve the quality of life and to reduce the cost of doing business, we do become increasingly dependent on them.

What is also a point of concern is that, in this dash to use the technologies, countries in the West are becoming increasingly exposed in relation to less well-developed countries. In the West, if critical systems are unavailable, we have gone past the point where we can easily return to manual or mechanical systems. If you compare our situation with that in less developed areas, the impact there is far less. They have not yet come to expect the systems to be available.

SUMMARY

To date there have been no publicly identified, direct attacks on information systems that have been initiated by terrorists. For this we should be thankful, but we should also consider why. The fact is that, to date, our dependence on high-technology systems is not so great that an attack on them would achieve the aims of a terrorist. That is to say that the populace may be made uncomfortable or delayed by an attack on high-technology systems, but they are unlikely to be terrified. What we can also be sure of is that terrorists will increasingly use the Internet and other high-technology systems to support their planning, fund-raising, communications, and publicity machinations.

> When terrorists think that the time is right and they will be able to achieve the effects they desire, we can expect to see attacks on elements of the infrastructure.

We need to be aware of the likely indicators of the high-technology systems and devices that we are responsible for and may have to investigate by terrorists, and make sure that we consider this type of attack when carrying out an investigation.

REFERENCES

1. *Government Hacker Warning Is a Sign of the Times.* http://insight.zdnet.co.uk/internet/security/0,39020457,39203968,00.htm
2. Hurst, P. (August 2, 2004). UK Terror Attack Plan "in Suspect's E-Mails." *The Scotsman.*
3. Sharrock, D. (2005, September 9). Belfast's Non-Jury Court Tries Islamist Suspect. *The Times.*

23

The Future of the High-Technology Crime Investigator Profession

The objective of this chapter is to discuss the future of the high-technology crime investigator profession.

INTRODUCTION

One can see some parallels between the high-technology crime investigator professional and high-technology crime investigator manager, and that of the ISSO and CISO. Both are relatively new, with the ISSO and CISO professions being less than 20 years old at best. As the InfoSec-related professions matured, a certification program was established to bring the profession into a similarly held professional level of that of the certified public accountant, for example.

> The profession of high-technology crime investigator is a relatively new one. Because of the technical nature of such a profession, it requires more skills than that of the general investigator.

The InfoSec professions are still developing and include portions of the high-technology crime investigator tasks. They have some commonality, and there is some crossover of experience required for both to be well-rounded professionals. For example, to conduct high-technology crime investigations adequately, the high-technology crime investigator must understand systems, their vulnerabilities, threats, risks, and basic protective measures that need to be taken to protect the systems and the information that they display, store, process, and transmit.

The Certified Information Systems Security Professional examination (started in 1989) includes a "10-domain body of knowledge." One of these is "Law, Investigations, and Ethics." As the high-technology crime investigator profession matures, a formal and globally accepted certifications program should be one of the goals of the profession.

LACK OF TRAINING, MANAGEMENT SUPPORT, AND SOMETIMES EVEN INTEREST

In 1995, Dr. Kovacich conducted a small, fairly informal survey of his fellow High-Tech-Crime Investigation Association members that was used for the first edition of this book. The purpose of the survey was to determine their preparedness, the level of support that was available, and their capability to investigate high-technology crime successfully. The members were asked to answer questions on a number of topics, and their responses indicated that at that time, more than three quarters of them came from law enforcement backgrounds, with the remainder being employed in businesses as investigators, auditors, or security personnel. They had a vast level of experience (an average of nearly 18 years each).

It is worth remembering that at the time of the first survey, the technological world in which we work was very different, as (to some extent) were the skills that a high-technology crime investigator needed.

- In 1995, the World Wide Web was still in its infancy.
- Most users only had access to limited bandwidth.
- The diversity of high-technology devices was still very limited compared with those of today.
- At that time there were 16 million people who had regular access to the Internet, whereas today there are estimated to be more than one billion!

HIGH-TECHNOLOGY CRIME INVESTIGATION UNITS AND LAW ENFORCEMENT

In the 10 years since the survey was conducted, there have been a number of significant developments:

- Law enforcement high-technology crime investigation units now exist in a number of countries.
- Considerable time and effort have been expended in ensuring that these units are able to work together to catch high-technology criminals.
- International protocols for the exchange of data and for assistance in investigations have been developed and, although they may not be perfect, this is a huge step forward.
- In many countries, laws have been brought onto the statute books that specifically address high-technology crime and, although these laws require constant updating to address the changes in technology and the criminal use of it, the law in this area is now better defined.

A problem that was identified during the initial survey was the lack of management support for the type of work that these units undertake. In this regard, in many ways, nothing has changed, probably with one exception. It is understandable that the law enforcement resources that are funded in a geographic area will be expected to address the issues that concern the citizens of that area. For example, if there is a high level of burglary or car theft in an area, the pressure will be on the law enforcement agencies to address these problems, because they affect the people that are funding the law enforcement officers.

> High-technology crime is still seen by many as a "victimless crime" and has no geographic borders, so a crime that may be investigated in one area will normally have been perpetrated by someone in a different jurisdiction. So who should put the effort into the investigation?

Law enforcement agencies are also often measured by statistics. If you can show that you have made a number of arrests and that car crime and burglary have reduced as a result, this will be considered to be a success. How do you quantify or measure the effect that a law enforcement investigation has had on crime when no one knows what the real level of crime is in the high-technology world?

The equipment and tools that are required for these units are also relatively expensive, as is the training that is required to use them effectively. Given the low visibility of most high-technology crime and the subsequent investigations, gaining and retaining support for the units will continue to be a problem. The future development and growth of this type of unit may rely more on the requirement for support to conventional crime investigations such as robberies and murders where, with the widespread use of high technology in our everyday lives, the potential for evidence to be stored on a computer or a cell phone has increased hugely.

An exception is that of pedophile crimes. These have very much become prominent in the high-technology world of the Internet, and investigations into this type of crime have the almost universal support of law enforcement management and the public.

> Adding resources to law enforcement high-technology investigation units remains a problem. They require a highly motivated and well-trained staff who, unfortunately, have skills that are also now in high demand in the commercial sector, which can afford to pay considerably higher salaries and are often perceived to offer better working conditions.

In addition to the law enforcement high-technology crime units, there are now also similar units in the military and increasingly in large business organizations. There are also independent, commercial high-technology investigation organizations that perform investigations for organizations that do not have their own resources and either cannot get law enforcement assistance or do not wish to involve them.

TRAINING

At the time of the initial survey, only 50% of those interviewed advised that they had received some training in high-technology crime-related topics. The majority of the respondents had received training in computer crime and computer crime investigation, with one respondent receiving systems security training. At that time the training was primarily provided by the American Society for Industrial Security, the FBI, the High-Tech-Crime Investigator Association, or the Management Information Systems Institute. All respondents believed the training was useful.

In the intervening period, from when the survey was conducted until now, the situation has changed considerably, and largely for the better. There has been increasing recognition by employers of the need for adequate training in the use of the tools and techniques required to conduct high-technology crime investigations. There has also been a recognition and an understanding, particularly among law enforcement and military investigators, that despite the wealth of experience that they may have, it is also important to obtain professional and academic qualifications. Fortunately, academia has responded to the need and a suitable range of courses is now increasingly available.

In the original survey, approximately 75% of the law enforcement personnel that contributed stated they had received some training in high-technology crime–related topics. They had received training in one or more of the areas of computer crime, computer crime investigation, Internet break-ins, electronic intercepts, telecommunications crime (PBX fraud, cellular phone fraud, and so forth), search and seizure of computers, data processing for law enforcement, or computer security.

At the time of the first survey, training was provided by SEARCH (The National Consortium for Justice Information and Statistics), FLETC (The Federal Law Enforcement Training Center), the High-Tech-Crime Investigators Association, IACIS (The International Association of Computer Investigative Specialists), MCI, the FBI, New York State DCJS, US Secret Service, US Customs, NYNEX (an aerospace company), and Motorola.

Many of these, particularly the government-based organizations, are still providing first-class training to meet the needs of federal, state, and local staff. They have now been joined by an ever-increasing number of universities, computer forensic equipment and software manufacturers, and independent specialists in providing education and training in the subject. The biggest problem now is the wide range of courses and the associated certifications to choose from. How do you select the course that is at the appropriate level and covers the range of material that you need? Well the answer to that is: through various user groups and contacts. Listen to your colleagues and take their advice.

In the initial survey, it was determined that a broad spectrum of high-technology crime-related training was required. Since the initial survey, in the technical areas the requirement has risen dramatically with the increasing connectivity and complexity of systems, their increased processing speeds and storage capacities, and the diversity of devices. Since the initial survey, the range of organizations offering training has increased dramatically, although it is refreshing to see that the majority of the pioneering organizations are still providing courses to meet the developing requirements. One of the difficulties that is more apparent now is that, for most investigators, it is not possible to be good at the whole range of topics and areas that may be encountered.

From the initial survey, the respondents indicated that the types of training they found most useful for them were hacker networking; bank fraud through computers, cellular phone and telephone fraud, latest methods to detect high-technology crime, fraud schemes, consumer-related computer fraud, Internet tracking of obscenity distributors, training in general and specific software and technologies, computer searching for evidence, all types of systems, bulletin board systems, current hardware, software applications, cloning programs, EPROM manufacturing, encryption techniques, high-technology crime search warrants, reviewing system audit trails, firewalls, networks, imaging, and counterfeiting with computers.

Although many of these topics are still valid, the technological developments in the intervening period have meant that things like bulletin boards, when they still exist, tend to be Internet-based, and things such as EPROM manufacturing is probably less significant. More significant at the moment are things such as phishing and pharming, handheld devices such as PDAs, mobile phones, and games systems such as X-Box and Play Station.

Hacking and illegally using satellite television channels is an area that also offers some challenges to the high-technology crime investigator.

This is part of a natural progression and the requirement will undoubtedly continue to change as new technologies are introduced and new applications are devised for the existing technologies. These changes just demonstrate that there is always a requirement to keep up to date with training and education on the topics that are of interest at the time. The underlying subjects, however, still need to be covered.

HIGH-TECHNOLOGY CRIME INVESTIGATIONS

In the initial survey, when the respondents were asked to identify the main problems that made it difficult for them to conduct high-technology crime investigations, they responded that they were:

- Lack of or the late notification of incidents by the victim
- Quality of training
- Lack of guidance and management support
- Poor communications with other investigators
- Lack of willingness of lawyers to take new types of crime to court
- Rapidly changing technology
- Range of different systems and their incompatible formats
- Insufficient training
- Lack of resources
- Time available

Once again, we have seen progress in some areas, but not in others.

> In most areas, organizations are more willing (or, in some cases, now legally required) to report high-technology crimes.

With the increase in the level of high-technology crime that is taking place, there is increasing recognition of this type of crime. As a result, the level of support and resources devoted to this type of crime has also risen. The quality and range of available training has improved greatly, and the legal profession has become accustomed to this type of crime. On the negative side, the diversity and complexity of computer systems has grown tremendously, and the different skills that are required have grown considerably. The resources that are required to investigate a high-technology crime are still at a premium, and, as a result, the amount of time that can be dedicated to any single investigation will still normally be the minimum required.

Computer crime is still happening and although it is becoming more complex, successful investigations are taking place. So it is probably true to say that the good guys are getting the minimum level of resources required to keep pace with the criminals.

THE BEST TOOLS TO ASSIST IN CONDUCTING HIGH-TECHNOLOGY CRIME INVESTIGATIONS

In the first survey, the respondents—both law enforcement and commercial investigators—indicated that the things that would most assist them in conducting high-technology crime investigations were:

- Quality liaison with the appropriate authorities
- Cooperation between law enforcement and technical specialists
- Reliable crime statistics
- Better training
- Better cooperation between agencies
- Dedicated investigative units
- More staff
- Knowing available technologies and having access to them

It is worth noting that the highly respected Norton Utilities tool was specifically identified at that time as an essential tool. Although a professional investigator would recognize the value of this type of tool in the modern environment, the development and use of specifically developed computer forensic tools is now essential and is expected in most cases.

> One thing that has certainly not changed is the recognition of the need for good liaison and communications between a range of groups and agencies.

THE BEST TOOLS TO ASSIST IN COMMITTING HIGH-TECHNOLOGY CRIMES

In the initial survey, the respondents believed that the best tools of the techno-criminal were:

- Social engineering skills
- Peer cooperation
- Inside information from employees
- Advanced off-the-shelf technology
- Easy-to-use software
- Computer expertise
- Lack of computer knowledge by law enforcement
- Poor and scarce law enforcement training
- More criminals learning about computers
- Poor security
- Victims' lack of knowledge
- Ease of access to the Internet
- High-technology crimes treated lightly by courts
- Non-face-to-face crime

In the intervening period, what has changed? In some areas, things have become much worse. We have seen increasingly more mobile workforces, with the result that employer loyalty has decreased in some cases. The availability of technology and the range of tools available to the criminal have increased, and the number of criminals using the Internet has risen sharply as well, partially as a result of the increased numbers of people using the Internet and partially as a result of the nature of crime: Criminals follow the money, and the money has gone online.

> The security of information systems is still only as good as the weakest link, and with the widespread use of broadband access by home users, access to systems has probably never been easier.

In other areas such as the level of police knowledge and training availability, there has been significant improvement. This also applies to detection and investigative tools and the laws that have been put in place to allow for the investigation and prosecution of high-technology crimes.

HIGH-TECHNOLOGY CRIMES INCREASING OR DECREASING?

The response to this question in the first survey was that all investigators believed that:

- High-technology crimes were increasing and were based on more people becoming computer literate.
- Computers were becoming easier to use.
- Techno-criminals have more money and less of a chance of getting caught.
- Techno-crime is financially lucrative.
- More information is being stored online.
- Hacker information is readily available.
- It is hard to trace techno-criminals.
- There is better cooperation among criminals than law enforcement and security personnel.
- Prevention and detection resources are not available.
- There is a lack of training and interest by law enforcement.
- There are inadequate controls.
- Internet access are easier and increasing in number.

Since the first survey, as noted earlier, we have seen a massive increase in the numbers of users of the Internet. Governments and businesses have increasingly had to use the Internet to remain competitive to gain access to the new population of potential customers. As a result, the number of potential targets and the amount of information that is available has increased dramatically, with the result being that the temptation for criminals has risen.

> Computers have become easier to use and the number of uses that they can be put to has increased as well.

With the increased level of usage and the resultant complexity of the systems, the difficulty in detecting and tracing criminals has also, in some ways, risen. However, to counter this, new detection and investigative tools have been developed to try to maintain some sort of balance.

There has also been considerable effort at both state and national levels to improve cooperation between commercial, local, state, federal, and national resources involved in the detection and investigation of high-technology crimes. In the mid 1990s, if you needed to get assistance from another organization, you would probably have had to start from scratch to try and find the scarce resources within the organization that could understand what you were talking about. Then you had to fight your way through a load of protocols (if they even existed) to gain assistance. Now, however, we have readily available contact lists and sets of protocols to enable mutual assistance.

CONFIGURATIONS AND SECURITY OF LAW ENFORCEMENT SYSTEMS

In the initial survey, one of the concerns of law enforcement officials was the protection of their sensitive information and the systems they used to process, store, and transmit that information. This was based on the information provided with regard to the systems they were using at the time. Then, approximately 80% of the survey respondents used systems that were operated by their agency, whereas nearly 20% worked on a shared system, or a system in which other organizations were responsible. Some of the interesting statistics from that survey are found in the types of systems that they were using. Their systems, at the time, were categorized as:

- Mainframe system (59%)
- LAN (64%)
- Dial-up (27%)
- WAN (36%)

Note that at the time of the survey, many of the respondents had access to and used multiple types of systems.

In the intervening period, the situation has clearly changed dramatically, but has it been for the better? For the investigator, the days of the mainframe are largely long gone, and it is more normal to have dedicated resources for investigations, but with access to corporate or organizational systems and the Internet for background and nonspecialist resources and information sharing. Investigators now have access to a huge range of shared investigative knowledge and resources.

Dial-up or wireless access is now expected, as a minimum, to enable investigators to do their job.

SYSTEMS SECURE?

In the initial survey, when the respondents were asked if they believed that the information maintained on their systems was adequately protected, more than half believed that the information was *not* adequately protected, whereas the remainder believed it was. Interestingly, the security of at least 25% of the law enforcement organizations had been outsourced.

From our personal experience, the outsourcing contracts that were set up at this time were often lacking in clarity with regard to responsibility or the ability of the organization that was outsourcing the task to inspect the measures that had been implemented to protect their information. The implication of this was that all the information stored, processed, and transmitted by law enforcement personnel had the potential to be read or modified, and the information could potentially be stolen and sold by others.

In the intervening period, the management and security of many more systems has been outsourced. The plus side is that we have all, hopefully, learned the lessons of the past, and the measures that are implemented to protect the information and the right of the outsourcing organization to test those measures have improved significantly. Having said that, these rights and measures are only as good as the interest that is taken in checking that the measures are effective.

CONCLUSIONS

In the initial survey, it appeared that the majority of respondents believed that they lacked the training, resources, and management support to address adequately high-technology crime issues. In addition, they believed that high-technology crime was increasing, because of cheaper, more powerful, easier-to-use computers and more computer users. It was noted at that time that the potential risk to their information based on outside personnel and/or agencies being responsible for maintaining and operating their systems was not adequately addressed, particularly by law enforcement personnel.

Since the initial survey, there have been changes. The perception that the situation was getting worse has proved to be correct. The number of users on the Internet, the number of organizations connected to the Internet, and the ease of use of systems and software have all probably exceeded the expectations of the mid 1990s. On the positive side, both law enforcement and commercial organizations have seen considerable, if only inadequate, additional resources applied to the problem. The development of easier to use systems and software has also benefited the investigator because new tools and techniques have been developed.

> The "good guys" have started to learn to communicate with each other and now pass on intelligence, evidence, and knowledge to each other in the same way the "bad guys" have been doing all along.

Comparing the Survey Results with Today's Environment

As stated earlier, that initial survey and the conclusions drawn occurred in 1995. A decade has past since then. As you read through this survey, do you believe that, in the intervening period, significant changes have taken place that would change the results of that survey? If you are an investigator in, say, the United States federal government, especially the FBI and since the events of 9/11, or in the commercial sector, you may say yes. If you are at the state or local level of law enforcement (where there is usually less money and a lower priority of such endeavors), you may not have noticed any meaningful improvements.

If you do not have optimism that the situation with regard to investigations is at least keeping pace with the developments by high-tech criminals, then you should probably look for a new career. The reality is that the future will most likely bring an ever-increasing demand from all areas for a greater number of highly trained high-technology crime investigators. In the future, this demand will probably not come so much from private citizens or even government agencies, but from the ever-increasing number of information-dependent businesses that are already tired of criminals attacking them and victimizing them at great cost to resources and losses in profits.

> As with other high-technology professionals, such as the InfoSec professional, high-technology crime investigator specialists will find that they are in ever-greater demand.

In the first edition of this book it was speculated that, although it would probably not happen in our lifetime, law enforcement specialists would find that the position of high-technology crime investigator within a police department would not be a dead-end job, but one that is highly sought after for visibility, career development, and the best steppingstone to promotion. This has come true in some areas and, as predicted, the high-technology crime investigator is developing into a formally recognized and distinct profession.

The profession, which was in its infancy in 1995, has followed the path of groups such as the industrial security profession with the Certified Protection Professional designation, the Certified Fraud Examiner, the Certified Public Accountant, the Certified Information Systems Auditor, and the Certified Information Systems Security Professional. In the high-technology crime area, there are now a considerable number of initiatives that are attempting to provide this recognized and distinct profession.

- The High-Tech-Crime Network (www.htcn.org/about.htm) has been around for more than 12 years and consists of law enforcement agencies and corporate security professionals from 15 countries. The membership includes organizations such as the Royal Canadian Mounted Police, FBI, Internal Revenue Service, US Marshals, Department of Defense, NSA, and law enforcement agencies from the United Kingdom, Germany, Belgium, and Switzerland, together with major telecommunication organizations within the United States.
- The SANS Institute founded the Global Information Assurance Certification (GIAC) in 1999 in response to the need to validate the skills of security professionals. They now offer courses and certifications such as the GIAC Certified Forensics Analyst.
- The Certified Forensic Computer Examiner certification was originally designed for law enforcement officers by the IACIS, but is now open to those with the experience and knowledge to complete the rigorous testing.
- The Certified Cyber-Crime Expert was designed for computer forensics investigators, information technology and security personnel, law enforcement officials, lawyers, and others who have the knowledge and tools to collect, handle, process, and preserve computer forensic evidence effectively. The certification requires successful completion of the Computer Forensic and Cyber Investigation course, and the successful completion of a practical and written exam.
- The Certified Computer Crime Investigator is another computer forensic certification aimed at both law enforcement and private IT professionals who seek to or who have specialized in investigations.

The basic requirements for the certification include at least 2 years of experience (or a college degree plus 1 year of experience), plus 18 months of investigative experience, a minimum of at least 40 hours of computer crime training, and documented evidence of participation in at least 10 cases.

- The Certified Computer Forensic Technician is another computer forensic certification aimed at both law enforcement and private IT professionals who specialize in investigations. The entry requirements include at least 3 years of experience (or a college degree plus 1 year of experience), plus 18 months of computer forensics experience, 40 hours of computer forensics training, and documented experience from investigating at least 10 cases.

- The Certified Computer Examiner, offered by the Southeast Cybercrime Institute at Kennesaw State University, is aimed at people with the appropriate computer forensics training and experience, including the gathering of evidence and its handling and storage. Applicants are also required to pass an online examination and carry out a successful examination of three test media.

- The International Information Systems Forensics Association (IISFA) is a nonprofit organization with a mission to promote the discipline of information forensics in the form of evangelism, education, and certification. Members of the IISFA adhere to the organization's code of ethics and can apply for Certified International Information Systems Forensics Investigator (CIFI). The CIFI certification was specifically developed for the experienced information forensics investigator who has practical experience in carrying out investigations on behalf of law enforcement or as part of a corporate investigations team.

- There is also a vendor organization, Guidance Software (www.encase.com/training/certifying.asp), that provides training in what is probably the most commonly used tool—Encase. They offer an Encase Certified Examiner Program certification program for the use of their products that is widely accepted in the industry as recognition of competence in the use of the tool.

- Increasingly there are colleges and universities offering courses that are relevant to the high-technology crime investigator at all levels— from bachelor's to master's to doctoral degrees. In the United States you can now acquire a bachelor of science degree in computer and digital forensics or an associate's degree/certificate in computer and network forensics, or a whole range of other, relevant academic degrees. In the United Kingdom, at the University of Glamorgan in Wales, and at Edith Cowan University in Perth, Australia, people are already graduating with a PhD in computer forensics. Surely this is the best certification that you can get.

> We have seen the increasing professionalization of high-technology crime investigations, which has been matched by an increasing demand for people in the industry to be properly qualified and certificated.

SUMMARY

In the time since the survey was conducted, there has been considerable change in the whole environment of high-technology crime. The Internet has seen massive growth in the number of users, and with it has come the inevitable move by commerce to try and meet the potential market. There has been considerable technological development that has in some way made the life of the high-technology investigator more difficult, because it has enabled criminal elements. On the other hand, these changes have assisted high-technology investigators through the development of more effective tools for detecting crimes and producing evidence that will stand up in court. The high-technology crime investigator is now receiving greater prominence as a profession, and with this recognition has come better support from management.

The balance between criminals' abilities to conduct crimes, and the ability of law enforcement and commercial investigators to detect those crimes and prosecute the perpetrators has, in the main, largely been maintained. High-technology crime investigators will always be faced with the reality that they are playing catch-up and are learning how to deal with the innovations of criminals. As a result, high-technology crime investigators will always have to think laterally and collaborate with all available resources.

24

Developing a Career as a High-Technology Crime Investigator

The objective of this chapter is to provide the high-technology crime investigator with a career development plan outline to be used in developing a career as a high-technology crime investigator.

INTRODUCTION

People who wish to develop a career as a high-technology crime investigator will have a range of backgrounds. Some will have a law enforcement background, some will come from the military, some will be from the information and communications technology arena, and others will be straight from education or from some other profession. As a result, how to develop your career as a high-technology crime investigator will be given in the form of generic advice and suggestions throughout this chapter.

QUALIFICATIONS

Increasingly, as the profession becomes more mature, there are suitable courses available and organizations are increasingly demanding that people they are considering for appointments or promotion have suitable academic qualifications. As little as 4 or 5 years ago, this would have been difficult for most people and would probably have involved considerable travel. Now there is a wide range of courses that are available in most of the developed world, but primarily in the United States and United Kingdom.

Courses do range in content to meet the diverse demands of the profession, but at least now and into the future, as skills are increasingly demanded, you should be able to find a suitable course within a reasonable distance from your location. In addition, there are online programs offered by technical schools and universities. There are also now a wide range of undergraduate degrees and master's degrees, and at least one University in the United Kingdom (The Security Research Group, School of Computing, University of Glamorgan, www.glam.ac.uk) is offering a research PhD in computer forensics. Its first group graduated in 2005.

A comprehensive (although no doubt incomplete) list of the universities, primarily in the United States and the United Kingdom, and the courses that they offer can be found at the Electronic Evidence Information Center Web page (www.e-evidence.info).

When you are selecting a course, do not forget to take into account the experience that you already have that may be relevant, and pick a course (at the appropriate level) that suits the area of high-technology crime you want to work in. Remember that in some academic institutes, professional experience in the relevant field will be taken into account for entry to both undergraduate and postgraduate degrees, even if you do not have the stated entry requirements.

We can assure you from personal experience that, on academic courses in this area, people, particularly from military and law enforcement backgrounds, are far more capable than they think they are. In most cases, they are very capable of gaining a good pass on degree courses.

In addition to academic qualifications, there are a large number of specialist courses provided by the manufacturers of specialist hardware and software, and by independent training organizations. These courses, many of which are evaluated, carry significant recognition within the profession. You will have greater credibility in the field if you are using tools for which you have received appropriate training.

CERTIFICATION

There is an increasing number of professional certifications for high-technology crime investigation professionals that are available (as mentioned earlier). This is both good and bad. Because there is a range of certifying bodies involved, there is pressure on them to make the testing that they carry out appropriate to the market, which is good for the profession. The downside is that too many certifying bodies will cause confusion and may be detrimental, because professionals will not know the most appropriate certification to obtain and will probably spend additional money and time to make sure they have one that is recognized.

In addition, because of various sponsors of various certifications, those in management looking for certified high-technology crime investigator professionals will be at a loss to determine which of the certification programs are truly adequate and recognized throughout the industry. As the situation settles down, it will become clearer, and people already in the profession will be able to give advice regarding the most relevant certification programs for specific areas of expertise.

> One must be cautious, when choosing a certification program, to avoid those that are not generally accepted and, in some cases, may even just be the latest in a range of money-making schemes taking advantage of current trends.

EXPERIENCE

This is always the "catch-22" of trying to get employment in a new area. Even with qualifications, employers only want to take on people who have relevant experience. In professions where there are large numbers of people employed, this is not normally a problem, because there will be apprenticeships and structures in place for professional progression. Unfortunately, in the high-technology investigation area, this does not normally apply outside the military and law enforcement. So how do you get some experience?

There are a number of ways that you can start to get experience. One example is that of a student who was studying for a PhD in computing. She decided that she wanted to work in the computer forensics area, so she got in touch with a number of government agencies, commercial forensic laboratories, and other universities that taught computer forensics, looking for advice and assistance. One of the universities that she contacted was carrying out research into computer forensic issues, primarily in support of law enforcement. Even though the student was not at that university, the spirit of cooperation that is still so often found in people involved in this area was present. She was invited to join in the research and gain some invaluable hands-on experience in looking at historic cases. From this work and the contacts that this student made with law enforcement agencies and commercial companies, she was offered a number of other opportunities to work on investigations, thus building her experience and knowledge.

Another way to gain some experience, if you cannot find some publicly spirited organization to help you, is to help yourself. Get hold of the most common tools (beg and borrow; don't steal); many of them are inexpensive or free to investigators. When you have some of the tools, start to use them and get to be competent with them.

Find out what they are good at and what they are not, and then start to get hold of some disks (from friends, colleagues, or from online auctions or computer fairs) and start to understand what information you can recover from disks and how hard it is. When you are comfortable with the tools and have some understanding of the problems that you will encounter on an investigation, you start to become a much better prospect as an employee than someone who has just completed the courses. Oh yes. Another benefit is that you have just demonstrated to a potential employer that you are self-motivated, persistent, and undaunted by difficult problems.

KNOWLEDGE

If you are to develop and maintain a career as a high-technology crime investigator, then knowledge is just as, or more important, than qualifications. The range of knowledge that you will need to have is vast. In reality, it is not possible to know everything that is relevant. All you can do is be good within one discipline and have knowledge of the other relevant areas.

> As you gain experience and standing in one discipline, you will get to know people who are good in other areas.

As you gain respect in your discipline, the people who are good in other areas will also seek you out. After all, a good investigator will want to know that the person in the computer forensics lab will do a good job and vice versa. When you are, perhaps, good at Linux problems, the people who are good at Windows or router issues will look you up.

How do you gain knowledge? There are a number of ways. The first is to gain experience from and exposure to a range of cases. As you identify and work to solve the problems and situations that you encounter in an investigation, you will develop knowledge. The next way to gain knowledge is through reading! Yes, it is still a good way to improve your knowledge. Acquire books, journals, white papers, and research publications. Do not be narrow in your choice of reading, because it is often true that research in one discipline can lead to enlightenment in another.

> One final thought here. Just because information is on the Internet, does not mean that information is true. Wherever you find information, always test it yourself to make sure that it is correct. In an investigation, you cannot, as a professional, rely on anything that you cannot prove to be correct.

Another way to acquire knowledge is to attend conferences, where, in addition to the actual lectures, you will be able to participate in workshops and network with the best in their fields. Finally, do some research of your own when you get the chance. We can all claim that we never have the time or the resources, but the truth is that most people in this field who are any good live and breathe it. They will always find the time to better themselves professionally. If you want to be the best, be like them.

RANGE OF CASES

If you want to develop your career and be a competent high-technology crime investigator, the wider the range of cases that you have been involved in (unsuccessful as well as successful), the better you will be. If you have only worked on financial investigations, you may become very good at them, but your knowledge of other types of crime may be limited. It is a personal choice if you prefer to be the financial crime investigation guru. However, we advise that one should be very good in one area, but have a reasonable or good knowledge of the other areas. The only way you can really do this is by getting involved in them.

> The more cases you have been involved with, the more you will have learned and the better your portfolio will be as an investigator.

Also remember that as part of this experience gathering, the more you can testify in court, the more your expertise will be requested as an "expert witness." As this happens, prepare for your demand and career to grow exponentially as the word gets around that you are not only good at what you do, but you are also good at testifying and explaining complicated high-technology matters in laymen's terms—a skill that is often lacking but much needed.

TECHNOLOGIES

It is almost a mute point, but you will need to keep up to date with high technology. You will not be much of an asset as a high-technology crime investigator if you don't.

> In developing your career, make sure that you keep up to date with new developments and have a good understanding of the types of high technology that you may encounter.

This is beneficial in a number of ways: The first is that your knowledge will be up to the job for any potential investigation. The second is that, as you are developing your career, it will demonstrate to current and future employers that you have a good breadth of knowledge and keep yourself up to date.

ASSOCIATIONS

This may seem to be a strange thing to include in a chapter on how to develop your career as a high-technology investigator, but trade associations are extremely important to the investigator. These associations are currently providing the certifications for our profession. It is also through the associations that a vast network of like-minded investigators can and do share knowledge.

> If you are a member of one or more of the high-technology crime associations, then you know most of them have a list server facility where investigators can post questions on problems they have encountered. You have access to the knowledge of all of the other investigators and researchers who have already encountered and found a solution to the problem.

For those of you who come from a security background, this will seem an alien concept—sharing information. When you have subscribed to the list server for a period of time however, you will build up a wealth of knowledge of the problems that you may encounter and solutions to them. This is knowledge that you cannot buy. Some of the associations that are prominent in the area are the:

- IACIS (www.iacis.info/iacisv2/pages/home.php)
- International Society of Forensic Computer Examiners (www.isfce.com)
- IISFA (www.iisfa.org/)

SUMMARY

In this chapter we have given you some ideas for developing a career as a high-technology crime investigator. The reality is that you will probably already be part of the way there in that you will have gained the academic qualifications, the certification, or have experience and been involved in a number of cases.

25

Marketing Yourself as a Successful High-Technology Crime Investigator

The objective of this chapter is to explain some of the more unique methods to prepare for a high-technology crime investigation job and to describe the "interview by portfolio" method to get that investigative position you've been looking for.

INTRODUCTION

The last chapter dealt primarily with career development and gaining experience to become a professional, certified high-technology crime investigator. After you have established your career development plan and hopefully even used project planning techniques to formalize your plan, you will be well on your way to gaining that "perfect" high-technology crime investigator position. Now you must put everything together to "sell" (or market) yourself. Consider yourself as any other product that must be sold to customers. You are that product, and you must devise a marketing plan to sell you to your potential employers.

MARKETING SUPPORT: TRAINING, EXPERIENCE, CERTIFICATIONS, ASSOCIATIONS, AND CONTACTS

Training

The issue of training is always contentious. An employer will want you to do as much on-the-job training as possible, rather than attend expensive academic or vendor-specific courses that you feel are necessary. If you attend a training course, make sure that you get the best benefit from it for your career that you can. Remember that when developing your portfolio to make yourself an attractive asset, there will be some courses and training that are more beneficial than others. If you have identified areas that you feel will improve your marketability and they are not considered to be necessary by your employer, think about paying for them yourself. After all, it is you that you are trying to market. If you want to get work in specific organizations or technologies, do your research and make sure that you are well qualified, because it is reasonable to be in the areas that are of interest to potential employers.

Experience

This is a tricky topic to offer advice on. There are a number of constraints regarding the experience that you can gain that will come about as a result of the type of training that you have and as a result of the type of work that the organization you are working for undertakes. If you are employed in a financial organization, the type of experience you will gain in that organization will probably be very different from what you would gain if you work in law enforcement or in government. It is worth keeping a record of the numbers and types of cases you are involved in, and it may be worth considering going to work in another department or for another organization if you identify that you need more experience in different areas that they deal with. Remember to break down the record of the experience you have gained into the different disciplines and types of investigation and the roles that you played in these investigations. For example, did you lead the investigation or cover a specific aspect of it? Also, identify the successes, failures, and the lessons learned from each case. This is not to suggest that you should catalogue them all in your portfolio, but if you have a record of them, you will be able to highlight the most significant when it is necessary.

It may well be worth capturing any suitable accolades that you receive as the result of the investigations that you are involved in. After all, you saying you are a superb investigator is one thing, but when other people have said it, it carries more weight.

Certifications

In the last chapter the development of your career was discussed and the subject of certification was addressed. It is a reality that when you are trying to market yourself as an investigator, professional certification is a benchmark that is understood by employers. If you want to promote yourself to best effect, it will be worth gaining suitable certification for the area of investigation that you want to promote yourself in.

Associations

There are an increasing number of professional associations that cater to all aspects of investigation. By joining suitable associations, you not only gain access to the material, resources, support, and networking they offer, but you may also gain knowledge of job vacancies in the field that you are interested in, because many of the associations post job vacancies on their Web sites.

Contacts

When you want to market yourself as a successful high-technology crime investigator, probably the best route you will have will be the network of contacts you have developed during the course of your career to date. These will be people who know you and can promote you in their organizations or can provide references for you from their experiences with you.

APPLYING FOR THE POSITION OF HIGH-TECHNOLOGY CRIME INVESTIGATOR, SUPERVISOR, OR MANAGER

Currently, there are very few, if any, positions in business or government agencies that have as a title "high-technology crime investigator." However, there are positions available for fraud examiners and investigators whose job description may include conducting investigations related to high-technology violations of policies, procedures, or laws.

If you have completed your career development project plan and have begun working the plan, you will be in a better position to compare your qualifications with job descriptions for an investigative position. This is because you would have conducted a self-analysis, a self-inventory of your current education, experiences, strengths, and weaknesses. If not, how do you know what you need to have vis-à-vis high-technology crime investigative-related education and experience? After all, if you don't know what you have, you cannot accurately determine what you need.

Once you start working your plan, you may be able to begin working in the high-technology crime investigative field. Using some of the sources and techniques explained in the previous chapter, investigators may find a position for which they believe they are qualified to hold. There is no reason not to apply for the position. If nothing else, it will give you the experience of interviewing, thus helping you to improve your interview skills. This is especially important if you are coming from a government agency position and are looking for a position in the private sector.

The more experience you have in interviewing, the more relaxed and confident you will become. Your confidence and more natural behavior will help you to obtain your desired position.

So, let's assume that you have found a position being advertised that calls for a high-technology crime investigator. What do you do next? The position will probably be advertised. Read the description of the job carefully to make sure that it is the position that you really want. If you are not so much interested in fulfilling that position as getting out of the job you currently hold, you should be sure you know what you are doing. You know the old saying about the grass being greener, so think carefully. Also, be sure that the position is the one you truly want to hold before you go through all the time and effort of applying for it, do the much-needed research on the company, and go through the interview process. You may be wasting time that could be better spent reading and studying topics that are listed on your career development plan. If you decide that the position being advertised is the one for you, you will probably see on the advertisement that a resume is to be sent in via e-mail or fax.

Today's businesses are usually inundated by resumes, and many of them use a computerized scanner to scan resumes into a database. If your resume is not easily scanned into the system, it may be trashed before it ever gets to be reviewed. Think about it. When a clerk scans the resumes into a computerized system, there may be literally hundreds of these resumes. Trashing one (the clerk will reason) would not be noticed, nor will it make a big difference. After all, there are hundreds of candidates to choose from.

In some cases, you have to take your chances and fax or send your resume via e-mail because the business does not want you to call, nor do they provide a mailing address. Sometimes, they do not even provide the name of the company in the advertisement. It has been known to happen that a person submitted a resume for a position only to learn later that the position was within the company where he was currently employed!

Before you submit a resume, change it. Undoubtedly you have a resume that is generic in nature. Sending the resume you created for any investigative-related job that you find available is the wrong approach. Your resume should be specifically tailored to the position that is advertised. If (hopefully) your resume is reviewed, the reviewer will probably be a human resource specialist, the manager seeking to fulfill the position, or both. In either case, the closer your resume identifies education, experience, and skills that match those of the job description, the better your chances are to be included in the number of applicants who will be scheduled for an interview. Your resume must give the impression that you are perfect for the job. Of the 50 to 1000 resumes received relative to that position, only a handful, maybe 5 to 10, of the most qualified applicants will be scheduled for the initial interview.

YOUR RESUME MADE IT PAST THE INITIAL SCREENING— NEXT STEP: THE INTERVIEW

Congratulations! You're resume has finally made it through the filtering process and you are asked to appear for an interview. You will probably find that high-technology crime investigator positions are very competitive, with very talented high-technology crime investigative professionals competing against you for those positions. So, you must be prepared. As with most job interviews these days, you will probably be subjected to a series of interviews consisting of members of the human resource department, information systems organization, auditors, and security personnel.

Interviews are what will put you back on the road to high-technology crime investigator job hunting or will offer you the challenges of the new high-technology crime investigator position. So you must be prepared!

There are many books on the market that tell you how to interview for a position. They offer advice on everything from how to dress to how to answer the "mother of all interview questions": What are your salary expectations? We assume that you have read those books and have prepared and practiced for the upcoming interview. We now want to show you how you can separate yourself from your high-technology crime investigator competition.

You have probably already interviewed more times than you care to admit. In all those interviews, you probably, as did your peers, walked in wearing dark, conservative business attire, were neatly groomed, and were prepared to answer any question thrown at you. The question is: *What separated you from your competitors?* What was it that made the interviewers remember you and choose you above the rest?

You probably answered most questions the most politically correct way. For example, What is your major weakness? Answer: My major weakness is that I have very little patience for those who don't live up to their commitments. When someone agrees to complete a project by a specific date, I expect that date to be met unless the project leader comes to me in advance of the deadline and explains the reason why that date can't be met. I believe in a team effort and each of us, as vital members of that team, must work together to provide the service and support needed to assist the company in meeting its goals.

Will the answer to that question be considered a weakness or a strength by the interviewers? Probably a strength, but that is how the game is played!

Most of us have been there, done that, and still didn't get the position. Why? Maybe because our answers "float" in the interview room air. They hang there, mingling with those of the other candidates before us.

The only real lasting evidence of the interview is what was written down by the interviewers and what impressions you, the prospective high-technology crime investigator, left with them. Many of the interviewers are "screeners"—human resource personnel who have no idea what high-technology crime prevention is all about. They are there because organizations do teaming today. They operate by consensus. Getting selected is much more difficult than it used to be. So, you need one thing, one thing that will have a lasting impression on the interviewers, one thing that will show them you have the talents, the *applied* education, the experience, *and* the game plan. You've done it! You've been successful in building an HTCPP before, and you will be successful again. You can prove that you can do it because you have your high-technology crime investigator portfolio.

Now you're probably thinking, *"What the heck is a high-technology crime investigator portfolio?"* You probably have seen movies in which models show up at the modeling studio and present their folder containing photographs of themselves in various poses. Sorry, but your photo will probably not help you get the high-technology crime investigator position. But think about it. These models took with them to their interview physical evidence (in the form of photographs), that *proved* that they were the best people for the position.

What you must do is develop your own portfolio to take with you, and show the interviewers *proof* that you've been there, done that!

Your high-technology crime investigator portfolio is something you should begin building as soon as you begin your first high-technology crime investigator job, or before! It should contain an index and identified sections that include letters of reference, letters of appreciation, copies of award certificates, project plans, metric charts you use for measuring the success of your high-technology crime investigations, investigations, and your high-technology crime prevention investigative program. Probably most important, the portfolio should include your high-technology investigative philosophy and crime prevention plan outline that you intend to implement as soon as you are hired.

Develop the outline, as detailed as possible, of an HTCPP, processes, functions, and similar material, and place it in your interview portfolio. Such an outline is probably the most important document in your portfolio and should be the first page after your index. All the other documents are just proof that what you plan to do, you've done before. This becomes increasingly important if the job you are applying for is a supervisory or managerial position.

In the case of someone who has never been a high-technology crime investigator, the prospective high-technology crime investigator can build the high-technology crime prevention plan and portfolio from the information provided in this book.

One question that may arise is: If I've never worked there, how do I know what I should do if I get hired? Again, do some research. Remember, if you really want this job, you have to work as hard to get it as you will once you do get it!

Your first stop should be the Internet. Find out about the company—"investigate" it. Information with which you should be familiar includes:

1. When was the company started?
2. What are its products?
3. How is the company stock doing?
4. Where are their offices located?

You should also stop by the company and pick up an application, available company brochures available, and so forth.

You should study the information, complete the application, and place it in your portfolio. Go into the interview knowing as much if not more about the company as the people interviewing you. This is invaluable, especially when you interview for more senior-level positions. These interviews will undoubtedly include members of executive management. Your ability to talk about their company in business terms and demonstrate an understanding of the company will undoubtedly impress them and indicate that you are business oriented.

All your answers to the interviewers' questions should be directed to something in your portfolio. For example, if they ask you how you would deal with downsizing in your department and what impact that would have on your ability to conduct high-technology crime investigations adequately, you should display the process chart or metric included in your portfolio that indicates that you have addressed this issue before or have an approach to dealing with the issue.

The portfolio can work for any new high-technology crime investigator in any company. The following is a sample portfolio outline, which can be used as a guide by a new or experienced high-technology crime investigator. In this case, it is the high-technology crime investigator applying for the GEC high-technology crime investigator position. It's up to you to fill in the details. Many of the ideas of what to put in your high-technology crime investigative portfolio will be found in this book.

You will note that the prospective high-technology crime investigator applying for the GEC position has done the research necessary to tailor an HTCPP for GEC. The beauty of building this type of portfolio is that it seems specific, and yet it's generic.

THE PORTFOLIO

We all spend a lot of time learning and gaining experience and attending courses and conferences, but if you want to make yourself an attractive proposition to a potential employer, you need to develop your portfolio. When you are filling out the application for a promotion or a new job, it's not the best time to think about building a portfolio. There are several reasons why you should develop a portfolio. First, it will help you to keep a record of significant career and self-improvement milestones, such as the courses you attended and the experience you gained over time. Also it can contain a list of the conferences you attended and any papers you presented or published. It is easy to add these things at the time, but trying to remember what you have done and when at some point in the future is not so easy.

Presenting papers at conferences and writing them for journals is not for everyone. The processes are time-consuming and require a level of confidence and experience in writing and public speaking.

The second point about a portfolio is that you should make it coherent. If you set out to develop the portfolio, the very act of creating it will highlight to you any areas that you need to gain additional knowledge or experience in. This will help you in deciding the actions that you need to take to be an asset to any organization.

SAMPLE HIGH TECHNOLOGY CRIME INVESTIGATOR PORTFOLIO OUTLINE

Table of Contents
   I Introduction
  II The Position and GEC Values
 III Strategic Objective
 IV Tactical Objectives
  V Transition Plan and the Future
 VI Why I'm the Right High-technology crime Investigator for the GEC Position
VII Examples of a Proven High-technology crime Investigator Record That Will Meet GEC's Expectations and Needs

I. Introduction
A. *Purpose:* To tell you about me, my high-technology crime prevention-related education and experience, and how I can establish and lead an HTCPP for GEC based on a cost-effective philosophy that

proves high-technology crime prevention investigative services and supports our internal and external customers (Note that a good technique to use during the interview is to use the words *we* and *our* in your discussions. This will help get the interviewers to look at you as a GEC team member. Approach the interview as if you already work at GEC.)

B. *Objective:* To convince you that I am the most qualified and best person for the position of high-technology crime investigator for GEC, and to demonstrate how we can establish a business-oriented HTCPP for GEC

II.   The Position and GEC Values

A. Customers
  1. Meet our customers' reasonable expectations.
  2. Show by example that we are the best in the industry in meeting any of their high-technology crime prevention needs.
B. GEC
  1. Establish and manage an HTCPP that supports business needs and requirements.
  2. Strive for an HTCPP that adds value to GEC products and services.
C. GEC suppliers
  1. Advise them so they can develop quality, high-technology crime prevention products that meet GEC needs at a reasonable price.
  2. Assist them in understanding our high-technology crime prevention needs.
  3. Direct them to bring only high-technology crime prevention products that can be integrated into the GEC HTCPP cost-effectively, with minimal maintenance.
D. Quality
  1. Establish and manage an HTCPP that provides quality service and support to its internal and external customers.
  2. Provide that quality service and support with least impact to cost and schedules.
E. Integrity
  1. Follow the rules, both the spirit and the intent.
  2. Always be honest.
  3. Demonstrate ethical conduct at all times.
F. Leadership
  1. Set the example.
  2. Help others.

III.   Strategic Objective

Build a comprehensive high-technology crime prevention environment that supports GEC's business needs at least cost and with least impact to schedules.

IV. Tactical Objectives

A. Define detailed milestones for GEC's comprehensive high-technology crime prevention environment identified as the GEC strategic objective.
B. Describe the current GEC high-technology crime prevention environment.
C. Identify the difference between the previous two entries.
D. Establish a master project and schedule to meet the strategic, tactical, and annual objectives as integral parts of GEC's business plans.

V. Transition Plan and the Future

A. First month
   1. Week 1
      a. Begin transition meetings with management to discuss expectations, goals, objectives, and budget.
      b. Begin familiarization with GEC processes and how systems are being used at GEC by all key departments.
      c. Begin review of GEC policies and procedures that relate to an HTCPP.
      d. Establish appointments to meet with applicable department heads to discuss their ideas related to an HTCPP, and how it may help or hinder their operations.
   2. Week 2
      a. Conduct one-on-one meetings with each department head.
      b. Hold in-depth interviews with peers in high-technology crime prevention-related organizations.
      c. Begin scoping the high-technology crime prevention level of effort required.
   3. Week 3
      a. Coordinate personnel and organizational issues with the human resource staff.
      b. Coordinate with internal customers.
   4. Week 4
      a. Finalize high-technology crime prevention plans, including strategic, tactical, and annual.
      b. Begin recruitment and hiring as applicable.
      c. Continue coordination meetings with applicable peers and executive management.
B. Rest of the year
   1. Develop, implement, and manage high-technology crime prevention projects.
   2. Develop high-technology crime prevention metrics and manage the HTCPP.

3. Continue working high-technology crime prevention issues with the GEC high-technology crime prevention team.
4. Continue evaluating potential high-technology crime prevention cost reductions based on a cost–risk assessment methodology.
5. Near year end, analyze successes and failures; validate goals and objectives; and plan projects for the next year.
6. Continue to evaluate various HTCPP processes; make changes where necessary to keep the program fresh, active, and viable.

C. Next year
1. Continue and refine first year goals.
2. Increase/enhance skills of organization/staff.
3. Ensure GEC's HTCPP becomes an integrated, value-added program.

VI. Why I'm the Right High-Technology Crime Investigator for the GEC Position

(This section includes the highlights of your resume, and a copy of the resume should also be inserted in this section. Remember, don't use a boiler plate resume. Tailor the resume for the GEC job based on the advertised job description.)

A. A bachelor's degree in criminal justice with a minor in information systems, which shows that I have the educational background to understand the academic and technical aspects of the profession
B. A master's degree in business administration, which shows that I have the business and management background to understand GEC from a business perspective
C. Experienced in supporting and providing services and support to similar customers
D. Enjoy the trust and confidence of other professional high-technology crime investigator's in both government agencies and business environments
E. Detailed knowledge of all high-technology crime prevention-related federal and state laws and regulations (Note: Identify all applicable federal and state laws that apply.)
F. A detailed knowledge of information systems, their threats, vulnerabilities, and associated risks
G. Enjoy the trust and confidence of corporate management wherever I have been employed
H. A proven HTCPP is already prepared, tailored for GEC and ready for implementation
I. Previous experience in coordinating related activities with the local district attorney, FBI, police, and US Secret Service
J. Experienced in high-technology crime prevention and management leadership roles (e.g., government standards, committees, working groups)

VII. Examples of a Proven High-Technology Crime Investigator Record That Will Meet GEC's Expectations and Needs

A. Functional costs averages. (In this section, list all the information related to past budget, tracking, and so on.)

B. Project management. (In this section, list samples of project management tracking, such as Gantt charts.)

C. Metrics management. (In this section, list the metrics you have developed or would use to management high-technology crime prevention functions.)

SUMMARY

Marketing yourself as a successful investigator is a combination of a number of elements. You need to show that you are highly competent, have the relevant training and experience, and have a good understanding of the profession.

A portfolio of your experience as an investigator will help you to convince any potential employer that you are the person they need. A well-written and thoughtfully prepared portfolio will show them that you are motivated and should help to convince them that you understand what they are looking for in a potential employee. This, of course, will only hold true if you have understood what it is that they are looking for in an investigator. However, the time you have spent in preparing the portfolio and the training and experience that you have gained should go a long way to satisfy potential employers. Remember:

- Prior to being interviewed for GEC's high-technology crime investigator position, learn all you can about GEC.
- Read books about how to prepare and dress for interviews.
- Prepare answers for the typical questions you will probably be asked and practice the interview process so your answers come across naturally and not as memorized, rehearsed answers.
- Develop a high-technology crime investigator portfolio to be used during the interview.
- During the interview, refer the interviewers to the portfolio.
- During the interview, use the words *we* and *our,* as if you have already been hired to work at GEC.

26

So, Are You Ready to Become a High-Technology Crime Investigative Consultant?[*]

This chapter describes how to determine if being a high-technology crime investigative consultant is right for you, provides a high-technology crime investigative consultant's business plan outline, and discusses running an international high-technology crime investigative consulting business.

INTRODUCTION

Being a high-technology crime investigative consultant is a very challenging profession, and these days it commands a very good salary, depending on one's education and experience, of course. But, there is a price to be paid. The price is constantly keeping up with high technology, new protection products, new malicious codes, attack techniques, defenses, and putting in many long days. However, these should be the fun, challenging parts of the job. The part that may not be so much fun is the people problems that arise when you are a corporate security employee manager investigator. Then there are the management meetings, performance reviews, and such, that have nothing to do with high-technology crime and investigation, but have to do with being part of a corporation.

> "If you wish to succeed, consult three old people."—Chinese Proverb

---

[*]Some of the information provided on consulting has been excerpted with permission from *Information Systems Security Officer's Guide: Establishing and Managing an Information Protection Program,* 2nd ed., published by Butterworth-Heinemann.

Also, some of the information in this chapter was provided by Steve Lutz, President, WaySecure, a successful international security consultant and high-technology crime and InfoSec specialist for decades.

No, managing a successful high-technology crime investigations unit is not a nine-to-five job. If you are a conscientious and dedicated professional, it can consume your life. So when one looks at the salary and benefits compared with the number of hours one works, job pressures, stress, time to commute to and from work, and lack of personal time, maybe that salary is not worth it. Add the fact that you are not your own boss. In fact, you may work for one of those "bad" bosses. You know the type, one who demands everything, takes credit for what you do, and blames you when things are not going right.

Some like the challenge of this type of job. Others don't see a way out and feel trapped. After all, their lifestyle has caught up with or even surpassed their salary. For those with more of a personal career plan, that sacrifice may serve them well. Those professionals may take such jobs for just a short period of time (e.g., 3 to 5 years). Their purpose is to build up experience and credentials for going out on their own as high-technology crime investigative consultants.

To be in any type of profession in which you work for yourself takes a special type of personality to succeed. After all, there is no one to continue to pay you when you are on vacation, no paid benefits, and if you decided to "hang around" the office and not work, you won't get paid for that either. There is no safety net or paid time off when you are sick. No work; no pay. For the independent consultant, the old saying "time is money" is certainly true. In addition, there is a constant need to maintain contacts (potential customers), keep up with high technology, and of course there is the almost constant travel.

Some high-technology crime investigators or managers may have the "connections" and believe that they are well thought of as high-technology crime investigative consultant professionals—being called upon to lecture at conferences, to assist others with their high-technology crime investigative needs, and the like. However, those who do so as a member of a large firm, such as a large accounting consulting firm, believe that they are the ones who draw others to them for help. In fact, it is usually not that at all. It is usually the large corporate name that brings these individuals to the high-technology crime investigative consultant.

Some high-technology crime investigator managers and technicians do not realize this fact. Then when they decide to go out on their own as high-technology crime investigative consultants, they find that what they thought was a great customer base on which to build their business trade turns out to be the customer base of their former employer. Furthermore, there are legal and ethical matters relating to "stealing" customers away from a former employer. When the shock of this fact hits them, they find themselves scrambling for clients.

Some advice for those who may be ready to take the high-technology crime investigative consulting plunge: Be sure that you *objectively* inventory your skills and potential client base.

Before you begin your high-technology crime investigative consultant career, it is strongly recommended that you have at least 2 years of your current salary (including funds for equivalent benefits) safely in the bank. That emergency fund will provide a year or more of income as you grow your business. If nothing else, it will be a good financial backup for some lean times or for the times you will want to take a break for 1 or 2 weeks to go on vacation. After all, you have to pay for your own days off now. Oh, and don't forget insurance for "errors and omissions," also known as professional liability insurance, general liability, and workman's compensation. Some clients require proof of some or all these policies before you set foot in the door.

All that being said, if you have the education, experience, business sense, and personality to handle being out on your own, consulting does offer its own rewards. These rewards include setting your own schedule and hours, being your own boss, taking vacation whenever you like, doing things your way—but wait a minute—that's not completely true. Your hours will be set by your workload and your clients. You will be able to do the work pretty much your way, but only that work that meets the clients' needs. And vacations can be cut short by an urgent client need. You really can't afford to postpone an urgent client request because you risk losing the client to a competitor. Payments from clients may be slow in coming, and they may be shocked by their bill for services rendered, causing you to negotiate or get your lawyer to negotiate for you. That means additional costs if you can't get your lawyer's costs ported over to the client. When such issues arise, you may eventually get your money, but you will probably never do business with that client again. How many clients can you afford to lose?

So being a high-technology crime investigative consultant looks great on paper, and it may do your ego good. After a while the real world takes over. It's a tough life and not for the faint at heart. Before you think about diving in, be sure you have a good business plan and one that is objective. Also, be sure you can support yourself and your family without work for extended periods of time. Yes, it sounds great, but maybe that corporate or government salary, working conditions, and boss weren't all that bad.

However, you have successfully worked your career plan and have developed the education and experience skills over the years that have given you the confidence to think about going out on your own as a high-technology crime investigative consultant. You have had articles published in magazines, lectured internationally, and developed a reputation as a professional high-technology crime investigator. If you think you are about ready for this career move, you need a plan.

HAVE A PLAN

If you decide to become an independent high-technology crime investigative consultant, the first thing you should do is develop a business plan *before you resign from your current job.* By developing a plan, you may ultimately decide that you don't or can't make it as an independent high-technology crime investigative consultant. There are many sample business plans available in books, and software programs can help you get started. Regardless of how you proceed to develop your high-technology crime investigative consultant business plan, you must be objective. If you are to assume anything, assume the worst. That way, you will be prepared for the "worst-case scenario" and be able to deal with it successfully. Your plan should be looked at as a project plan and, at a minimum, should address the following:

- Your business goals and objectives
- Why you want to start this business
- Education, experience, and skills. (Inventory them to ensure they will fit your consulting business. Be realistic.)
- How much money you need to begin
- How much money you have
- How you plan to get the money you don't have but need
- How you plan to survive financially when business is slow. (If you have a family or significant other, will they support you? If not, you may have to clarify your relationship–business priorities.)
- Whether you are willing to travel the majority of the time. (After all, you must go to customers, not them to you.)
- The steps you will take to begin the business and the costs for each line item or task
- Whether you will incorporate your business
- Your knowledge of the marketplace, your competitors
- Whether you offer better services at lower prices
- Competitor strengths and weaknesses
- Your strengths and weaknesses
- Competitive analysis
- Market scope
- Whether you will have a logo and business motto, and, if so, what are they and why?
- Whether you need a lawyer to assist you

- Whether you will have copyrighted material, trademarks, and trade secrets, and, if so, how you will handle those processes
- Whether you have standard invoices, proposals, confidentiality agreements, contracts, billing, and general business processes and forms in place and ready for use
- Whether you have trusted high-technology crime investigations specialists and high-technology specialists (e.g., systems programmers available to support your contracts as subcontractors)
- How you will obtain business
- How much you will charge for what work
- Awareness of the laws and regulations that affected you doing business

These are but a few of the many issues you should address before taking the plunge into the high-technology crime consulting service business. Remember, also, the guiding principles that you should employ:

- Confidentiality
- Objectivity
- Professionalism
- Respect
- Integrity
- Honesty
- Quality
- Efficiency
- Client focus

GETTING STARTED

After you have your business plan in place and have decided to become an independent high-technology crime investigative consultant, your plan should provide you with a step-by-step approach to getting started. Let's break down the high-technology crime investigative consultant business into sections (Fig. 26-1):

- Engagement setup
- Engagement process
- Assessment services
- Advisory services
- Security implementation
- Augmentation
- Legal issues
- International aspects

Figure 26-1   An example of the consulting components of a high-technology crime investigative consultant. *Only in countries where corporate espionage is legal. (Portions of this information were coordinated with and provided by Steve Lutz, WaySecure, an international security consultant.)

Engagement Setup

To begin, you need an "entry into the business" strategy. You must have established and continue to refine your information network (trusted contacts within your business arena who can tell you what is going on where). You must also use other sources to find your potential customers. Such other sources include referrals and marketing through brochures, pamphlets, lectures, books, articles, and your business Web site. The strategy should also include "cold calling" of potential customers and explaining to them what services you offer.

After you have made contact with a potential client, you must clearly and precisely communicate your services. You must "find their pain" and explain how you can help solve their problems. Try to make this a question-and-answer session during which a dialogue takes place. You should also use the opportunity to explain your experience by citing examples of your past services to clients, without providing specific names of course. Assuming the meeting goes well and they ask you for a proposal, you should provide one in the most expeditious manner possible. Be sure that you understand that each client requires a different approach depending on the size of the client (e.g., small, medium, or large organization), because the scale, tactics, and strategy will vary with each. In the proposal you should be precise. Include a project schedule that includes logistics requirements, roles and responsibilities (for both you and your client), and liability issues. Other matters to consider include:

- Understanding who you are dealing with, and being sure to get to the right level of authority to make decisions that affect your work
- Identifying their needs as specifically as possible
- Understanding their budget (size and cycle)
- Getting the "big picture"
- Being sure you have a clear understanding of their expectations and your deliverables before you leave the potential client
- Determining any time factors they want to consider
- If needed, exchanging encryption keys so correspondence can be done in private

As part of your engagement setup, you should have a specific written proposal prepared, as well as one in the standard format you have developed. Both should be on your notebook computer so they can be modified immediately to fit the situation. If you believe your specific written proposal is just right for your potential client, be sure to have several hard copies available to present to the potential client. The proposal, at a minimum, should include:

- Proposal structure
- Work to be performed
- Project schedule
- Timing and fees
- Roles and responsibilities
- Assumptions and caveats
- Legal issues

Engagement Process

After you begin, remember to document everything, including:

- Times and dates
- Who you spoke to
- What was said
- Any action items that resulted from the conversations
- Tasks you completed and their time and date
- Notable events that occurred
- All other matters that can be used to support your activities, position, time spent, and the like

> More than one consultant has found that they performed worked based on conversations with a client's employee and for which the client balked in making payments for that work because they considered it unauthorized (i.e., that employee had no authority to direct you perform that function).

It is imperative that you and the client both have a clear understanding of what is agreed to, when it will be accomplished, proof that it was accomplished, and the fees relative to completing the work. Notes help when discussing the work performed, especially in dealing with the billing process. An excellent technique to use during the engagement management process is to monitor the progress of the engagement on a daily basis. Constantly communicate with the client the progress of the task (or lack of it), and delineate why there are delays. If there are delays resulting from a fault on the part of the client, inform the client of the impact to the engagement and give choices such as:

- Ask for additional funding
- Abbreviate certain tasks
- Eliminate certain tasks

This technique helps avoid unpleasant surprises and misunderstandings. Use a *we* mentality. Approach your counterpart project manager and say, "Joe, we've got a problem. The project is behind because of this, this, and this. How do you think we can fix this?" If the project is screwed up, Joe has just as much to lose politically as you do monetarily. If there is a debate regarding why things aren't going well, the events are fresh in everyone's minds, and it's easy to sort out and correct or compensate. A common mistake is to wait until near the end of the engagement when things are way behind schedule, and inform the client, thinking that somehow everything might work out. This will end up, in a best-case scenario, as souring the client relationship; in the worst case, you'll end up in court arguing over who did what when.

> If there are delays resulting from your own performance or lack of planning, work extra hours and accept the loss. Do whatever you have to do to meet the objectives of the proposal, and don't complain about it. Make careful notes regarding why you miscalculated or undermanaged the engagement, and use that knowledge when writing your next proposal.

Assessment Services

You may want to break your services into various groups. One group may be "assessment services" (e.g., environment survey study to determine anticrime defenses). This should have been decided as part of your business plan. These services include such things as penetration testing, security test and evaluation of software and systems, and supporting documentation analysis.

Advisory Services

Advisory services, also previously considered as part of your business plan, may include the following:

- Risk assessments
- Technical security countermeasures
- Technical design review
- High-technology change management
- Systems and network security
- High-technology crime prevention policies, processes, procedures, and architecture
- How to establish and manage a high-technology crime investigator unit
- Evaluating the efficiency and effectiveness of a high-technology crime investigator unit

Security Implementation

The services to be considered for inclusion in your high-technology crime investigative consultant business plan, based on your expertise, include ensuring that products to be installed on systems don't make the systems and networks more vulnerable, and that any security software meets the needs of the business and operates as advertised.

A holistic approach means that you can cover the broad spectrum of the clients' needs from assets protection implementation, to protection evaluation, to inquiries and investigations. Such expertise is very difficult to get because of the many technical aspects you have to master. However, this expertise will put you ahead of your competition and may just give you that competitive edge to make your long hours and travel as a high-technology crime investigative consultant worth the effort.

Augmentation

Augmentation services include such things as termination surveillance and assisting in client investigations of employees (e.g., computer forensic services). You may also be requested to respond to incidents. If so, this should be addressed in your contract, as should billing for such responses, which often seem to happen after midnight.

Legal Issues

Legal issues may arise regarding your authority in conducting or assisting in high-technology crime investigations as well as issues related to your contract. It is imperative, to avoid legal problems later, that all matters be clearly and concisely stated in the contract. The last thing you want is a conflict in contract interpretations, delayed payments, and/or refusal to pay what you billed the client, not to mention the problem of your reputation, which will follow you (good or bad) from client to client.

> Above all, *never* begin an engagement without a signed contract. Make certain that the person signing it has the legal right to do so for the organization (usually an officer or director).

International Aspects

More and more high-technology crime investigative consultants are working all over the world and with foreign clients. In dealing with such clients, it is important to:

- Avoid slang, colloquial terms.
- Learn as much of the foreign language and culture as possible.
- Make positive comments on the food and architecture.
- Use local hand gestures and volume of speech (which should be such that those in the back can hear you).
- Understand the foreign governments where you will be working.
- Understand the latest terrorist threats in the region.
- Explain security terms in local context.
- Don't complain about their country or culture, or brag about yours.
- Avoid political discussions or remain neutral if you are dragged into such a discussion.

QUESTIONS TO CONSIDER

Based on what you have read, consider the following questions and how you would reply to them:

- Do you want to be an independent high-technology crime investigative consultant?
- If so, what are the pros and cons as they relate to you?
- Do you believe you have the education, experience, and reputation necessary to be a successful high-technology crime investigative consultant? If so, list your "assets" in detail.
- Do you plan on becoming a high-technology crime investigative consultant in the future?
- If so, should you begin planning today?
- If so, what would be your business plan?
- Do you have the financial resources to get started?
- If not, how will you get these resources?
- What services would you offer?
- Why do you think you could succeed?

SUMMARY

Being an independent high-technology crime investigative consultant is not for everyone. One must have not only the education and experience in the high-technology crime investigative profession to be successful, but also the required personality, self-discipline, and confidence. The bottom line is that it's not really better being an independent consultant, just different. New headaches replace old ones and different benefits arise. The real change is in lifestyle and sources of stress. The new boss is the client, and some can be better or worse than your old boss. The good part is that you only have to deal with a bad "boss" for the duration of the engagement.

Some high-technology crime investigators and managers working for corporations believe they can succeed, but have not conducted sufficient objective analyses to validate their beliefs. Prior to beginning a career change from a corporate high-technology crime investigator and/or manager to an independent high-technology crime investigative consultant, you should develop a detailed business plan and supporting project plan. In doing so, you may find that being a consultant is not something you can do. It is better to find that out now, before you make the career change.

27

Conclusions and Final Thoughts

This chapter provides, as the title states, some final thoughts on the topic of high-technology crime investigations and the profession of the high-technology crime investigator.

INTRODUCTION

The profession of the high-technology crime investigator is still very much in its infancy. The challenges of high-technology crime investigators are many. Among the topics they must know and understand or understand the limitations of their knowledge are:

- People
- Relevant laws and regulations
- High-technology devices
- Investigative techniques
- Project planning
- Report writing
- Evidence seizure and collection methods
- Forensic laboratory procedures
- Quality control procedures
- Patience and empathy
- InfoSec
- E-commerce
- Office politics
- Who they know who knows what they do not know
- Every high-technology environment where they will work

WHAT IS THE PROFILE OF A SUCCESSFUL HIGH-TECHNOLOGY CRIME INVESTIGATOR?

We believe a profile of a successful and professional high-technology crime investigator is a person who, among other things:

- Enjoys "playing" with high-technology devices, equipment, and games
- Enjoys working with people, especially technically oriented people
- Enjoys the challenge of "the hunt" and chasing the high-technology "bad guys"
- Takes each investigation as a personal challenge to his or her ability
- Has the attitude that if the investigation does not end in a successful identification of the miscreant, the miscreant is smarter than the investigator. This is a major driving force in the investigator's relentless pursuit of knowledge and the miscreant.
- Keeps current on technology and related crimes and understands the implications of new technology, the opportunity to use it as a tool for criminal deeds, and has a basic understanding of its implications in conducting a related investigation
- Keeps current on latest investigative tools, techniques, and related sources of information
- Is an active member in a high-technology-related association and is constantly networking with peers to keep abreast of current and related events
- Helps others in the profession
- Enjoys constant change and gets bored if there are no changes
- Is customer support oriented and driven to meet all expectations
- Accepts and uses new, unique investigative methods
- Loves working in the global information environment
- Loves conducting high-technology investigations
- Loves life and has fun as a high-technology crime investigator professional

When you read through this list, think of how many of the entries you can honestly say describe you. Those that do not will adversely affect your ability to be a successful high-technology crime investigator professional, to get the job done, and to enjoy yourself in the process.

Not all people are made of the stuff required to be a successful high-technology crime investigator. Many people, for example, do not like confrontation. Being a high-technology crime investigator means that you will probably be involved in many confrontations. How you handle them affects your ability to get the job done. As a high-technology crime investigator, conflict is unavoidable.

"LOVE IT OR LEAVE IT!"

It takes a special kind of personality to be a high-technology crime investigator. Throughout this book we have described and discussed the world in which the high-technology crime investigator must work, the miscreants who are the high-technology crime investigators' adversaries, how to plan to defend against them and conduct successful investigations, as well as the many other challenges and issues.

You may be a high-technology crime investigator, an investigator wanting to transition over to the high-technology crime investigator profession, an investigator wanting to add the high-technology crime investigator expertise to your resumes, or someone considering a career as a high-technology crime investigator. The high-technology crime investigator profession is one that you must really enjoy to be successful. You must at times—most of the time—"think outside the box." You will constantly be challenged by the changing global environment, new high technology, sophistication of the miscreants, your tools, and the miscreants' tools.

It is also vitally important to be objective and yet take it personally when you are "on the hunt." You must identify the miscreant and build a good case for disciplinary action or prosecution. If you cannot identify the miscreant, you have lost that battle. This means not only that the miscreant has won, but that this time, the miscreant outsmarted you. For a professional high-technology crime investigator, this is unacceptable! The thought of some scum bag loser outsmarting you, the professional high-technology crime investigator, is unconscionable! That should be your attitude.

On the other hand, you must also realize you can't catch them all. Such is the nature of the environment, the hardware, the software, and the protection mechanisms in place (or often not in place). So, at the same time, try not to get an ulcer or high blood pressure over any of it! For a true high-technology crime investigator professional, this may be easier said than done. Think of it as a game—sometimes you win and sometimes you lose.

If you do not have the personality to be constantly challenging yourself to keep up with everything while also enjoying the work, do the profession a favor and find another one. Eventually you will give the profession a bad name because of your lack of skills, lack of aggressiveness, or poor attitude.

HOPES FOR THE FUTURE

The global information environment has brought with it the opportunities for mankind to make great strides, bringing all people of the world closer together through global communications, which leads to better understanding and, potentially, world peace. As a constructive tool, it can help alleviate suffering, help groups collaborate to identify new cures for deadly diseases, provide us with entertainment, and generally make life much easier. However, in the hands of juvenile delinquents and global miscreants, it can "take" from those who honestly labored for their possessions, destroy businesses, and cause major disruptions, chaos, and death (through such things as telemedicine).

NEVER GIVE UP!
NEVER SURRENDER!
—From the movie "Galaxy Quest"

An Wang (1920–1990) was quoted as saying, "When we enter society at birth, we receive an inheritance from the people who lived before us. It is our responsibility to augment that inheritance for those who succeed us. I feel that all of us owe the world more than we received when we were born." A professional high-technology crime investigator strives to do just that.

Thus far, the high-technology miscreants are winning the high-technology war, and the situation is not likely to change significantly in the foreseeable future. It is part of the global information war that is taking place and one that has already started to intensify as we have moved into the start of the 21st century. It is the new crime scene, the new battlefield.

Index

Numbers in italics indicate pages on which figures appear.